PLURALISM IN THEORY AND PRACTICE

PLURALISM IN THEORY AND PRACTICE

RICHARD McKEON AND AMERICAN PHILOSOPHY

Edited by Eugene Garver
and Richard Buchanan

Vanderbilt University Press
Nashville

First Edition 2000

04 03 02 01 00   5 4 3 2 1

Library of Congress Cataloging-in-Publication Data

Pluralism in theory and practice : Richard McKeon and
American philosophy / edited by Eugene Garver and
Richard Buchanan.—1st ed.
       p. cm. — (The Vanderbilt library of American
philosophy)
       ISBN 0-8265-1340-9 (alk. paper)
    1. McKeon, Richard Peter, 1900– 2. Pluralism. I. Garver,
Eugene. II. Buchanan, Richard, 1950- III. Title. IV. Series.
    B945.M4564 P57 2000
    191--dc21   00-008762

Published by Vanderbilt University Press
Printed in the United States of America

Contents

Contents

◆ Preface ◆

Richard McKeon is a pivotal but neglected figure in twentieth-century American philosophy. In a career that spanned seven decades, he published more than 150 articles and eleven books; inspired generations of students, many of whom went on to distinguished careers in a wide variety of fields; and received most of the honors possible for an American philosopher, including an invitation to deliver the Paul Carus Lectures in 1964. He was an important educator, instrumental in developing the General Education program of the University of Chicago in the era of Robert Maynard Hutchins and in developing the cultural and philosophical projects of UNESCO in the early years of that organization, including the preliminary studies for the Universal Declaration of Human Rights. He was a pioneer in the study of medieval philosophy and the history of science when those disciplines did not yet exist in the United States, and he was a central figure in the resurgence of rhetoric as an intellectual art and in the development of the so-called "Chicago School" of literary critics. Yet, McKeon's philosophic position appears isolated among his contemporaries, and in the decade following his death in 1985, his work was neglected among philosophers. Despite his many accomplishments and a well-deserved reputation for scholarly brilliance, McKeon's philosophic position is seldom explored in depth, his wide-ranging contributions to philosophy and the humanities are not fully known, and his lasting influence remains difficult to determine.

There are three reasons for this situation. First is the inaccessibility of his work. Until the recent publication of several anthologies of some of his most important essays, McKeon's works were scattered among so many journals and conference publications in the United States and abroad that the full range and scope of his thought was known to very few individuals. A reader who appreciated one side of his thought was frequently unaware of its extension in other directions or of its connection to a consistently developed body of work that expressed a broad vision of the nature of the philosophic enterprise. Second, McKeon wrote in an idiom so different from that of other major twentieth-century American philosophers that just reprinting his articles addresses only part of the problem of coming to understand his approach to philosophy. His work is characterized by a mixture of philosophy and scholarship, expressed in a style of writing that consistently challenges the casual reader with unusual ideas and juxtaposed views. Third, and perhaps most important, is the nature of the problems McKeon investigated, which were philosophically important but not the ones that occupied most other philosophers of his time. He investigated pluralism, the diversity of cultures, and the problems of communication and community when these were unfashionable subjects. He also explored and problematized the relationship of philosophy and the history of philosophy, philosophy and rhetoric, and a variety of other subjects that had little significance to most of his contemporaries. As a result, McKeon appears relatively isolated in his own time in giving attention to problems that are now closer to the main lines of inquiry in philosophy and the humanities.

Charles Wegener once remarked that he introduced McKeon at a conference by saying that McKeon had two contradictory reputations. For some, he was regarded as a dogmatic Aristotelian, for whom philosophy consisted in repeating what The Philosopher said. For others, he was a modern sophist who had no philosophic convictions of his own but regarded philosophy as a matter of being able to advocate any position, as the occasion demanded. These dual accusations show the difficulty that contemporaries had in understanding McKeon's conception of pluralism and the philosophic enterprise. But they also foreshadow the relevance of his work today, as the problems of pluralism and cultural diversity increasingly require new approaches in philosophy and the humanities.

However, the goal of this volume of essays is not to vindicate McKeon's work in the context of subsequent history. We have no interest in simply arguing that McKeon's work should be of interest to contemporary philosophers and those interested in the development of twentieth-century American philosophy, or even that his work would have found a more receptive audience today than when he was writing. Instead, the authors explore newly popular and urgent philosophic problems with a challengingly different approach that emerges from the work of Richard McKeon. Along the way, they do seek to bring McKeon to the attention of a new generation of philosophers and students by looking critically at his work as significant philosophy, situating his inquiries in the context of American philosophy of the twentieth-century, with its characteristically practical emphasis. The focus is on contemporary philosophic problems addressed within the context of the authors' own philosophic projects, using McKeon and his ideas as a point of departure or, in some cases, investigating McKeon's work as fertile ground for shaping the direction of new inquiry. The contributors to this volume regard McKeon's work as an excellent place to reconsider the history of American philosophy in this century and from which to move on to new problems and concerns.

The central theme of this volume is pluralism in theory and practice, and the authors discuss pluralism as a philosophic concept and as an objective fact of human experience. However, in keeping with the spirit of McKeon's conception of the philosophic enterprise in the twentieth century, the essays in this volume are also exceptionally diverse. At least in part, they represent the pluralism of modes of philosophizing that held

McKeon's intellectual attention and that are characteristic of philosophy today. Furthermore, they reflect the scope, if not the full range, of
McKeon's work, with essays that address problems in the areas of philosophy, education, and practical action, shaped in diverse historical and cultural circumstances. It is important to the spirit of McKeon's philosophy
that the contributors to this volume include both professional philosophers and those whose academic affiliations are in disciplines such as rhetoric, English, design and technology, and the social sciences. It is also
important that the contributors have experience in theoretical investigations in their disciplines as well as practical action in educational administration, government, and industry in the United States and abroad.
McKeon believed that knowing, doing, and making are interrelated and
interdependent in our time and that they are at once local and global in
significance. Taken together, they represent three approaches to the same
problem: the unity and diversity of truth.

> These three—the understanding of order in nature, in the rela-
> tions of men, and in knowledge, the education of men sensitive
> to the marks and uses of that order, and the appreciation of
> differences in the modes in which peoples express that order
> and seek their fulfillment in accordance with it—are the three
> related aspects of a problem which we all face in our individ-
> ual lives, our communities, and in the world relations in which
> all communities have been placed.[1]

Wayne Booth has noted that studies of metaphor have recently increased
faster than the birth rate, and Alasdair MacIntyre has pointed out something similar for discussions of moral dilemmas. Discussions of pluralism,
too, are growing at an exponential rate, with different intellectual and political purposes. For example, after the change of regime in South Africa,
the Afrikaaners rallied on the banner of "pluralism" as a way of upholding their traditional privileges and resisting majority rule. In fact, there is
now a thriving pluralism of discussions of pluralism, with participants in
different threads of the discussion unaware of the existence of the others.
Pluralism in literary criticism has been explored extensively by Wayne
Booth, a student of McKeon, and by Kenneth Burke, one of McKeon's
life-long debating partners. Isaiah Berlin has celebrated the pluralism of ultimate goods, and others have drawn attention to the pluralism of interest
groups, of conceptions of the good life, and of religions. However, in addition to these kinds of pluralism, there is also a pluralism in recognizing
the ultimate diversity of modes of philosophizing—a kind of pluralism
that is at once more radical and more difficult, if not impractical in initial
appearance. This is the kind of pluralism that McKeon made fundamental in his own philosophic inquiry. A pluralism of philosophy, itself, provides a way of connecting the diverse forms of pluralism that others have

identified, and in the long run it may not be as impractical as it appears on first consideration.

In one of many surprises in McKeon's philosophy, pluralism is closely related to objectivity. On the one hand, he often observes that pluralism is an objective fact of human experience. On the other hand, he observes that objectivity is a desired outcome of communication and discussion and, further, argues that objectivity is a fundamental goal and principle of being human. To understand this seeming paradox, we require a better interpretation of the term "objectivity" than is commonly found today. Objectivity is often interpreted as a reference to physical and material existence, oriented toward the underlying processes and materials of nature and toward one of the specialized meanings of "empirical" in contemporary philosophy and science. With this meaning, objectivity is the bête noire of postmodernist theory, since it seems to imply an ultimate reality which undermines the evident fact of pluralism and the deep ambiguity of values and meanings that we encounter in cultural life. This use of the term, however, is no longer entirely relevant to the problems faced in contemporary circumstances. An alternative meaning is needed that better expresses the communal dimension of communication. Such is offered by John Dewey, who writes that language "may be directed by and towards some physical existence. But it first has reference to some other person or persons with whom it institutes *communication*—the making of something in common. Hence, to that extent its reference becomes general and 'objective.'" This is a bridge to the meaning of objectivity in McKeon's philosophy of culture and communication. Human beings come together around common issues or problems, and their different interests and perspectives are often an obstacle to collective action. But a well-conducted discussion leads to agreement on a course of action, and sometimes to mutual understanding, if not to agreement on issues of ideology or philosophic belief. A speech—or a succession of speeches and discussion—is the mediated ground for public agreement on what shall be done. Indeed, the final judgment that follows from discussion is what Dewey means by the making of something in common. The outcome has reference to some physical existence, but it is formed as "objective" in the essential matrix of the immediate cultural environment, where conflicting concepts, interests, and assumptions about the world constitute the ecology of culture. Discussion forms an object, which is the transformation of the subject of discussison into a product that is held in common as the outcome.

However, objectivity is more than a methodological issue for McKeon. It is a principle of the unique standing of the individual in community and culture. "A world community, like a cosmology, provides the conditions of our being, thinking, acting, and speaking. Objectivity is the inclusive principle of indifference by which it is recognized that being is grasped only in what we think, say, and do about it."[2] For McKeon, the pluralism of perspectives is an unavoidable reality of life. However, the effort to form our individual perspectives through thought and action brings us into touch with being human and being with other human beings. For McKeon, an understanding of pluralism gives us access to whatever may be grasped of being, itself.

> The unity of an ongoing philosophy of experience and humanity is a product of a plurality of perspectives focused on common experience rather than a consensus of opinions stated in a common belief. The universality it achieves is not a specification of generic inclusions but an expression of individuality or particularity placed in its context and traced through its coherences.[3]

It is no accident, therefore, that many of the essays in this volume grapple with the themes of unity, system, community, and culture at the same time that they address problems of pluralism. The empirical fact of pluralism, if it is anything more than the casual differences of opinion, preference, and desire that usually pass for pluralism in the common understanding of the term, forces us to examine principles in a new way, opening a host of problems for which McKeon's philosophy has continued relevance. Whatever the merits of his position and his arguments on this matter, his work on pluralism and objectivity is timely today.

Similarly McKeon's exploration of the relationship between philosophy and the history of philosophy is also timely. It may have been unfashionable to assert the philosophic importance of the history of philosophy in the 1930s, 1940s, 1950s, and even the 1960s. Journals such as the *History of Philosophy* and the *History of Philosophy Quarterly* did not exist during most of McKeon's career. But the history of philosophy is respectable today, and it is even regarded by some people as more than historical. In many cases, the interpretive turn in philosophy has been a turn to the history of philosophy, and McKeon's work has contemporary relevance for this enterprise. When Edwin Curley organized a conference on Spinoza in the late 1970s, he cited McKeon's doctoral dissertation, published in 1928 as *Spinoza: The Unity of his Thought,* as one of the primary background readings. The relationship between philosophy and the history of philosophy is a focal issue in McKeon's work because that relationship is so complicated and contested. It may seem easy to know when a writer is engaged in philosophic investigation and when he or she is engaged in the history of philosophy, but experience suggests the opposite. Often we make a philosophic argument by producing a coherent interpretation of Aristotle, Spinoza, or Wittgenstein. McKeon took that common experience seriously. He did not assimilate philosophy to history, as did Hegel or Collingwood in their different ways. But he did force reflection on the relationship between philosophy and its history, as many of the essays in this volume attempt to do. These essays enact that complex relationship by treating McKeon, himself, as a historical figure whose texts need to be analyzed and by using the results to pursue further philosophic problems.

McKeon also wrote about rhetoric and the relationship between rhetoric and philosophy long before the existence of a journal called *Philosophy and Rhetoric* and long before rhetoric reemerged as a respectable philosophic subject. For much of their history, philosophy and rhetoric were enemies, competitors, and collaborators. It is only in the recent past that philosophy has thought itself able to ignore rhetoric. The interpretive turn in philosophy has, in many cases, been not only a turn to history, but an unacknowledged turn to rhetoric. Initially, McKeon stood almost alone in pointing to the philosophic significance of rhetoric, though now the value of rhetoric for philosophy and of philosophy for rhetoric is more evident, as in the work of Chaim Perelman, Stephen Toulman, Jürgen Habermas, and others. Again, McKeon's explicit attention to rhetoric and its intellectual history offers a useful resource in contemporary inquiry, as several of the essays in this volume demonstrate.

The essays in this book are not organized in sections with discrete themes. Rather, they present an unfolding of contemporary philosophic problems, beginning with the difficult relationship between philosophy and the history of philosophy and ending with the unity of commitments necessary to bind together a pluralistic community. Along the way, the contributors discuss themes of philosophy, education, and practical action in a variety of interrelations.

In the first essay of this collection, Richard Popkin meditates on the relationship between philosophy and the history of philosophy in his own life, in McKeon's life, and in twentieth-century American philosophy. He draws the ominous conclusion that while the quality and quantity of work in the history of philosophy have improved dramatically during his own career and that of McKeon, the impact of the history of philosophy on most American philosophy is still minimal, with little excuse for the continuing ignorance that it represents. Walter Watson continues the collection with an essay called "McKeon: The Unity of His Thought," a title that recalls McKeon's doctoral dissertation and first book, *Spinoza: The Unity of His Thought*. Watson provides an overview of the methods and interests that unify a body of work that is exceptionally wide ranging, and he poses a challenge as to whether there can be a system in McKeon's vision of pluralism.

The essays that follow place McKeon in different historical contexts, seeking both to evaluate his work and appropriate it for different purposes. David Depew discusses McKeon in relation to pragmatism and John Dewey, examining the way Dewey and McKeon treat the problems of philosophy and relate them to "the problems of men"—a phrase coined by Dewey. Depew's essay gives an interesting account of why Aristotle occupies a special place in McKeon's thinking and why McKeon, at the same time, is not an Aristotelian. His essay suggests why McKeon called his own approach to philosophy one of pluralism, following William James's use of the term, rather than employing Dewey's term, pragmatism. This points toward McKeon's concentration on the political and practical, as in Horace Kallen's cultural pluralism, and his shift away from James's concern for the pluralism of religious experience. One could say that McKeon's interests are found more in an urban pluralism suited to New York or Chicago than in the more aristocratic version of pluralism that James developed in Cambridge.

This provides an interesting transition to the next essay, in which Donald Levine compares McKeon's pluralism with that of another writer from Harvard, the social scientist Talcott Parsons. Levine uses the genre of comparative articulation to discuss their work, exploring neglected historical and philosophic dimensions of their thought. His essay usefully situates McKeon's pluralism alongside a very different sort of pluralism that leads to another conception of the relationship between theory and practice.

In contrast, Dennis O'Brien, a former university president, uses the genre of the memoir as a way of raising questions about the relationship between philosophy and its history and philosophy's relationship to personal history. His paper raises important questions about philosophy as an educational project and as a research program—and to the philosopher as thinker and teacher. It is common to accuse pluralism of leading to relativism; O'Brien shows what is wrong with that accusation. In the next essay, Charles Wegener also employs the genre of memoir but focuses on the difficulty of examining a philosopher in order to discover the truth. He offers the case of the Parmenides as an example of a series of dialectical exercises between philosophers. The arguments of the Parmenides are arguments about ideas as well as arguments about a theory of ideas, showing how philosophy and its history are mixed together in our thought, making truth an elusive goal in discussion.

In the two essays that follow, both Garver and Buchanan treat McKeon's work as a text and as a point of departure for addressing philosophic problems in the context of their own work. Eugene Garver discusses philosophic pluralism as a means of enriching contemporary discussions of more apparently practical forms of pluralism, relating McKeon's work to discussions in contemporary philosophy. Both philosophy and democracy were Greek inventions, but politics and democracy have been radically transformed in this century. Part of the problem for philosophy is how to redefine itself in ways that are coordinate with the changes in democracy—as theory changes, practice develops in new ways. Garver also offers suggestions to explain McKeon's seeming lack of influence as well as an evaluation of what he regards as McKeon's successes and failures.

Richard Buchanan discusses how metaphysics in the twentieth century has been relocated within a philosophy of culture and communication, oriented toward the problems of how we order, disorder, and reorder our experience in an ongoing search for values and understanding amid the ecology of culture. He explores the role of rhetoric in this transformation and focuses on McKeon's "circumstantial metaphysics" as a way of understanding culture as an activity rather than a state or ideology. Buchanan's essay, with its discussion of perplexity and objectivity in McKeon's work, provides an overview of McKeon's philosophy that contrasts with the view presented by Walter Watson in his first essay.

While the former essays address broad problems in philosophy, the remaining three essays address issues of individual and community action. In his second essay of the volume, Walter Watson addresses issues in the development of the community of scientists, looking specifically at McKeon's investigations of the history and philosophy of science. This essay provides a careful reading of McKeon's work in the area and presents an account of the significant contributions that he made before such a field existed in its own right. Turning from the problems of science to those of personal action, Thomas Farrell presents a case study of successful and unsuccessful "confessions" and shows the rhetorical and philosophic conditions for success. It is common to accuse pluralism of being incompatible with commitment, and Farrell's paper shows the complexity of that accusation. Farrell's essay, along with those of Garver and Buchanan, explore the ways in which philosophy and rhetoric intersect.

In the final essay, Wayne Booth also discusses the relationship between pluralism and commitment. However, he shifts the focus from the personal commitment of the individual pluralist to the unity of commitments necessary to bind together a pluralistic community. Booth's essay is a fitting conclusion to the volume, since it raises problems that were of deep concern to McKeon and that continue to be important for our culture at the end of the twentieth century.

Half of the essays included in this volume began as papers delivered at a conference that ran from March 13 to 14, 1992, held to discuss McKeon's contributions to the University of Chicago during the university's centennial celebration. The conference, entitled "Pluralism and Objectivity: Departures from the Philosophy of Richard McKeon," was organized by Donald N. Levine, Richard Buchanan, and Douglas Mitchell. The participants were former students and colleagues of McKeon and represented a wide range of fields and disciplinary interests. Funding was provided by the Earhart Foundation and by the College of the University of Chicago. In addition to thanking the organizations and the many individuals who made this conference possible, we also want to thank Joel Orlan, executive director of the American Academy of Arts and Sciences, for his strong encouragement and support.

PLURALISM IN THEORY AND PRACTICE

PHILOSOPHY AND THE HISTORY OF PHILOSOPHY

Richard Popkin

I knew Richard McKeon only slightly. As a graduate student at Columbia University a couple of academic generations after he had been there, McKeon took the trouble in 1952 to recommend European contacts to me. He did so, I suppose, not only as one who had traveled the road to France before me, but on the strength of his commitment to the history of philosophy, which, under the influence of Herbert Schneider, Paul Oscar Kristeller and John Herman Randall, was thriving at least as well during my time there as it had in the days of Frederick Woodbridge, McKeon's sometime mentor. Indeed, McKeon played a role in bringing into existence the *Journal of the History of Philosophy,* of which I became editor. In the mid fifties, the American Philosophical Association (APA) commissioned two committees, one in the central division and one in the Pacific, to look into the feasibility of such a journal. McKeon, together with Julius Weinberg and one or two others, was on the central division committee. The final push for the journal occurred in 1960 through the catalytic energies of Ed Strong, Herbert Scheider, and John Goheen. It was edited from Claremont Graduate School where I had just became a member of the faculty and which had strong links to Columbia.

At the same time that professional history of philosophy was developing, a counter movement among professional philosophers devoted to moving the profession in precisely the opposite direction was gaining strength.

As everyone knows, the movement to dehistorize professional philosophy waxed as the history of philosophy, in spite of an abundance of superb work, waned. As one who devoted his academic career to the history of philosophy, I could not help but be dismayed by these developments for reasons suggested in the following essay. It comforts me to know that McKeon would have felt likewise. It gives me great pleasure, therefore, to present my apologia for the history of philosophy in his honor.

Philosophy and the History of Philosophy

Many current philosophers see no reason to study the history of philosophy. The number of courses in the subject in most English and American universities has declined steadily in the last fifty years. [1] The knowledge of the history of philosophy required in most graduate programs in philosophy has diminished greatly. Many philosophical practitioners decry the teaching of a litany of dead or false theories. Instead, they want to deal only with what they consider true philosophies. For many, the history of philosophy is seen as "a brief introduction to the history of human stupidity" which lasted until Bertrand Russell, Ludwig Wittgenstein, and Martin Heidegger came along. And once that had happened, then why should one look back to a deluded past?

Along with this attitude, there has also been a general view that historical research about previous philosophers is of quite limited value, unless it illuminates the researcher's arguments. Otherwise, it is not of philosophical concern and can be left to historians, philologists, literature professors, and others who might be concerned with historical gossip about intellectuals of past times.

In contrast, the early nineteenth century saw Georg Hegel in Germany and Victor Cousin in France make the history of philosophy the core of advanced philosophical study. By seeing how philosophy had developed, one could then find the best or the better philosophy of the present age.

In all other areas of humanistic study—literature, art, music, etc. . . , the history of the subject is considered an important part of understanding the present-day writings, art works, and musical productions. The field of the history of science has grown in the last half century into an important area of study which helps us understand what present-day scientists are doing and how their work relates to past endeavors and to other kinds of human activities. There are now ongoing studies of the sociology and anthropology of science as well as its history. Up to now, these studies have been supported by the scientific community and have been largely underwritten in the United States by the National Science Foundation.

If other areas of human concern make use of their own historical background in order to understand where they are at present and where they are going, why is that so-called creative philosophy is actually hostile to studying its own history and discourages many efforts to see what it is doing in a historical perspective?

A key element of this hostility stems, I think, from the fact that philosophy, unlike other human intellectual and cultural activities, conceives of itself as timeless. Philosophy seeks *Truth;* it does not matter when and where this may take place. Benedict de Spinoza had explained why some writings can be understood apart from any historical knowledge, while others, like the Bible, he said, can only be understood in historical context. He used the example of Euclid's geometrical writings, but could have just as well used his own philosophical work, *Ethics.* "We can follow (Euclid's) intention perfectly and be certain of his true meaning without having a thorough knowledge of the language in which he wrote . . . We need make no researches concerning the life, the pursuits, or the habits of the author, nor need we inquire in what language, nor when he wrote, nor the vicissitudes of his book, nor its various readings, nor how, nor by whose advice it has been received.

"What we here say of Euclid might equally be said of any book which treats of things by their nature perceptible."[2]

Presumably, some writings, mathematical and philosophical, need no historical context in order to be understood because they deal with "things by their nature perceptible." However, mathematicians saw soon after Spinoza's time that Euclid's writings were part of Greek intellectual history and needed to be seen in terms of the problems that concerned mathematicians of that time. By now the critical edition of Euclid's *Elements* provides a wealth of information to make clear why Euclid did not take certain steps which became important later on and why he presented material the way he did. Euclid's *Elements* is now happily ensconced in the history of mathematics, and, as also is Isaac Newton's *Principia Mathematica,* a landmark in the history of mathematics and physics, to be studied in terms of its times and its contents.

Why does the same thing not happen to philosophical texts? Philosophers *doing philosophy* act as if the texts they are philosophizing about need nothing beyond the text to understand them. The most they see as relevant is not data about past times but what other contemporaries also doing philosophy have to say about the same texts. Many present-day discussions about Spinoza are about his arguments and how they are interpreted by contemporary philosophers, without reference to the wealth of historical materials that might elucidate what Spinoza might have been saying.

Other fields, even mathematics, recognizing that they are developing, are proud of the progress they are making or of the new and different orientation they are now presenting. They see that by considering what they are currently doing in terms of previous historical developments they can underline what is new, interesting, and important about present work and point to possible future lines of inquiry.

One can say philosophical work does this to some extent. It is almost always presented in terms of solving or resolving problems posed by previous historical figures, such as Plato, Aristotle, René Descartes, George Berkeley, David Hume, or Immanuel Kant, or even recent ones like Russell, Wittgenstein, Heidegger, and Jean-Paul Sartre. But as soon as a historian asks whether the actual historical figure said or meant what is claimed he or she said, an antihistorical outlook is set forth. It does not matter, we are told, if Plato said such and such. It only matters if his argument leads to a particular conclusion or position and if a present-day philosopher finds grist for his intellectual mill in the supposed argument or position of a previous person. Hence, there is no need to read the earlier thinker in the original language (even though much present-day philosophy is quite emphatic about the need to take great care about linguistic usages). There is no need to know if the terminology has changed in meaning over time. There is no need to know the context in which the argument was put forward. There is no need to know if there are clarifying materials about what the previous philosopher intended in his or her other writings, correspondence, etc. . . . We are told that a text says what it says, and any other information is irrelevant. Some have gone so far as to contend that it does not matter when a text was written or who it was written by. All that matters is the study of arguments. This becomes a kind of intellectual chess game taking place outside of historical time and space.

But who is to decide what arguments should be studied? As Constance Blackwell's article on the history of the history of philosophy shows,[3] development of what is considered the canon emerged historically from the Renaissance to the early nineteenth century. The texts studied in the Middle Ages and in the Scholastic universities of the sixteenth and seventeenth centuries were put aside, and new authors, like Francis Bacon, Descartes, and John Locke were studied instead. This kind of development has continued up to today with curricula being revised as new philosophical perspectives become dominant and as new thinkers are seen as important philosophers.

Not only is this kind of historical development going on in the study of philosophy and the study of philosophical arguments, no matter how ahistorical the practitioners may be, there is also a continuing increase in available philosophical texts to be studied. Some of the availability is due to decisions of publishers and their academic advisers trying to make money by packaging what they think will be studied in years to come, some to scholars employing the very best historical techniques to find the best texts, and some to scholarly sleuths discovering hitherto unknown texts.

During the late nineteenth century, and more during the twentieth century, massive projects have gone on to publish *all* of the writings and correspondence of Descartes, Spinoza, Gottfried Leibniz, Locke, Berkeley, Hume, Kant, Hegel, Friedrich Nietzsche, and others both in their original languages and in translation. Anyone working on such projects needs a great deal of historical training, not just an eye for arguments. Partly because of such projects, and partly due to the work of people adept in intellectual detective work, important works and letters of Descartes and some others have been turned up, some of which are now studied in the canon (such as Descartes's *Conversations with Burman,* Berkeley's *Philosophical Commentaries,* Hume's *Abstract of a Treatise of Human Nature* and his *Letter to a Gentleman.*) Unpublished writings of Wittgenstein, Russell, Heidegger, and other recent philosophers keep appearing. Some of this material throws significant light on texts already studied. So that it is not just timeless arguments that are the philosophical corpus, but revised and amended texts. Further, new information about authors of important philosophical arguments keeps being discovered in various archives. So, there is a continuous developing body of information that even the most ahistorical philosopher will find him or herself using in analyzing and evaluating arguments.

Instead of using modern examples, consider what is happening in the study of Plato's texts. He wrote dialogues and presented arguments within them. Many people just study the arguments. Others, as Gerald Press's article on Plato shows,[4] see the need to ask, if the arguments were intended as abstract timeless entities or part of dramatic interchanges, a play of ideas, in which nonphilosophical elements may have been just as important as the arguments? Most philosophers would say, "Who cares?" It is the arguments that are of interest, and not the setting they are in. But in the case of a great dramatic author like Plato, is it possible to make the separation? Some of the arguments may be part of the dramatic irony, some to represent the silliness or acuteness of various characters.

Many thinkers wrote their philosophical works in the course of many years and during changing conditions in the worlds in which they lived. Can one fasten on *an* argument as a timeless, independent entity, rather than what a historical personage said at a particular time under such and such circumstances? Of course one can, and it is done all the time in current philosophy teaching, discussion, and writing. But is that the best way of understanding the argument and the author of the argument (who may, like many of the people we know, have a developing and changing intellectual life and perspective)?

When one looks at current philosophical discussions, both the reader and the author need and make use of historical guideposts to place the material in an intellectually meaningful perspective. References are given to previous works by the author or others that set the stage for the present discussion. Indications that one is making use of terms and concepts in one manner rather than another are presented. And often some contextual apparatus appears, indicating that the present author's concerns grew out of a discussion that took place in some historical setting or grew out of the present author's reading a particular book or article. Material from the rich Russell archives at MacMaster University, from the Wittgenstein archives, and others keeps adding to the understanding of twentieth-century thinkers.

Two philosophical writings that appear on first sight to be presented completely ahistorically are Spinoza's *Ethics* and Wittgenstein's *Tractatus*. The latter was published only when Bertrand Russell wrote a preface to it, so the reader (and the publisher) could tell what issues the work dealt with. Spinoza deliberately decided to present his theory in geometrical form from the aspect of eternity. In form it looks as if all the reader has to do is learn the definitions, the axioms and the postulates, and then see if the propositions logically follow. Some readers do this and write articles about the good or bad or confusing logical development of the text. Others, including Spinoza, get more interested and excited by the meaning and import of what is being "demonstrated," namely, the pantheistic system, the denial of the explanatory power of supernatural religion, the way mind and body relate, etc. . . . . Spinoza wanted to make sure that readers realized the import of what was being presented, and so he added explanations, lengthy notes, and discussions apart from the logical apparatus. At the end of Book I, he offered a diatribe against traditional religion, claiming that the monistic system being developed ruled out the kinds of explanations offered in Judeo-Christian theology. Spinoza also added introductory essays putting his views in the context of what Descartes and others had written. Hence the ahistorical character of the work eroded as the author saw that he and the reader had to be part of a historical context. Spinoza's great achievement only becomes clear if one realizes how completely he differed from Jewish and Christian theological writers, and from Descartes. Recent research into the reception of Descartes's ideas in the Netherlands and into the intellectual ferment going on in the Amsterdam Jewish community are leading to new interpretations of Spinoza's contribution. Data continues being found about Spinoza and his times which helps in understanding the ahistorical arguments and text which he left us.

Wittgenstein in the *Tractatus* presented his thoughts in a numerical ordering and in aphoristic statements. The very title has historical resonance, to Spinoza's *Tractatus*. A reader around 1918 or 1920, like Bertrand Russell, (who had had previous discussions with the author) could place some of the statements in the context of what Russell, Gottlob Frege, and others had been discussing. Others could recognize phrases from previous authors, such as St. Augustine and Sextus Empiricus. Wittgenstein occasionally mentioned a name, like that of Arthur Schopenhauer, into his text. By now, when much more of Wittgenstein's writings are available, and much more is known about his intellectual development, one can claim, as some historians of modern philosophy do, that Russell actually misunderstood Wittgenstein since he did not know about the Viennese background of some of the text's discussion.

Spinoza and Wittgenstein are both now historical figures. New research into their lives and times has proved of much interest to current thinkers. New interpretations relating Spinoza to the situation of the time in the Netherlands, and relating Wittgenstein to the fin de siècle intellectual world in Vienna, have been rewarding both to those seeking to understand these thinkers, even if the argumentative structure in the works is unchanged.

The present-day ahistorical philosophers, who deplore the study of the history of philosophy, are also, nonetheless, themselves historical personages. They had teachers, and they know that their teachers did various things as historical individuals (such as advising governments, defending political positions, and advocating various creeds). The present-day philosophers have read certain books. They had interchanges with other thinkers. They wrote their philosophical works at a specific time for a specific audience. At present they may be able to presume that their auditors or readers have the background to understand them. But in a week, a month, a year, a decade, a century, it will be necessary for historians of philosophy to provide some background for new generations of readers, such as dates of works, sources of quotations, terms, or references to other relevant writings. Future readers may have to translate philosophical writings and determine what corresponds to today's thinker's ideas in another linguistic context. (This is happening all the time nowadays with the translations of French and German twentieth-century texts into English and English and American texts into French and German.)

No matter how hard ahistorical philosophers try, they cannot avoid being in history and being part of some historical developments. Why is this frightening? or objectionable? or irrelevant? If philosophy is supposed to be the quest for eternal truth, it is a quest that goes on in human history, carried on by various people in many different times, places, and cultures. We today could not be in contact with other truth seekers unless they left historical traces of their efforts and we had historically developed tools for finding and interpreting their traces.

I think the fear comes from two sources, one in seeing one's own philosophical achievements as part of previous developments, and hence probably about to be followed by other developments; and the other, the traumatic possibility that even our thoughts are relative, only to be understood in terms of historical and cultural features. Kierkegaard asked how can an eternal consciousness be based on a historical moment? He showed that it cannot be in any logical or rational or scientific manner. So Kierkegaard claimed it required a miracle for this to occur. The ahistorical philosopher cannot escape his historical existence; yet he believes his thoughts can and that placing his thoughts *in context* can only have deleterious results.

The argument surrounding the importance for philosophical understanding of Heidegger's Nazi activities revolves, in part, around whether these activities tell us something about the value of his thoughts when they are seen in such a context. In the discussion of this, which is far from over, important problems are being raised about the extent to which any person's thought can be separated from its context and from the moral or immoral world in which it was set forth. Some insist that Heidegger's arguments are *totally* independent of his political activities and are in no way questioned or invalidated by the facts about his life during the Nazi period. Others insist that his philosophy is both a theory and a practice which cannot be understood apart from the individual who wrote the philosophy and the individual who performed certain actions.

Maybe the only reason we do not have similar arguments about the views of Spinoza, St. Thomas Aquinas, and Kant is that we do not know enough about their politics. However, recent studies on Hume's racism and Kant's racism may lead to re-evaluating portions of their thought, or at least to reconsidering their ideas as part of their social messages.

It has been claimed that the history of philosophy is actually just the repetition and annotation of a basic set of ideas formulated in the ancient Greek and Hellenistic worlds. Some have said all philosophy is just footnotes to Plato and Aristotle. Others, like myself, would claim all philosophy is just footnotes or readaptations of ideas of Plato, Aristotle, Epicurus, the Stoics, Sextus Empiricus, and Plotinus.

Does this denigrate the present *doing* philosophy? I think not. Basic ideas need to be constantly adapted and interpreted to the changing human world and changing human concerns. This can best be done through an appreciation of what has gone on in philosophy's past, rather than by a rejection of the prior history and prior understandings.

Mathematicians and scientists seem able to accept their historical existence and see themselves as following in the footsteps of predecessors, yet making contributions that they think are significant. They seem to accept something like the Marquis de Condorcet's view about the potential infinite perfectibility of human understanding and see themselves as participating in an ongoing enterprise that makes continuous progress. They are also willing to accept great changes in basic assumptions, in ways of gaining evidence, and interpreting evidence.

The scientists, mathematicians, and teachers of literature, the arts, and music all seem willing to accept the fact that they are part of the intellectual and cultural life of a civilization at a given time and place. They are willing to accept that social and political forces act on them determining what will be financed by society, what will be permitted by society, and what will be encouraged by society. They seem to accept that patronage is part of the game and that they will prosper or fail depending on whether any person, or group, is interested in furthering their work.

Why are philosophers so different? Mostly they act as if they are in the so-called Ivory Tower, unaffected by social and political forces. They may be dealing with different sorts of problems that seem to change very little over centuries. But these are problems that concern human beings in history. In this century, we have had glaring examples of philosophy being used for political ends in Nazi Germany and in the Soviet Union. Less glaringly political and social forces have affected philosophy's role in France and Italy. In England during this century, philosophers have been political figures of some importance. In the United States, there has been a retreat on the part of most philosophy teachers from active roles in society, and the society seems less interested than in Europe in what philosophers are currently doing. At the present moment, a lot of what philosophers used to do in action and reaction to society has become the province of literary critics, political scientists, sociologists, and scientists.

Perhaps understanding the problems of philosophy and its position over the centuries in terms of the history of philosophy will enrich and improve the ongoing *doing* of philosophy and aid us in appreciating where we are and where we may be going intellectually.

MCKEON
The Unity of His Thought

Walter Watson

In "A Philosopher Meditates on Discovery", McKeon gives an account of the insight that seemed to him to have influenced his work in philosophy more than any other.[1] He says that the insight occurred in 1921,[2] which was before his study in Paris from 1922 to 1925, and that it had its background in the crossed influences of Woodbridge and John Dewey and its occasion in the reading of one or the other or both of two paradoxes. The first paradox, from Cicero's *De Finibus*, was that all philosophies except the Epicurean are particular expressions of the same truth, and the second paradox was from Plato's *Protagoras* and stated that "the good are sometimes bad and sometimes good," modified to "the true is sometimes false and sometimes true."[3] The insight is formulated as follows: "The recognition, therefore, that there is a sense in which truth, though one, has no single expression and a sense in which truth, though changeless, is rendered false in the uses to which it is put, was attractive in spite of the fact that it ran counter to my most fundamental convictions at the time."[4]

Pluralism

McKeon's early recognition that the truth has no single expression is also noted in the account of his philosophical formation that he gives in "The

Circumstances and Functions of Philosophy." He says that he was presented by his professors with a choice among various modes of philosophizing, which he enumerates, and continues,

> It did not seem necessary to me to assume that one of these modes of philosophizing was the unique true philosophy, or that what other philosophers said and did had to be thought to be odd, absurd, or meaningless, as it was said to be in the light of the true philosophy. The later revolts of neopositivistic, analytical, linguistic, and existentialistic philosophies provided further diversifications of materials and orientations with even less temptation to be converted to the new testaments.[5]

The preface to McKeon's doctoral dissertation, *The Philosophy of Spinoza,* contains his first formulation of this principle of pluralism: "Perhaps great philosophers and seekers after truth have been led by their divergent systems and terminologies to express in varying forms insights into a truth which is, for all that, at bottom one." McKeon's later conception of the philosophy of culture retains this pluralism, turning philosophic oppositions into supplementary solutions to cultural problems:

> The oppositions developed in a philosophy of culture will be turned into supplementary solutions of the particular problems of divergent cultures and of the common problems which make them parts of a common culture, and the unity of a philosophy of culture will be a pluralism of activities and communications directed to increasing and enriching the known facts and the practicable values which constitute the culture.[6]

It would seem, then, that the idea of pluralism is the generative idea of McKeon's philosophy and that the philosophy can be understood as the development of the paradox of a pluralism that affirms the truth of philosophies that are themselves opposed to one another.[7] There are, of course, other philosophers besides McKeon who have developed the idea of pluralism—Stephen Pepper and Wayne Booth, for example. In fact, anyone, no matter what his philosophy, can become a pluralist without abandoning the principles of his philosophy.[8] Eugene Garver even goes so far as to assert, "We are all pluralists today."[9] But McKeon, if not our only pluralist, is our preeminent pluralist and is likely to remain so. No one else has worked out the grounds and consequences of pluralism so fully and with such erudition, novelty, and suggestiveness for future inquiries. In what follows I propose to seek the unity of McKeon's thought in its pluralism and to understand the specific form of this pluralism as a consequence of the fundamental features that pervade his work.

Let us begin from the problem of why, according to McKeon, there are many philosophies. In *"Pride and Prejudice:* Thought, Character, Argument, and Plot," par. 1, McKeon distinguishes three possibilities with respect to a literary object of discussion:

> Yet a literary object of discussion is not simply an entity; nor is it a variable entity which takes its characteristics from the perspectives in which it is considered. It may, however, be variously considered—in itself as an artificial object, or in terms of the underlying circumstances which condition it and constitute its subject matter as a natural object, or in terms of meanings and references which it employs as a communicative object, or in terms of the ideas and values which it embraces as an intelligible object.

Thus what is in one sense the same object can be considered in different ways, and the result is a plurality of objects. We may be reminded here of the source of the plurality of disciplines in Aristotle's philosophy. The disciplinary perspective determines how the object is considered, but within the perspective the object itself determines what is true of it. McKeon contrasts this approach with an objectivist approach in which the mind simply conforms to the object and, on the other hand, with a relativistic approach in which the object takes its characteristics from the perspectives in which it is considered. The same threefold distinction is used in McKeon's last article, "Pluralism of Interpretations and Pluralism of Objects, Actions, and Statements Interpreted," par. 2. At this time in his life McKeon did not hesitate to schematize the arguments of the participants in a conference before the conference had taken place.

> Some participants will argue that there is only one true interpretation or criticism of a literary work, and their conception or philosophy of criticism will permit them to say that other proposed interpretations are false or pseudo-interpretations. Others will argue that more than one interpretation of a literary work can be made without affecting its unity or identity. Finally, some will argue that critical pluralism yields a variety of interpretations and a variety of related objects judged. In what follows I shall explore the grounds, ramifications, and

consequences of the position that critical pluralism is a plurality of judgments joined to a plurality of objects judged.

McKeon's pluralism is not a perspectival pluralism, in which the object acquires characteristics from the perspectives in which it is considered; nor a pluralism of hypotheses, in which different hypotheses are advanced with respect to the same object not yet fully known; nor what Wayne Booth has called a methodological pluralism, in which different formulations imperfectly reflect an object that exceeds and includes them all; but a disciplinary pluralism, in which different objects result from various ways of considering the same object.[10]

The facts about an object thus depend on the principles that determine how it is considered, and McKeon repeatedly asserts the interdependence of facts and principles. "Observation depends on thought no less than thought depends on observation."[11] "Whether or not it is supposed that certainty is possible in human and natural investigations, it must remain no less true that the nature of things, in so far as we know it, is determined by philosophic principles than that philosophic principles are determined, in so far as they are adequate, by the nature of things."[12] "Facts are not encountered as such in primary experience. The discovery of facts is by formation and invention as much as by information and encounter."[13] "Facts are as much determined by orientations as orientations are determined by facts."[14] "Facts are conditioned by men's philosophies in as definite a sense as philosophies are conditioned by relevant facts."[15] There is no escape from the sway of philosophic principles, which, together with the object, determine what facts are true of the object. Because the possible philosophic principles are plural, the expressions of truth are also plural.

When one turns from a semantic study of the multiple facts to inquiry into their object, McKeon recommends destroying the facts in order to see the object.

> It is well, in order to be able to see an object, to destroy the facts with respect to it, but you can't focus unless you have the facts there to destroy. This is exactly what happened in our most prestigious sciences—this is the way in which an advance is made, by changing the facts so radically that the school children of the next generation get the notion that the established truths and the geniuses that found them in the previous generation were simple-minded dopes: Because their facts are all gone.[16]

The process by which, from the confused whole of immediate experience, we make selections, propositions, orderings, and systems is sketched by McKeon as follows:

An initial immediate experience is a confused whole from which selections and simplifications are made in perspectives determined by attention and interest. They are stated in particular propositions and generalized in universal propositions. They fit into a compendent whole or are isolated into irrelevancies; they are ordered in inferential sequences or are opposed in contrarieties or contradictions. Neither existence or experience is *ab initio* an ordered whole of constituted facts or of spaced or sequential events. Occurrences, observations, errors, illusions, and fictions are all facts; and errors are sometimes as illuminative of experience as controlled, well-grounded experimental observations. A coherent system of relations may cease to apply to relevant facts, and an incoherent, opaque system of variables may be reinterpreted to become relevant and fruitful.[17]

Philosophy as Doctrine and as Power

What, if anything, prevents McKeon's philosophy from becoming just one more among the many philosophies whose truth it affirms or, on the other hand, from becoming simply the sum of these many philosophies? His philosophy is expressed primarily in a large number of separate articles. The published bibliographies list eleven books and 158 articles.[18] In what sense is a unified philosophy expressed by these many and diverse writings? Looked at in one way, the writings are highly unified, for their thought and style are so characteristic and distinctive that they are easily recognized as the works of a single unique and powerful mind. Looked at in another way, there is an irreducible plurality in the different writings, for they differ in their approach and content and do not fit together as parts of a single doctrine. They seem to call for a further synthesis. Andrew Reck in his book on American philosophers active since World War II did not include a chapter on McKeon "because his major work is yet to be published."[19] Do the articles then lead toward a synthesis that has not been, but might be, realized, or does their very diversity somehow exhibit the unity of McKeon's thought? In the one collection of his articles that McKeon himself published, *Thought, Action, and Passion,* it is through the diversity in their themes and techniques that McKeon weaves his articles into a unity.[20]

The articles were published over a span of nearly sixty years, and we must first consider the possibility that any differences among them reflect a developmental sequence. We are familiar with this method in its application to the philosophies of Plato, Aristotle, Immanuel Kant, Edmund Husserl, Martin Heidegger, Ludwig Wittgenstein, and others.

McKeon, however, enjoyed making fun of this method. Commenting on its application to Aristotle, he says,

"After the history of the stages of the evolution of Aristotle's philosophy has been worked out, he has early, late, and middle periods but he no longer has a philosophy. He begins with Plato's philosophy, ends with Theophrastus' philosophy after going through a period which is a melange."[21]

McKeon rejects in advance the application of this method to himself. In "Criticism and the Liberal Arts: The Chicago School of Criticism," he points out that his early paper on imitation, "Literary Criticism and the Concept of Imitation in Antiquity," as well as an unpublished paper on grammar, use the same fourfold paradigm of discrimination-assimilation-composition-resolution that was made explicit thirty years later in "Philosophic Semantics and Philosophic Inquiry."[22] When McKeon was asked by James Ford in 1982 whether there had been a development in his thinking in the sixteen years that had elapsed since the latter paper, McKeon replied, "What I wrote in the early articles and in the late articles is exactly the same; there's been no change. There have been alterations of vocabulary. . . . I have sometimes used paradigms with three terms, four terms, sixteen terms, but they can be translated into each other."[23]

Similarly, it would seem that one can discern vintages in McKeon's students: first those who saw in the ontological argument a touchstone for philosophic differences, then those who saw the contrast between Plato and Aristotle as fundamental, then those who focused on the semantic matrix, and finally those who turned from semantics to inquiry, arts, and topics. But when asked if he could discern vintages in his students, McKeon replied in characteristic fashion that the differences were more a matter of attitude towards his philosophy: at one extreme were the system-builders who extend and fix, at the other the diggers who work at some small part. Asked where Paul Goodman belonged, McKeon replied that he was a revolter, one who argued against McKeon's suggestions, and that Hippocrates Apostle was the same.[24] Rather than a change through time we have essential types: system-builders, diggers, and revolters.

But even if McKeon, like Socrates, can truly say, "I have always been the same,"[25] it is also the case that the sequence of his writings is remarkable for its continual development and novelty. It would indeed be strange, and hardly complimentary to McKeon, if his philosophy underwent no development in over a half century of philosophic activity. McKeon himself notes some of these developments in various contexts. In "A Philosopher Meditates on Discovery" he says that the steps by which his insight into the pluralism of philosophic truth was bodied forth in a broad interpretation of its significance were "slow and meticulous."[26]

At the end of the discussion following "The Organization of Sciences and the Relations of Cultures in the Twelfth and Thirteenth Centuries," he notes a change from an early semantics that refuted interpretations different from his own to a more subtle method that used these interpretations to indicate things in the text that before he had not suspected.[27] In his "Spiritual Autobiography" he says, "I have been impressed by the recurrent conviction that the significant part of what I know in relation to what I do, always has been acquired during the past year."[28] McKeon's philosophy is always the same, and develops from year to year.

Leaving this paradox unresolved for now, let us turn from the chronological sequence of the articles to their content. In general, each article is elaborately structured by a set of terms that take on definite meanings in the context of that article and that permit definite conclusions to be reached. But if the terms and statements are taken out of this context, they become ambiguous. McKeon is a contextualist in the sense that each of his articles develops its own intellectual context. The terms that structure the articles do not always have exactly the same meanings but are rather topics or places that take on definite meanings in relation to the particular materials being treated.

There are many recurrent sets of such terms in McKeon's writings, and four principal ones. The set *things-thoughts-words-actions* is used again and again in many different ways.[29] The semantic rubrics *selections-interpretations-methods-principles* are repeatedly used to order philosophic differences.[30] The four liberal arts, *grammar, rhetoric, logic, dialectic,* appear in many forms and guises.[31] The components of McKeon's philosophy of culture, what Douglas Mitchell has called the "grand dimensions" of his philosophy, are the interdependent arts of *topics, semantics, arts, inquiry,* and they serve to order what McKeon is doing in his various courses and articles.[32] If one examines the way these recurrent sets of terms are used in different contexts, one finds in them both the sameness and also the fluidity and openness of the rhetorical topic. Not only are they given different content in different contexts, but the topics themselves are related to each other in endlessly varying ways. Insofar as they are empty places, they can be reduced to each other or differentiated into new places. Sets of two or three terms are expanded into four or more, or these in turn are condensed into a smaller number; whole sets are differentiated from one another or merged with one another; they are applied to each other or to themselves to generate new distinctions and matrices without limit. Rather than some set of fixed meanings, there is at the core of McKeon's philosophy this fluid source of indefinitely many sets of fixed meanings.

Because even the terms that are used to order the multiple contexts of McKeon's philosophy—topics, semantics, arts, and inquiry—are themselves topics, McKeon's philosophy does not constitute a single system with well-defined parts such as the systems we attribute to Aristotle, St. Thomas Aquinas, René Descartes, Kant, or Georg Hegel. The systematizing terms are themselves ambiguous, so the system includes indefinitely many modes of its own systematization. It cannot be adequately expressed in a single definitive book employing a single unambiguous schema, or in a set of books or articles ordered by a single unambiguous schema, but it is appropriately expressed by indefinitely many articles each exhibiting an unambiguous form of ambiguous schemata. The "major work" in which McKeon's philosophy is expressed is precisely the totality of his articles. A brief selection of his articles cannot for this reason do justice to his philosophy, for it conveys the impression of a set of particular doctrines rather than of a capacity to generate indefinitely many doctrines.

The ways in which McKeon characterizes his philosophy as a whole reflect the paradoxical unity of the articles. It is most often a philosophy of culture,[33] but it is also a humanism,[34] a philosophy of communications and the arts,[35] and a philosophic rhetoric.[36] These different characterizations are all appropriate and not inconsistent, yet they also suggest that philosophy in its nature resists being pinned down by a single name just as it resists expression in a single work.

McKeon's philosophy is not a doctrine but is instead a power. What stands in the way of our realizing this is the very authoritativeness and definitiveness of the articles themselves. We suppose that each one is a final statement of his views and part of a system of unambiguous meanings. It is only when all the different articles on a given subject or making use of a given commonplace are studied in their relation to each other that we begin to see the power that lies behind the authority of the articles. McKeon's philosophy is like rhetoric, conceived, as it was by Aristotle, as the power to use in any given case the available means of persuasion. Each of the speeches produced by the rhetorician reveals something of the power of rhetoric, just as each of McKeon's articles reveals something of the power of his philosophy. But just as it would be a mistake to identify any one speech of the rhetorician, or even all of them taken together, with his art of rhetoric, so it would be a mistake to identify any one of McKeon's articles, or all of them taken together, with McKeon's philosophy. The unity of his philosophy is not to be found in any one article, nor in all of them taken together, but in the single power or art that produced them all.

The Schema of All Philosophies

What is the scope of this power or art? McKeon's philosophy seeks to comprehend within itself the full range of philosophy and culture that have in fact existed. Its scope or domain is the whole of culture, particularly the culture and philosophy of the West. Taken together, his writings provide an account of what is most significant at every stage of the cultural history of the West from Hellenic times to the present. Further, in approaching any problem, McKeon characteristically reviews the entire history that is relevant to it. His paper on the Bertrand Russell case reviews the history of similar judgments in the past, beginning with ancient Athens.[37] As a propaedeutic to a philosophy of method, McKeon glances at the entire history of theories of method from the first uses of the word to the present.[38] In his 1972 commencement address, "Where We Are and Where We Are Going" he glances at the history of education from Hellenic times to the present as a way of clarifying where we are and where we are going. A parallel historical sketch of the circumstances and functions of philosophy precedes the account of his own philosophical activity in "The Circumstances and Functions of Philosophy."

The inclusive scope of McKeon's philosophy is joined to accounts of the particulars that are remarkably accurate, perceptive, and novel. Whatever one's philosophical persuasion, and whatever one may think of pluralism or of McKeon, it is always instructive to read his accounts of thinkers and cultures. Here, for example, is a sentence on the philosophy of Plato: "Three political agents are sharply distinguished in the philosophy of Plato: the lawgiver, who in his formulation of the laws is divine and wise; the statesman, who may be wise and good in his administration of the laws and nonetheless fails, although he succeeds in achieving prosperity for the state, to make men good; and the philosopher, who might analyze the bases of law, educate men, refute Sophists, and in the happiest contingency rule the state."[39] In the literature on Plato, a great deal has been said about the philosopher-king, but how much attention has been given to the fact that the political dialogues distinguish the approaches of the lawgiver, the statesman, and the philosopher, and to the need for, and significance of, this distinction?[40]

Although McKeon's historical studies are valuable simply as histories, they are pursued not merely for their historical value but for the sake of future inquires. The effect of viewing cultural institutions in relation to their history, of understanding their origin and mode of constitution, is first of all that they are seen not as given or fixed, but as generated under specific conditions and embodying specific philosophic principles. When asked how history should be taught to undergraduates as a part of general education, McKeon replied by sketching a history of histories, of the conditions under which they arise and of how they are constituted. Thus, history appeared not as something given with determinate characteristics, but as a human art occurring under certain conditions and constituted in certain ways and susceptible of being other than it is.[41] The effect of taking cultural products back to their origins and exhibiting them as human constructions is one of liberation from what may have been unreflectively accepted or supposed fixed by the nature of things. A new domain is gained for the mind, which acquires power to understand and order and control what was formerly viewed as external to it. McKeon points out that taking into account problems treated by past philosophers has the effect of removing history and time from the determination and resolution of philosophic problems:

I learned by this process of backing through the history of Western philosophy that the relation of philosophy to the history of philosophy has been a persistent and varying exemplification of the reflexivity of knowledge: philosophers who take into account problems treated by past as well as by contemporary philosophers remove history and time from the determination and resolution of philosophical problems, while philosophers who are convinced that philosophy and philosophical problems have been newly discovered in the recent past give history and time a function in the determination and resolution of problems. For the one group, Plato, Aristotle, Augustine, William Ockham, David Hume, and Immanuel Kant are contemporaries in living discussions, while dead issues are found as frequently in contemporary journals as in ancient manuscripts; for the other group, philosophy and philosophical inquiry did not exist until it was made possible by Kant, or Friedrich Hegel, or Gottlob Frege, or Edmund Husserl, or Ludwig Wittgenstein, and there is no philosophical profit in reading works earlier than the date of the chosen disclosure and innovation.[42]

If history and time are removed from the determination and resolution of philosophic problems, and if past philosophers are contemporaries in living discussion, it is because philosophic problems are persistent as well as emergent and the solutions to them depend on principles that are independent of the historical context of their occurrence. "In the history of philosophy the occurrence, persistence, modification, and recurrence of philosophic positions escape the warfare of controversy and refutation."[43] If the whole of the past is to be made relevant to the future, it is through these recurrences. Here we may note a second feature of McKeon's pluralism that distinguishes it from other possible pluralisms. It is not a pluralism of different and incommensurable philosophies reflecting existentially different worlds, nor a provisional pluralism that will diminish as philosophies are replaced by the scientific truth about the nature of things, nor a pluralism of partial glimpses of a transcendent reality, but a pluralism of essential types of philosophic thought.

McKeon's histories characteristically disclose atemporal patterns that can be lifted out of their historical circumstances and that make them at least implicitly relevant to contemporary problems. The approach leads to the development of a schema of essential possibilities for philosophy at any time, to what McKeon has called his semantic schema. The semantic schema is a basic device for understanding and interpreting all philosophies and thus making them relevant to future inquiries.

The semantic schema should therefore help us to understand McKeon's own thought and its unity, for it presumably identifies the respect in which his philosophy remains the same even while it develops and changes. McKeon tells us, however, that when he is doing semantics, as distinguished from inquiry, he is not standing anywhere,[44] and thus would have no semantic profile. On the other hand, in "A Philosopher Meditates on Discovery," he says that the semantic schematism must be neutral, not in the sense of being conceived and stated apart from the methods it treats, but in the sense of being susceptible of statement without distortion in each of the methods.[45] In semantics, McKeon has no profile and all profiles.

As to the method he uses in inquiry, as distinguished from semantics, McKeon professes different methods in different articles. In "The Philosophic Bases of Art and Criticism," McKeon says of the essay itself, "It is an essay in the dialectical mode of criticism."[46] In *Freedom and History,* he says, "The present analysis, thus, employs a method of inquiry."[47] Similarly, at the end of "A Philosopher Meditates on Discovery," he says, "The course of inquiry which I followed and the exposition which I have just given of it, thus, employ the problematic method."[48]

In subsequent papers that identify their own method, the method is rhetorical or operational. In "Dialogue and Controversy in Philosophy," McKeon says, "The preceding analysis of dialogue and controversy was made from the point of view of the rhetorical or skeptical tradition in which the fundamental assumptions are that knowledge is advanced best by the free opposition of arguments, that a common truth may be given a variety of statements from different perspectives, and that there is an element of truth in all philosophic positions."[49] In "The Uses of Rhetoric in a Technological Age: Architectonic Productive Arts," he says, "The history of the development of culture in the West sketched in the preceding paragraphs is an application of the methods of rhetoric to the discovery of ourselves and our times."[50] In *"Pride and Prejudice:* Thought, Character, Argument, and Plot," he says, "This essay has used the art of rhetoric."[51] In the interview with James Ford, 1982, McKeon says, "The method that I use, when I'm doing philosophy and not Semantics, is an operational method. It is, therefore, as *if* I were being a Sophist dealing with the Aristotelian system."[52] The other elements in his profile, he says, are Aristotelian, but the method is operational: "When I'm doing Inquiry . . . I am using reflexive principles, because I have a multiplicity of sciences, operational method, because I am doing the construction, essentialist interpretation, and problematic selection."[53] Thus, here too McKeon's philosophy resists any limiting formulation of its unity that would make it inadequate to the full range of philosophic possibilities. McKeon uses all methods and one method, for it is characteristic of the operational method that it uses all methods and tests them by their consequences.

Paradoxicality

The attempt to state the unity of McKeon's philosophy has encountered multiple paradoxes. Opposed philosophies may all be true even in their denial of truth to each other, while a true philosophy may be false. McKeon's philosophy is always the same and yet develops from year to year. His philosophy cannot be expressed in any determinate set of books and articles, and yet is expressed in a determinate set of books and articles. He has no fixed paradigm, and yet his paradigm is "fixed, necessary, and conclusive."[54] His philosophy is fully situated in history and yet ahistorical. His philosophy exhibits a single semantic profile and all semantic profiles.

Further paradoxes can be added. McKeon's own philosophy is pluralistically open and tolerant of differences and yet fully committed and intolerant of differences. McKeon derives his pluralism from Cicero and Plato and his semantic profile from Aristotle and the Sophists, yet he says, "I have always been a neoteric."[55] A text has no fixed meaning, and McKeon is interested in taking Democritus as an idealist and Plato as a materialist,[56] and yet the semantic paradigm depends on fixed meanings derived from his readings of Democritus, Plato, and the rest.

These paradoxes may remind us again of Socrates' *Apology* and serve to warn us that McKeon's philosophy is no ordinary philosophy that can be easily understood or restated in familiar terms.[57] In general, those who attempted to restate McKeon's views when he was around to correct them were told by McKeon that they had not understood him.[58] McKeon does not conceive paradoxes to be obstructive, however, but generative. McKeon begins "Love, Self, and Contemporary Culture" with the paradoxical observation that, "Philosophical problems are stated most clearly and comprehensively today in paradoxes and dilemmas." "The Flight from Certainty and the Quest for Precision" begins, "The paradox of philosophy in the modern world is that it is at the center of everything that is said or done and yet totally removed from anything but philosophy."[59] Again, McKeon's "Spiritual Autobiography" begins from paradoxes in the relation of the facts of narrative to the ideas of argument, and asserts,

"The power and significance of autobiography and confessions have their sources in these paradoxes, however much they may distress those who seek simple meanings of what is said and simple separations of the facts of narrative from the ideas of argument."[60]

Inquiry that begins from problems stated in paradoxes does not aim to resolve the paradoxes, but to construct places in which both sides of the paradoxes may be developed. After two pages of stating paradoxes at the beginning of "Arts of Invention and Arts of Memory: Creation and Criticism," McKeon says,

> The function of critical inquiry is not to resolve such paradoxes but rather to construct places in which the varieties of poetry and of criticism may be developed as statements of common unstated experiences and of common encountered problems of poetry and criticism, which are named differently and are put in different contexts in different modes of making and knowing.

Dilemmas likewise are not resolved but used to advance inquiry:

> The dilemmas of philosophy and history, together with the dilemmas of the history of philosophy and the philosophy of history which are their theoretic counterparts, cannot be resolved. They would not be dilemmas if they could be. They can, however, be used to advance inquiry rather than stop it.[61]

Paradoxes yield a plurality of doctrines, whereas antinomies yield a single doctrine. Discussing the possible relations of critical doctrines, McKeon says,

> The critical doctrines that emerge may be different but analogous, and the relation between them may be stated, not in an antinomy, in which one must be true and the other false, but in a paradox, in which both doctrines may be derived, paradoxically, sometimes using paronyms rather than synonyms or homonyms, from a single doctrine; and the implication of a paradoxical derivation is that the consequences of the derivation are unexpected or novel. Antinomies yield one critical doctrine and many pseudocriticisms. Paradoxes yield a plurality of critical doctrines which in turn yield many interpretations of the same literary work, and raise the question whether the work interpreted remains the same or should be considered more than one work characterized by

the different properties uncovered in the different interpretations.[62]

In the sciences, paradoxical truths have displaced self-evident truths and self-contradictory antinomies.[63] McKeon traces their use back to the fourteenth century[64] and finds that twentieth-century physics and technology provide a model for the treatment of paradoxes.[65]

McKeon's pluralism is developed from paradoxes and is itself paradoxical. Strictly speaking, the paradoxicality does not reside in the relation between the horns of the paradox (if I may follow McKeon in attributing horns to paradoxes as well as to dilemmas), but in the relation between received opinion *(doxa)*, what everyone knows, on the one hand and the joint assertion of both horns of the paradox on the other. Received opinion supposes that both horns cannot be true, yet this is what the paradox asserts. The paradox thus generates a double tension, one between its two horns and the other between the joint assertion of the two horns and accepted opinion, that is, between McKeon's philosophy and accepted opinion. In this respect, McKeon's philosophy continually operates with the tension between the two meanings of commonplaces, for commonplaces as places of discovery are used to explode commonplaces in the sense of what everyone knows.

We may note here a third aspect of McKeon's pluralism that differentiates it from other possible pluralisms: it is not a logistic pluralism that reduces philosophies to their irreducible elements in order to determine what is verified or verifiable and what is not, nor a dialectical pluralism that finds a higher truth through the reconciliation of philosophies that seem to be opposed to one another, nor a resolutive pluralism that seeks to understand the reasons for the differences of philosophies and how these differences may be made to function in the resolution of common problems, but an agonistic pluralism that develops tensions and oppositions in order to test positions by their consequences.

The same method can be discerned in McKeon's philosophy, in the style in which it is expressed, and in the man himself. It is a method which sets McKeon's philosophy apart from all others and places it in opposition to whatever is commonly accepted. The style admirably captures this aspect of his philosophy, for it is no commonplace style, but one that presents a sustained challenge to the reader. As the challenge is met, the style and the thought become clear. The mystique, too, which surrounded McKeon while he was alive, and which tended to divide people into true believers and infidels, can be seen to have its source in the same contrast between McKeon with his paradoxical wisdom on the one hand and everyone else on the other. McKeon's students in their various ways tend to retain some sense of the superiority of what they are

23

doing to the accepted commonplaces of the time. But even the zealous disciple who studies all of McKeon's articles does not acquire his wisdom in so far as it resides not in the written articles but in the power to write them, and McKeon remains unique and superior to all. Here again one is reminded of Socrates and his statement, "Rightly or wrongly, men have made up their minds that in some way Socrates is different from the multitude of men."[66]

It is tempting to try to dissociate whatever one finds excellent in McKeon or his philosophy from those aspects of the man or his philosophy that one finds objectionable. One may think the philosophy acceptable but the man intolerable. Or one may think the content of the philosophy appealing but the style rebarbative. Or one may think that McKeon would be a great teacher if he were not a bully.[67] (Here again one is reminded of Socrates and of Alcibiades' accusation, "You are a bully, as I can prove by witnesses, if you will not confess."[68]) It will doubtless be possible for interpreters of McKeon to separate what they find valuable in his philosophy from the features they perceive as faults, but if one wishes to understand McKeon's pluralism in its origin and unity one must take the opposite course, and see what are perceived as faults and as essential conditions of his achievement. McKeon provides, perhaps, a noteworthy example of the human capacity to return good for ill, for the compensation for narcissistic injury has in his case resulted in a benefit to all mankind, although even in receiving the benefit we are reminded of the injury from which it came.

The Influence of McKeon

I have been seeking the unity of McKeon's thought in its pluralism. This pluralistic unity can be fully realized in the work of no individual philosopher nor even in that of the profession as a whole, but only in the activities and communications of the culture. An individual philosopher such as McKeon may, however, develop a philosophy of culture in accordance with which, as we noted at the outset, philosophic oppositions are turned into supplementary solutions to cultural problems, and the unity of the philosophy will be the pluralism of activities and communications directed to increasing and enriching the facts and values that constitute the culture:

> The oppositions developed in a philosophy of culture will be turned into supplementary solutions of the particular problems of divergent cultures and of the common problems which make them parts of a common culture, and the unity of a philosophy of culture will be a pluralism of activities and

24

communications directed to increasing and enriching the known facts and the practicable values which constitute the culture.[69]

The pluralistic unity of a philosophy of culture is not something that now exists; it is yet to be attained, projected rather than achieved. A new kind of philosophy for the future may be unified in communication and cooperation among a plurality of perspectives focused on common experience:

> The philosophy of culture opens up the possibility of a new kind of philosophy for the future which will be unified in communication and co-operation without the need of consensus in a common ideology. Common problems will be treated by considering consequences of statement and action rather than by constructing and relating imputed antecedents in individual, national, or cultural characters. The possibility of agreeing on common solutions of common problems for differing reasons and by application of different methods will be subject to control by reference to concrete facts and values. The common experience of mankind may be made a source of diversified but coherent facts and values.
>
> The unity of an ongoing philosophy of experience and humanity is a product of a plurality of perspectives focused on common experience rather than a consensus of opinions stated in a common belief.[70]

Here we may note a final respect in which McKeon's pluralism differs from other possible pluralisms: its functioning does not depend on the creativity with which philosophers respond to one another's arguments, nor on the physical elements that are the ultimate causes of all thought, including our philosophies, nor on the grand design of which pluralism is a component, but on itself, on its actualization in the activities and communications of the culture.

During his lifetime, McKeon engaged in activities and communications appropriate to his conception of the philosophy of culture. He wrote many reviews of books by his contemporaries, and in "An American Reaction to the Present Situation in French Philosophy," he surveyed the diversities within the then current French philosophy. He was advisor to the United States Delegation to the first three General Conferences of UNESCO, in 1946, 1947, and 1948, and participated in the UNESCO studies of the foundations of human rights and of the idea of democracy. In 1954 he conducted, under the auspices of UNESCO and the Indian Philosophical Congress, a series of eighteen roundtable discussions at Indian universities on human relations and international obligations. He was president of the Western Division of the American Philosophical Association in 1952, of the International Institute of Philosophy from 1953 to 1957, and in 1966 gave the Paul Carus Lectures.

There was, however, a certain one-sidedness in McKeon's interactions with his contemporaries, for there was little contemporary examination and discussion of his work. This was a natural consequence of the difficulty of his philosophy and its difference from the philosophies being pursued by most of his contemporaries. From the standpoint of the philosophy of culture, the effort to establish one's philosophy as the one true doctrine appears rather futile, but if one is engaged in developing and promulgating the true doctrine, then a nondoctrinal philosophy appears empty and sophistical, hardly a philosophy at all. Similarly, the turn from debate and refutation to discussion of common problems seems premature if the discussion aims to reach agreement on the truth. Everyone knew of McKeon, and he was the subject of the most widely varying judgments, but few devoted much attention to the examination and criticism of his work.

In the long run, however, the very reasons that led to his lack of influence during his own lifetime assure his important and continuing influence. The acceptance of pluralism greatly enriches the content of philosophy and at the same time makes more evident its functioning in all cultural activities. McKeon's articles, even though addressed to his contemporaries, often seem to be oriented to future readers and to invite the kind of careful textual analysis that he himself practiced on the works of his predecessors.

But if McKeon had little effect on those whose philosophies were already formed, the opposite is true of his effect upon students. McKeon profoundly influenced many generations of students in diverse ways. He did not, however, and here again one is reminded of Socrates, produce a school or a recognized group of disciples. The reason for this again lies in the peculiarity of his philosophy, for if his philosophy is a power rather than a doctrine, what is the disciple to make his own and to teach? To transform oneself into another McKeon is not a feasible project. One can indeed devote oneself to expounding his writings and their significance, and this is an important task. But the usual effect of McKeon on his students is that each takes from his philosophy what he will and makes use of it in his own way, and this is an appropriate mode of influence for a pluralistic philosophy such as his.

There is, however, a problem that in closing I would like to propose for future consideration, and this is how to teach McKeon's philosophy. The same peculiarities that make his philosophy resistant to reduction to a commonplace form make it difficult to teach in a customary way. It would seem that it should be taught as a set of arts rather than as a doctrine, and that these arts can best be taught not by studying the philosophy as such but by using it to structure the study of other cultural materials. This is, indeed, how McKeon taught his philosophy. He normally made no use at all of his own writings.[71] But his pluralistic philosophy lends itself admirably to the design of courses and curricula, and McKeon excelled in this. Perhaps the best known of the courses he designed was the philosophic integration course in the University of Chicago College: Observation, Interpretation, and Integration.[72] McKeon himself taught a section of this course the first year that it was offered, in 1943–44, and it was my good fortune to be a student in that section for the first two quarters, before I was inducted into the army. McKeon was also influential in the design of the three-year humanities sequence in the college.[73] A design for a course in Latin literature and Roman culture is among his publications.[74] His four new liberal arts have inspired a number of courses and programs.[75]

But now that McKeon is no longer with us, and the nearest approximation that we have to the living person is his writings, it would seem that we should find ways to use them effectively. We cannot expect the writings taken by themselves to produce the excitement and the insight and the mastery that are characteristic of the courses designed with their help, for McKeon's ideas come to life in relation to the materials they order. Nor can we expect the writings taken by themselves to convey the intellectual exhilaration that was characteristic of McKeon's personal teaching, for they cannot compel our interest and attention as did the living person. No philosopher, perhaps, is adequately represented by his writings. Is the philosophy of Plato, for example, adequately represented by his dialogues? He tells us that it is not. And yet we think we are able to use the writings of philosophers to apprehend their philosophies. How, then, can McKeon's writings best be used to apprehend his philosophy and to make whatever merits it possesses effective in the world? The future of McKeon's philosophy depends not only on the publication of his writings, but also on the discovery of how best to use them.

In summary, then, I have sought to present the unity of McKeon's thought as its pluralism. McKeon conceives pluralism to result from the various ways in which the same object may be considered. He expresses the pluralism not in a single doctrine or system, but in a plurality of articles each of which embodies an unambiguous form of ambiguous topics. The unity of the articles lies in ambiguous topics made unambiguous by a single power or art. The scope of this power extends to all philosophies and to the whole cultural history of the West, a range of materials that is ordered by the semantic schema. The semantic schema is a single schema that includes the plurality of opposed philosophies. The unity of the opposed philosophies in a single philosophy is a paradoxical unity that sets McKeon and his philosophy apart from accepted views and opinions. The paradoxical unity of his philosophy is to be realized in the future as a pluralism of activities and communications directed to the solution of cultural problems. In our own time, the provocative novelty of his pluralistic treatment of a wide range of cultural materials has led, as might be expected, not to a school of followers united by a common doctrine, but to diverse appropriations of his thought that are united by their common indebtedness to McKeon. This book presents some of the many ways in which McKeon's philosophy has been influential in our time.

BETWEEN PRAGMATISM AND REALISM
RICHARD MCKEON'S PHILOSOPHIC SEMANTICS

David J. Depew

Richard McKeon was a graduate student at Columbia University when its philosophy department, presided over by John Dewey and Frederick A. Woodbridge, was in its *floruit*. After a sojourn in France studying Medieval philosophy with Etienne Gilson and Leon Brunscwig, McKeon began teaching the history of philosophy at Columbia. In 1935, he was summoned to the University of Chicago at the behest of its *enfant terrible* president, Robert Maynard Hutchins, who had been put onto McKeon by their mutual friend, the contentious neo-Thomist Mortimer Adler. At Chicago, McKeon served as dean of the recently organized Division of Humanities, as well as professor of philosophy and classics. As dean, McKeon had important, and delicate, responsibilities in the reform of undergraduate education that became known as the Hutchins College. Thus McKeon, having been educated at Columbia in its glory days, played a role in bringing the University of Chicago into what has seemed to many to be its glory days.

In these bare facts lies the germ of the tale I want to tell. It is a tale of two universities, of two philosophy departments, and of one man's answers to questions that were sharply debated within and between these institutions at a particular juncture of American intellectual history. My claim will be that McKeon's project of philosophical semantics, and his proposal for a philosophical rhetoric, can profitably be interpreted as a creative, if somewhat baroquely elaborated, resolution of quarrels that throughout the twenties and thirties pitted self-described realists against self-described pragmatists in American philosophy departments, nowhere more intensely than at Columbia. This is a context to which McKeon himself hardly alludes, whether in his autobiographical or scholarly writings. So the story I want to tell must be limned by reconstructing the circumstances in which McKeon came to maturity as a philosopher and by guessing at how he threaded his way through them. I will end by suggesting that McKeon's silence about these matters obliquely reflects the very position about philosophy that he came to adopt, and so mutely testifies to the interpretation I am placing on his work.

I

Classical pragmatism—the pragmatism that culminated (and ended) in Dewey—was rooted in Charles Sanders Peirce's recognition that all real thinking is problem-solving. No real problem, says Peirce, no real thinking. From this it followed that well-founded belief is the temporary cessation of genuine puzzlement through successful inquiry—"a demi-cadence," as Peirce put it, "in the symphony of our intellectual life." It also followed that ideas are dynamic instruments or tools of thinking, not inert pictures of a static reality. As Peirce's defection from William James's rhapsody on this theme indicates, however, what McKeon was to call the "problematic" conception of methodological thinking was only a necessary condition for full-blown pragmatism. What was needed in addition was eagerly provided by James. It was the claim that inquiry, ideation, and belief formation are organic functions. Thus, when A. O. Lovejoy, a realist opponent of classical pragmatism, characterized the pragmatic movement in terms of the view that "knowledge consists of those general propositions . . . which have in past experience proved biologically servicable to those who have lived by them," he was doing no more than commenting on Jamesian remarks like the following: "Taking a purely naturalistic view of the matter, it seems reasonable to suppose that, unless consciousness served some useful purpose, it would not have been superadded to life."[1]

Unlike Peirce, James had more than vague ideas about the evolutionary etiology of mental traits. He was in fact explicitly Darwinian about them, claiming "that new modes of thought and conceptual innovations spring up in the mind as spontaneous mental variations. We come to accept them as representations of the environment only if they continue to meet the test of survival."[2] Yet, in his environmentalism James was very far from social Darwinism. Unlike Oliver Wendell

Holmes, Jr., his Harvard contemporary, James did not think that people are necessarily up against the wall in a brutal struggle for mere life. For he believed that there had long been, as there still is, selection pressure for learning skills themselves. Reasoning that any adaptation that yields a capacity for reacting creatively to a wide range of environmental contingencies will, *ceteris paribus,* be more valuable than one that dictates only fixed reactions to relatively stereotyped occasions, James argued that the human mind is a highly valuable adaptation, the spontaneity and creativity of which allows us to respond flexibly to the contingencies and indeterminacies of experience by way of versions of the world that guide and shape further experience. James was, on this score, among the founding fathers of what I call Progressive Darwinism: Darwinism in the service of democratic ideals.

The degree to which Dewey was affected by this idea cannot be exaggerated. Yet, Dewey did not believe, as he perhaps unfairly thought James did, that such an account allows each of us individually to count as true whatever helps us get up in the morning. Rather, what Dewey called "the influence of Darwinism on philosophy" should lead us to favor a range of redescriptions of experience in which individual life is characterized as social and in which social life is described in interactive and cooperative terms that foster ongoing projects of social reconstruction through communal experimental inquiry and democratic decision making. This shift from individual reinterpretation to collective reconstruction is what Dewey meant when he remarked, in an autobiographical sketch far more insightful than most instances of this generally self-serving genre, that James did not "fully and consistently realize . . . the return to a biological conception of the *psyche*" that he was primarily responsible for reintroducing to a post-Darwinian world.[3] By focusing on humans as social animals, Darwinian adaptationism, as Dewey understood it, provided a way of articulating a new Aristotelian naturalism, in which, in an open, unfinished world, humans appear as problem-solving animals, and their linguistically mediated social environment seems as natural to them as water to fish.

In Dewey's opinion, the consequences of this view for philosophy are great. If beliefs are adaptations, and adaptations are, by their very nature, referentially tied to the particular environmental conditions and needs to which they respond, "interest shifts from the wholesale essence back of special changes to the question of how special changes serve and defeat concrete purposes," as Dewey puts it in "The Influence of Darwinism on Philosophy."[4] This means that outside of their relevance to a real problem-solving situation, or what Dewey calls "inquiry," ideas lose their meaning. Transcendental illusions, that is to say, will accompany thinking outside of a real problematic context, and not just, as Kant thought, thinking beyond the bounds of empirical sensibility. In the naturalistic space thus secured by evolutionary psychology and episte-mology, the problems of philosophy are not to be "dropped," but "re-constructed" by translating them into a fruitful vocabulary for social reform. When Dewey claimed that reconstruction in philosophy would turn its practitioners toward "the problems of men" and away from "the problems of philosophers," he was suggesting the primacy of tech-nical-practical reason over contemplative *theoria* that was built into his adaptationist theory of mind. In homage to Marx, whose affinities to Dewey were first noted by Dewey's student Sidney Hook, I will call this aspect of classical pragmatism the primacy of praxis.[5]

By the thirties, another implication of classical pragmatism began to come to the fore, an aspect that by the early fifties would virtually de-fine (or redefine) what it meant to be a pragmatist. As the penetrating work of C. I. Lewis made vividly clear, thinking does indeed take place in and through conceptual frameworks of various sorts, as Kant and Hegel had argued. (Atomism, for example, roughly approximates such a framework, as does Aristotelian essentialism or Platonic transcenden-talism.) But, according to Lewis, and even more his student W. V. O. Quine, there simply is no matter of fact about which conceptual frame-work is the privileged medium for encoding basic truths about the world and human experience. The term pragmatism was soon assigned to this doctrine of conceptual relativism. Rudolf Carnap was alluding to this way of taking the term when he proclaimed that he had taken a prag-matic turn in recognizing that it is neither true nor false that numbers (for example) exists, although if you do adopt a framework of numbers it is as true as anything can be that two plus two equal four, and as false as anything can be that it equals five.[6]

Dewey's later philosophy, I believe, is increasingly vexed by the con-ceptual pluralism latent in his own philosophy. Especially after his ex-tended visit to the Far East in the twenties, Dewey's stock formula about the problems of men displacing the problems of philosophers came to imply that philosophers had not only been wasting their (and everybody else's) time by obsessively trying to decide which conceptual framework is *the* privileged medium for representing the world as it objectively is, but were actually adding to the world's woes by doing so. For so long as one harbors, however secretly, the conviction that one way of putting things is in principle capable of trumping all others, one will be placing constraints on communication, thereby increasing the chances of the sorts of misunderstanding that lead to violence, sometimes on a world-wide scale. If unreconstructed philosophers were a negative force in the world, reconstructed philosophers could be a positive force—but only if their belated recognition of conceptual pluralism leads them to offer their services as interdisciplinary and cross-cultural translators, inter-preters, and conceptual therapists.

It was in this context that Dewey began to use the term "communication" as an architectonic concept.[7] The problem was that in practice Dewey himself was not much of a conceptual pluralist.[8] He still seemed to hope that everyone everywhere would adopt the semi-Darwinian argot in which he had formulated the problems and priorities of the Progressive era. In my view, it was primarily the tension between the primacy of praxis and the relativity of conceptual frameworks that turned Dewey's intended masterwork, *Experience and Nature,* into the flop that he himself recognized it to be. As Richard Rorty has insightfully shown, Dewey retreated in this work from genuine pluralism by elevating his preferred adaptationist vocabulary to the status of a metaphysical first principle, when he might have (and in Rorty's view should have) become a full-fledged relativist by abandoning his pious attachment to philosophy altogether instead of fruitlessly attempting to reconstruct it.[9]

II

To more fully appreciate what pressures led Dewey in this direction, we must turn to his relationship with his professional philosophical colleagues in the period roughly between the mid-twenties and the mid-thirties. Sensing that philosophy could no longer preside serenely over an increasingly irrational culture, or indeed find a secure place as a professional discipline in the modern university, if it were reconstructed in Dewey's prescribed manner, the majority of American academic philosophers, led by Lovejoy, Roy Wood Sellars, Morris Raphael Cohen, and Woodbridge, had by about 1930 categorically rejected both of the pillars of pragmatism that I have been describing: the primacy of praxis and conceptual pluralism.[10] When they described themselves as "realists," these men meant different, often contradictory things. But whatever differences might have cropped up between commonsense realists, new realists, critical realists, Brentanean realists, Aristotelian realists, or any other sort of realist (including the strange poetic realism of George Santayana), all American realists meant to affirm that the human mind is capable of contemplatively grasping the world the way it uniquely and actually is. By calling themselves realists, they were proclaiming precisely that they were *not* pragmatists.

The fact that Dewey, America's preeminent philosopher, held views that were perceived to have a potential for destroying professionalized philosophy was felt especially keenly at Columbia, where Dewey had taught since leaving Chicago in 1904. This circumstance provoked an effort within the Columbia department to push Dewey back toward a more conventionally contemplative position. Woodbridge, chair of the department, sometime dean of the college, and editor of the *Journal of*

Philosophy, the profession's journal of record, was an Aristotelian realist who tried hard, and in part successfully, to get Dewey to recognize the Aristotelian element in his (Dewey's) own thought. Woodbridge (who had long before been taught by the great German Aristotelian F. A. Trendelenberg) confessed in an autobiographical sketch that "Aristotle has said everything which I have ever said or shall ever say."[11] McKeon says of him that he "taught that ideas are not inventions constructed by the mind, but discoveries forced upon us by compelling realities whose natures are basically intelligible."[12]

What Woodbridge wanted Dewey to recognize was that Aristotle, Aquinas, Dewey, and Woodbridge himself all shared "the same" philosophy of mind, but simply differed about the biological machinery that supported it—a purely empirical, and at least for philosophers, relatively trivial issue. Dewey acknowledged that, in proclaiming that "By nature all humans have a desire to know," Aristotle too thought that inquiry was grounded in a largely naturalistic problem-solving impulse. He denied, however, that he shared Aristotle's and Woodbridge's philosophy of mind. For in his view, to agree with Woodbridge that the range of adaptive capacities we collectively call mind remains "the same" whatever material or organic conditions undergird them (a view curiously reminiscent of the functionalisms that flourish in contemporary American philosophy departments) would be to concede three crucial points. First, it would reify and substantialize quite disparate capacities, biasing the issue in question toward Cartesianism. Second, it would be to miss the whole point of the Darwinian revolution. For Dewey, as for Darwin, there could be no difference between the nature of a thing and its mode of generation or coming to be. So it could hardly be a matter of indifference how the various powers we call "mind" came to be. Finally, if Woodbridge was right, the mind would be capable of transcending its own natural and social conditions and engaging in private contemplative knowledge, as indeed Cohen and Sellars were insisting that it could. In privileging *theoria,* Dewey thought that the drift toward philosophical realism was a way of deflecting the progressive political implications of pragmatism and of maintaining a priestly caste of philosophers. This would let philosophers go on endlessly attacking their inconsequential "conceptual" problems, and guessing at the uniquely correct conceptual framework in which the world was encoded, without doing anything about real and pressing ills. In *Experience and Nature,* accordingly, which is to a considerable degree a response to Woodbridge, Dewey tried to rebut this threat by showing that the problems of metaphysics could only be resolved by assuming his own version of Darwinian adaptationism. To put the matter this way, however, was for Dewey to become something of a metaphysician himself. It was from this time that Columbia pragmatists began calling themselves "empirical naturalists," thereby nesting in one of the professional pigeon holes that pragmatism was ostensibly designed to destroy.

III

McKeon was a graduate student in an atmosphere dominated by the realist-pragmatist debate, and in particular by its local version at Columbia. This was an atmosphere in which younger faculty members and doctoral candidates vied with one another to mediate the differences between Woodbridge and Dewey. It was an atmosphere in which John Hermann Randall was soon to write a book about an Aristotle who sounded a lot like Dewey and in which Ernest Nagel, who, like Hook, had been the realist Cohen's student before he was Dewey's, would help nudge pragmatism toward playing the philosophical underlaborer on behalf of the hegemonic role of scientists in reforming society—an elitist attitude hitherto monopolized by realists, which stood in stark contrast to the plebian participatory democratic impulses of classical pragmatism and foreshadowed the subsequent assimilation of pragmatism to expertise-oriented logical empiricism in the forties and fifties.[13]

For his part, McKeon studied with Dewey just after the latter's return from his extended stay in China and Japan, and thus at a time when Dewey was most alive to intercultural communicative problems and to the possibility of cultural pluralism. Throughout his life, McKeon tried hard to honor his Deweyan inheritance by recognizing ineliminable interpretive diversity. Together with Dewey's mature stress on preserving and expanding the conditions of communication, conceptual pluralism forms the cornerstone of his own philosophy.

If McKeon had more success than Dewey in actually being a conceptual pluralist, it was in part because it was a perspective that was natural to him. Recalling his early years studying the history of philosophy, McKeon says that he was delighted to find himself exposed by Gilson to a whole range of positions that he had not previously known in any detail. "It did not seem necessary to me," he wrote, "to assume that one of these modes of philosophizing was the unique, true philosophy, [just as] the later revolts of neopositivistic, analytical, linguistic and existentialist philosophies provided further diversification of materials and orientation with even less temptation to be converted to the new testaments."[14] It was also from Gilson, and not from Woodbridge or Dewey, that McKeon acquired a taste for what is called "the perennial philosophy"—the idea that all great thinkers, by the very fact that they are great, participate in a timeless conversation in which a finite number of possible philosophical positions are accessed again and again, and in which, in spite of differences, there is, as McKeon puts it, "a homogeneity in the discussion inasmuch as they raise the same or comparable questions and give different answers to them."[15]

McKeon's academic genealogy as well as his uncompromising conceptual pluralism should allow us to count him as a pragmatist rather than a realist, as these terms were then understood, were it not for the fact that McKeon declined to acknowledge, as Dewey forthrightly did in proclaiming the primacy of praxis, that the contemplative stance of philosophers is itself no more than an ideological reflection of static, hierarchical, authoritarian societies. Historical materialist talk of this sort would have sounded a bit Stalinist (and in consequence hostile to professional philosophy) in the ideologically charged cultural environment in which McKeon was working. Indeed, McKeon sounds like a card-carrying realist (and orthodox anticommunist) when he confesses that he had "never felt attracted to the use of pragmatic principles or dialectical methods, preferring to treat theoretical and practical questions separately rather than to assimilate theory to practice or practice to theory;"[16] or when he asserts that the problems of philosophy, which Dewey had invidiously contrasted with "the problems of men," now "have greater importance beyond philosophy than they have ever had before;"[17] or when he says that "we have found no means of making explicit and effective the underlying common values which would save values from the relativism into which they fall when they are naturalized and localized in cultures;"[18] or finally when he proclaims, in an explicitly anti-Deweyan remark, that "The cultivation of scientific method and 'real problems' may be the excuse for the neglect of truths that have been discovered and of errors that have been exposed."[19]

I am now in a position to restate my main contention a bit more precisely. I believe that McKeon's philosophy splits the difference between realism and pragmatism. He agrees with realists that contemplation, and so philosophical inquiry, has priority over practice. At the same time, he forthrightly proclaims that pragmatists are right about conceptual pluralism. Just what this position amounts to remains to be seen. But whatever it might mean, it probably seemed to McKeon to have practical advantages as well as theoretical ones. It was a way of keeping philosophy professional while at the same time making it profoundly useful. For if a discipline, even a science, could be devoted to studying the many ways in which equivalent or at least comparable truths could be encoded and translated, philosophers could lend a hand to policy makers in disentangling substantive differences from mere matters of formulation, thus preventing the latter from freezing up into dangerous ideological fixations of belief. Without being liquidated into praxis, philosophy could thereby acquire something that would have seemed important to a man whose first studies were, after all, as an engineer—an applied side.

These reflections yield some clues about why Hutchins may have brought McKeon to Chicago in the first place. The fact that a student of the Thomist Gilson came to Chicago at the behest of the truculent Thomist Adler might encourage one to believe that McKeon was also a Thomist, or at least a secular Aristotelian. It is a myth that has bedeviled McKeon's image ever since. The fact of the matter is, however, that whatever Hutchins or Adler might have hoped, it was sufficient that the new dean of the Division of Humanities be an intellectualist, a moral realist, and a studiously anticommunist liberal. McKeon fit that bill to a tee. Conceptual pluralism combined with ardent philosophical intellectualism supported liberal values, liberal education, and liberal institutions without in the least flirting with moral scepticism. It also meant that McKeon could be counted on by Hutchins and Adler to at least tacitly acquiesce in their efforts to rid the University of Chicago of the remnants of the praxis-centered pragmatic Progressivism that, in the person of such figures as George Herbert Mead, had taken root in Chicago in Dewey's day.

The intellectualist spin that McKeon and his allies managed to put on the humanities curriculum of the undergraduate experiment known as the Hutchins College testifies to McKeon's effectiveness as an academic politician. At a time when undergraduate education was a hotly debated topic, Hutchins, as is well known, was interested in integrating the undergraduate curriculum and stripping it of its overly disciplinary and preprofessional cast. In his view, the allegedly liberating aims of the liberal arts were to be achieved by inviting students and faculty to jointly interpret, on a nonexpert basis, the great texts of the Western civilization. These were conceived, as in Medieval universities, as including both the quadrivial mathematical and the not-so-trivial verbal arts, and therefore as embracing the foundational texts of the natural and social sciences as well as those of the literary and humanistic tradition. It was a distinctly intellectualistic program, which has given a certain cast to a Chicago undergraduate education to this day, long after Hutchins's way of institutionalizing this vision has disappeared. What was most novel, I think, about this program for undergraduate education was that the freedom allegedly granted by theoretical wisdom was no longer to be associated with authoritarian teaching. Indeed, in a quirky reversal, the democratic and participatory pedagogy of the pragmatic movement, which had been developed during the Progressive period at Chicago and at Columbia, was to be reoriented toward an intellectualist rather than toward a pragmatic and "progressive" goal, in large part as a way of immunizing reflective students against nonliberal political ideologies of all sorts. In institutionalizing such a curriculum, the Hutchins College was to a considerable extent the McKeon College.

IV

I can say little more to support my interpretation of McKeon without leading the reader some way into the icy waters of the interpretive scheme that he spent much time devising as a method for parsing and comparing philosophical claims. Beginning from so simple a distinction as that between holoscopic (whole-oriented) and meroscopic (part-oriented) thinkers (Plato was holoscopic, Aristotle meroscopic), what McKeon called "philosophical semantics" eventually ballooned into a sixteen-fold categorial matrix characterized in the following way by McKeon's friend and colleague Elder Olson:

> [McKeon] produced no philosophy, as such, of his own, no system of doctrines. What he did produce was something that I have likened elsewhere to a Copernican Revolution; not a philosophy, but a metaphilosophy, which, in its systematic display of the oppositions and correlations of diverse philosophies, adumbrated a matrix from which all valid philosophies were generated, as well as a general dialectic explaining how the diverse dialectics operated. He produced a key—hinting at the key—to all philosophy.[20]

McKeon's philosophical grammar begins from the fact (already known by Aristotle) that every argument has (1) terms or elements, (2) premises, (3) inferences, and (4) conclusions. Rather in the manner of Kant, McKeon puts a slightly more categorial spin on this fact when he claims that every argument has a *selection* of materials with which to work, *principles* from which to proceed, a *method* by means of which it can get from premises to conclusions, and an *interpretation* of what the method establishes. Following Walter Watson, McKeon's most fertile and insightful successor in the art of philosophical semantics, we may say that each of these four rubrics constitutes an "archic variable."[21] In turn, these archic variables may take any of four values. The matrix thus generates sixteen categories, between which (if no constraints interfere) there will be 256 possible combinations. By identifying one value for each variable, what Watson calls an "archic profile" may be produced for any argument that has a significant conceptual dimension (even when it is not produced by someone who happens to be a professional philosopher). Since most philosophers tend to favor the same archic variables throughout their careers, we can also draw up archic profiles of philosophers themselves, that is, of the general tenor of their entire oeuvre. (The greatest geniuses are, of course, their own best refuters. Thus one might gain insight by representing the difference between middle and late Plato, or early and late Wittgenstein, as a change in the value of one or more archic variables.) Summed up, the full matrix looks something like this: (I have taken the liberty of replacing some of McKeon's preferred names for his rubrics with terms I believe are more connotative.)

Selection	Principles	Methods	Interpretations
Thoughts	Holistic	Dialectical	Noumenal
Things	Reflexive	Problematic	Essential
Rules	Elemental ("Simple")	Computational	Substrative
Terms	Creative ("Actional")	Agonistic	Phenomenal[22]

Why, we may well ask, are there exactly four values for each archic variable? McKeon says that Aristotle had four causes, or explanatory factors, and that he could not hope to improve on him.[23] The idea behind this cryptic statement, it seems to me, is that the four horizontal lines of the matrix correspond to the four main positions in classical Greek philosophy as Aristotle distinguishes them in the introductory etiological books of his various treatises. Aristotle assigns to Democritus an emphasis on material causes, to Plato a stress on Aristotle's formal cause, to the Sophists a stress on efficient cause or agency, and to himself the explanatory primacy of the final causes. In itself, this is obviously an inadequate account of why archic variables take four values. Its implicit reference to Aristotle's efforts to parse the history of ancient Greek philosophy into a number of distinct voices (an effort renewed by Hegel at the very birth of modern history of philosophy) does, however, provide something of a clue about how one might construct at least an inductive argument for this fourfold scheme. The insight is that the development of classical Greek philosophy arises from an unconstrained, leisured dialogue about the most important problems that confront reflective human beings, a dialogue that tends, accordingly, to embody in itself a fairly full range of archic profiles. Following this clue, one might find deeper insight into the genesis of McKeon's thinking by performing a thought experiment: Let us represent philosophical semantics in at least its elementary phases as an attempt to analyze the four main voices in the Greek dialectic between innovation and tradition, as the ancient epic-heroic religion came into conflict with more rational, civic forms of discourse, and then see what might have happened after that.

Consider Protagoras, the paradigmatic Sophist. Sophists—the first professional teachers of Greece, the founders of rhetorical study, the inventors of humanism—do not challenge the old epic and tragic worldview. Inventive as they are, they want to defend the continuity of modern with traditional life. Thus Protagoras, the head of Pericles' brain trust, proclaims that poetry—its invention, its interpretation, and its criticism—is the most important part of *paideia* (education or upbringing).[24] Protagoras wants the old epics to do what they have always done: encourage young males to live a life no less combative than those of Achilles or Odysseus. Let the young contend for preeminence with one another, then, as fiercely as the heroes of old in the logomachies, or verbal battles, of modern civic culture. According to Protagoras, every man can be such a hero in a modern democracy, because all are free to compete in the discursive battles of civic life. However, the most successful word warriors will secure the willing assent of their hearers by making it appear that the bill of goods they are selling is simply an expression of the hearer's own most cherished views. It is persuasion by solicitation. One person's framework attracts others into it.

Given these facts, we may now draw up Protagoras's archic profile. It runs smoothly along the bottom horizontal of the matrix. Leaving selection aside,[25] we may say that the Sophist's principles are *creative* or *actional* insofar as the *arche,* or beginning point, of any argument is an act, often a speech act: I assert, I posit, I challenge. His method is *agonistic,* as befits one who thinks of himself as a warrior in words. I thrust, you parry. One of us carries the day. This is the method of debate. In general, the interpretation that one places on a conclusion depends on the ontological region, site, or level at which the argument comes to rest. The clue to Protagoras's ontology is that for him the best warrant for the persuasiveness of my argument is the very fact that I have persuaded you. This stress on what actually appears shows that the Sophists' interpretation is *phenomenalistic* about things or *existentialistic* about persons. If this were not so, something fixed in the nature of things, but not immediately available in experience itself, would constrain my argument and your acceptance or rejection of it. There would be (as Plato's Socrates in fact insists there is) another court of appeal. But this is precisely what the Sophist denies. Protagoras takes appearance to be the really real. He is a phenomenalist. What you see is what you get.

Archic profiles make themselves useful by their explanatory, or at least diagnostic, power. In Protagoras's case, we may see why McKeon thinks that the sophistic profile is the home of the rhetorical tradition, and why periods (our own may be one) in which rhetoric expands toward cultural hegemony and methodological universality are times in which components of this profile, whether terminist selections, actional principles, agonistic methods, or phenomenalistic ontologies, cease to be confined to the limited sphere to which more sober types typically want to consign them. Contemporary debate about whether scientific theories are social constructions illustrates the rhetorical profile in its hegemonic or universalizing style. This debate cannot even be formulated, let alone resolved, outside of the so-called "rhetorical turn in science studies." We may also see why Protagoras can be considered a theorist of democracy, and why latter-day Protagoreans present themselves as defenders of often more radical kinds of democracy than those we presently enjoy. It is precisely because there is no higher or lower court above the lived world or beneath it that argument can preserve, indeed enhance, the giddy autonomy and ungrounded responsibility of both speaker and hearer: their ability to bind up human time into shared projects, and hence their ability to live a distinctly political life.

Not everyone, of course, agrees with the Sophists. Since the primitive mythology on which the appropriations of the Sophists are based is itself false, scientistic sorts can be counted on to rise up saying that the heroic, if egalitarian, anthropocentrism of the Sophists' project is mistaken. It must, therefore, be replaced with a materialistic, causal account of how things work, with attendant doubts about the intelligibility and viability of a civic life based on mere myths. For scientistic folk, valid conclusions are not reached by trying to solicit the consent of an audience, but by computing units that are added and subtracted until the truth is arrived at by some sort of algorithm. Whatever does not add up is to be dismissed as ungrounded, untrue, illusory, meaningless or nonexistent. There is a strong implication that social discourse, and especially narrative discourse, is full to the brim with this sort of flotsam and jetsam. To find the truth, you must strip off the veil and look unblinkingly at the clanking machinery behind the theatrical sets and the wordy display. You must liberate yourself from illusion through value-free knowing. This is the voice of the materialist enlightenment. Having arisen in Ionia and Sicily in the sixth century, this archic profile becomes in fourth-century Athens the fully mature voice of Democritus and Empedocles. Democritus's principles are simple, atomistic units. They are combined computationally to form the complex furniture of the world. As for interpretation, what you see is precisely what you do *not* get. For the level at which causality operates is below the visible world, hidden, as Democritus says, at the bottom of a deep, dark well. McKeon calls this an entitative interpretation. I dub it substantive.

The restoration of elements of this archic profile to prominence in the early modern period constitutes the birth of modern science. In point of fact, classical modern science is, to a large extent, an effort to encode the world in the archic profile of ancient materialism. Hobbes's *Leviathan* is a *locus neoclassicus* of this kind of thinking. Hobbes not only puts people into a physical world conceived explicitly along Galileo's lines, but, in his denial of dualism, contends that persons are themselves "nothing but" (the signature phase of the reductionist) atomistically conceived points of self-interest. Actions originate from drives and compulsions rather than from spontaneous assertions of freedom. They are exposed to the competitive force field exerted by the self-interest of other such atoms. And they necessarily, indeed deterministically, follow a trajectory that yields the best deal possible under the circumstances. The influence of this model on modern economics, politics, and most recently biology is hard to exaggerate.

We may now imagine a third voice, a voice troubled by both Sophists and scientists. This is the voice of Plato, who asserts that Protagoras is right to think of human values as more important than physical facts, and who therefore opposes scientism, but who also thinks, quite unlike Protagoras, that the right values cannot be had if the old poetic heritage is retained, under any conceivable reinterpretation or reappropriation. The old poets, and their modern avatars, the tragedians, are as false as a Democritus might think. Democritus is also right to say that the truth about the world lies beyond the illusory appearances of social life. But he, and the whole line of scientific thinkers from Thales to Empedocles, is wrong to assume that the truth is to be found in the material underworkings of nature, a new cthonic realm below. Rather, it lies in a new sort of Olympus above, in the divine sphere of ideas, which we contact with our reflective mind (*nous*). Plato's voice is the voice of idealism. His dialogues begin with a confused comprehension of the whole. Through dialectical regress, the interlocutors, where they are not mired down by worldly attachments, ascend to blinding clarity that is achieved only when they realize that behind, and above, phenomenal experience lies a realm of transcendent beauty apprehended lovingly by the mind. Plato's principles are holistic, his method dialectical, and his interpretation noumenal. Christian appropriations of this otherworldly vision eventuated in the neo-Democritean revolt against it in early modernity to which I have already referred.

Finally, let us envision a fourth, somewhat belated voice—that of the peripatetic scholars, who by the later fourth century were trying to settle the Athenian cultural wars by professionalizing inquiry, turning it into a problem-solving industry. For McKeon, what most saliently distinguishes Aristotle's work from that of Plato's academy is his effort to mark off the problems that arise in each separate field of inquiry so that appropriate disciplinary criteria and methods for solving these problems can be found. Once a disciplinary field is marked off, and criteria appropriate to it laid down, data can gathered and problems can be enumerated. Sorting inductively through this data yields first principles or definitions, whose explanatory fecundity is rooted in their identification of the essential, constitutive properties of the phenomena under investigation, by reference to which the puzzles (*aporiai*) that have been accumulated during the course of inquiry may be resolved. Problem-solving success itself reflexively warrants our confidence in the essential definitions that produce solutions to the range of problems falling within the range of the subject matter. To think well, Aristotle says, is to follow the track of the problem at hand, until what John Rawls calls "wide rational equilibrium" is established. In this way, Aristotle could be scientific without being scientistic; dialectical without being totalistic; and rhetorical without being sophistical.

In the classical Greek dialogue that I have sketched, there seems to be a natural alignment between principles, methods, and interpretations. It seems as fitting that Sophists should have actional principles, agonistic methods, and phenomenal interpretations as that Platonists should have holistic principles, dialectical methods, and nounmenal interpretations. One of McKeon's richest insights, however, is that the values of archic variables can float freely and that in postclassical phases of culture archic elements are shuffled and reshuffled as each intellectual tradition tries to respond to challenges by conceding some things in order to retain others. Post-Aristotelian Greek and Roman philosophy clearly exhibit this phenomenon. Academic scepticism, for example, arose out of an epistemological crisis within Plato's academy. Plato was right, the argument goes, to think that knowledge, if we could get it, would be the perfect grasp of perfect Forms. Trapped in the empirical perceptual conditions to which we seem to be subject, however, academic skeptics concluded that we cannot get any knowledge at all. They thus combine the sensory phenomenalism of the Sophists with Plato's dialectics to show that the ascent to knowledge can never take place. The Stoics, meanwhile, whom the Sophists called "dogmatists," inherited what was left of Aristotle's school in late antiquity. They were much more impressed, however, with mathematical and computative conceptions of rationality than the Peripatetics. (The Stoics virtually invented the propositional logic that came to fruition in the early twentieth century.) So they replaced Aristotle's problem-solving methods with computational ones. Cicero's unique blend of philosophy and rhetoric, meanwhile, comes from using the method devised by the New Academics, who were his teachers, to find a path between Platonism and the sort of academic scepticism that is nothing but epistemologically disillusioned Platonism. The New Academy abandoned the positive dialectics of the Old Academy and the negative dialectics of the academic skeptics by using the agonistic method of debate to find a way of fixing reasonable opinions by weighing probabilities, thereby arriving at a probabilistic analogue, in a mutable world, of Aristotle's problem-solving method, which was as biased toward immutability as Plato's. That is the source of Cicero's hope for a new birth of philosophy—or so, in any case, McKeon argues.

V

Coming closer to home, I think that another of McKeon's most fertile insights was his recognition that the classical pragmatists, in whose philosophical shadow he himself came of age, all used the Aristotelian problematic method or method of inquiry. (An indication of this is their insistence that organisms are well adapted by evolutionary history to be problem-solving beings.) Well-known differences among the founders of pragmatism can then be elegantly explained by their having opted either for different principles or interpretations. Both James and Dewey insist that all problem solving begins and ends in action, just as evolutionary adaptation begins with spontaneous variation and ends with adaptive behavior. They employ actional or creative principles—and precisely not the contemplative, allegedly self-evident reflexive principles of their realist opponents (including, ultimately, Peirce). Dewey's complaint that James puts too subjective a spin on how organisms solve problems can then be rewritten as Dewey's preference for a more essentialist and less phenomenal mode of interpretation: for more Aristotle, as it were (with whom, as we have seen, Dewey was preoccupied) and less John Stuart Mill (to whose memory James dedicated his volume of lectures, *Pragmatism.*)

This story can be protracted by taking note of the gradual displacement of problem-solving conceptions of scientific inquiry by computational theories of scientific method in the United States during and after the Second World War. As I have argued elsewhere, this shift was facilitated by an explicit assimilation of pragmatism to logical positivism during the forties.[26] One marked effect of this shift was that, in an environment marked by the rise of a national security state, of managerial forms of capitalism, and of a privatistic, utility-maximizing, consumption-oriented economy, meritocratic communities of expertise displaced the problem-solving conception of participatory democracy favored by Dewey. Among the results were an enormous rise of pseudoscientific theorizing in the social sciences, the degrading of public discourse into media *techne,* and the transformation of the schools into meritocratic sorting factories.

The beginnings of this shift were visible at Columbia, where Ernest Nagel was turning Dewey's philosophy of science into something closer to logical positivism, as well as at the University of Chicago, where the pragmatist logician Charles Morris facilitated dialogue between his tradition and Viennese neopositivism by offering the University's sheltering arms to the refugee Rudolf Carnap. In his famous *Logische Aufbau der Welt,* Carnap's aim had been to screen off the cacophonous rantings of pseudotheory from verifiable scientific claims by using rules to compute truth values on the basis of atomic statements. Here was a modern expression of the voice of Democritus: computationalism under a linguistic or term-oriented mode of selection, rather than under Democritus's mode of "things," or Locke's "new way of ideas." Eventually, Carnap was forced to moderate his original program by recognizing that an indefinitely large number of linguistic or conceptual frameworks might equally efficiently aggregate the same data. Under the tutelage of American philosophers, Carnap called this conceptual relativism a turn toward pragmatism.[27] In point of fact, the computationalist method embedded in the resulting pragmatized positivism meant that problem-centered classical pragmatism was now effectively dead.

McKeon not only articulated his interpretive matrix during the time Carnap was his colleague, but curiously enough called it by the same name that Carnap, Morris, Quine, and others were using to describe their inquiries into the relationship between empirical data and conceptual frameworks: "philosophical semantics." We might advance our aim of locating McKeon's work in its time and place by speculating on whether in bestowing the same name on his quite different enterprise McKeon may have been criticizing Carnap more than paying him a compliment. For as his matrix expanded, McKeon might well have reflected that in restricting meaningful, useful, truth-functional languages to those whose connectives could be computed by some sort of rule-governed, algorithmic process, Carnap was arbitrarily restricting discourse to an impoverished subset of conceptual frameworks, no matter how pragmatically open to alternatives he seemed to be. McKeon seems to me to reaffirm his Deweyan legacy by intimating that a society that links free speech to democracy must put all discursive frameworks, and not just those that can be computed, into play. The matter is some importance. For constriction of discursive possibility space will always be attended by the illusory assumption that there is some one nondiscursive reality that is to be captured by some one right semantical framework. The discovery of conceptual relativity as a deep philosophical truth about our way of using language to interact with the world, that is to say, cannot be made until the full possibility space of discursive pluralism has been recognized and welcomed.

"The most significant philosophical discovery of the present century," Watson has proclaimed, "is the fact of pluralism, that the truth admits of more than one valid formulation, and, secondly, of the reason for this fact in arbitrary or conventional elements, inseparable from the nature of thought itself."[28] Watson attributes this discovery to McKeon. What, we may ask, was the significance of this discovery in McKeon's own eyes? Certainly, he thought that the practical problem solving he took to be the essence of political and social praxis would be facilitated by making it illegitimate for any contributor to a discussion to insist that his or her most cherished conceptual framework is the only one in which the most salient aspects of the problem at hand can be expressed. He probably also thought that problem-solving power increases roughly as a function of the engagement of multiple frameworks. This practical, pragmatic, solidly liberal point seems to me to have been less important to McKeon himself, however, than his belief—a belief preserved and expanded by Watson—that all frameworks are equally valid vessels of theoretical truths, and that the discovery of conceptual pluralism is itself, as Watson says, a philosophical truth. So construed, the implications of conceptual relativity for reconstructing the discipline of philosophy are in many ways quite the opposite of those drawn by Dewey. For Dewey, conceptual relativity entails the primacy of praxis. For McKeon, and certainly for Watson, it grounds the possibility of first philosophy.

The very fact that great thinkers, by virtue of their greatness itself, have been able to understand one another suggests to McKeon that they are already pluralist enough to be able to translate each others' claims into their own preferred terms, even across the gulf of ages, and so to generate the genuine conversation that in McKeon's view takes place among them. McKeon professes his faith in what has come to be called "commensurability" between different discursive paradigms when he says, in a passage I have already quoted, that there arises among great thinkers "a homogeneity in the discussion inasmuch as they raise the same or comparable questions and give different answers to them."[29] The explicit discovery of conceptual relativism cannot help but enhance this conversation by making mutual comprehension easier and translations less distorted. This proposition slides rather easily, however, into another. To be able to talk about the same thing in what all participants now recognize as different ways may also make it possible, perhaps for the first time, for thinkers to arrive at least at some identical conclusions precisely by setting aside the conventional aspects that *ex hypothesi* they now recognize. Watson raises this very possibility when he writes, "With this discovery the very thing that was formerly thought to be a scandal and a disgrace to philosophy, namely, that philosophies do not agree, turns out to be its great virtue, for through it *are revealed essential features of all thought, present everywhere indeed, but nowhere so clearly as in philosophy.*"[30]

Note that in saying this Watson seems to be asserting that it is philosophical claims—claims about the ontological and epistemological foundations that precede, and indeed make possible, the inquiries of the special sciences and arts—whose validity and soundness are enhanced by the discovery of conceptual relativity.[31] The insight we are to derive from deploying McKeon's semantic matrix is not what conceptual pragmatists from C. I. Lewis to W. V. O. Quine made of it. They held that conceptual relativity means that apart from their uses in encoding first-order claims frameworks have virtually no reference at all. They are arbitrary and conventional because, as Quine famously put it, "to be is to be the *value* of a variable," and not to be a variable itself.

Moreover, for most conceptual relativists the utility of different conceptual schemes is that they encode different first-order truths, not the same ones in different "form." Indeed, the postmodern pragmatism associated with Rorty radicalizes the conceptual relativity of earlier pragmatists just because it makes the expression of difference and otherness the whole point, regarding the imposition of sameness as little more than an ideological tool. From this perspective, it is difficult even to imagine what sort of truths could conceivably remain "the same" over different formulations. Yet in spite of this, Watson's view is that McKeon's philosophical semantics at last makes it possible for philosophers to state the same deep truths about the conditions of the possibility of knowledge in different, but ultimately commensurable, idioms. Truth-functional business, it seems, can be done at an explicitly conceptual level. To hold this view, Watson must flatly deny Carnap's claim that nothing important can be said about "second-order" categories apart from their first-order uses. And so he does. Watson wants to assure us, in fact, that among the things that can be said at this higher level is that McKeon's semantic matrix puts first philosophy, after its many false starts, at last on the path to *strenge Wissenschaft,* and not on the road to self-destruction, since it allows us to affirm that all the philosophers who participate in the "Great Conversation" not only can understand one another, but can in principle come to a number of agreements.

One who affirms this also appears to be committed to the view that philosophy should continue to preside over culture, as Plato said it should, but turns the tables on the standard objection to that claim by asserting that its right to so preside depends on the discovery of conceptual relativity rather than being undermined by it. We know that Watson takes this position because he is brave enough to say so. And although there is a different, more practical and rhetorical direction in which McKeon's work can be interpreted and developed, as I will show below, we may suspect that McKeon, with his hankering after a *philosophia perennis,* takes it too. If so, our conclusion will be as follows: McKeon may well have disagreed with the realists of his day on the matter of conceptual pluralism, and especially on their touchingly naive belief that the ultimate truth about the world can be encoded in only one interpretive framework. But on the matter of the primacy of *theoria* over *praxis,* and maintaining philosophy as a foundational discipline, he sided with the realists, defenders of the traditional cultural aspirations of philosophy, against his mentor Dewey.[32]

VI

McKeon's philosophical pluralism has never been well-received by the professional philosophical community. On the other hand, his approach has sometimes intrigued rhetorical theorists, who have seen in his work an effort to elevate the categories, methods, and indeed the worldview of rhetoricians to central status in making, interpreting, and criticizing discourse of all kinds, and in resolving the problems of a pluralist society. There is no doubt that McKeon had an abiding interest in, and considerable knowledge of, the history and philosophy of rhetoric. Moreover, one of his most distinctive theses, as we have seen, was that at several periods in the history of the West the rhetorical approach initiated by the Greek Sophists has been elevated to hegemony over other spheres of culture, functioning as what McKeon, following Aristotle, calls an architectonic art. In such times, the fertile and fluid logic of commonplaces, which are aimed at illuminating and judging complex particulars, displaces formal logic, with its emphasis on the universal and necessary.

Cicero's expansion of the scope of rhetoric in the troubled days of the Roman Republic occurred in one of those periods. An expanded rhetoric was to restore vigor to public discourse, which had been abandoned by thumb-sucking sectarian philosophers. The humanism of the Renaissance, which was directly influenced by Cicero, placed rhetoric and the probabilistic logic of commonplaces on a similar footing. McKeon clearly thinks that ours, too, is a time in which commonplaces can to serve as a fertile source of discovery and innovation. "As we enter into the final decades of this century," he wrote in 1971,

> We boast of a vast increase of output in all arts, and we are puzzled by the absence of interdisciplinary connections and by the breakdown of interpersonal, intergroup and intercultural communication. We need a new architectonic productive art. Rhetoric exercised such functions in the Roman republic and in the Renaissance. Rhetoric provides the devices by which to determine the characteristics and problems of our times and to form the art by which to guide actions for the solutions of our problems and the improvement of our circumstances.[33]

48

Calls for the expansion of rhetoric to serve as the primary medium of argument, and for its topical and tropological methods of analyzing and assessing arguments to become canonical in every sphere of discourse, I will call programs for "universal rhetoric," in homage to Hans Georg Gadamer's parallel calls for "universal hermeneutics." Such calls typically arise when diversity in an expanding social realm runs ahead of social integration, when incommensurability among paradigms in the realm of theory overtakes unification among the sciences, and when plurality in the sphere of values seems to stultify common action. McKeon was very concerned about problems like these. After the Second World War, he became involved with the United Nations in trying to find ways to facilitate communication and common action in the new world *ecumene* that had been created by the collapse of European imperialism and the rise of a new multicultural international order. It was in these contexts that McKeon raised the call for rhetoric to become a new architectonic art.

McKeon's project, like Cicero's, depends on allowing rhetoric to intersect with philosophy. There are at least two ways, however, in which McKeon might have meant this. He might have been trying to elevate rhetoric to the architectonic status of philosophy, shifting the focus from inaccessible universals to the resolution of complex cases calling for judgment. Alternatively, he might have been using rhetoric to revitalize the claims of foundational philosophy in a world that was more shot through with pluralism than philosophers had previously assumed, and in which, accordingly, the fact of pluralism had itself become a philosophical problem. In introducing a collection of McKeon's essays on rhetoric, Mark Backman argues for a version of the first view. He claims that McKeon's "essays on rhetoric constituted the critical core of his intellectual activities;" that "McKeon rejects the notion that rhetoric and philosophy are separate disciplines;" that McKeon "passed from a rational philosophy founded on universalizing vocabularies and derived from fixed principles of being to a rhetorical philosophy based in the circumstances of experience;" and that McKeon would approve of Rorty's distinction between systematizing and edifying philosophy and would locate himself among the edifiers.[34] I believe that these statements are misleading, and that the second way of looking at McKeon's work is closer to the truth.

As I have argued, McKeon can profitably be seen as responding positively to Dewey's recognition of diversity and his call for "reconstruction in philosophy." But his solution to the problem of pluralism was not to proclaim the primacy of *praxis* over *theoria,* and not, accordingly, to replace a theory-oriented philosophy with an action-oriented rhetoric, as Backman suggests it was. It is quite true that McKeon called for use of commonplaces as instruments of discovery and judgment.[35] "It is a long time," he wrote, "since topics have been used as an art of invention in rhetoric . . . A reconstituted verbal art of invention, adapted to our circumstances and arts, might be used to shadow forth the methods and principles of an archetectonic productive art generalized from invention in language to discovery in existence."[36] It is also true, at least in my view, that McKeon's semantic rubrics are best conceived as commonplaces that function interpretively and inventively in this new productive art, and that in these roles they have a considerable amount of power.[37] Yet the fact is that McKeon himself drew back from endorsing a purely practical use of his semantic system, probably because he did not want to undermine or eliminate the classical distinction between *theoria* and *praxis,* as Dewey had done. Anyone who holds, as both Dewey and Marx did, that *theoria* is entirely an ideological fiction that functions to preserve social class hierarchies will believe that eliminating the theory-practice distinction cannot help but improve the quality of free discourse. Someone who doubts this, however, as McKeon plainly did, will believe the exact opposite: that collapsing the theory-practice distinction will have a devastating effect on freedom of speech and thought. With the philosophical realists of his day, McKeon was unwilling to accept that consequence; and I suspect that he would continue to resist it in the postmodern cultural environment in which we find ourselves today.

Certainly, in calling for his new architectonic art, McKeon commends the rhetorical tradition, especially when it follows in Cicero's wake, for recognizing and reveling in a multiplicity of interpretive frameworks. But the ineliminable plurality of interpretive frameworks entails for McKeon not that foundational truths—truths more secure than the shifting first-order claims for which they provide a stable context—are unavailable. On the contrary, the main thrust of his argument is that, when the arbitrary and conventional elements in which speech is necessarily encoded are recognized, the same deep truths are capable of expression in quite different, and only seemingly contradictory, frameworks. In consequence, McKeon's universalized rhetoric does not use philosophy as an *ancilla rhetoricae.* It uses rhetoric as an *ancilla philosophiae.*

Support for my interpretation comes not only from the argument that I have been building in this essay, but from the fact that we have McKeon's word for it in the very essays Backman anthologizes. He says, for instance, that while the universal rhetoric of Cicero's time was aimed at reorienting praxis, and the universal rhetoric of the Renaissance had a poetic or productive orientation (*poeisis*), "there is every reason to think that the art *we* seek is *rhetoric with a theoretical orientation* (*theoria*)."[38] McKeon puts a theoretical spin on Cicero himself when he writes, "I read Cicero [as saying] that all philosophies . . . are particular expressions of the same truth, and that, insofar as they succeed in ex-pressing that truth, they differ only verbally."[39] His reason for insisting on this is that in a world that had passed through two ideologically in-stigated wars, and numerous revolutions, and countless bloodbaths, McKeon was convinced that we need to see "what is common is con-stant and common" in diverse value systems, and not merely to appre-ciate difference.[40] He was convinced that this cannot be achieved if the fact of pluralism is used to undermine the traditional aims of philosophy and its pretensions to preside over culture. On the contrary, it can only be achieved if philosophers resolve to retain and enhance their dominant position by taking pluralism seriously.

McKeon was insightful enough to see that ours is an age that needs an architectonic rhetorical art, or a universalized rhetoric, or a rhetoric of inquiry. To some extent, moreover, the age has got what he thought it needed. The revolt against computationist neopositivism, the first stir-rings of which are enshrined in Thomas Kuhn's *The Structure of Scientific Revolutions,* has swelled in recent decades into a mighty cho-rus of "social constructionist," largely rhetorical, analyses of science. In philosophy itself, heretics such as Rorty have reacted—some would say overreacted—to the scientistic, positivized versions of pragmatism that triumphed in the fifties by asserting, in the name of pragmatism itself, much that McKeon would recognize as a Protagorean archic profile. When Rorty (who was once McKeon's student) proclaims himself a pragmatist, he does not intend to return to Dewey's old biocentric nat-uralism, redolent as it still is with naive faith in the power of science. Rather, he means to say that the only warrant for the claims people make is the fact that they have persuaded other people to accept these claims.[41]

On the whole, however, the growing, fractious family of universal rhetorics that have now arisen are not much like McKeon's. In spite of Backman's attempt to view McKeon's work through the eyes of con-temporary rhetorics, those rhetorics are likely to display his project as preserving the very "logocentric" assumptions about discourse that uni-versal rhetorics have succeeded lately in calling into question. They will show, for example, that McKeon is still committed to the primacy of identity over difference, and, at least tacitly, to as mysterious and as nu-minous a source of "onto-theological" sameness as, say, Martin Heidegger. In consequence, those who have been sensitized to the dan-gers of intellectualizing communicative problems, and who have in con-sequence recognized the ideological power of what Kenneth Burke called "terministic screens" to hide the most salient considerations rather than to uncover them, are not likely to be impressed by the ana-lytical machinery McKeon invents or the uses to which he puts it—nor will those who have insisted on the situatedness of all discourse, or its role as an instrument in social negotiations, or its tenacious connections to class, race, and gender. For it can be argued that *theoria* facilitates the suppression of diversity no less when it tries to absorb plurality into a grand multicolored vision than when it tries to repress it in favor of one transcendent, realist framework.

Rhetorical analysis of the sort cultivated by contemporary rhetoricians of inquiry can even be deployed to support my contention that McKeon's project is tilted away from its considerable potential as an instrument of rhetorical and invention and oriented instead toward philosophical preoccupations. For an explicitly rhetorical critique of McKeon's own discursive practices will identify the workings of *pathos* and *ethos* in his performances as speaker and writer and will not restrict itself to the *logos* that philosophers, including McKeon himself, have always wanted audiences to regard as uniquely relevant to the judgment of their arguments.

We may begin by noting that theoretically oriented speakers, especially philosophers, generally have a bias against narrative history. Ever since Plato, they have thought of mathematics, and of mathematical physics, as the most epistemologically high-grade form of discourse and of history and personal narrative as the least. In McKeon's various attempts at first-person narrative, the same bias, even if it is denied in theory, is hard to overlook in stylistic practice. What purports to be a "spiritual autobiography," for example, is little more than a maddening attempt to keep deferring the subject.[42] We never learn much about McKeon himself. For the most part what we get is a lot of reflexive throat clearing about the nature of narrative and various ways to write an autobiography.[43] What passes for a story is mostly confined to a memorandum about McKeon's policies as dean. One can almost feel a palpable fear that revealing the contingent events that have shaped one's life or conditioned one's ideas might deflate the authoritative voice in which the philosopher wants to impart abiding, noncontingent truths to others. Such is the *ethos* of McKeon as speaker and writer. McKeon's Great Conversation literally collapses time, the unique, narratively constituted identities of the participants, and the burdens of concrete persuasion into an eternal present. The same triumphs over the different as fully as in Gilson's *philosophia perennis*.

In this essay, I have tried to illuminate McKeon's work by situating it in the historical context out of which it came. In this respect I mean to agree with Nietzsche, who thought of philosophies as involuntary confessions extracted from their authors, and with Dewey, who recognized that, just as there is no difference between the nature of something and its mode of coming-to-be, so there is no difference between the meaning of a proposition and the circumstances of its production and reception. Such a rhetoric can find productive uses for McKeon's analytical rubrics as commonplaces, tools for inventing context-sensitive en-thymemes. But it will find rather less use for them as pigeonholes into which philosophical arguments can be thrown.

Dewey's great defect was that, unlike Marx, he did not recognize the opacity of discourse. His confusion of pragmatism with scientific exper-imentalism led him naively to assume, with many nineteenth-century thinkers, that the scientific method is inherently self-purifying and free from the ideological distortions that plague other discoursive forms. McKeon's pluralistic semantics offers ways to break through Dewey's limitations. To take full advantage of his achievement, however, it is in-sufficient to acknowledge conceptual diversity and discursive pluralism simply by integrating claims into a philosophical rose window framed in a Completeness Proof. Dewey's admirable stress on the deep connection between democratic life and the primacy of practice will be honored when the fact of conceptual pluralism is used instead to give voice to dif-ference rather than sameness.[44]

THEORY AND PRACTICE REVISITED

REFLECTIONS ON THE PHILOSOPHIES OF RICHARD MCKEON AND TALCOTT PARSONS

Donald N. Levine

Richard McKeon and Talcott Parsons were two of the most powerful voices of the academic world in the twentieth century.[1] In themselves, their oeuvres remain continuously generative; considered together, they stand to offer a fresh approach to certain vexing problems of contemporary thought. Although intellectual biographies of the two men reveal striking parallels, the philosophies which they created bring notably different slants to the interpretation of culture. If those different philosophies are brought together in a complementary way, I shall argue, they can throw new light on the perennially problematic character of the relationship between *theoria* and *praxis*.

Why McKeon and Parsons?

Like Emile Durkheim and Max Weber, Richard McKeon and Talcott Parsons were contemporaries whose works were mutually relevant yet who took no documented notice of one another. McKeon lived from 1900 to 1985, Parsons from 1902 to 1979. Both men received their undergraduate education on the East Coast—at Columbia University and

Amherst College, respectively—and proceeded to pursue a critical portion of their graduate studies in Europe, McKeon at the University of Paris for three years (1922–25), Parsons for a year each at the Universities of London and Heidelberg (1924–26). The early careers of both men were marked by strife and ambiguities of status. Such loud objections were raised when President Hutchins proposed the appointment of McKeon to the Department of Philosophy at the University of Chicago in 1930, that for some time McKeon refused to let himself be considered further there. When he did finally come to Chicago in 1934, it was through appointments in the departments of history and classics. Although Parsons received his doctorate in economics and began to teach at Harvard in the Department of Economics, his intellectual inclinations led him to affiliate with Harvard's controversial new Department of Sociology in 1930. His appointment was backed by the chairman, Pitirim Sorokin, but the initiative was turned down by President Lowell, a decision reversed only after energetic intervention by supporters of the young Parsons. However, as Parsons's work developed in ways that Sorokin did not appreciate, the chairman came to turn against him, first by keeping him at the rank of instructor after an initial three-year appointment, later by opposing his promotion to tenure—which again was saved only through friendly colleagues outside the department.

After these turbulent beginnings, both men established themselves solidly by the late 1930s at the institutions where each would spend the rest of his life as a prominent scholar, a powerful teacher, and a devoted citizen. In addition, both came to play significant roles as administrators, roles in which they would gain renown for instituting rare and innovative multidisciplinary programs. As dean of the Humanities Division, McKeon established four interdisciplinary committees, including the Committees on the History of Culture and on the Analysis of Ideas and the Study of Methods; Parsons established and long presided over Harvard's famed interdisciplinary Committee on Social Relations. Despite their predilection for interdisciplinary work, moreover, both men received the highest awards within their home disciplines. McKeon served as president of the American Philosophical Association, Western Division, in 1952, and later as the APA Paul Carus Lecturer; Parsons was honored as president of the American Sociological Association in 1949.

The intellectual biographies of McKeon and Parsons also exhibit striking parallels. The early works of both men concentrated on recoveries and fresh interpretations of significant classical figures—medieval philosophers, Spinoza and, in particular, Aristotle for McKeon; for Parsons, Werner Sombart, Alfred Marshall, Vilfredo Pareto, Durkheim, and, in particular, Max Weber. From early on, the work of both men included a mission to do battle against naive positivist assumptions about science—this in the 1930s, long before it became fashionable to do so. Both also strongly objected to economistic theories of action by arguing for the interpenetration of cultural ideals with economic motives.

Perhaps most remarkable is the fact that each developed a succession of categorical schemes for organizing the universe of Western culture, initially in the form of dichotomies, then in trichotomies, and finally in quadripartite schemes that evolved in ever more involuted and exponential ways. McKeon began with an opposition between holoscopic and meroscopic methods in the late 1930s; proceeded to develop a semantic schema anchored in the tripartite distinction among logistic, dialectic, and problematic methods in the postwar years; then developed through the 1950s toward the complex four-by-four matrix illustrated in Figure 1.[2] Parsons similarly began with a presenting dichotomy, between what he called positivistic and idealistic theories of action in the 1930s; shifted to an analytic framework anchored in the three-part distinction among cognitive, cathectic, and evaluative orientations in the postwar years; and thence, through the 1950s and beyond, moved toward the complex four-by-four matrices illustrated in Figure 2.[3] Indeed, while the scholarly credibility of both men stemmed from their pioneering work on classic authors, like Aristotle and Weber, and their analyses of substantive problems, like the bases of literary criticism or the meanings of freedom and history for McKeon, and for Parsons, the physician-patient relationship or the origins of fascism, many of their students remember them chiefly for their later four-fold schemas for organizing the universe. For McKeon, this included four commonplaces (things, thoughts, words, and deeds); four semantic variables (principles, methods, selections, and interpretations); four universal arts (interpretation, discovery, presentation, and systematization); and four modes of thought (assimilation, discrimination, construction, and resolution). For Parsons, this included the four subsystems of action (behavioral organism, personality system, social system, and cultural system); the four functions of all action systems (adaptation, goal attainment, integration, and pattern maintenance); and the four media of interchange (money, power, influence, and activation of commitments).

Introducing a volume of essays on Parsons that appeared in 1991, the editors conclude: "Parsons is one of the few genuinely modern and global minds of the twentieth century."[4] That is surely true, and Richard McKeon is just as surely one of the few others. Although several other twentieth-century thinkers could be described as quintessentially modern, I can think of none who have been so resolutely global as these two. They were global in four senses. First, they were catholic in their intellectual sweep: McKeon ranged widely as well as deeply across all branches of philosophy, from metaphysics, philosophy of

Figure 1

Quadripartite Schemata in McKeon*

MODES OF PHILOSOPHIC INQUIRY

Modes of Being Being	Modes of Thought That which is	Modes of Fact Existence	Modes of Simplicity Experience
Being and Becoming——————	—Assimilation and Exemplification— (models)	—Reality and Approximation——	Categories of Thought (Ideas and presentations)
Phenomena and Projections————	—Discrimination and Postulation——	—Process and Frame——	Categories of Language and Action (Symbols and rules)
Elements and Composites————	—Construction and Decomposition (constituents)	—Object and Impression——	Categories of Things (Cognition and Emotion)
Actuality and Potentiality————	—Resolution and Question—— (causes)	—Substance and Accident——	Categories of Terms

SCHEMA OF PHILOSOPHIC SEMANTICS

Principles	Methods	Interpretations	Selections
Holoscopic	Universal	Ontic	
Comprehensive————	—Dialectical———	—Ontological———	—Hierarchies (transcendental)
Reflexive—	—Operational—	—Entitative———	— Matters (reductive)
Meroscopic	Particular	Phenomenal	
Simple—	—Logistic—	—Existentialist———	—Types (perspective)
Actional—	—Problematic——	—Essentialist———	—Kinds (functional)

BASIC DIVISIONS OF PHILOSOPHY

Theoretic	Physics	Philosophy	Logic
Practical	Ethics	Poetry	Rhetoric
Poetic	Logic	History	Grammar

BASIC PROBLEMS

Whole	Universal	Reality	One
Part	Particular	Process	Many

* Source: "Philosophic Semantics and Philosophic Inquiry," in *Freedom and History and Other Essays* (Chicago: University of Chicago Press), pp. 250, 253.

Figure 2

Quadripartite Schemata in Parsons*

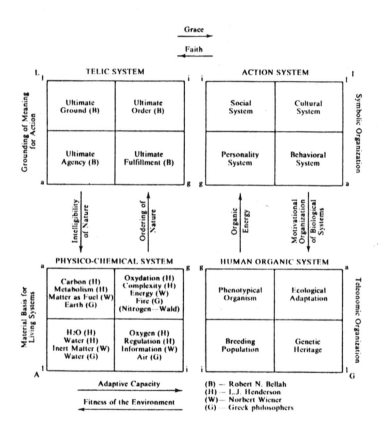

Source: *Action Theory and the Human Condition* (1978), p. 382.

Figure 2 *(continued)*

Quadripartite Schemata in Parsons*

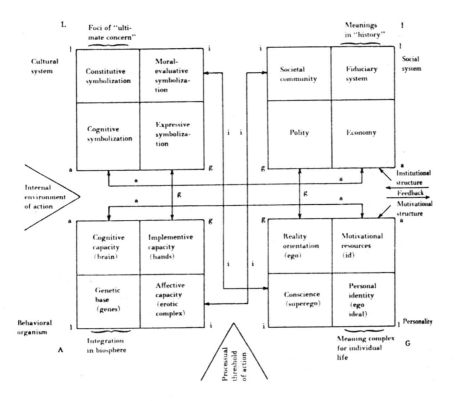

science, and logic through moral and political philosophy and aesthetics, and on to literature, education, and the history of culture as well. The scope of Parsons's investigations touched nearly every subfield of sociology, from small groups, socialization, and medical sociology through organizational analysis, stratification, and sociocultural evolution; and beyond sociology his learning and creativity ranged from biology, cybernetics, psychoanalytic psychology, and anthropology through economics, political science, linguistics, and religion. Second, both provided a global perspective on world history, McKeon with his sweeping interpretations of the history of Western culture, Parsons with his daring reintroduction of a perspective of societal evolution. Third, both had a flare for architectonic issues; they stand almost alone in the twentieth century for turning repeatedly to questions regarding the global organization of the intellectual disciplines. Fourth, they were ecumenical in the sense of promoting international scholarly discourse; both played significant pioneering roles in linking American thought with European traditions and then in working during the Cold War years to build bridges between Western scholars and colleagues in the Soviet bloc.

Finally, both men left highly ambiguous legacies, legacies that remain "essentially contested." Both have aroused detractors who consider their lifetime reputations inflated and hold that little of their work will endure. Others claim that the detractors either have not read or certainly not understood their works, and that in due course these profound pioneers will come to be appreciated. Followers of McKeon claim he anticipated by decades, and in more sophisticated form, positions associated with deconstructionism and related movements of recent years, and Walter Watson[5] has suggested that McKeon's writing seems written for future readers rather than for his contemporaries; while in the volume on Parsons mentioned earlier, Mark Gould argues that Parsons's *Structure of Social Action* of 1937 was published "sixty years ahead of its time."

Beyond debates about their enduring value, the works of both men have been beset by controversies regarding the extent to which their oeuvres are unified or not. Watson depicts this matter in the form of a double paradox: McKeon's work proceeded by stages, inspiring students who distinctively manifested the emphasis of each stage, yet McKeon claimed his work was the same throughout, only to contradict himself by referring at other times to its continual development and novelty. Similarly, Parsons had followers who worked chiefly with the ideas of one or another stage, some of whom accused him of betrayal for abandoning earlier positions as he evolved new ones. Parsons himself claimed that there was an essential unity in his lifelong effort to develop a comprehensive theory of action, although as his theory evolved he kept referring to what he called radical new insights and fundamental break-throughs in this theory.

The Semantic Project and the Voluntaristic Project

Behind the comprehensive philosophical schemas that McKeon elabo-rated, Watson has identified a core generative idea: "the idea of plural-ism, that the truth, though one, has no single expression," and that philosophers "can be unified in communication and co-operation with-out the need of consensus in a common ideology."[6] Like McKeon, Parsons strove to develop comprehensive schemas for analyzing the di-versities of human experience. And beneath Parsons's theoretical edi-fices, one can also identify a core generative idea: the notion that human action is doubly animated, by dispositions to pursue goals through in-strumentally rational adaptations and by dispositions to follow moral guidelines that ultimately express symbolic ideals.[7]

These contrasting generative ideas are issued in philosophies of culture in which notably different conceptions of culture were embod-ied. For McKeon, the central axis of cultural variation was cognitive. Whichever categories he used to analyze culture, and in whatever direc-tion his analysis turned, McKeon's take on culture turned mainly on the various cognitive forms through which philosophers and others appre-hend the world. He anchored the sources of values in the truths and hy-potheses about the world found in the "framework and conclusions of the natural sciences, the social sciences and the human sciences."[8] Nearly every time that McKeon broached a discussion of some moral or political value, he treated the topic by examining differing cognitive rep-resentations of the value in question. Thus, in his luminous discussions of the concept of freedom, he analyzed the different meanings it assumed when treated by the dialectical method, the problematic method, or the logistical method,[9] and showed how an initially ambiguous definition of freedom could be made unambiguous through semantic analysis of the principles, methods, and interpretations through which it is configured.[10] Such analyses typically concluded by arguing that persons or communi-ties can agree on common courses of action while yet holding different beliefs about the world.

What social scientists who study culture may find neglected in McKeon's work is a systematic analysis of the ways in which different value-orientations animate culture. And what McKeon omitted consti-tutes precisely the dimension that Parsons made the linchpin of his phi-losophy of culture. In an early essay, Parsons wrote: "The positivistic reaction against philosophy has, in its effect on the social sciences, manifested a strong tendency to obscure the fact that man is essentially an active, creative, evaluating creature."[11] This formulation displays Parsons's proclivity to equate human agency with a commitment to normative orientations. Thus, when analyzing the great systems of culture Parsons concentrated on the types of value-orientations embodied in various societies, such as the particularistic-achievement value pattern of traditional China[12] or the value system of contemporary United States, which he described as "instrumental activism."[13] The same was true when he analyzed microstructures, such as the roles of the physician, the parent, or the businessman.

In following his proclivity to emphasize value-orientations, some critics have argued Parsons did not pay the cognitive dimension its due.[14] Thus, despite the array of meanings Max Weber associated with the concept of rationality, when Parsons discussed rationality he limited it solely to its technological and economic usages, that is, to the form of instrumental rationality. This is not to say that Parsons did not make significant contributions to understanding the cognitive cultural institutions; simply consider his pioneering analyses of science, ideology, and philosophy in *The Social System* or the analysis of what he called the cognitive complex in *The American University*. Nor is it to say that McKeon failed to illuminate the role of normative symbols in promoting cohesion within communities or the rich diversity of meanings of terms like justice and freedom. The point here is that although both thinkers appear to be presenting comprehensive philosophies of culture, they end up treating culture in a somewhat one-sided manner, with McKeon making the cognitive dimension foundational to all else at the expense of the normative, and Parsons doing the reverse.

This tendency to reduce the cognitive or the normative dimension of culture to the other leads to a peculiarity that both philosophies have in common. McKeon, for all his celebration of human reason, offers us no criteria for evaluating the cognitive forms he so brilliantly analyzes; and Parsons, for all his celebration of human agency, gives us a philosophically impoverished conception of practice and the ways it can be informed by reason. For both of them, the domain of rational choice, understood not in the circumscribed sense employed by economists but in the classical sense of choice informed by reason, appears to be neglected. The central task of this paper is to suggest ways to remedy that neglect by pooling resources supplied by the two of them, with results that point to hitherto unexplored terrain.

Practice and the Theory of Action

Two of the announced goals of *The Structure of Social Action*, the grand synthesis which climaxed the early work of Parsons and propelled his subsequent work, were to rekindle belief in the efficacy of human reason and to restore appreciation for the role of ideals and norms in directing human conduct. The irony is that Parsons never linked these two objectives by explicitly discussing the relationship between reason and moral choice. The closest he came to attending to the question of the use of reason in directing action was when he analyzed the problems of the sociological profession,[15] where he identified a need to separate the pure discipline of sociology, with its distinctive theoretical and research tradition, from sociological "practice" (his quotation marks). Such practice consists of the application of the discipline's findings to activities like helping disturbed people or enhancing industrial productivity. Parsons advocated the institutionalization of a role wherein professionals could work full-time as applied sociologists. Accordingly, he urged the profession to set up special structures to mediate the applied functions in order to protect the integrity of the pure discipline while maintaining high standards for its applications. Parsons presented his position on this matter without engaging in explicit philosophical argument; he simply presumed the importance of preserving the integrity of pure theoretical work and that the practical contribution of sociology would take the form of its "application."

This conception assumes a radical division within sociology between pure theoretical work and applied practical work, and it assumes that in this division the theoretical work is cognitively superior to the practical and should be completed prior to its application. The model for this conception is that of physiology as a pure theoretic discipline in relation to medicine as its applied form, or between physics as a pure discipline and engineering as its applied form. One of the few voices within sociology to question this conception was that of Morris Janowitz,[16] who glossed this view of the relation between sociology and practice as one that embodies an "engineering model." Over the past century this outlook has come to be accepted by the majority of professional sociologists, so in his remarks on the profession Parsons was simply giving voice to a widely shared point of view.

Anyone schooled in the thoughtways of Richard McKeon would know better than to accept such an assumption uncritically. Although Janowitz was not so schooled, he had been influenced by McKeon's one-time mentor John Dewey. From Deweyan pragmatism, Janowitz derived an alternative he called the "enlightenment model," which blurs the distinction between pure and applied sociology and sees the sociologist not as an outside expert, but as part of the social process. Had Janowitz delved more deeply into Dewey's arguments, he might have been led to maintain that the notion of a cognitively privileged and antecedently secured body of theory was a superstitious relic, an obstructive vestige of the quest for certainty pursued by Western philosophy since Hellenic times. Had Janowitz, not to mention Dewey, enjoyed access to the distinctions available from McKeon's semantic analyses of philosophic systems, he might have broached a still more differentiating critique. But even the limited degree of dissent which Janowitz expressed in his espousal of an enlightenment model was little heeded by the sociological profession. The engineering model probably remains the dominant orientation among professional sociologists to this day. I turn now to consider what a portrayal of the relation between theory and practice that departs from the work of Richard McKeon might look like.

Six Views of the Theory-Practice Nexus

What is the right way to conceive of the relation between theory and practice? The import of McKeon's philosophy is that such a question *must* be asked, but it is absurd to expect there can be only one valid answer for it. Both terms are multiply ambiguous, and both their meanings and their proper relationship depend on certain generative assumptions that possess some inexpungible degree of arbitrariness. What is more, when carrying out some inquiry about them, it is best not to restrict their meanings by imposing some rigorous definition in advance but to let their varying meanings unfold in the course of using them and seeing how they are used in different ways.

So instructed, I direct my inquiry to recovering the fundamental alternative ways of conceptualizing practical knowledge in relation to theoretic knowledge.[17] And I find that relationship to take three distinct forms. Theory can be construed as *foundational* for practice, as *disjunctive* from practice, or as *inseparable* from practice. Each of these forms exhibits two primary variants. In examining these six views of the theory-practice nexus, let us begin with what is closest to us, the conception articulated by Parsons which is so widely shared that I call it the SPS position: the position of standard professional sociology.

The SPS position holds that theoretical knowledge is required to provide a rational foundation for practice in that it supplies scientifically warranted means to employ in pursuit of stipulated goals. Its classic formulation in modern philosophy is Kant's notion of the hypothetical imperative: if you want x, then you must do y. Max Weber's essays on objectivity and ethical neutrality contain the classic exposition of this position for modern sociology. Weber argued that although the goals of action could not be set by reason, pure science was needed for rational action by virtue of its capacity to provide not an authoritative selection of the best means toward one's goals but an analysis of the costs and benefits of various alternative means. This use of reason—as a calculus of optimal means—was what Parsons referred to as *instrumental rationality,* and in his own theory of action it proved to be the only type of rationality he seriously considered.

There exists, however, another mode of using reason in which theoretical knowledge figures as foundational for practice. This mode might be designated as *diagnostic rationality.* In the mode of diagnostic rationality, theoretic reason provides ends for action by establishing standards of well-being for persons or collectivities. Here the analogy with physiology/medicine is taken, not just to indicate the best means for attaining a goal, such as repairing a broken bone or relieving an aching back, but as a model for establishing criteria of a healthy organism. Theoretical science establishes limits within which an organism can survive and/or function adequately, such as normal temperatures and blood-pressure levels for various species and its subtypes, by age and gender, and the practical application of this knowledge works to diagnose given specimens of the species to determine their level of health.

Within the social sciences, diagnostic rationality was pioneered by Auguste Comte. Comte insisted on regarding society as a natural being and so advocated basing directives to action on prior theoretical knowledge about society's natural course of development. Armed with that knowledge, statesmen could assist society in reaching its normal state with the least pain and disruption. A century ago, Freud and Durkheim both attempted to generate diagnostic criteria for directing therapeutic interventions with personalities and with societies, respectively. Both Freud and Durkheim used the medical model to legitimate a quest for scientifically grounded knowledge of normal and pathological conditions in human conduct. Through studying social systems of a certain type, Durkheim argued, one could arrive at formulations regarding what conditions were normal to its existence and essential to its functioning.

In contrast to these views that would base rational practice on a previously secured foundation in theoretical knowledge, there stands a quartet of positions which challenges that view of the theory-practice nexus and which in fact holds that efforts to reduce practical knowledge to a process of applied theory are misguided at best. Philosophers who articulate these four positions are Aristotle, Kant, Marx, and Dewey. Two of them see theory as separate and distinct but not as an appropriate guide for practice; while the other two regard a disjunction between theory and practice as illegitimate.

The great architect of the disjunctive conception of theory and practice was Aristotle. McKeon helped generations of scholars grasp the several respects in which Aristotle worked to distinguish the theoretical sciences *(epistemai theoretikai)* from the sciences of human action *(epistemai praktikai)* — of ethics, economics, and politics. Those distinctions need to be made, Aristotle said, because every science needs to limit its attention to a certain class of things in order to demonstrate their essential attributes.

With respect to their subject matters: insofar as they deal with substances, the theoretical sciences contend with things that exist by nature, while the practical sciences work with a different class of things—*ta prakta* (things done). Actions do not occur by nature, they are made by humans (as are *ta poieta* [things produced], which form the subject matter of yet another group of disciplines, the productive sciences *[epistemai poietikai])*. Things existing by nature differ from human actions in two fundamental respects. Natural substances have an internal principle of change, whereas in actions the principle of change is external to them—in the will of the actor. What is more, the properties of natural substances are invariable, whereas human actions result from deliberate choice and so are variable.

The sciences of action differ from the sciences of natural substances in their methods as well as in their subject matters. The methods employed in studying natural substances include the establishment of true generalizations by means of induction and the demonstration of valid consequences by means of deduction. The propositions of natural science take the form of necessary universals because the essential characteristics of natural substances are invariable. For several reasons, the form taken by inquiry in the practical sciences diverges from that taken in physics. Since human actions are based on choice, not on natural necessity, their properties cannot be so securely grasped. What is more, because people differ so radically about what they consider good, inquiry into the nature of good action has to take into account the variety of opinions people hold. Finally, since the circumstances of action differ from situation to situation, knowing the best thing to do demands, above all knowledge of particulars: what counts in practice is not general rules but knowing what to do to the right person at the right time to the right extent and in the right manner.[18]

Methods geared to demonstrating universal propositions are therefore out of place in the practical sciences. The method suited for determining the right course of action is what Aristotle called deliberation *(boulesis)*. Inquiry proceeds by examining the diverse opinions people hold about an issue, and its successful resolution depends on traits of good character possessed by the deliberating parties. Deliberative excellence involves the selection of worthy ends and the determination of suitable means by means of sound reasoning in a moderate amount of time. The conclusions of deliberative inquiry cannot be expected to reach the precision and certainty attainable by the natural sciences, and it is the mark of an educated person to realize this.

Another difference between the two kinds of sciences concerns the faculties needed to prosecute them. The generalizations of natural science come from exercising the faculty Aristotle called intuitive reason *(nous)*. Showing the logical consequences of those generalizations involves what he called scientific knowledge *(episteme)*. On the other hand, deliberations about the good life involve a different sort of mental ability designated as *phronesis,* which may be translated as practical wisdom or prudence. In deliberating about laws and policies, a special variant of this, which he termed political wisdom *(politike),* is needed. In contrast to the states of mind that generate theoretical knowledge, *phronesis* is concerned with the "ultimate particular fact."[19] Perhaps we can refer to the kind of reason Aristotle claimed for practice as *deliberative rationality.*

Finally, the ends, or purposes, for which the two kinds of science are pursued also differ radically. The motivation for studying natural substances is to understand the world, for the sheer aesthetic pleasure and for the relief from ignorance such understanding affords. By contrast, the reason one studies human actions is for the sake of learning how to live well and how to cultivate the dispositions that promote good action, which is to say how to pursue the *aretai,* or excellences.

Kant also holds to a principled separation between the domains of theoretical and practical philosophy, but he does so for reasons that in many respects are the reverse of Aristotle's. For Kant, too, theoretical and practical knowledge differ in their subject matters, forms, ends, and methods, but Kant fills these distinctions with radically different contents. Where Aristotle found the subject of practical science to be variable human actions, Kant finds it to be a kind of law—laws of freedom. Where Aristotle faulted theory as a guide to practical decision making because of its universality and because the essence of practical wisdom is to understand particulars, Kant faults knowledge of human conduct from a theoretical perspective as a guide to practice because merely theoretic knowledge of what humans in different societies actually do cannot be universal enough to provide categorical imperatives for action. Where Aristotle found the method of practical philosophy to be a necessarily imprecise form of deliberation about variable things, Kant finds it to involve a kind of reasoning that can yield apodictic certainty. Where Aristotle considered the end of practical philosophy to be the pursuit of happiness, or at least *eudaimonia,* Kant considers it to be knowledge of how to live in accord with duty. Kant's practical reason can thus be glossed as a kind of deontological rationality.

Although Aristotle and Kant took pains to distinguish the knowledge involved in rational practice from theoretical knowledge, both of them deemed it important to preserve theory as an independent and dignified domain. Aristotle lauded the pursuit of theoretic contemplation as the highest form of human excellence, and Kant celebrated the theoretical domain which Copernicus revolutionized and Sir Isaac Newton championed. In the views of authors like Marx and Dewey, however, to protect a separate, distinct, and privileged domain of theory is to promote obfuscation and mystification.

Although Marx acknowledged the historical existence of a distinct domain of theoretical knowledge separate from practical concerns, he considered that domain detrimental to human well-being. The division of labor is the great source of human alienation, and the division of labor really takes on this alienating form only at the point when mental work gets separated from physical labor. From that moment onward, intellect flatters itself that it has hold of something supremely important. Theoretical work becomes the activity of an elite group that is exploitative in several ways: by deriving support from the exploited labor of working class people, by detracting mental energies from attention to the economic and social miseries of the populace, and by buttressing the position of an exploitative upper class.

For Marx, then, the disjunctive conception of theory/practice contributes to human self-alienation. Since true consciousness can only be consciousness of existing practice, there can be no legitimate basis for a principled separation between theory and practice. Rational practice begins with an acknowledgment of true human needs—for eating and drinking, clothing and housing, but also for expressing oneself creatively in work—and any intellectual activity that does not minister to the satisfaction of these needs represents false consciousness of some sort. One might refer to the use of reason implicit in Marx's philosophy as sensuous rationality. Abstract theories of society are useless, distracting, or manipulative mystifications. "Social life is essentially *practical,* [and] all mysteries which mislead theory into mysticism find their rational solution in human practice and in the comprehension of this practice."[20]

Like Marx, John Dewey interprets the idea of a separate domain of pure theory as the residue of an elitist social structure. He, too, believes that the mysteries of pure theory find their resolution in human practice. But Dewey regards the effort to establish a list of absolute human needs as itself a kind of alienation, just another byproduct of the age-old, all-too-human wish for certainty. Dewey eschews any and all efforts to secure entitative foundations, including those lodged in a reified conception of practice or in antecedently established notions of history and societal structure.

In his view, theory is simply a name for a special kind of practice, so the quest for a theoretical knowledge either prior to or segregated from practice must be rejected as a reflection of human fears and uncertainties. Accordingly, Dewey aspired to develop a logic of inquiry that reveals the underlying unity of theory and practice. In science as in daily life, action proceeds from undertakings that transform a problematic situation into a resolved one. In daily life as in science, action gets initiated in situations marked by indeterminacy or conflict, in which felt difficulties prompt efforts to formulate problems, suggest hypotheses, and carry out activities designed to test those hypotheses.

What Dewey finds harmful about disjunctive and foundational notions of the theory-practice nexus is not so much their ideological functions in upholding privilege but their effect in preventing the great resources of scientific intelligence from being harnessed for improving human experience. Against the notion of mind as a spectator beholding the world from without in a joyous act of self-sufficing contemplation, and against the notion that theory can disclose the characteristics of antecedent existence and essences, and therewith determine authoritative standards for conduct, Dewey propounds the view that reality itself possesses practical character and that this character is most efficaciously expressed in the function of intelligence. This notion of reason in practice is one he would call pragmatic rationality. Figure 3 summarizes the types of relationship between theory and practice just presented.

Playing with Pluralism

Inspired by the spirit of McKeon's approach to historical semantics, if not employing the terms of his schemas, the foregoing reflections challenge the hegemonic view of standard professional sociology as represented by Parsons. They subject the notion that pure sociology should inform practice through the logic of instrumental rationality to a fivefold critique.

From the viewpoint of diagnostic rationality, the SPS conception of the theory-practice nexus can be faulted for failing to provide norms about normal or healthy states. For example, it might lead one to apply propositions about group process to eliminating the authority of leaders, without considering whether or not authoritative leaders comprise a normal and healthy part of group functioning. From the viewpoint of deliberative rationality, that conception can be faulted for neglecting the importance of particulars in action and the imprecise nature of practical decisions—for example, looking for universally valid processes to heighten morale in organizations without considering the nuances of local life and the difficulties of verbalizing certain aspects of interpersonal rapport. From the viewpoint of deontological rationality, it can be faulted for shortchanging the ability of reason to provide normative injunctions independent of empirical circumstances—using instrumental calculations to optimize the elimination of allegedly inferior peoples without considering whether there is not a rationally prescribed duty to resist such objectives. From the viewpoint of sensuous rationality, it can be faulted for deflecting attention from urgent social needs, spending millions to do research on poverty instead of on programs to alleviate

Figure 3

Conceptions of the Theory-Praxis Nexus

THEORY-PRACTICE RELATION		EXEMPLARY AUTHOR	TYPE OF PRACTICAL RATIONALITY
FOUNDATIONAL	Theory provides lawful regularities to be applied in practice	Weber, Parsons, SPS	Instrumental
	Theory provides standards of health or normality	Durkheim, Freud	Diagnostic
DISJUNCTIVE	Theory concerns necessary universals; practice involves variable particulars	Aristotle	Deliberative
	Theory concerns laws of nature; practice concerns laws of freedom	Kant	Deontological
INSEPARABLE	Separate theory reflects alienation from sensuous needs	Marx	Sensuous
	Antecedent theory fractures unity of experience	Dewey	Pragmatic

poverty through job training and job creation. From the viewpoint of pragmatic rationality, it can be faulted for deriving its problems, concepts, and methods from antecedently formulated theories, when appropriate concepts and methods can only be identified as plausible responses to problems that emerge in indeterminate or conflictual situations—as when one brings a set of standard procedures demonstrated to enhance communication among staff members when the chief presenting problem in their office is a lack of time to deal with crises in their families.

This kind of work—identifying shortcomings in a position by appeal to the insights of plausible alternative positions—can be construed as a first-level engagement with pluralism. We could just as readily confront any of the others with critical arguments from the remaining five. Yet this is not the only way in which McKeon's work can be utilized, for it opens up at least two more advanced ways to employ a pluralistic vision. In these other modes, the point is not to engage alternative perspectives or principles in order to open up new ways of looking at a commonplace issue, but to see how those different positions relate among themselves. As George Kimball Plochmann has observed, "essay after essay of [McKeon's] begins with some variation on the theme that there are great discrepancies in the traditional philosophies, and it is important to lay them out in order to resolve them."[21] I shall call them, first, the mode of cyclical history, and second, following Watson's usage in *The Architectonics of Meaning,* the mode of reciprocal priority.

McKeon exhibited the cyclical mode chiefly when representing the broad historic shifts of attention to different subject matters in Western cultural history. Originally shown in the opening pages of *Freedom and History,*[22] he traced a series of epochal changes, starting in the Hellenic period when philosophers debated about being—when the atoms of Democritus, the Ideas of Plato, and the substances of Aristotle were considered existent things which provided principles for science and had some bearing on morals and politics. In the succeeding Hellenistic epoch, philosophers tired of the inconclusive debates about being and shifted their concern to the nature of thought. Stoics, Epicureans, Academics, and Skeptics sought their basic principles in the criteria of knowledge, criteria by which truth or probability might be achieved. Under the spreading Roman rule, philosophers found epistemological debates as unfruitful as their predecessors had found metaphysical disputes and turned to examine how people talk and how people act. At the same time, Sextus Empiricus proceeded to analyze the signs used in various sciences, and Cicero appealed to consequences in practical action. The coming of Christianity reawakened interest in doctrines about being, a concern codified by St. Augustine. Then Boethius shifted attention to the problem of knowledge, after which Cassiodorus and Isidore of Seville engineered the linguistic turn, and the court of Charlemagne revivified interest in philosophy by attending to problems of practical action. This cycle of shifts in subject matter, from being to thought to words and deeds, took place five times in the history of the West—most recently in the cycle beginning in the seventeenth century, when modern science began with a new interest in the nature of things, after which Kant reoriented philosophy to the problem of knowledge, leading to our century with its interest both in the nature of symbols and the patterns of action and experience.

The cyclical mode offers an ideal type for a conjectural history of shifts of attention and emphasis. The operative principle is the notion that a certain approach gets cultivated until its fruitfulness is exhausted and its omissions become too glaring. How might could one adapt such a conjectural grid to the vicissitudes of approach to the theory-practice mode in sociology during the past century? It began with some strong statements of diagnostic rationality—Durkheim's about normal and pathological states, Thornstein Veblen's about stage-appropriate conditions, Pareto's about optimal equilibria. This was replaced by a concern for using social science to organize publics and inform public opinion, as the statements in the 1920s by Dewey and Park show. During the 1940s and 1950s, sociologists attained an unprecedented level of professional respectability and shifted to an appeal to instrumental rationality based on their specialized expertise. The 1960s saw a good deal of revolt against this engineering model and a renewed appeal to Marxian doctrines against alienated instrumentality. The shortcomings of directly sensuous rationality became apparent in the 1970s and 1980s, as writers like Jürgen Habermas came to emphasize deliberative rationality and others, insisting that the horrors of Nazi genocide be confronted, invoked the need for deontological rationality.[23]

In addition to relating different approaches in terms of this model of cyclical manifestations, McKeon offered a model by which any given perspective, deeply pursued, could find some kind of place for the main thrust of the others. This kind of mutualized accommodation has been represented aptly by Watson's felicitous phrase, *reciprocal priority*.

In the mode of reciprocal priority, one position is taken as central, and the others are confronted, redefined, and assimilated in accord with its perspective. So if we were to take the position represented by what I have called instrumental rationality, we could in principle find some way of accommodating each of the other five. Thus, from the viewpoint of instrumental rationality, diagnostic rationality might be criticized as purporting to advance scientific grounds for what are in fact conventionally based norms, but the norms it suggests could be used as goals for directing the analysis of means. Deliberative rationality would be criticized for leaving too much to opinion, since rigorous scientific methods are now available to assess various outcomes. However, this does not mean that the precision of physics can be expected in measuring human affairs, so their results must be stated in probabilistic terms; and there is no reason why those results cannot be discussed by an informed public in open democratic process. Deontological rationality would be criticized for ignoring immoral consequences in its quest for rationally grounded motives for action, but its efficacy in setting the normative ground rules for honest inquiry and open discussion would be acknowledged. Sensuous rationality would be faulted for failing to appreciate the complexities of action situations and human dispositions, but its caution about getting lost in alienated procedures could be appreciated. Pragmatic rationality would be hailed as a close ally and perhaps faulted only for failing to appreciate that to tie optimal actions so closely to the particularities of situations is to undermine the quest for generalizations about factors that structure the contexts of action.

Confronted with a plurality of positions about the relationship between theory and action—or anything else—then, the philosophy of Richard McKeon opens up the three options we have just considered: to use the other positions to generate criticisms of the one chosen, to see them in a cyclical progression as giving rise one to another, and to use a chosen position to translate others so as to assimilate their congenial features while rejecting their incompatible ones.

The work involved in pursuing these options can demand a great deal in maturity of mind and strength of intellect. But there is some sense in which one responds to this work with amusement, regarding it as some sort of game—which is why I have called this section of my paper "Playing with Pluralism." There remains something ultimately unsatisfactory about it; namely, its apparent difficulty in providing any rational ground for choosing one position rather than another. McKeon's philosophy seems to be excellent for clarifying the cognitive alternatives in our culture, and certainly consistent with the criticism of degraded versions of those alternatives, but provides no criteria for selecting one alternative over another.

Selecting a Mode of Thought

Indeed, that does seem to be the prime weakness for which this philosophy has been faulted. The only advice McKeon ever gave about which approach to select was his reported comment that one picked an approach "that feels most comfortable."[24] His indifference in this regard parallels Max Weber's advice regarding ultimate values: only hearken to your inner demon. But what if you have no clear demon, or what if two demons are warring in your breast, or what if you suspect that your demon is inappropriate due to changing circumstances, or what if new prophets appear, or when forgotten truths are recovered; what then?

McKeon's failure to specify criteria for selecting a cognitive approach may be connected with his relative inattention to the normative dimension of culture. This can be made clear by considering some features of Parsons's theory of action. In an earlier phase of work on culture, Parsons analyzed cultures with respect to the general value-orientations they embodied, values to which he gave such names as universalisticascription and particularistic-achievement patterns. In later work, he came to focus on the generic needs of boundary-maintaining systems of action, needs which he came to refer to in terms of the functions of adaptation, goal attainment, integration, and pattern maintenance. Different value-orientations, then, came to be viewed as differentially relevant to one or another of these generic system functions.

Through the same logic that relates the selection of values to the functions of action systems, one can also find criteria with which to assess the differential relevance of diverse cognitive approaches. Let us return to the authors whose views we sketched above and encapsulate their respective approaches to the theory-practice question by referring to the different meanings they ascribe to practice.

For Aristotle, practice refers to a human process involving choice, and the choices are made with respect to some end or purpose. Since all human activities aim at some good and the higher or more general good directs the lower or more particular goods, the chief task of practical philosophy is to articulate the ideal ends of human action. In *Ethics,* this turns out to be the cultivation of the *aretai,* or human excellences; in *Politics,* the establishment of laws which will promote justice as well as the cultivation of excellence. Durkheim sees a similar agenda for sociology. Although he differs from Aristotle in rejecting the notions of common opinion as a point of departure for discourse about the good, he aspires to use his social science in practice by establishing conceptions of the normal and the pathological that will provide the reasonable ideals toward which human decisions should be oriented.

For Kant, practice also refers to human action that is subject to choice, but Kant's emphasis is on the subjection of those choices to imperatives that guarantee freedom—of the inner exercise of will in ethics; of the external exercise of will in jurisprudence. The task of a philosophy of practice, accordingly, is to ground the principles which generate ethical and juridical norms.

The meaning of practice changes considerably in Marx. For Marx, practice refers to the satisfaction of human sensuous needs, so the task of a philosophy of practice is to show how those needs are historically met and frustrated and what must be done to overcome those obstacles to their complete satisfaction. Dewey also connects practice with the satisfaction of human needs, but what Dewey understands by practice differs from what Marx meant by the term. Practice for Dewey consists of efforts to cope with anything that impedes the enjoyment of experience, whether it be of a material or an intellectual character. Dewey's formula for practice is couched not as the satisfaction of needs, but the solving of problems. That formula would also cover the kind of practice entailed in Max Weber's notion of instrumental rationality.

The question now before us is whether it is possible to determine if one of these meanings and its attendant agenda is superior to another. I have argued that it is not possible to do so without departing from the limits of McKeon's philosophy, but that such a determination could be derived from the conceptual resources of Parsons's theory of action. An immediately transparent way to do so would be to make reference to familiar Freudian schema for analyzing the parts of the personality. The part of personality that presents bundles of imperious needs that clamor for satisfaction Freud called *das Es* (the id). Another part deals with the solution of problems posed by the relations among the different parts of the personality and its relations with the reality outside the individual, *das Ich* (the ego). Yet another part confronts the individual with duties and norms that are to be obeyed, *das Überich* (the superego). Finally, what he sometimes designated as a part distinct from the superego provided general ideals for the person to follow, the ego-ideal.

While Parsons accepts this schema for the analysis of psychic structure, he interprets it as a refraction at the level of the personality system of the four-function schema that pertains to all systems of action. The ego deals with the function of adapting to reality in order to attain goals. The id provides general motivational resources available to energize action. The superego is concerned with normative integration, and the ego-ideal with pattern maintenance (see Figure 2, bottom right). What Parsons offers to a philosophy of culture, then, is a way of connecting different dimensions and systems of cultures with the satisfaction of different kinds of systemic needs. At the global level of culture, he connects the functions of adaptation with science, of goal attainment with art, of integration with ethics and law, and of pattern maintenance with religion.

Returning to the construal of meaning at the personality level, we could say that Aristotle's concern with excellence and Durkheim's with standards of health and normality represent alternate approaches to the specification of ego ideals, which afford alternate ways to fulfill the function of pattern maintenance. Kant's concern with the specification of norms corresponds to the superego of the individual, fulfilling what Parsons calls the function of normative integration. Marx's identification of practice with the satisfaction of needs corresponds to one ego-id interface, that involving the function of goal attainment; while Dewey's identification of practice with problem solving and the SPS position correspond to another ego-id interface, the identification of resources within the personality and the more general system function of adaptation.[25]

Parsons's schema thus suggests one rational way to select one of the cognitive modalities so brilliantly typologized by McKeon. It would take a form something like that represented in Figure 4. If the system problem concerns adaptation or resource generation, use instrumental or pragmatic rationality, for that is the kind of reasoning that specifies the costs and benefits of alternate means. If the problem has to do with goal attainment, use sensuous rationality, for that is the kind of reasoning that applies to whether or not resources have been effectively mobilized to satisfy needs. If the problem concerns integration, use deontological rationality, for that is the type of reasoning related to compliance with obligatory norms. If it has to do with pattern maintenance, use deliberative or diagnostic rationality, for that type of reasoning clarifies the ultimate values which govern the system's orientation.

It should be clear that the above suggestions are offered in an illustrative and exploratory mode. Whatever the status of these particular suggestions, I hope the way of thinking they configure indicates what might be gained by connecting the analyses of values Parsons found embodied in action systems with the diversity of cognitive orientations McKeon identified in philosophical outlooks.

Figure 4

Types of Practical Rationality (*après* McKeon) in Relation to Action System Functions (*après* Parsons)

	INSTRUMENTAL	CONSUMMATORY
EXTERNAL	Adaptation *Instrumental rationality* *Pragmatic rationality*	Goal-attainment *Sensuous rationality*
INTERNAL	Pattern Maintenance *Deliberative rationality* *Diagnostic rationality*	Integration *Deontological rationality*

ONE MIND IN THE TRUTH

RICHARD MCKEON, A PHILOSOPHER OF EDUCATION

Dennis O'Brien

> ". . . to be of one mind is not to be of one opinion."
> RICHARD MCKEON, "COMMUNICATION, TRUTH, AND
> SOCIETY," 99

Mark Backman properly comments that Richard McKeon was "edifying."
"Awesome" or "terrifying" would have been my personal reaction, but
Backman is being technical. He cites Richard Rorty. The mainstream of
philosophy has been "systematic." Philosophers in the mainstream lay out
systems, refuting rivals, and constructing powerful proofs of their own
views. In contrast to the majority there are edifying philosophers on the pe-
riphery who have kept alive the historicist sense that this century's "superstition" was the last century's triumph of reason, as well as the relativist
sense that the latest vocabulary . . . may be just another of the potential infinity of vocabularies in which the world can be described.[1] McKeon as
"edifying" *in sensu Rortiano* helped explain to me the fascination and frustration which I (and many of my contemporaries) felt in our studies at
Chicago during the 1950s. Personal history may help to set the philosophical issues I wish to raise in this essay.

The University of Chicago has traditionally had a more open-door
policy toward graduate students than many other great graduate centers.

If one evinced interest, showed some modicum of talent, and could pay the tuition, one could enroll. (In my case this was most fortunate since I had taken virtually no philosophy courses as an undergraduate.) The result of "open admissions" was that there were lots of philosophy graduate students on hand. I leave it to the faculty of the era to decide on talent, but in terms of interest I was fascinated at the number of Roman Catholics (some current, lots of ex-) among the students. Presumably the multiplicity of Roman Catholics was due to the general reputation of Messrs. Robert Maynard Hutchins, Mortimer Adler, et al. as Thomistic fellow travelers. To be sure, neither of those famous people were available in the philosophy door at the university, but the medievalists among us were not (entirely) frustrated by what we found. We discovered McKeon. (As a nonphilosopher undergrad, I had, of course, never heard of him.)

It was by no means the case that the raft of ex–Roman Catholics wanted straight-line Scholasticism—and they certainly would not have obtained anything like it at the Chicago of the fifties. On the other hand, most were sufficiently concerned with traditional religious/philosophical issues to be wary of the dominant scientific positivism which seemed to blanket the American philosophical landscape. Chicago somehow or other seemed to be interested in the historical tradition of philosophy and thus not wed to some modern valueless "scientific" dogmatism.

While I was considering taking graduate work in philosophy at Chicago, I somehow extracted an opinion from someone at my undergraduate school (Yale) about the Chicago department. I was told that it was a bad place to study philosophy because they—McKeon in particular—were not interested in philosophy but only in the history of philosophy. We certainly did read much from the history of philosophy. Later, when I started teaching at Princeton, I had the impression there that philosophy had started with Bertrand Russell; at Chicago it seemed the subject stopped with *Principia Mathematica*.) Given such heady information and being utterly naive in the ways of graduate study, I made an appointment to see this Richard McKeon and confronted him with the negative appraisal from New Haven. It was my first confrontation, but more or less like all the rest. McKeon snorted (politely) and went on at some length about the fact that it was the others that were only interested in the history of philosophy and that he (and Chicago) were peculiarly concerned with philosophy. I did not understand his argument at all; perhaps I was baffled enough to enroll and see if I could discern the actual state of affairs.

I recount this personal history of myself and comrades because it relates to the problems of McKeon's approach to philosophy—or the history of philosophy or whatever he was up to. Many of us chose Chicago because it seemed to be open to the historical tradition with which we were still struggling. In so far as McKeon was "edifying" as described, he obviously rejected the systematizing scientism of prevalent positivism. This rejection gave legitimacy to our desire to discover value in traditional moral, religious, and metaphysical systems. But if McKeon gave legitimacy to the historical philosophers, we began to wonder whether he gave legitimacy to philosophy. Maybe the Yalies were correct.

McKeon was very much into "Ideas and Methods," the name of the special program which he created and supervised and under which rubric he offered a series of courses. During my second year in graduate school, the students presented a burlesque of the philosophy department. It was brilliantly titled "Philosophy Phollies," and the plot (?) centered on one Richard McBean. McBean sang a long refrain called "I Got Plenty of Methods." The lyrics went something like this: "Don't need logic, don't need ethics, don't need philosophy / I got plenty of methods and methods plenty for me." The point was that we were always doing what McKeon called "historical semantics," an intricate set of changes and variations which allowed one to "translate" from one philosophical perspective to another. If you knew philosopher A's method (logistic) as distinct from B's method (problematic), you could see why A was right—but so was B! Democritus or Descartes saw things this way and so—so what? We wanted to do "philosophical semantics" and find out who was right and wrong in these conceptual capers. In short, while we did not like the systematic philosophy of the day, we wanted to rummage in history for the True philosophy. What we got was plenty of methods.

Fashions in philosophy change. (McKeon was right on that score.) Although the systematic spirit probably still commands a majority vote, the inroads of the edifying have been remarkable. A variety of postmodernist views have arisen which emphasize the "historicism" of the philosophical voice and develop "hermeneutics" which proclaim a "potential infinity of vocabularies." The modernist tradition being rejected by *post*modernists is exemplified by Descartes, who fancied philosophy as the activity of dis-embodied, a-historical mind. Feminist critics have been most acute in debunking Descartes and re-embodying philosophy. (Gendered philosophy obviously requires a body.) More broadly, deconstructionists and their "multicultural" allies have demanded that philosophy be reoriented to the vital histories of peoples, races, sexual cultures, and subcultures. The trend of the varieties of postmodernist thought is, then, determinedly against the transcendent, definitive, scientific thrust of positivism—if not of Western philosophy overall since Plato. To the extent that McKeon's historical semantics seemed to reject system in favor of historical transformations, his philosophical approach would appear to be as timely and as modern as postmodernism can be.

Postmodernist thought, however, has presented precisely the problems which troubled myself and my graduate student colleagues in the fifties. If one rejects the transcendent and the systematic, does one not reject philosophy in favor of some "aesthetic" ideational dance, an embrace of relativism such as Richard Rorty proclaims. Although deconstructionism or neopragmatism may make McKeon's historical semantics trendy, do they confirm our suspicions about the lack of philosophy?

The Roman Catholics (extant and ex) at Chicago appreciated the openness to history favored by McKeon but doubted that his project would ground their beliefs. Susan Bordo has put forward a similar objection to the deconstructionist project as a background for feminist thought. She has argued that in escaping the transcendent "dream of Descartes" (the myth of the transcendent view from *nowhere*) deconstructionism creates a new transcendent, the protean knower who has the dream of being *everywhere*.[2] If systematic philosophy rests on transcendent mind, the philosophic persona of the postmodernist is "the mythological 'Trickster,' the shapeshifter: 'of indeterminate sex and changeable gender . . . [who] continually alters her/his body, creates and recreates a personality . . . [and] floats across time' from period to period. . . ."[3] Bordo believes that the view from everywhere is as empty as the dream from nowhere. If one does feminist philosophy, shape-shifting as the ideal will be rejected. If the urge is to grounded, embodied doctrine, shape-shifting transcends the transcendent into emptiness.

Anyone who has spent anytime reading McKeon will recognize that his essays "float across time from period to period." Repeatedly he will approach the most pressing of immediate problems by a scholarly review of just about everything that one might even remotely imagine as past precedent.[4] What is the result of these remarkable historical excursions? Clearly it rejects Descartes's deductive dream, but Susan Bordo's concern about the Trickster might well apply to the McKeon project. Certainly there were those of us who regarded the intricacies of methods, principles, interpretations, and the whole machine as "tricky." Could one really move with protean assurance from one philosophy to another, reveling completely in the body of Aristotle or Spinoza or Dewey?

It is worth emphasizing that when McKeon was *in* a philosopher, teaching Aristotle or Plato, the world was wholly defined by the system at hand. If McKeon had not been such a compelling expositor from the inside, I doubt that his shape-shifting across the history of philosophy would have been so intriguing. One can always "translate" between philosophical quarrels by an equitable misunderstanding of all positions. One of the significant differences between McKeon's project and the multiculturalist, deconstructionist projects currently being advanced is McKeon's assessment of the meaning of "variety" in philosophical systems. McKeon seems to hold a paradoxical position: each position when taught from the inside was compelling, but no position seemed definitive against another—despite the polemic which has marked the history of the subject. McKeon seemed to advocate the philosopher at hand—along with all the rest of the philosophical literature.

Multiculturalism: Politics and Philosophy

I cite contemporary multiculturalism because it makes highly controversial, reformative claims upon the prevailing (truth-seeking) philosophy of higher education—most particularly on philosophy and the humanities, but even on the sacrosanct transcendent of the natural sciences. One should recall that McKeon was also in the midst of the radical reform at the University of Chicago. While President Robert M. Hutchins is the one most associated with that "great books" reform, McKeon, as dean of the Division of Humanities, was in many ways the mastermind of the programs on the ground. Since this is an essay on McKeon as a philosopher of education, the contemporary multiculturalist arguments serve as a comparison and contrast to McKeon's own schema for education.

Before attending directly to McKeon as philosopher-dean of higher education, it is important to note the historical background of McKeon's work during the '50s when historical semantics was being developed and purveyed. When I was studying at Chicago, McKeon was in the thick of his involvement with UNESCO. His concerns could certainly be labeled multicultural, but they were not so much concerned with the nature of university study as in pressing political concerns. Far from being a simple exponent of Western civilization, McKeon was seeking ways of creating the widest cross-cultural/cross-political dialogue.[5] Given the Cold War tensions, he sought a means of discovering common agreement about action across apparently antagonistic ideological systems. Did McKeon's quest for peace through historical semantics, however, imply reducing ideas to action, truth to historical position, philosophy to ideology? I think not, and if we understand his approach we may well have educational diversity and digest Truth as well.

During the UNESCO period, McKeon certainly had an overriding political context for handling diversity. Given an ideological conflict between East and West, McKeon sought to demonstrate that ideological difference did not demand difference in action. The context of the present paper is not political, however, but educational—and I believe that McKeon's real contribution is in that context. While there may be overwhelming practical reasons for prescinding from theoretical concurrence in international conflict, in an educational setting such a strategy may well appear as the abandonment of proper Truth and legitimacy. Thus, in the current educational discussion of diversity, one of the dangers often claimed is that education has been reduced to politics and diversity to the polemics of eternally warring genders, races, or classes. If so, education would be international politics extended—quite the reverse of McKeon's ultimate hope that international politics might conform to the process of education.

McKeon addressed the problem of diversity and unity in thought and action in many publications. He is consistent in rejecting the systematic approach to the problem. In his mind, this approach attempts to discover a vantage point above the historical moment from which one could derive a satisfactory theory which would then be implemented. Whatever the ultimate value of such an approach, McKeon judged it to be practically empty. He claimed that his approach was set by Frederick Woodbridge and John Dewey:

> In the teachings of Woodbridge and Dewey the problem of the one and the many is restated in terms appropriate to the problems of our times—not as a problem of essence and existence, nor as a problem of reality and appearance, but as a problem of truth and modes of formulation.[6]

As he goes on to say in the same passage, he wanted to root his work in "the experience and the problems of our times . . ." It is this problematic approach growing from the historical moment that leads to regarding his work as "edifying," nonsystematic, and, at least in statement, akin to postmodernist historicisms. Does historicism in McKeon (with a nod to pragmatists like Dewey) lead to the relativism of neopragmatists like Rorty? McKeon sees the problematic character of historicism:

> The problems of an age arise in what is said—in the communications of the age—and they cannot be formulated accurately, intelligibly, or effectively without taking into account how they arise and in what context they are stated.[7]

But if the problems lie in communication arising from peculiar contexts, the problem of commonality and truth becomes acute.

> The consequences of beginning with communications . . . run[s] contrary to the sense . . . that communications would be adapted in form and structure to the subject matter they set forth or to the thoughts that they express. Yet, recognition that the discovery of truth and the formation of thought are evidenced in communication need not lead to skepticism or relativism.[8]

Contemporary exponents of diversity often claim that the historical, ethnic, and gender origins of artistic or ideational constructs are wholly constitutive so that only this gender, this race, this class, or this individual can understand and interpret it aright. Such emphasis on origin and context lead directly to various forms of sociological or psychological reductions of truth to ideology and argument to emotional display. How does McKeon propose to avoid such relativistic conclusions?

McKeon construes the problem of diversity as a problem of communication. Communication is certainly the proper setting for the dominant defense of diversity of voices. Postmodernist thought champions hermeneutics, the interpretation of texts. Older metaphysics which sought direct confirmation of theory in Being is rejected along with epistemologies which would pretend to the stance of the de-gendered, unlocated knower. For the postmodernist, Truth is a function of authored texts; Truth is always contextual. McKeon seeks to escape from multicultural relativism through an analysis of communication. His strategy is to locate the fundamental aspiration of the communication demanded in both dogmatic and diverse visions of society. Uncovering the basic aspiration and structure of communication, even and especially in situated voices, establishes in McKeon's view the basis for a larger community and the pursuit of Truth.

Given the centrality of communication, McKeon conceptualizes communication in four dimensions: a relation of persons, the assumption that communication implies change, the guidance of change by some ideals, and a conception of the objective circumstances in which communication about change toward the ideal would occur.[9]

Communication is obviously a problem of relation. Most apparently, it is a relation of understanding between two or more persons, though it may also be a communication between the true self and some false image of the self. Thus, women are often urged to "communicate with their true feelings," e.g. anger, obviously a relation between conscious and unconscious within a single person. Communication is attained when the right relation is obtained between persons or a person and the true self. Communication becomes an overriding aim and desideratum, when it is ascertained that right relations do not exist between or within persons.

The simple existence of nonrelatedness will not lead to emphasis on communication, however, without an implied belief that change is possible toward the ideal of right relation. If one supposed that human social relations were biologically fixed, any ideal would be fantasy and any urge for change utopian. One would not emancipate the slaves if everyone (including the slaves) believed in Aristotle's natural slave.

Finally, of course, the aim of communication, changing forms toward the ideal, can only be understood against current objective circumstance. It is only because the current circumstance is assessed against present hindrance and future possibilities for action that communication is genuinely expressive or truly effective. If one lacks connection to objective circumstance, the tension which demands change will be regarded as neurotic. Those who demand a new voice will be regarded as projecting inner malaise on external circumstance or hypothecating fanciful solutions to genuine issues which demand more realistic remedies.

It seems obvious that in describing the aspirations of new voices, the issue of Truth remains ever present at the margin. One is urged to make contact with a "true" self, women should communicate their "true feelings," an "authentic female community" should be established to replace the "false" image of masculinity. Blacks are urged to reject the false image of white masters. In pursuing a cultural cause, its prophets must presumably read "the signs of the times" and judge correctly the bars to progress and the possibilities for a better life. It might be simple enough, then, to suggest that all historicisms which demand a situated voice are established within the culture of truth. Relativism and skepticism cannot be the assumption or the outcome of such historicisms without destroying the claim to legitimacy. The argument is a form of the standard self-refutation lodged against situated claims to Truth.

Simple self-refutation is, however, both practically and theoretically unsatisfactory. The historicist is unlikely to give up her situation, fearing that the Truth lurking at the margin is none other than the old transcendent, and she will have none of Him. If necessary, madness or depression may be more authentic to her project. The truth alluded to in the description of the feminist aspiration (and I emphasize again that similar structures will occur in all claims for a situated voice) may be regarded as an internal standard of authenticity, which has only a nodding verbal allegiance to the traditional transcendent theories of Truth.

There are two unacceptable solutions to the dilemma of historicism and truth. One, of course, is simply to abandon the basic idea of a situated voice and admit that, in the end, it is the transcendent which judges all: men and women, black and white, Christian and Jew. The other is withdrawal into either private madness or communal cultism. Only those of particular gender or grace can gauge the truth of the self expressed or the cult formed. Infallibility is internally generated and self-guaranteed by birth or baptismal rebirth.

Withdrawal seems a desperate stratagem, but it has certainly been adopted. It is difficult to see, however, how it can fulfill the essential aspiration of any situated voice since it would fail to create the community of interest intended. Authenticity may be purchased at the price of the communicable—which would appear to jeopardize the basis of any new community or cult. A primal scream may be emotionally satisfying, but it is something less than self-understanding and a shaky base for communal action.

I raise the strategy of withdrawal because I believe that in the diversity debates of today, it is important to make sure that cultism is not the diversity sought. This point is acute for the educational context. Adding new voices to education would presumably enrich some sort of dialogue of understanding; if cultism is the base, however, then the educational context is indistinguishable from the political. The state is constitutionally incompetent to adjudicate religious controversy. Religious practices and private enthusiasms lie beyond state action unless they somehow infringe on the public peace. (You may primally scream provided you do not keep the neighbors awake all night.) A cultic understanding of diversity within education would, however, dissolve educational dialogue in any form in favor of a political order (at best). In an educational community, such diversity seems unacceptable on its face and would certainly dissolve any standards for intellectual discourse.

McKeon poses the problem of communication in terms of two forms of social organization: the unitary and the pluralistic society.[10] Postmodernists will have no trouble identifying the unitary society. It is any old hegemonic culture in which the truth being known, values are set, freedoms expressed as adherence to those values, and decision is made by those specially possessed of the truth. Unitary societies preclude discussion of truths. If you know the truth, you do not need to discuss it. Few deliberate about arithmetic.

The ideological assumptions about the nature of truth, expression, values, and so forth within unitary societies seem prima facie to be too narrow, but McKeon does not argue against such organization on mere historical results.

> The facts of history and contemporary observation are evidence to the contrary to the assumption that truths, values, freedom, and agreement are not achieved in an authoritarian society or with a unitary conception of truth is without attraction to uncommitted minds. Science has flourished under despotisms . . . the arts have flourished and waned under highly diverse conditions.[11]

The real problem for the unitary society is reflexive: it cannot coherently carry forward its own aspiration to create and sustain community. Unitary societies are caught in inner contradiction. (The fact that they are unstable may be regarded as the ground for the failure of historical evidence to bring decisive judgment on the value of dictatorships.) Unstable societies show their instability by failing to conform to their own model and thus may prove fruitful in spite of themselves. McKeon believes that the solution to the temptation of the unitary society is neither historical condemnation nor mechanical safeguards. "[T]he processes of unitary communication will be stopped . . . only by the clarity and efficacy of communications which provides and employs alternative ways of making men of one mind."[12]

One can assess the ultimate failure of the unitary model by examining the conditions of its opposite, specifically the issue of truth in a pluralistic society.[13] The allure of the unitary society is that it claims to be the only possible framework for a society interested in truth. Thus, critics of diversity in contemporary educational debates suggest that diversity is nothing but a fast retreat into skepticism. If each individual has her own truth, there is no Truth at all worthy of the name. Education becomes fashion, class struggle, international politics, or religious polemic. If McKeon can gives us a theory of truth in a pluralistic society, he would solve a deeply felt issue in contemporary educational debate.

McKeon differentiates the two societies by the relation between the four dimensions of communication. In a unitary society, there is "a simple equation of the four functions of communication established by control of communication."[14] In contrast,

> A pluralistic society is one in which the four dimensions of communication function independently, and the basis of truth in a pluralistic society is communication which facilitates the statement and discussion of differences, and the clarification and utilization of agreements . . . the basic problem of a pluralistic society is to use unity to promote diversity and diversity to strengthen unity.[15]

In the unitary society, the four factors of community are strictly co-variant. Values are directly deduced from known truths; the inculcation of true values is the measure of freedom—all else is license; leadership in the unitary society rests with those who know the truth and enforce the values which flow therefrom.

While it is tempting to find models of unitary society in historical despotisms, it is more useful to note that scientific disciplines can also be regarded under the unitary model. In physics there are known truths which determine the value of specific scientific claims; what is known as valuable science determines the limits of freedom of thought versus license, and in some sense the community of physicists acts to enforce the sense of common undertaking, which is the physics community. The recent controversy over cold fusion illustrates how a group of certified experts can be called upon to establish truth and determine the value of the physics.

The example of physics is, of course, imperfect. One can regard the physics community as much more pluralistic than the unitary model suggested. The physics analogy does suggest, however, the central role of known truth and its experts in linking the factors of community. One of the features of a pluralistic society is the rejection of the life of theory as the model for the life of society. Truths are not already known, experts are not established via the known truths, common values cannot be directly deduced from uncertainty and dispute, individuals cannot be freed by known value since the values are in dispute, and, so, freedom exists to choose and deliberate. It is this state of affairs which McKeon describes as the independent function of the four factors of communication.

To anyone obsessed with the unitary vision of society, the falling apart of the four functions may at first appear as the abandonment of any satisfactory standards of truth, value, freedom, or community. McKeon obviously disagrees with any such assessment and would attempt to locate the genuine community of the pluralistic society in its structure of communication.

Communication is *the* unrecognized problem for the unitary society. It is obvious in pluralistic societies that people do not generally agree on any of the four factors. One may, in fact, regard pluralistic societies as collections of miniunitary societies. Paradoxically, the glue which holds the large pluralistic society together will be discovered in communication within the minisocieties. Unhappily for sheer cultic diversity, the discovery of commonality within the various subunities is grounded on a habit of communication which cannot finally be limited at the lab door or the portals of the parish.

Each generation must acquire the truths and values of the society or societies into which it is born. If one is born into a unitary society overall or the local parish in a pluralistic society, in either instance the society must communicate its truths and values. This is the process we call education—or more accurately, it is a process which finally collapses into education. Unfortunately for the ideal of a unitary society (large or small), education in a unitary way of life undercuts its own ideal. It is not that one need abandon the beliefs of the unitary group, it is that beliefs into which one has been educated cannot be held in the manner which a unitary society desires.

The best illustration of the inner failure of the unitary ideal because of education is in Socrates' scandalous suggestion of the noble lie in the *Republic*. Having most carefully "educated" the various classes of citizens into their social roles, Socrates says that it is now necessary to convince each class that they were born into that role as gold, silver, and brass.[16] Being born to a role establishes the necessity to which the unitary society aspires; if, on the other hand, the guardians were to realize that they had only learned these roles from others, they may well begin to wonder why these roles and not others, why these teachers and not others. Freedom arises in the detachment between self and any role which has been inculcated by education. If, then, communication (inculcation) in truth, freedom, value, and social order is the only way that any truths, freedoms, values, or societies can be created, the idea of the unitary society collapses (unless one can pull off the noble lie). Once inculcation (an educative moment) is self-consciously recognized, the fact and devices of pluralism must either be made clear or any and all societies will dissolve. (This is, of course, the next step in the *Republic,* when the philosopher comes inside the state rather than constructing one ab extra. The problem of intergenerational continuity raised at the beginning of book V—as a new starting point for the dialogue—leads directly to the need for the reflexive wisdom of the philosopher-king. With the internalizing of philosophy, one learns that philosophic education can ground community without the noble lie of natural necessity.)

The noble-lie argument is roundly condemned as Socratic subterfuge, but it is interesting to note the persistence of arguments from natural determination in modern diversity debates. One is not born gold or silver, but we are urged to believe that sexual orientation or gender wisdom is genetically determined. While that claim may have a validity, it is interesting that communication remains a central issue. Feminists are urged to discover and proclaim their true self (given by nature). Whatever the natural base of the discovery of sexual ideology, it seems clearly to be subject to education in a manner that discovering biological sex difference is not. In the feminist scenario, one is bound to discover a diremption of self and sexual identity, which makes the sex role learned at some level of function.

The point made here about education is stated by McKeon at the conclusion of the article which has been the basis of this exposition:

> We have tended in our analysis of communication to reduce the minds of men to opinions and to neglect active attitude and ability by concentrating on what is passively received. Communication is education, and education should train men to judge all communication . . . [17]

In so far as every society must communicate/educate in order to make (its) truth known and effective, it creates the "active attitude and ability" which is at the essence of being educated. Being educated cannot be "passively having opinions."

The problem posed by a pluralistic ideal of society is communication across diversity. "Communication is education," as McKeon rightly claims, and education is not finally inculcation of opinion. Education is a habit of mind relative to opinions, even one's own. The philosopher-king has opinions, but this habit of mind relative to the opinion has been established through the self-conscious awareness of what education can or cannot accomplish.

There are certain methodological truths which arise from appreciating the difference between having an opinion and having an educated opinion. One of the things that education cannot accomplish is bypassing communication; there is no education by pill, program, or golden nature. Education and communication as active abilities establish their own metavalues which create the educational/communication community. It is in this sense of a community of active education that "men are of one mind." They do not hold out the unity of opinion as a condition of society as in the unitary society, but for all that they may be "of one mind."

> Men are of one mind when they possess reason to judge statements of truth, understanding to appreciate statements of their own values and those of others, desires ordered under freedom, and love of the common good for which men are associated. *When men are of one mind in these abilities,* they can be of different opinions without danger to society or to each other.[18] (italics added)

In his paper for this collection of essays, Walter Watson suggests that McKeon did not offer a philosophy as much as a power. True enough, one supposes it is the power of education as a distinct way of assessing and appropriating opinions. If one wished to derive the truths of McKeon's work, they would not be truths of doctrine, but truths about what it means to have, hold, or discover a doctrine. Such truths would themselves not be doctrines. However, unless one is willing to accept biological determination or some other natural determinant for communication and community as in the Noble Lie subterfuge, one will have to accept the truth of education as *the* method for knowledge and value. Allegiance to education/communication is the unitary belief of a pluralistic society.

In the current heated controversy over diversity of viewpoint in education, McKeon's subtle analysis should receive attention. He is clearly on the side of diversity. His life's work consisted of affirming the value of seemingly abandoned philosophies and intellectual cultures wholly forgotten. His ability to be inside now this and now that seemingly contradictory position was frustrating to his students looking for the Truth once and for all. No more shape-shifting, let us get at the Answer! But he thought that one could not bypass communication in education—even, and particularly, philosophical education. Systematic philosophy as traditionally practiced shadowed the ideal of the unitary society, while McKeon held that if wisdom was to be attained, it would have to be the result of the exquisite exercise of communication across and between powerful diversities. Only then would the wisdom achieved be the product of education, not the outcome of current intellectual fashion.

Where McKeon differs from some of the current advocates of diversity is in the seriousness with which he takes diverse opinions. Since he is convinced that the transcendent and systematic ideal is impossible—it cannot communicate the very truth it claims—the only road to truth is through living in the diverse voices of the tradition and today. To live in the many voices for educational needs, however, means that one brings along the metavalues of education. One does not enter into the other voice as a tourist or a temporary votary of the local cult, one never forgets the vocation of philosopher, the active attitude and ability of the educated mind. One has already learned the metatruth that values are learned and truths must be communicated. The diverse voices so highly valued and so necessary in the search for truth and value submit to the conditions of communication and the ideal of education.

Susan Bordo worries about whether the shape-shifter is the ghost of the old transcendent. The empty fleeting spirit of old dogmatism will certainly not ground the voice of feminist perspective. McKeon would reply that in creating the grounded voice one cannot bypass education in that ground. But educating the grounded voice finally transcends the voice itself—not to a doctrine which supplants the feminist insight—but to a wisdom which recreates the value. One moves feminism from biology to philosophy. All worthy views are grounded, but in the context of communicated/communicable value. McKeon offers a guidebook to communication within and between grounded values. "The basic problem of a pluralistic society is to use unity to promote diversity and diversity to strengthen unity."[19]

What was McKeon up to? Philosophy? History of philosophy? Historical semantics? I think it is clear that McKeon basically was a philosopher of education—and particularly a philosopher of education in philosophy. The maddening indirection of his shape-shifting, the multiple schemas and transformation tricks, his categorization as edifying, all point to a common concern about how one teaches philosophy—not just technical school philosophy, but how one teaches the final wisdoms buried in grand science, comprehensive religions, and deep literatures. The prevailing model for education in philosophy has been the unitary model. One reaches some ultimate principle by Cartesian meditation or Humean inspection and deduces truth and virtue therefrom.

When McKeon's students arrived in the 1950s, the unitary model was in force throughout the Anglo-Saxon philosophic world. Almost. A notable exception that was to have increasing importance was the work of Ludwig Wittgenstein, which was just then being published for general circulation.[20] Wittgenstein had rejected the unitary model in its Russellian form as early as the *Tractatus*—despite the fact that Russell did not seem to realize that fact and happily mislead two generations of interpreters through his introduction to the work. By the time of *Philosophical Investigations,* even Russell could see that Wittgenstein had a radically different idea of philosophy from the prevailing unitary-scientific notion. (Russell disliked the whole idea and accused Wittgenstein of abandoning philosophy altogether—a judgement lodged by McKeon's critics.)

Wittgenstein thought that the task of philosophers was not to demonstrate truths in the manner of physicists, but somehow to give insight about deep linguistic puzzles. There was no direct method, then, of pursuing the subject of philosophy—if it was a subject at all. His solution was to invent language games through which one could gain perspective on the puzzling grammar so prevalent in philosophical discourse. (And not only traditional philosophical discourse: Wittgenstein was equally concerned with foundational theories in psychology, mathematics and so on. Foundational theory in any area was for Wittgenstein an example of philosophy and likely to be "language on a holiday.")

It would be interesting to pursue a detailed comparison of the task of philosophy as carried forward by Wittgenstein and McKeon, what I wish to accomplish here is only to point the similarity in their common turn away from any unitary theory of philosophy. For both McKeon and Wittgenstein, there was a philosophical task to be accomplished, but it could only be accomplished by communication—and this communication turns out to be insight by indirection. We learn by arraying our problem against a variety of language games or the variety of philosophic systems. A straightforward (deductive) assault on the special wisdom of philosophy fails in its method of grounding even if one ends by uttering right opinion. As Wittgenstein says, "There is no common sense answer to a philosophical problem. One can defend common sense against the attack by philosophers only by solving their puzzles, i.e., by curing them of the temptation to attack common sense."[21]

Wittgenstein's invented language game is McKeon's arrays of extant philosophical language games. To do philosophy is not to deduce, it is to array for the sake of insight and wisdom. To be sure, Wittgenstein saw the task of philosophy as largely curative of extant metaphysical cramps while McKeon seemingly had a more constructive view of the ends of philosophy. Despite the significant difference, however, both should be regarded as philosophers of philosophical education since they raise in the most acute fashion the peculiarity of philosophical problems.

McKeon believed that philosophical foundations underlay all the intellectual disciplines and many of the quarrels therein. If that were the case, what sort of *general education* should be proposed for those who pursue the various disciplines? Organization, methods, and principles of the sciences would seem to be a necessary completion of any curriculum. But because the problems were philosophical and foundational the pedagogy could not be didactic, it had to be indirective in the array of variations. Thus the (in)famous Ideas and Methods. There was indeed a common curriculum, a community of scholars. Universities need not be collections of ideological cults—but the hopes for the community would lie in education as communication within the assumptions of a pluralistic society.

My conclusion: Richard McKeon was first and foremost, early and late, a philosopher of education—and of the necessity of philosophy in education.

MEMOIRS OF A PLURALIST

Charles W. Wegener

I think of myself as one of Richard McKeon's students, and in that epigonic band I place myself in something like the second or third generation. For when I first encountered McKeon, there were already some grizzled graduate students on the verge of actually acquiring a Ph.D., if not already in possession of one. I mention this because I have the distinct impression that diverse generations came away having learned somewhat different things. My generation was the one that knew that Aristotle knew everything and what he did not know Plato did. So, in trying to explain to you how I function pluralistically, I turn to Plato.

It has long seemed clear to me that Plato was a pluralist; that he knew there were radically different ways of talking and thinking about the world; and that since the world as thought and the world as existent as experienced are two sides of the same world, radically different modes of thought entail radically different worlds. So he encountered in his world not only a plurality of opiners and opinions about the world, but a plurality of worlds. I think the dialogues can be read as a series of explorations of the paradoxical (in both senses of paradoxical—paradox and paralogism) situation inherent in accepting that in our world there is a plurality of worlds or that the world exists, is encountered, and is known in a plurality.

While this is true, I think, of all the dialogues, in the so-called later dialogues it emerges in a strikingly sophisticated form—"sophisticated" meaning self-conscious, explicit, intellectually controlled, and urbane. In most cases, of course, in the processes of inquiry developed in such dialogues as the *Theaetetus* or the *Sophist,* this plurality functions as a way of identifying the options which the world offers us with respect to itself, and the point of articulating options is to set one's own course among and with respect to them—to order and thus to constitute a world which explains its own plurality.

This is a procedure with which, in another form, we are familiar with in our other Hellenic guru, Aristotle. But in one of Plato's later dialogues, as I read it for the purpose in hand, the process takes an unusual turn. You will recall that Parmenides, in the dialogue that bears his name, encounters a very young Socrates distinguished equally by intellectual brilliance and intellectual avidity. Ostensibly, at least, the dialogue is the advice he gives, from his age, his experience, and his wisdom, to the young and too eager youth. That advice, in sum, has two parts, a diagnosis of the young man's overeagerness and a prescription for supplying the discipline which will at once reorder his priorities—as we might say—and equip him for the enterprises with which he is now prematurely (and therefore incompetently) engaged. I presume to paraphrase the sage.

Socrates, you are commendably eager to discover the truth and to determine how the world is and can be justly ordered in the realization of goodness and the enjoyment of beauty. I say 'commendably' because your eagerness is an avidity not only comprehensive—a total dedication of your activity—but intellectual, that is, the activity in which your eagerness is manifest shows that you already know what most people learn only tardily and many never, that the enterprises of truth, goodness, and beauty are enterprises of intelligence conditioned through-and-through by the possibilities and necessities inherent in the objects of intelligence and their concomitant intellectual functions. But you have not yet come to see that determining the truth in and with respect to the world and the ordering of that world by and to goodness and beauty are consequent upon and conditioned by the form of the world, that is, by what there is to be known, to be good, to be beautiful—its pluralities and unities, the modes of relation in and among them, the stabilities and instabilities, differentiations, conjunctions and identities inherent in both these formalities and so on. These objects of intelligence and the grounds and forms of intellectual function you have neglected to explore, in your eagerness to get on with the proper business of intelligence. I do not question that propriety, but I can offer what is also proper to the functioning of intelligence—an organized set of exercises in its formalities necessarily preliminary to its inherently purposive deployment.

Now this is a turn taken by many of those strange reflective enterprises we sometimes call philosophies. But here the turn has some unusual features, two of which seem to me to be relevant. The first of these is apparent in what has already been said: the priority of what I have loosely called (following, curiously enough, Gilbert Ryle) the formalities of ideas (or of formal ideas) is a literal priority. That is, Parmenides is not saying—or at least not merely saying—that certain questions, problems, ideas, and intellectual activities are "logically" prior to or presupposed by others: he is saying that one who is interested in certain activities should first engage in other activities. In other words, the priority is educational, curricular—disciplinary in the sense of disciplining. One might argue that such a literal, propaedeutic priority is not unusual—there is a sense, for example, in which Descartes enjoins us to meditate on philosophy first—that is, before undertaking the reconstruction of knowledge and practice.

But at this point the second feature of interest here emerges. Whatever one may say of the actual temporal prerequisite of Descartes's meditations (not the book but the activity), one would hardly call them mere exercises, a training of intellectual muscle, a gymnastic of thought. It is true that we might be said to emerge from them prepared to play, but surely their function is also to determine the rules and the object—in the sense of both substance and purpose—of the cognitive game. By contrast, the "hypotheses" which constitute the latter portion of the *Parmenides* are—or at least seem to be on their face—not only "inconclusive" but so problematic as to carry inconclusiveness to the point of conclusive self-negation—a kind of intellectual black hole. In the face of these impressions it is not surprising that commentators on the dialogue have found it very difficult to live in the extraordinarily active state of closure-oriented nonclosure they articulate. It is clear to most of them that the hypotheses cannot be mere exercises. It is tempting to conclude that they must somehow contain a doctrine—or at the other extreme, that, being mere exercises, they are some sort of elaborate and rather tedious joke—probably of the "in" variety—and can thus be in effect ignored.

We might be tempted to say that similar things have been said of other deconstructions, but the "hypotheses" of the *Parmenides* are constructions rather than deconstructions: it is only taken as a whole that they lead to the astonishing conclusion that "whether one is or is not" (or perhaps "whether or not there is unity") "it and the others, both in relation to themselves and to one another, both are and are not in every way, and seem and do not seem to be." Taken separately they articulate radically diverse universes, any one of which, in and by itself, is at least conceptually and perhaps imaginatively possible. And whatever else we might say of them, surely we can see that, as we suggested earlier, the enterprises of determining the truth and of the purposive ordering of the world by and to goodness and beauty in and with respect to each of them will necessarily also be radically different. Nor is it apparent how one is to choose among them (if we assume them incompatible), or how they are to be reconciled if we assume them ultimately consistent. And something like the same consequence would seem to follow for investigation and realization of the true, the good, the beautiful. Yet it seems equally obvious that these othernesses, these diversities, are systematically generated, so that in some way they would seem to be systematically related—to be, that is, not simply or absolutely external to each other. But to say that, of course, is to return to the very problems of unity and multiplicity which are the proximate subject of the hypotheses, to disappear into the black hole of paradoxical, paralogical self-destruction, a radical epoche subjectively quite uncomfortable.

At this point let us imagine an intervention in the dialogue between Socrates and Parmenides by a stranger named McKeon from a land even more westerly than Elea. I hope that the arbitrariness of this move will leave no doubt that this intervention is entirely mythical. The McKeon of this dialogue is as mythical as are its Parmenides and its Socrates: all of them being creatures of mine invented for the purpose of explaining to you how I function, something for which I would not like you to hold Socrates, Parmenides, or McKeon responsible. I use them partly for convenience of exposition, but more importantly because, while it is the case that I am solely responsible for what my mythical characters say and do, I would also have you understand that I did not work this all out in a totally uninhabited intellectual environment.

In any case, this McKeon in the dialogue makes a fairly long speech, which we may thus summarize. "It would be more appropriate in this company for me to ask for guidance than to offer it, but I wonder if I might suggest an alternative approach? I assume what might be called the postulate of pluralism in something like the form you have advanced—namely, "that the enterprises of truth, goodness and beauty are enterprises of intelligence conditioned through and through by the possibilities and necessities inherent in the objects of intelligence and their concomitant intellectual functions" and that from and on this ground it is possible to "articulate radically diverse universes any one of which, in and by itself, is at least conceptually and perhaps imaginatively possible," with the consequence that "the enterprises of determining the truth and of the purposive ordering of the world by and to goodness and beauty in and with respect to each of them will necessarily also be radically different." Further, I agree that a disciplined, systematic, and

95

appreciative exploration of these diversities is the properly propaedeutic exercise to reflective inquiry. My alternative, then, is a two-fold suggestion. First, I suggest that these diversities be explored in the forms in which they have actually been elaborated in the human enterprise at large, in, that is, what is vaguely and misleadingly called the history, the career, of thought, of ideas, or (even) of philosophy. For such an exploration we shall require a heuristic hermeneutic meeting two requirements. It must resemble your hypotheses, Parmenides, in that it will be a set of devices for disclosing or discovering *intellectual* functions in the construction and ordering of worlds. And it must resemble your hypotheses in another respect—it must at least attempt to be systematically exhaustive and comprehensive. So my second suggestion is that such a hermeneutic may be elaborated by starting from the parts and wholes of consequential thought, of inferential connection, with, of course, the full recognition that the postulate of pluralism requires that commonplaces of statement and inference be appropriately transformable into commonplaces of being and existence. I say that a hermeneutic *may* be elaborated on such a ground; as proof of that possibility I offer what I think is a version of such a heuristic."

No doubt there then ensued a long and interesting conversation, but at this point I abandon the myth for the memoir of which it is a translation, but first I must make it clear that pluralism as I understand it and practice it both is and is not a phase of my intellectual life. It is a phase in the sense that it is a propaedeutic, but it is not a phase in the sense that it is merely one of the ways in which I function (or, at least hope that I function) intellectually. That is, all my intellectual practice is pluralistic in the sense that it is always informed by the awareness of articulable alternatives to the process of thought in which I am engaged. Sometimes that awareness is in the foreground, so to speak, of my thinking, sometimes in the background, but it is never absent. But this is not an awareness of other views, other opinions, other doctrines, except insofar as those are indices or materials of alternative modes or processes of thought. That is, it is an awareness which in the form of a question would always be *how* would this be alternatively thought about, *how* alternatively intellectually placed, *how* might this inquiry or inquiry of this sort be alternatively identified, be alternatively possible, be alternatively formulated and conducted?

To say, with my mythical Parmenides as emended by my mythical McKeon, that this functional awareness is developed in and by a "disciplined, systematic and appreciative exploration of these diversities in the forms in which they have actually been elaborated in the human enterprise at large" and that such an exploration is an exercise properly propaedeutic to reflective inquiry is to say that the learning and, subsequently, the teaching of what we vaguely call philosophy has been and is for me a series of exercises in practicing alternatives which I have found available in the world around me not only in so-called texts but in the living practice of other ambulatory and orally competent sources. I could develop at some length how that worked and works out for me in my education, and how I have tried to work it out educationally, pedagogically, but any such development is necessarily so much an account of circumstances as to be misleading with respect to what is essential to these exercises, whatever their materials and occasions may happen to be. With respect to the essentials, I would make three points I think characteristic of my practice. Before I do that, however, I am constrained to remind you that my practice is, strictly speaking, all I purport to be telling you about in this memoir. But it is also the case that these features of it do not seem to me to be accidentally associated in what I do, and as such they may be of more than merely biographical or autobiographical interest.

First, as I have already said, what I am concerned to elicit and to practice is ways of thinking, modes of inquiry, processes of thought. On the one hand this requires, as I said, that what is thought about and what is thought about it in the sense of views, opinions, doctrines—conclusions, if you like—be treated only as indices or materials of alternative modes or processes of thought. This amounts to detaching, one might say, the thinking from its content insofar as that is a function of context and circumstance broadly defined. On the other hand, it is obvious that thinking is always of something, is always contextually and circumstantially conditioned. Here there are many interesting hermeneutical questions into which I cannot now enter. Suffice it to say that in my own practice I do not judge that I am capable of practicing a given mode of thought in "disciplined, systematic and appreciative exploration" until I can exercise it in contexts and circumstances quite different from that in which it was developed and in which I find it and formulate what I am doing in a different language.

Second, it is important to emphasize that this pluralistic practice is not only disciplined and systematic but, as I just said, appreciative. Since, following our mythical mentor, we are using a hermeneutic derived from and oriented to the discovery of inferential processes, it follows that what is to be appreciated in the exercise of any mode of thought is its inferential cogency, including, of course, its devices for locating and differentiating various forms of such closure. Again there are here many hermeneutical and other problems which I cannot discuss, but bluntly put the sense in which the practice I am attempting to articulate is systematic exercise does not mean that it abstracts from, suspends, or somehow brackets the question of truth. On the contrary, it proceeds on the assumption that truth is determinable only within the members of the plurality being explored and that, therefore, practicing them is an activity of determining and articulating truth and truths.

In those terms, to say that in this sort of thinking we somehow abstract from that strange form of substantive reference what we call truth is to say that we are not thinking at all. Put another way, it is only within some articulated system of distinctions with respect to thinking and assertion that forms of reference, including truth, kinds of truth, and truths can be identified and determined. Radically reflective thought—and that is what we are engaging in—is not, therefore, a process which is somehow accredited in the way of truth after it is completed by some criterion, standard, or device external to its own cogency as reflectively determined. That is, accreditation becomes problematic and determinable in the process itself and has no functional meaning outside of an activity of a determinate form. We might say, with a considerable sacrifice of precision and subtlety, that truth is not an attribute of philosophies precisely because a vital part of the philosophic enterprise is to tell us what we mean by it.

Mention of the philosophic enterprise should serve to remind us, however, that our mentors are agreed that this pluralistic practice is an exercise, a propaedeutic not only to the determination of truth and truths but of goodness and beauty as well. In other words, it is to be instrumentally preliminary to engagement in philosophizing, in consequential thought functionally oriented. The third relevant feature of my practice as I reflect upon it here, then, is the way in which I have discovered—made determinate for myself—what kind of thinking is mine; what sort of thinker I am; what sort of inquiry I can appropriately, effectively and satisfyingly engage in; what sort of contribution I can make to the human enterprise, of which after all philosophizing is a part, by my thought.

In my experience, for what it is worth, this is a complex and difficult exercise in reflective self-determination. It is tempting, of course, to consider it a self-discovery, in which, in one way or another a "self" or a mind or whatever finite center one wants to postulate, becomes aware, makes explicit or refines and stabilizes by reflective correction what it is already directed, predisposed, or committed to. We all know that it has been said, though perhaps not well said, that we are all born Platonists or Aristotelians: on this showing pluralistic practice is a way of discovering our individual fates. Versions of Bradley's well-known remark that "metaphysics is the finding of bad reasons for what we believe on instinct" are easily constructable with various determinations of instinct—commitment, intellectual/cultural environment, personal history along other lines. But all these have in common the assumption that the problem is to discover and to do—or to do and discover—what comes naturally or is congenial. As explanations of what happens, they are of course subject to many difficulties, but it is as accounts of what happens—that is, of what is to be explained—that I find them inconsistent with my practice and in that sense with my experience. That is, it seems to me that they do not incorporate the sting in the tail of Bradley's aphorism—namely, "but to find these reasons is no less an instinct," a remark which I choose to interpret here as pointing to the presumption of pluralism with which I began—namely, in the words of my Parmenides, that "the enterprises of truth, goodness and beauty are enterprises of intelligence conditioned through and through by . . . intellectual functions." Operationally what this means is that however one may explain how such choices are made and thus account for them, the only way they can be arrived at is by a process of actual reflection with its own rationality, that is, its own disciplined procedures in which alternatives become formulated, criteria emerge, and relevancies are determined. It may be that in the end we simply come out where we went in, but that does not obviate the necessity of the journey.

This journey issues, in the nature of the case, in the consideration of why one philosophizes at all, to what end or ends is this activity oriented? As a personal or individual or what I would call an ethical question, there is much to be said about this matter, not merely in an autobiographical mode but in what might be described as the conscientious mode, taking Kant's point that conscience is the function of making sure we are taking into account all the relevant considerations in the right proportions and weighing them as best we can. The pluralistic discipline—probably better denominated the discipline of pluralizing—offers a wealth of material for this sort of reflection, for in this connection it amounts to a series of alternative versions of philosophical activity and its place among other activities of knowing and doing—amounts in other words to alternative accounts of what the relevant considerations may be and how they are to be proportionately weighed.

But these questions may also be stated—more relevantly for the purpose of this conference—as questions about the place of philosophical activity not in individual activity and activities but in human activity at large, about, that is, the function of philosophy and philosophizing in culture and cultures. More particularly, of course, the question would be what consequences does a pluralistic stance, a pluralistic understanding of philosophizing—what I have called the discipline of pluralizing—have for that function?

It would, I think, be apparent from the sketch I have given of my pluralism that the function of philosophy in culture (as in individual activity) is something that can only become determinately understood and practiced within a philosophy—that is, in one of the intellectual modes which pluralism explores. The postulate of pluralism as earlier formulated—"the enterprises of truth, goodness and beauty are enterprises of intelligence conditioned through and through by . . . intellectual functions"—does not commit us to the view that intellectual functions are wholly and simply constitutive of culture: as with all other questions of truth, goodness, and beauty, the sense in which these enterprises are conditioned by intelligence and intellectual function or in what sense they are enterprises of intelligence is something only intelligence can undertake to analyze in one of its determinate forms, as is indeed the converse question of by what and how the functioning of intelligence is itself conditioned—that is, conditioned not by itself. Thus intellectual alternatives are not necessarily identical with cultural alternatives, so that a plurality of intellectual modes need not entail a plurality of cultures. That plurality is recognized and becomes problematic within, we are likely to think, a culture. You will remember that when I construed the dialogues of Plato pluralistically, I said of them that they "can be read as a series of explorations of the paradoxical . . . situation inherent in accepting that in our world there is a plurality of worlds or that the world exists, is encountered, is known in a plurality." Plato's world is his cultural world and it is in that culture that he encountered Parmenides and Gorgias and elaborated his own philosophy—in order, of course, that it might be encountered by Aristotle and reconstructed by Richard McKeon. Given all this we might without further analysis (in some mode of analysis) be more likely to think then that intellectual plurality is a plurality of cultural elements than that cultures are a plurality of intellectual elements. We should note that this latter position would seem to entail the consequence that problems of incompatibility and incoherence of cultures or of cultural elements are philosophic incoherences and conflicts in a very strong sense.

I shall return to this possibility, but before I do allow me to make a suggestion from my own practice. It follows from what I have said about philosophies and cultures that what I can say about philosophical pluralism and cultural pluralism would be consequent upon working out a position as to the cultural function of philosophy. Since I cannot do that here, I must necessarily proceed dogmatically, hoping that what I have to suggest may not be wholly unintelligible.

From my vantage point, then, I think of the cultural function of philosophizing as primarily critical. For me, philosophizing is one intellectual function among many—the radically reflective and thus radically critical function. Since here I am perforce dogmatic, I may as well be aphoristic as well, so I suggest that philosophizing is one of the ways in which we attempt to keep the human enterprise on the rails, so to speak. Of course, such an arcane intellectual activity can function that way only insofar as the enterprises of truth, goodness, and beauty—enterprises which taken together constitute the human enterprise, the enterprise of culture—are enterprises of intelligence. But this reference to what I have grandly called the postulate of pluralism should remind us even as we construct our critical philosophy of culture that as pluralists we presume intelligence gives, in reflection, different accounts of itself. In our pluralistic propaedeutic, we have tried to appreciate each of these accounts, but appreciation means that we have also come to see how each sets standards for itself, how each mode of thinking can be done well or badly in its own terms. I should think that we might probably conclude that from the point of view of keeping the human enterprise on the rails, the important thing is to be able to distinguish doing well from doing badly within each pluralistic alternative and to encourage the practitioners of modes other than our own to do well what they do as it is to explain, in and from whatever mode of philosopohical functioning we may have adopted, that the sort of thing that they are doing will not do. I venture to suggest that the widespread adoption of this stance in philosophical communication would amount to a revolution—perhaps a minor revolution but nonetheless a revolution—in communicative style and function not only among philosophers but in the intellectual world at large. It might allow us to recapture something of that Platonic sophistication in communication from which I began—an acceptance of plurality appreciatively self-conscious, explicit, intellectually controlled and urbane. Intellectual control would be supplied for us by the use of our hermeneutics of pluralism as heuristic devices—topics, if you like—for placing, understanding, and appreciating the work of others both from the inside and from our own position. Such a pluralistic stance would be urbane if only because, of course, it entails an appropriate modesty with respect to the claims of whatever philosophizing of our own we undertake, since at the least we would recognize that the burden of keeping the human enterprise on the rails is shared with all the philosophic schools.

This modest view of philosophizing and its role in culture is not just a matter of temperament grounded in a native caution or a concern to avoid intellectual hubris. You will recall that earlier I described my pluralizing discipline as a process of "detaching thinking from its content insofar as that is a function of context and circumstance, a process completed only when I can exercise a given mode of thought in contexts and circumstances quite different from that in which it was developed and in which I find it *and* formulate what I am doing in a different language." Clearly, here, there is postulated a certain independence of context and circumstance: philosophies are modes of intellectual functioning which, while always instantiated and contextualized, admit of many instantiations and contextualizations. It may be that they cannot exist or function outside of a cultural context, but they are not exhausted in any one of them. Ultimately it is on this detachment from circumstance that their critical power rests. The very image I have used—"keeping the human enterprise on the rails"—suggests, rather more strongly than I like, that continuity within the many-cultured human enterprise which philosophies in this sense attempt to articulate.

But need we postulate such a continuity and such a detachability? Must not our pluralism provide for that possibility in which instantiation is, so to speak, itself the principle of our philosophizing, the principle which makes intelligible the human enterprise, being indeed the ground of culture itself? The mythical McKeon of my dialogue sounds more like myself or Parmenides, but there is another McKeon—perhaps equally mythical—who talks much of operationalisms, pragmatisms, and rhetorics. In this sort of philosophy, philosophies become *persuasions* in that sense in which we say that someone is of the Platonic or positivist persuasion. Persuasions in this sense are the attributes of agents, of persons, of groups, and of cultures and the diversities of philosophies become ineluctably associated with and expressive of the diversities of persons, peoples, and communities as they encounter each other in operation, in action.

The function of philosophizing thus becomes itself persuasion in the sense that it becomes a set of devices for finding amidst these diversities common ground for the resolution of conflict and the identification of common problems in the interest of pursuing a common course of action. The hermeneutical devices of what I have called my pluralizing discipline thus become rather more like rhetorical than dialectical topics—they are the places in which one may find those considerations which will effect communication to adjust cultural conflicts and create cultural communities in which human living is defined and shared.

I am reminded of a saying attributed to Antisthenes: "If you intend a boy to live with gods, teach him philosophy; if with men, rhetoric," for surely all I have discovered here (if it is more than simple confusion) is another version of the ancient tension between philosophy and rhetoric, and in those terms I am asking whether McKeon's teaching was a divinity or a humanity. Bluntly put, the question raised for me about pluralism and pluralistic practice by my own practice is whether pluralism must be rhetorically formulated and practiced? If that is the case, does it require that all philosophies become operationalisms, rhetorics? Conversely, if pluralism can and must be formulated and practiced philosophically, as I have called it, does it follow that operationalisms and rhetorics are not philosophies and, therefore, do not enjoy membership in the plurality of pluralism? Is it another form of this question to ask whether pluralism can in fact be formulated and practiced neutrally, or have we discovered that pluralism is as plural as philosophy? But I must stop before we all disappear into the Parmenidean black hole, muttering to ourselves "whether plurality is or is not, it and the others, both in relation to themselves and to one another, both are and are not in every way, and seem and do not seem to be."

Postscript—1998

This memoir is here reprinted as written to be read at the conference in 1992, save for a very few editorial changes. While of course I now would say what I had to say somewhat differently, I do not find anything I now would not say. I add this postscript in order to make somewhat clearer how I think this paper, couched in a personal manner as it is, bears on other questions about McKeon and, especially, about pluralism.

In the memoir I described the McKeon who appears there as "mythical," partly because I did not want to get involved in historical questions as to which others then present might have different recollections. In any case, historical accuracy seemed irrelevant to my purpose. In a sense that remains true with respect to what I shall add here, but still it is important to note that whatever there is of historical data and account here (and in the original paper) claims to be no more than how one student reconstructs after many years what he understood McKeon to be saying in one phase of his teaching—roughly the late thirties and the forties shading into the early fifties (1938–1951). What I have to say about later developments in his thinking is based upon more distant observation.

It is easy to say that during this period McKeon developed and propounded a pluralistic view of philosophy and philosophizing. Of course it was much more than a view: it was an elaborately articulated analysis. Of what, then, was multiplicity predicated, what was it that was plural, or in what way did his account show philosophy to admit of plurality?

In the memoir I attributed to my mythical McKeon the suggestion that a hermeneutic designed for the "disciplined, systematic and appreciative exploration" of the diversity of philosophy might be

> elaborated by starting from the parts and wholes of consequential thought, of inferential connection, with, of course, the full recognition that the postulate of pluralism requires that commonplaces of statement and inference be appropriately transformable into commonplaces of being and existence.

This formulation was intended to parallel one attributed to my mythical Parmenides

> [D]etermining the truth in and with respect to the world and the ordering of that world by and to goodness and beauty are consequent upon and conditioned by the form of the world, that is, by what there is to be known, to be good, to be beautiful—its pluralities and unities, the modes of relation in and among them, the stabilities and instabilities, differentiations, conjunctions and identities inherent in both these formalities

and so on. These objects of intelligence and the grounds and forms of intellectual function you [Socrates] have neglected to explore. . . .

Among other things, I intended to suggest that the Platonic or Parmenidean plurality would be disclosed by the use of metaphysical or ontological instrumentalities such as "being" and "unity" supporting diverse modes of inquiry, whereas the basic instrumentalities for articulating intellectual plurality in McKeon's practice at this time were logical elements and combinations implying a grounding ontology.

That parallel (and its inversion of analytical direction) may or may not make sense, but there can surely be no doubt that McKeon schematized his heuristic of philosophical diversities with instrumentalities derived from logical analysis. It was during this period (late forties) that he first published—by making use of them in his teaching—the matrices in which he attempted to articulate the plurality with which he was concerned. The relation of the two matrices to the traditional minor and major logics, and thus to the Aristotelian *Organon,* was clear. Of course, they constituted a major feat of generalization in which Aristotle's logic became merely one possibility among others, and the courses in which he first made public use of these brilliant schematisms were courses in logical theory using as texts such full-blown logics as those of Mill, Bernard Bosanquet, F. H. Bradley and W. E. Johnson. In these courses, students were invited to explore these treatments using the matrices—testing, so to speak, whether they illuminated what these logicians were doing as they did Aristotle. Always, of course, the analysis led beyond technical questions to methodological and metaphysical implications, but the proximate context was logical in a very strong sense.

When McKeon first formulated these mathematical models I do not know, though he clearly indicated that he had made use of them for some time before he exposed them to public view. But certainly his preoccupation with logical and methodological questions and their close relation to metaphysics was not something that began in the forties. In the early thirties he had several times offered a course called "metaphysics and method," and while that title disappeared from his repertory in the period with which I am here concerned, it would not be a bad title for some of the logical courses, except that it would more accurately reflect the trend of his teaching were it reversed to method and metaphysics. During this period, one of the persistent items in the student scuttlebutt which always surrounded him was that he had in mind to write—and perhaps had already written in part—a history of logic. (I leave it to others to investigate the relation of his medieval studies and even, perhaps, of his work on Spinoza to these later developments.)

In our present intellectual/philosophical environment (what used to be called "the intellectual temper of the age") it may be difficult to understand how normal an intellectual orientation in which logic was so prominent seemed in the years I am discussing. It is an exaggeration, but no more, to say that much of the first half of the century was, at least in western Europe and the United States, philosophically dominated by logical and methodological analysis centered on mathematics and the natural sciences. Perhaps this was particularly true of the period in which McKeon was educated and achieving intellectual maturity—the years of the Great War and the years between the wars. The period was not only rich in its inheritance from the later years of the previous century of influential logical formulations, some of which I have already mentioned, but it had been profoundly shaken by the impact of a new logic—symbolic, mathematical, calculative. Graduate students in philosophy today may find it difficult to believe that their counterparts in the thirties and forties were expected to have more than a verbal acquaintance with such arcane matters as the sentential calculus, to be able to distinguish between material and strict implication, to be able to construct truth tables, and perhaps even to understand what sense could be attributed to the statement that "a false proposition implies all other propositions."[1] Some of them were, in fact, fascinated by the debates concerning the reducibility of mathematics to logic, by analysis of problems of the consistency and parsimony of deductive sciences and their postulate sets, perhaps gaining some understanding of what mathematicians and logicians mean by "elegance." Given all of that, it is not difficult to understand why Henry Sheffer's invention of "the stroke" and consequent reduction of the number of primitive postulates set forth in *Principia Mathematica* was considered a logico/philosophical coup of no small importance accomplished in papers beautiful in their power and lucidity.

Star status in academic philosophy—another indication of where intellectual interest was focused—was enjoyed by Sheffer at Harvard, along with, of course, Alfred North Whitehead and C. I. Lewis. It would be difficult to deny the same prominence to Ernest Nagel at Columbia or to Alonzo Church at Princeton. Importations from Europe were influenced by all sorts of factors arising from the political turmoil on the continent, but among the most prominent were other logicians and philosophers of science such as Hans Reichenbach, Alfred Tarski, Carl Hempel, and Rudolph Carnap, McKeon's colleague at Chicago, whose name should serve to remind us that the positivism of these days was *logical* positivism. If, for Carnap, philosophy was "the syntax of the language of science," that syntax was "logical." And it is worth noting that the Wittgenstein who was influential in this period—at least in the United States—was not the Wittgenstein of the varicolored books but of the *Tractatus Logico-Philosophicus.* There were, of course, other stars, including some luminaries of sustained brilliance. John Dewey was still active. Yet, again, one should note that one of the major works he published in this period was the most elaborate of the many reformulations of logic he attempted in his long career, *Logic: The Theory of Inquiry.*

In such an intellectual milieu, McKeon's logical orientation is hardly surprising though certainly not inevitable.[2] But its sources are of interest only because of the direction in which it led him in developing his account of philosophical pluralism. Here one should distinguish, I think, between the concept of the project he undertook and the particular form it took at various times in his teaching and writing, such as the matrices. In the memoir I stressed the sense in which I understood it to function as propaedeutic to finding one's own way philosophically and functioning in a community in which philosophical divergences manifest themselves more or less directly in how one's fellow citizens think and carry on their work.[3] Here, however, I am more concerned with pluralism as such, that is, as I said above, with what, in his analytical project emerged as "plural, or in what way did his account show philosophy to admit of plurality?" Another way to put those questions would be to ask what it is that is put into systematic interrelation in such schematization as is represented by his matrices and the distinctions which they develop? Bluntly, what is philosophy, philosophizing, and a philosophy as members of this plurality?

This is no easy question, but as an initial formulation one might say that what McKeon was attempting to articulate and interrelate as alternatives were radically reflective accounts of the methodical and systematic deployment of intelligence, including the conditions and materials of intelligent activity and the ways in which the activity of human intelligence may be connected to that, other than itself, with respect to which it functions. This rather clumsy formula attempts to include, in somewhat different language, the logical and metaphysical emphasis I think characteristic of his pluralistic analysis, while at the same time, I would hope, suggesting, by employing a language of activity and function, something of its breadth and power. It was never narrowly logical or traditionally metaphysical. (But the formula is probably suggestive, if at all, only to someone who knows his work—particularly that of this same phase in his career—already, because the richness and cogency with which he was able to invest the philosophical texts to which he addressed himself beggars description and even suggestion.) If nothing else, his account requires us to rethink what is functionally—i.e., in any analysis of the deployment of intelligence—meant by metaphysics, by what is at stake, so to speak, in issues of principle and first principles. Bradley observed that someone "who is ready to prove that metaphysical knowledge is wholly impossible . . . is a brother metaphysician with a rival theory of his own."[4] Any account of pluralism must, as McKeon's did, give an account of those analyses which repudiate metaphysics in virtue of the discovery of other ways of discharging its function in the operations of intelligence, just as it should shed light on why it was that Carnap, given his logical predilections, would dismiss Dewey's *Logic* as psychology.[5] A pluralism which begins by outlawing intellectual possibilities or loading the dice against some in favor of others is dubious indeed.

However, if the formula does serve to shed light on what, to my mind, is of the greatest importance in McKeon's pluralism, it is because it emphasizes that philosophies and philosophy should be thought of first as reflective activities—efforts to grasp and formulate the activity of intelligence. That is, what gets related and what is plural in this pluralism is modes of deployment of organized intelligence. In this plurality, philosophies are not primarily identifiable by the results of that employment but rather by the characteristic and complex analysis they offer of the activity of intelligence and that activity itself. Philosophies are not congeries of doctrines ("Aristotle taught that the world is uncreated and that. . . .") or the working out of attitudes ("Plato's philosophy is a defense of traditional morality. . . ." "Pragmatism is the philosophy of the young, the strong and the virile. . . .[6]) It is not that doctrines and attitudes are not attributable to philosophers and philosophies, rather that they are to be understood as what they are in the light of what is primary in philosophical activity—the context of argument that issues in assertions and manifests attitudes.

The ambiguity of the term argument itself illustrates the problem of grasping the nature of the members of this plurality. Argument in this analysis primarily means neither debate/controversy or a proof/consideration advanced in support or contestation of a thesis or a course of action. Rather, it means a developing structure of cogency of inquiry and proof as a subject matter is discovered and explored, problems raised, and systematically resolved. Its sense then is much closer to its literary meaning, as when one speaks of the argument of the *Iliad*. In this sense the *Republic*, or Aristotle's *Metaphysics*,[7] or one of the Kantian critiques should be said not only to have an argument but *to be* an argument—a sustained articulation of intelligence. And it is *an* argument, that is, one of the marks of a philosopher at work is a text which is as a whole an argument, a sustained consequentiality of parts or phases. To pursue the literary analogy, one might say that in such an articulated context, to detach doctrines would be analogous to saying that what emerges in *Hamlet* is that he dies. The dramatic power of that conclusion—the quality of his death as it is a function of a complex structure of antecedent events—is thus simply lost, as is the meaning and force of what emerges in argument in this sense. Of course, one of the plots, or patterns of argument, is that of debate or the evaluation of assertions as these are impugned or supported by arguments, but that is only one plot among many.

It is this pluralism—this plurality of ways of conducting and grounding argument in this sense—that I tried to describe as a functioning intellectual attitude in my memoir. I think that all the consequences I discussed can be said to follow from or at least be consistent with a pluralism of philosophical arguments and argumentation. The problem of philosophical truth, for example, becomes the problem of how arguments differently conducted, variously grounded, and possessed of an explicitly examined integral cogency can be related to each other—clearly it cannot be by simple assertion and denial. Something like translation is more appropriate. But how is that possible? So also, if philosophies are modes of argumentation they clearly must enjoy some sort of independence of the circumstances in and with respect to which they function. Thus I argued that

> what is thought about and what is thought about it in the sense of views, opinions, doctrines—conclusions, if you like—[is to] be treated only as indices or materials of alternative modes or processes of thought. This amounts to detaching, one might say, the thinking from its content insofar as that is a function of context and circumstance broadly defined. On the other hand, it is obvious that thinking is always of something, is always contextually and circumstantially conditioned. Here there are many interesting hermeneutical questions. . . .

And so on—I repeat myself no more except to make my final point.

No doubt there are many difficulties with this plurality and this pluralism. At the same time, it was clearly in itself an extraordinary intellectual feat. It had antecedents—as McKeon himself would (sometimes quixotically) point out—but none that attempted the rigor, precision, and range of his analysis. Yet more important for the discussion of pluralism is, I think, the conception of the intellectual world and philosophical activity therein which he tried to articulate in what I have called a logical—quasimathematical—hermeneutic. Philosophizing, I suggested in the memoir, is "one intellectual function among many—the radically reflective and thus radically critical function," a function within a culture, a plurality of different accounts of ambient common activities. But I also tried to suggest how philosophizing might be thought of not as a form of cultural activity but as the "ground of culture" itself, pointing out that in such a view philosophies become "persuasions" (and thus always more or less obviously moralities) and

[t]he hermeneutical devices of what I have called my pluralizing discipline thus become rather . . . rhetorical than dialectical [i.e., "logical"] topics—they are the places in which
one may find those considerations which will effect communication to adjust cultural conflicts and create cultural communities in which human living is defined and shared.

In the terms McKeon, at least at one time, might have employed, this
is—very broadly—a shift from logic to rhetoric. It is a shift which nearly the whole of the Western intellectual/philosophical community made
in the decades immediately following the period I have been discussing.
It would be interesting (and perhaps even amusing) to trace the process
by which a tidal wave of ordinary language analysis, existentialism, deconstruction, and their intellectual cousins swept away the traditions I
outlined, leaving a few philosophers of science largely talking to themselves. Within a few years—to simplify—one moved from a situation in
which there was grave doubt that the social sciences were sciences at all
to one which it was discovered that science and mathematics are things
we do and therefore are subject to all the vagaries, confusions, and limiting conditions of human activity as well as, of course, exemplifying the
protean creativity in which we make ourselves and the world in which
we function.

I see in this many questions; two of interest in this context. (1) Why
and how did McKeon make this shift? (2) A question I asked in the
memoir: is pluralism as plural as philosophy? Are there many pluralisms? The first of these I leave to historians and biographers, if they
are interested. Did he follow where the argument led? If so, what is the
argument? Or is it perhaps the point that the argument ought not or
cannot be followed? As to the second, I have tried to offer evidence that
the answer must be affirmative. It follows, I think, that pluralists will, in
their practice, be as diverse as philosophers, so that a conference of pluralists will be no better babble. A conference of pluralists about pluralism would seem to compound the problem, but as to that any reader of
this volume has evidence to consider. No doubt a plurality of standards
will be applied.

PLURALISM AND THE VIRTUES
OF PHILOSOPHY

Eugene Garver

Becoming aware of the irreducible diversity of ways of thinking and living is like becoming aware of one's own mortality. What difference does the recognition that I am going to die make to how I see the world and how I choose to act? In some ways that recognition has consequences that are utterly pervasive: if I was immortal, everything would be different. Thus, in the *Phaedo* Socrates argues that we have to re-orient the idea of virtue around preparing for death. In other ways, though, thought and action go on in pretty much the same way regardless of my final end. Socrates' preparing for death does not prevent him from acting courageously when military courage is called for, and does not prevent him from spending his last hours doing what gives him most pleasure, engaging in philosophic argument. Sometimes remembering that we all die is a useful topic for reflection, and sometimes thinking about mortality is quite unproductive.

The recognition of diversity seems just like our awareness of mortality. The fact that there are irreducibly many ways of thinking and acting seems alternately completely consciousness-transforming and utterly banal. All my thoughts are completely different from what they would be if I, or my way of thinking, were alone in the world. If there were a single ultimate end, be it salvation, happiness or pleasure, my deliberation would be different from how I deliberate in the presence of plural and possibly competing final goods. On the other hand, my thinking goes on for the most part as though it was the only way to think. When I think, I think about *something,* and that fact that there are other things that I am *not* thinking about seems trivially true but precisely not relevant to my current thinking. In any particular act of deliberation, I must posit a single end, since otherwise I could not deliberate; the fact that my deliberation must exclude other possible ends cannot affect my thinking. If it did, I could never do any productive thinking at all.

I want to ask a practical question: Could my thought and action be *better* if I took the irreducible diversity of modes of thought seriously? For the purposes of this paper, I want to define "pluralism" simply as the reflective and intelligent response to the predicament of diversity, the recognition that mine is not the only attractive and defensible way of thinking and acting, and then to ask how practical pluralism could be. What is an appropriate response to the irreducible diversity of modes of thinking, acting and being?

Pluralism and Pragmatism

What difference does it make to my thinking and acting when I recognize that the way I go about things is not the only way possible? What is an appropriate response to the irreducible diversity of modes of thinking, acting and being?

Since the invention of liberalism and the separation of church and state, people have wondered whether tolerance is a merely external or second-order value that does not affect one's central virtues and duties, but instead allows us to live together in peace with those who persist in error—or whether the duties of tolerance and justice affect one's ultimate purposes.[1] But the question has a more generalized form. There are any number of human activities, including moral action, scientific inquiry and philosophic reflection, for which the same problem periodically emerges. In each case, the question is whether coordinating one's activity with others is a distinct concern from carrying out the activity in the first place, or whether it transforms the activity. Is the coordination of my moral choices and actions with others a central part of my moral life, or a set of external constraints on what virtue or duty otherwise demands? Are the organizational and persuasive activities of a scientist part of her work as a scientist, or simply the price she must pay either to be left alone or to get others to join her in her work? Does the philosophical recognition of a permanent diversity in ways of thinking philosophically create duties of tolerance, modesty and politeness that leave one's own thought unaffected, or could an awareness that one's own thinking is not the only possible valid mode of thought transform how one thinks, and transform it for the better?

I propose to address these questions by looking at the work of Richard McKeon. McKeon's life project is a continuation of the kind of social inquiry to which his teacher John Dewey devoted his own life, an attempt to formulate a relation between theory and practice appropriate for what William James called a pluralistic universe. In this essay I want not to report on or explicate McKeon's own contribution so much as pursue a line of argument inspired by his work. That line of argument starts with pragmatism.

There is a tension at the heart of pragmatism which re-enacts the ambivalence concerning whether the awareness of diversity is trivial or revolutionary. Starting with Peirce, pragmatism brings the good news of science to the rest of human activities. While in some respects the method of scientific inquiry codifies ordinary intelligent conduct, in other ways science goes against and tries to reform usual human habits. People think, Peirce says, only because doubt is painful. People do not want truth; they just want their doubts to go away. Science, though, values true belief over stable belief, and therefore values continued inquiry over settled opinion. Therefore science takes what is a means for the nonscientist, and turns it into something that is its own end. Science, while it may begin as practical problem-solving, becomes counter-intuitive as it reverses our expectations and transforms our values. Science makes reason and the pursuit of truth into autonomous, rather than instrumental, goods, and so opposes and threatens democracy as much as it proposes to enrich it. Dewey says it well:

> The value of any cognitive conclusion depends on the *method* by which it is reached, so that the perfecting of method, the perfecting of intelligence, is the thing of supreme value. The natural man is impatient with doubt and suspense: he impatiently hurries to be shut of it. A disciplined mind takes delight in the problematic, and cherishes it until a way out is found that approve itself upon examination. The scientific attitude may almost be defined as that which is capable of enjoying the doubtful; scientific method is, in one aspect, a technique for making a productive use of doubt by converting it into operations of definite inquiry.[2]

Just as the liberal state begins as a way of allowing people to practice a diversity of faiths without killing each other, but seems eventually to become an independent source of allegiance competing with those initial diverse religions, so the scientific gospel according to pragmatism begins by serving existing needs, and then criticizes and replaces those needs.

McKeon's career-long exploration of pluralism continues the critical side of pragmatic reform and proposes its own transvaluation of values. It makes the pragmatist initiative even more paradoxical and radical. According to ordinary opinion, differences in scientific or philosophic theory make for differences in conduct but McKeon, like Dewey before him, insists that agreement in action does not require prior agreement over doctrine. Differences in practice do not follow from differences in theory, nor are they overcome by theoretical agreement.

McKeon's single most fundamental insight is that there is a diversity of philosophic methods. That diversity is made possible by the space opened up once there is no simple connection between theory and practice, principles and consequences. If there is a diversity of ways of thinking, then we can draw the radical conclusion that method cannot simply be the codification of preexistent behavior called rational. Where the pragmatists' exposition of science ran contrary to the prescientific habits of mankind, McKeon's pluralism goes further by running against the traditional practice of philosophy itself.

Insistence on the irreducible diversity of ways of thinking is a much tougher-minded response to diversity than the more usual alternative of making rationality into a more minimal—formal or procedural—idea, the pragmatist strategy that corresponds to liberalism as minimal morality, a coordinating sort of justice that is agnostic with regard to the good.[3] The strategy of minimal rationality and minimal morality makes the encounter with diversity as inconsequential as possible. It proposes to let preexisting actions, faiths, values and desires continue with as little interference from outside as possible.

One reason minimal rationality is such a tempting response to diversity is that it is hard to imagine any coherent alternative. McKeon's work did not have immediate appeal because it seems unlikely and paradoxical that we could fruitfully address problems of practical diversity by a detour through worrying about philosophic diversity. Diversity at the heart of rationality is the most radical form of diversity imaginable, so radical that it seems hard to keep calling it rational.

The diversity of ways of thinking can be interpreted modestly if those ways of thinking are considered merely instrumental to the truth they lead to, through, for example, separations of contexts and methods of discovery and justification. There is nothing threatening in the claim that there are many useful methods of thinking, so long as the products of those methods submit to a single ultimate and independent judgment.

Pluralism becomes more radical if that common end is taken away. The diverse modes of thought are at least partly constitutive of their results. When thought and action are partly constitutive of their results, then there is no common measure of success. The grudging concession to diversity that characterizes minimal morality and procedural rationality always founders against autonomous values of politics, science, and rationality itself. Finding a minimal common ground of respect for rights may sometimes resolve practical controversies between intractably opposed conceptions of the good. But it is no universal solvent for all practical encounters with diversity, and looks increasingly impotent against the forms of ideological and cultural diversity that set today's moral and intellectual problems. In many cases money, agreement, or empirical confirmation can act as a universal solvent and a common measure to pacify disputes between divergent modes of thought, but that sort of pragmatism fails when confronted with ways of thinking and acting that are their own end.

McKeon takes his stand on the ultimate diversity of methods of thinking. He does not follow the easier route of searching for a common, universal, and therefore minimal rationality underpinning an apparent diversity of thinking. Nor could he have any time at all for the incoherent "Romantic" idea that logical principles such as that of noncontradiction or excluded middle are merely "Western" conventions or prejudices successfully overcome by the more spiritual peoples of the East or uncontaminated indigenous cultures. There are diverse modes of thought; there is no common measure of success or truth that can be stated apart from these modes of thought, and yet different ways of thinking are not insular. They can talk to each other and be understood by each other.

The recognition of radical or ultimate diversity of methods of thinking is a novel idea in philosophy, made necessary by the increasingly unavoidable experience of practical diversity.[4] But this new philosophic idea has a counterpart that is a commonplace for practical thought and action. The most narrowly pragmatic reading of practical diversity is that different people have different ideas about what will satisfy them, but ultimately their end is the same—happiness, satisfaction, pleasure—rooted in a common human nature. That reading of diversity finds confirmation in the increasing homogeneity of the practical world of automobiles, soft drinks and computers. That minimal interpretation of diversity fails when we see that for our most important desires, *how we secure an end is part of the end.* I not only want to *have* something, I want to *achieve* it. Our highest desires are to achieve things, not just be consumers. (This is also true of our most destructive purposes, those that liberalism and tolerance were originally designed to thwart, the desire to convert others to the one true faith, to usher in the messianic age and the end of history.) Whenever we want to do something and not simply want some result to exist, however, there is no longer any neutral, common, external measure of practical success. This interpretation of diversity finds confirmation in the increased fragmentation of the practical world that confounds expectations of homogeneity. The easy liberalism of the peace treaty, the *modus vivendi,* minimal morality, and the right prior to the good founders against these more practical sorts of goods, just as the easy pragmatism which codifies and makes more efficient the means we use to achieve predefined goals founders against the discovery of autonomous scientific values.[5] That foundering, I will argue, is the engine of philosophy and of history.

Pluralism and the Rediscovery of Philosophy

If we can understand what consequences the recognition of diversity has for philosophy, we might be in a position to address more immediately practical varieties of diversity that have been the subject of so much recent attention: the diversities of cultures, interests, beliefs, and values. Every moment in human history that can be called "philosophical" is an encounter with diversity, with the one and the many, although rarely in as radical a form as today. Contemporary pluralism is a rediscovery of philosophy itself. Philosophy begins in Plato's hands as a confrontation with new forms of diversity, new and upsetting theories of the gods, outside experts such as Sophists, *nouveaux riches* and ambitious young men, the need to integrate competitive and co-operative virtues.[6]

To re-enact Plato, and to re-enact philosophy, is to consider the relations among three kinds of virtues. First, there are the ordinary practical virtues, courage, temperance, justice, and perhaps piety, with its modern extensions such as loyalty and patriotism. Second, there are the virtues of philosophic and scientific inquiry. These virtues are valued because of their tendency to lead to truth. Yet these virtues can be in opposition to the original practical ones. This is the tension that I mentioned before at the heart of pragmatism, and it is the beginning of philosophy. Dewey notes this tension between seeing the second set of virtues as valuable because they fortify the first set of virtues and seeing them as valuable in spite of the fact that they upset the first set. (These remarks would not be a bad description of Plato's dialogues.)

A certain group of men, perhaps relatively not very numerous, have a 'disinterested' interest in scientific inquiry. This interest has developed a morale having its own distinctive features. Some of its obvious elements are willingness to hold belief in suspense, ability to doubt until evidence is obtained; willingness to go where evidence points instead of putting first a personally preferred conclusion; ability to hold ideas in solution and use them as hypotheses to be tested instead of as dogmas to be asserted; and (possibly the most distinctive of all) enjoyment of new fields for inquiry and of new problems.

Every one of these traits goes contrary to some human impulse that is naturally strong. Uncertainty is disagreeable to most persons; suspense is so hard to endure that assured expectation of an unfortunate outcome is usually preferred to a long-continued state of doubt. 'Wishful thinking' is a comparatively modern phrase; but men upon the whole have usually believed what they wanted to believe, except as very convincing evidence made it impossible. Apart from a scientific attitude, guesses, with persons left to themselves, tend to become opinions and opinions dogmas. To hold theories and principles in solution, awaiting confirmation, goes contrary to the grain. Even today questioning a statement made by a person is often taken by him as a reflection upon his integrity, and is resented.[7]

Third are the virtues of communication, of understanding others, including keeping the conversation going and treating with respect those with whom we disagree. These are virtues associated with the arts of rhetoric which McKeon did so much to bring to the attention to philosophers. Socrates sets the problem for philosophy by arguing that the unexamined life is not worth living, that only the philosopher is truly courageous, temperate, just and pious, and, further, that the philosophic life is a life spent in conversation, in exposing the errors of others and in knowing oneself through speaking to others. Socrates claims that the three sets of virtues are the same.

Socrates' thesis seems evidently false much of the time. Ordinary practical virtues need no help from either science or community, when the unreflective consciousness can do well without consideration of any grounding for the virtues or worries about alternatives. Hegel referred to such people and times as unhistorical. They could just as well be called unphilosophical. Philosophy could in such circumstances only be an unwelcome subversive force. Similarly, there are times when scientific virtue does fine without communication, as in Williams's presentation of Descartes's "project of pure inquiry" as a solitary thinker confronting the universe, where to think scientifically is not to be part of a community, and great scientists are not known for possessing the ordinary practical virtues.[8]

There are other times, however, when those three sets of virtues seem to need each other, when effective moral action requires powers of reflection and justification, or the ability to consider possible ways of life or proposals for action other than one's own. There are times when scientific progress demands attention to practical consequences or to the ethical qualities of scientific practitioners, or when such progress depends on effective communication with adherents of rival research programs, or with the beneficiaries or consumers of scientific results. There are times, that is, when the virtues of action, of thought, and of communication are not independent of each other. Those moments can be called philosophical. Ours is such a time.

While questions of how to respond to diversity are always at the heart of philosophy, the contemporary encounter has a rare depth to it that demands new sets of virtues. Onora O'Neill describes the contemporary situation calling for pluralism this way:

> The modern circumstances of justice are ethical diversity: people have variously constituted capacities to reason and to act and varying forms and degrees of independence from one another and from the institutions and practices that constitute their *Sittlichkeit*. Plurality without coordination is the classic condition in which the problems both of order and of justice arise; modern plurality is more radical because we cannot assume a homogeneous *Sittlichkeit* either within or beyond boundaries. Principles of justice are redundant where there is only a single agent, or where a preestablished harmony (a well-entrenched total ideology?) coordinates agents. . . . Modern circumstances of justice include the plurality not just of agents but of ideologies.[9]

Plurality without coordination is also the classic condition in which the problems of philosophy arise. Each encounter with new forms of diversity forces us to rediscover ways in which reflection can be a practical act and ways in which considering how others think and act is part of one's own deliberation about what it is best to do. Today we find partisans of the one and of the many, those who worry about the increasing fragmentation of society and anarchy of multiculturalism, and those

117

exercised over increased homogeneity and hegemony of advertising and late capitalism. While it has been popular to look to the Greeks for unity and an integrated life against modern fragmentation, I here want to emphasize the opposite, and look among the Greeks for sophisticated responses to diversity and for understandings of pluralism as the response to diversity and integrity, one and many. Aristotle may have been the first to articulate in theory what Plato dramatized and what the Greeks discovered in practice—that true political community is founded on difference, not unity—when they invented the polis and substituted political ties for ties of force and blood.[10] But we are now in a position to make good on that discovery in a way unimaginable to the Greeks. That is what Dewey meant by saying that the "problem of a democratically organized public is primarily and essentially an intellectual problem, in a degree to which the political affairs of prior ages offer no parallel."[11]

With O'Neill, I believe that the current problems of philosophy are as radical as they are because "we cannot assume a homogeneous *Sittlichkeit* either within or beyond boundaries," that is, because we cannot assume either that there is or is not a connection among the virtues of action, of knowledge, and of communication and rhetoric. The tension between pragmatism as the codification of good behavior securing existing goods and as the grounds for reform and the transvaluation of values is the engine of philosophy and of history. The engine of history and philosophy is the shifting interrelations among the three kinds of virtues: practical, theoretical, and rhetorical.

Pluralism, Belief, and Argument

I want to approach this deep philosophical and practical diversity by recalling Kant's three maxims of unprejudiced, enlarged and consecutive thought. I want to quote Kant's account of three maxims at length to show that these three maxims demand intellectual *virtues,* not just obedience to rules, and to marvel at the radical idea that fulfilling such maxims can be done in irreducibly diverse ways.

The following maxims [of common human understanding] may serve to elucidate its principles: (1) to think for oneself; (2) to think from the standpoint of everybody else; (3) to think always consistently. The first is the maxim of *unprejudiced* thought; the second of *enlarged* thought; the third of *consecutive* thought. The first is the maxim of a never passive reason. The tendency to such passivity, and therefore to heteronomy of the reason, is called *prejudice;* and the greatest prejudice of all is to represent nature as not subject to the rules that the understanding places at its basis by means of its own essential law, i.e. is *superstition.* As regards the second maxim of the mind, we are otherwise wont to call him limited (whose talents attain to no great use). But here we are not speaking of the faculty of cognition, but of the *mode of thought* which makes a purposive use thereof. It indicates a man of *enlarged thought* if he disregards the subjective private conditions of his own judgment, by which so many others are confined, and reflects upon it from a *universal standpoint* (which he can only determine by placing himself at the standpoint of others). The third maxim, viz. that of *consecutive thought*, is the most difficult to attain, and can only be attained by the combination of the former and after the constant observance of them as grown into a habit.[12]

There is no guarantee that cultivating the intellectual virtues that allow us to develop and act on these three maxims would produce unanimity. Once again, we have a paradox, since common opinion no doubt finds difference and dissent to be signs of irrationality. As McKeon puts it,

> To be of one mind is not to be of one opinion. Men are of one mind when they possess reason to judge statements of truth, understanding to appreciate statements of their own values and those of others, desires ordered under freedom, and love of the common good for which men are associated. When men are of one mind in these abilities, they can be of different opinions without danger to society or to each other.[13]

To be of one mind without unanimity is to recognize others' thoughts as rational without having to agree with them or abandon our own. Something of the distance between this robust pluralism and minimal rationality can be seen in the difference in the meaning of "consecutive thought" according to a purely formal logic and minimal rationality and according to a conception in which thinking consecutively is the most difficult maxim to fulfill, and where thinking consecutively depends on the mind's being always active and able to take a universal standpoint. Successful thinking depends on the existence of other minds and on seeing them as mind and other. The virtues of thought depend on the virtues of pluralism.

With that sense of diversity in mind, I want to recall a second feature of pragmatism. In addition to the tension between discovering efficient means to existing ends and finding new autonomous values in inquiry itself, the pragmatist maintains that we should treat ideas as hypotheses rather than absolute claims. The great benefit of treating ideas as hypotheses is that it separates advocacy from belief and commitment. Pragmatism thus makes into a theory of rationality the same tactic that the liberal offered as a theory of politics, a retreat from commitment to supposition for the sake of argument. When ideas are hypotheses, we can neutrally specify conditions for testing them, determining when they should be used and when abandoned. We do not have to take the defeat of ideas personally. When liberalism formed conditions for admission to citizenship in the new state, people, factions and faiths could enter by agreeing to submit to neutral tests of when one set of beliefs should carry the day, and agreeing to being a good loser. This is the liberal as hypocrite, and the philosopher as Sophist, advancing many ideas in the experimental spirit of science but fully committed to none of those ideas. Religious wars may have been destructive, but at least they showed that people were willing to kill, and sometimes to die, for their ideals. The political liberal is accused of having no morals at all because he or she refrains from making absolute and exclusive moral claims. That is what happens, it seems, when one treats ideas as hypotheses.

McKeon in his own practice often looks like a chameleon: a scholar who presents other views while having none himself, a Sophist whose clients are Plato, Aristotle, Spinoza, and Kant. In deliberation, theoretical or ideological differences are no bar to practical agreement, and so the liberal and the pragmatist are peacemakers. Collingwood notes the connection between pluralism and this severing of philosophic argument from advocacy and belief: "The characteristic outcome of supposal is pluralism. Just because the work of art is merely supposed, the world of art was a pluralistic or monadic world, consisting of an indefinite number of works of art all ostensibly independent of one another and having no such structure as would make them into a single coherent world."[14]

The encounter with diversity makes it hard to maintain one's own commitments reflectively. I could think other than as I do, and so how can I be committed to the way I think? It looks as though awareness of the existence of alternatives prevents full commitments. Without more sophisticated, and more rhetorical, relations between supposal and assertion, it looks as though awareness of diversity is incompatible with full confidence in one's own ideas. Hence Williams's suggestion that reflection can result in the loss of knowledge.[15] It is as though the encounter with diversity acts as an Iago destroying our unreflectively secure knowledge while offering not certainty but permanent suspicion and madness in its place. Small wonder that some people hope to hang on to their security by killing the messenger before Iago's news can become infectious; thus the passion directed against "fragmentation." But once the secret of diversity is out, it is too late to recover. With a sufficient monopoly of force, one could suppress diversity. Therefore, as I noted before, some of our most destructive projects come from the encounter with diversity, such as the will to convert others to the one true faith.

Thus the first result of the encounter of philosophy with diversity. Diversity forces a retreat from dogmatism and monism. Such a retreat looks like sophistic, or relativism, because it separates advocacy from commitment. Pragmatism and pluralism, consequently, depend on more complicated and sophisticated relations between doubt, hypothetical supposal and assertion or belief either dogmatism or sophistic can conceive. My initial question, What difference does it make to my thinking and acting when I recognize that the way I go about things is not the only way possible?, is thus a question about the relations between the virtues of practice, of reflection, and of communication.

Pluralism and the Possible and the Actual

I propose to search for this new variety of cognitive states and activities which lie between knowledge and supposition by looking at their "objective correlatives," modalities between the actual and the possible. Without philosophic reflection, the perception of diversity leads naturally to seeing plural systems as options, and ultimately to the kind of romantic pragmatism recently celebrated by Rorty, in which the encounter with diversity leads to a kind of free play that reduces practical to aesthetic value. Liberal therapy consists in the conversion of dogmatism into relativism, also called disenchantment. Jonathan Sacks describes this picture of modern theoretical, practical, and rhetorical virtues this way:

> Modernity privatizes the religious domain. Liberal theologies, accommodating themselves to social and intellectual change, translate statements about external reality into propositions about believers themselves, and propositions about authority into the vocabulary of personal choice. Religious language, instead of describing a given external and objective order, now designates a chosen internal and subjective reality. Once this move is made, pluralism becomes an intellectual possibility. Statements of objective truth clash in a way that statements about subjective perception do not. When religion no longer contests the public domain, coexistence takes the place of conflict. Because ultimate realities have been internalized, religious movements can see their differences as matters of interpretation rather than truth.[16]

Such relativism is often rebutted by the second-most simple-minded answer, the notion that these plural modes of thought, far from open to free choice, are fixed, whether by history, nature or the unconscious. In an impersonal possibility space, all hypotheses are equally possible, but I am fully constrained, stuck with the way of thinking and living I find myself with. The other might be intelligible or rational, but not something that makes truth claims on me. These alien ideas might be worthy of respect, but my respect for others does not have much to do with how I lead my own life. Relativism is replaced by historicism and incommensurability.[17]

If history presents an irreducible variety of modes of thought, then in the one case history is a set of *possibiles* with no nonarbitrary connections to the actual; in the other, history produces the actual world we live in, with no possibilities left over. Either my own identity, as philosopher and citizen, is completely unaffected by these possibilities and is instead left up to my unencumbered self, or my identity is fully given and so is no longer *mine*. Gellner has a concise way of framing the problem: "The task facing the theory of knowledge is to combine the idealist insight, concerning the active, context-bound, historically specific nature of mind, with the realist awareness of the nonautistic nature of genuine knowledge."[18]

The interesting and unprecedented problem of pluralism—both as a philosophical and as a practical problem—is a problem of the possible and the actual. I can recognize that my position is one among many, without the others being alternatives for me. My two more simple-minded responses to plural modes of thought both rested on the unexamined assumption that if there are various possible ways of thinking, all these must be possible for me. If they are not possible for me, then they are not really possibilities. If I cannot find a fallacy in Aristotle's defense of slavery, I am committed to embracing it. If I cannot embrace it, I had better not decide that he offers a valid argument.

Making the relations of the supposed and the asserted, the actual and the possible, problematic can help us avoid the antinomy that principles are either given, and so irrational and arbitrary, as Foucault has it, or freely chosen, and so irrational and arbitrary, as his Romantic opposition thinks. In contemporary legal discussions, religious affiliation is said to deserve special protection and deference, or the opposite, alternatively because it represents one's deepest choices or something given and outside one's control. There is personality or impersonality. In neither case is character or rational choice possible. Thus, while Richard Rorty recommends treating philosophy as a matter for private irony, and hopes to "josh" people out of their commitments to principles—how else could one regard things that alternately seem necessary and arbitrary than by both personal and political detachment?—people do not always welcome such joshing.[19] But character in a sense robust enough to do justice to Kant's maxims is not simply a matter of behavior. *Êthos* is revealed in the sorts of things I take as possible options, and the things I regard as impossible for me.[20]

Not all possibilities, thus, are potencies which can or should be realized, and I have no duty to spend my time rejecting all impossibilities: I need spend no energy showing to myself and to others that I reject Aristotle's justification of slavery, but it would be unethical to regard a contemporary proposal to re-institute slavery with equanimity.[21] Before I said that a full confrontation with diversity requires modalities of belief between supposal and assent, and then suggested that we could make progress in filling out what that means by looking at the varieties of the possible. I find helpful a distinction Bernard Williams, borrowing from Newman's rhetorical *Grammar of Assent,* develops between "*real* and *notional* confrontations.*" This is a distinction that should already be familiar to pragmatism from Peirce's attacks on Descartes for conflating doubting in principle or a bare possibility of doubting vs. a real doubt.

A real confrontation between two divergent outlooks occurs at a given time if there is a group of people for whom each of the outlooks is a real option. A notional confrontation, by contrast, occurs when some people know about two divergent outlooks, but at least one of those outlooks does not present a real option. The idea of a 'real option' is largely, but not entirely, a social notion.[22]

The real/notional possibility distinction is a practical distinction, not about the true or the good but about what *I* should do. That there is such a distinction between what is possible and what is possible for me shows the irreducibility of practice to theory, of practical reason to theoretical reason. As McKeon says, "If practical problems are treated as if they were theoretic oppositions, reason enters in their resolution only as it is used to destroy an opposed position concerning policy, science, or society."[23]

It is for this reason that the virtues of belief and supposition are irreducibly ethical virtues. The virtues of reflection and communication are distinct from the virtues of practice, but they are ethical and practical virtues nonetheless. The logical ideas of contradiction and consistency have practical counterparts, such as conflict and agreement, and so do other logical properties such as possibility and necessity, but those practical ideas are not reducible to their theoretical analogues. As Wittgenstein puts it, "The *civil* status of a contradiction, or its status in *civil* life: there is the philosophical problem."[24] Hume, otherwise an ally on the reductive side of liberalism, sees the impossibility of reducing practice to theory, what is possible for me to what is possible, that is, takes into account the costs of entertaining ideas hypothetically for the sake of argument.

Whatever speculative errors may be found in the polite writings of any age or country. . . . There needs but a certain turn of thought or imagination to make us enter into all the opin-

ions which then prevailed, and relish the sentiments or conclusions derived from them. . . . [But the] case is not the same with
moral principles as with speculative opinions. . . . I cannot, nor
is it proper I should, enter into such sentiments . . . and where
a man is confident of the rectitude of that moral standard by
which he judges, he is justly jealous of it, and will not pervert
the sentiments of his heart for a moment, in complaisance to
any writer whatsoever.[25]

Just as failure to distinguish the actual from the possible results in
philosophic relativism, so too the discovery of alternative possible moral
principles leads, unless prevented by better thinking, to ethical relativism. Once one sees that different people have different moral ideals,
those ultimate ends seem exempt from rational discussion. My commitment to my own ultimate ends begins as constitutive of who I am and
ends as an arbitrary and irrational attachment. What was my character
becomes my personality. Goods beyond price become goods beyond reason, and then quickly become the irrational attachments of the conventional good soldier or the fanatical reformer.

But if I cannot assume that, because something is possible or rational, it is possible or rational for me, and if possibilities that are not possibilities for me are not for that reason simply to be ignored, then there
are new intellectual and moral problems associated with the discovery
of possibilities that are not possibilities for us. Here are new challenges
to pluralism, requiring theoretical, practical and rhetorical virtues for
which neither practical nor philosophic heroes of the past offer models.
Lee H. Yearly nicely articulates one set of those new practical problems
of the possible and actual, which he calls "spiritual regret."

Spiritual regret arises when we understand both that different but legitimate ideals of religious flourishing exist, and that conflicts among
them are deep enough that no single person can even come close to exhibiting all of them. Each of us must be a limited specialist in the human
good. Moreover, the specializations available to us will usually be determined by forces beyond our control. Spiritual regret arises, then, when
we face confrontations, and thus choices, that fit between the notional
and the real. A notional confrontation occurs when I ask myself if I can
imagine, without ceasing to be me, incarnating the excellences of a
T'ang dynasty Buddhist monk. A real confrontation occurs when I ask
myself what I can say to my child's desire to move into a Tibetan
monastery in New Jersey. To be tempted by a religious excellence and
yet to understand that you cannot, and should not, pursue it is at the
heart of spiritual regret.[26]

Like the relation between hypothetical supposal and full affirmation,
the distinction between real and notional possibilities is in one respect
nothing new to philosophy, but in another way it has an urgency unique

to the contemporary situation. Diversity is such a problem today because diversity is not a purely external problem about our relations to others. That is why the set of questions I raised at the start are so difficult for us. As Rorty puts it, "Most of us identify with a number of different communities and are equally reluctant to marginalize ourselves in relation to any of them. This diversity of identifications increases with education, just as the number of communities with which a person may identify increases with civilization."[27] Liberalism may have begun when different sorts of Christianity had to live together within a single state, but such liberalism could afford the easier solution one's own religious faith and practices being unaffected by the tolerance towards those who were too strong to convert or kill. Once diversity is found within communities and within individual deliberators, pluralism must be more radical.

Kant's three maxims of thinking for oneself, thinking from the standpoint of everybody else, and thinking always consistently are more difficult to fulfill in such circumstances. What does it mean, first, to think for oneself when the self is not given but emerges out of this encounter with diversity? Socrates already gave an answer that collapsed practical, theoretical and rhetorical virtues into each other. One finds one's own wisdom by testing others and exhorting them to stop running after money and chasing wisdom instead. But he substituted the paradox that only the philosopher is courageous, temperate and just for the tension that I have called the engine of history and philosophy. The distinctness of persons disappears. There is no reason to single Socrates out as the wisest of men. If I resist the Socratic reduction, pluralism means that I have to come to terms with diversity to determine my own identity and *êthos,* and come to understand my own ethical identity by seeing that others have distinct ethical identities.

Next, what does it mean to think the standpoint of everybody else when the distinction between what is possible and what is possible for me forces me to distinguish the standpoint of everybody else from the standpoint of no one at all? Minimal morality and minimal rationality have consequences that are not so modest after all. As MacIntyre observes: "Even since the Enlightenment our culture has been far too hospitable to the all too plainly self-interested belief that whenever we succeed in discovering the rationality of other and alien cultures and traditions, by making their behavior intelligible and by understanding their languages, what we will also discover is that in essence they are just like us."[28] Rawls's veil of ignorance not only separates the right from the good, but substitutes calculation for communication, eliminating the rhetorical virtues, and probably the practical ones as well, as the veil of ignorance, like the Socratic reduction, removes the distinctness of persons. If we resist that reduction, what does the "standpoint of everybody else" mean?

What, finally, does Kant mean when he says that thinking consistently is "the most difficult to attain, and can only be attained by the combination of the former and after the constant observance of them as grown into a habit?" This obviously is not the consistency of procedural rationality. It must be more ethical, something like Wittgenstein's "civil status" of contradictions, and of consistency. Theoretical, practical, and rhetorical virtues cannot be separated. Only then can consistency be a habitual product of self-activity and taking the standpoint of everyone else.

Thus a second preliminary indication of an answer to the original question, what difference does the consciousness of diversity make? Just like the complicated relations between supposal and assertion demand a rhetoric in which *êthos* is central, the complicated relations among the possible, the actual, and the possible for me demand a conception of practical reason not reducible to theoretical reason as Plato and Rawls sought to do, because the practicable, the possible for me, is not reducible to some combination of the actual and the possible. Whatever pluralism will ultimately look like, we can no longer come to terms with diversity by seeing it only outside us. The one and the many are implicated in each other. Practical, theoretical, and rhetorical virtues must all be ethical.

Ideas as Hypotheses vs. Thinking Categorically

I have framed my two problems of pluralism, the problems of the hypothesized and the affirmed and of the possible and the actual, as practical problems, issues of understanding what it is to have a character or *êthos*. They are equally theoretical problems about what it is to have philosophic principles. Like one's character, one's principles seem necessary from the inside and arbitrary to the outside.[29] The new relations I have demanded among understanding, belief and assertion pose a challenge for a new intellectual virtue, turning on difficulties of applying terms of assessment such as "voluntary," "choice," "freedom," and "necessity" to the *principles* of thought and action, instead of to actions themselves. What are the appropriate cognitive and practical attitudes, and corresponding moral sentiments, for the pluralist to exercise towards philosophical principles, one's own and others'? That question is a new way of making more concrete and manageable the original question of what difference the awareness of diversity should make to our thinking, and its first redaction in the relations among the three kinds of virtues, practical, theoretical, and rhetorical. It is the hope of philosophy since its Socratic invention that knowing how to deal with principles will tell us how to deal with selves and others, since they too are principles.[30]

Dewey finds pluralism practically urgent but theoretically unproblematic, because ideas are hypotheses. On that account, partisans who think that ideas have systematic values in addition to their value as hypotheses are simply wrong. His reconstruction in philosophy will help people to abandon these unnecessary and impossible ambitions, much as earlier liberal movements towards tolerance promoted modesty by separating church and state, ethics and politics. The instrumental side of pragmatism sees progress issuing from the translation of recalcitrant phenomena such as moral principles and personal and communal identity into more manageable matters of interest. I cannot defeat people who worship false gods, so I must live with those people. But living with them should not make me waver in my own faith. However, the condition of success is for me to treat others as less than fully rational. We can live in peace so long as we treat each other's principles not as principles at all but as preferences. Diversity might demand new practical and rhetorical virtues of respecting others and maintaining communities without unanimity, but no theoretical virtues emerge alongside: my own thinking and acting should go on as before. There are times when the effect of the encounter with diversity *should* stay only skin-deep.

Success for this "end of ideology" sort of pluralism, which will resolve practical problems by asking people to restrain their dogmatic impulses in the name of public peace and progress, looks more unlikely each day. Perhaps in Dewey's time one could dismiss those who resisted the pragmatic overtures as primitives who still irrationally held to religiously inspired messianic dreams, but today the resistance to pragmatism seems too powerful and too thoughtful to be purely vestigial. The resistance to reducing science to problem-solving and politics to maximizing given preferences rejects the transformation of philosophic systems into mere hypotheses whose multiplicity is tested against a single world by a single rationality. Plato already gave us reason to be skeptical about the reduction of politics to problem-solving not only by asking repeatedly about just who the experts are, but also when Socrates observes, in conversation with Euthyphro, that while disagreement over measurements and quantities do not produce anger and enmity, disagreements concerning the goods have this peculiarly unirenic character. Consistently reducing other people's principles to preferences is an unstable solution. It violates Kant's maxims by exempting oneself from the judgment one applies to others. The more I do unto others as I would have them do to me, the more my own principles too become mere preferences. "It is hard," Rorty rightly says, "to be both enchanted with one version of the world and tolerant of all the others."[31] If I cannot defend my desires and purposes in public with public reasons, I have no right to them. This is the liberalism of the unencumbered self, in which the right is not only prior to the good, but determinative of the content of the good. Seeing my own thought as only one possibility among others, I can no longer be committed to it, and so can no longer even think it, except playfully and aesthetically. No wonder the pluralism of a peace treaty, the end of ideology, and the *modus vivendi* is appealing. The trouble is, we can no longer pretend that it fits our world.

There are no neutral data to resolve disputes among distinct ultimate principles and systems just because principles are categorical, not hypothetical as the reductive side of pragmatism would have it. Pragmatism is not radical enough to confront today's "problems of men." As Charles Taylor puts it,

> I articulate what were formerly limits to intelligibility, in order to see these in a new context, no longer as inescapable structures of human motivation, but as one in a range of possibilities. That is why other-understanding changes self-understanding, and in particular prizes us loose from some of the most fixed contours of our former culture.

> Debate is not between two propositions which are rivals in the ordinary way that empirical hypotheses are—say, the big bang theory versus the steady state cosmologies. In this latter case, the truth of each is incompatible with the truth of the other, but not with its intelligibility. But here the clash is sharper. The whole strength of [one theory] lies in the supposed unintelligibility of a rival account.[32]

Plural hypotheses are easy to understand, but the idea of plural systems, like that of plural truth, seems almost a contradiction in terms. These clashes of intelligibility, as Taylor calls them, one of the things meant by the popular current term, incommensurability, are the radical challenge diversity poses to philosophy. As I said before, the new relations among understanding, belief and assertion forced on us by diversity pose novel problems of intellectual, practical and rhetorical virtue, turning on difficulties of transferring terms we use in assessing actions, such as "voluntary," "choice," "freedom," and "necessity," to *principles* of thought and action. We know what it means for actions to be chosen, but choosing to believe, taking responsibility for one's beliefs, being free to believe—those are different matters for which the usual alternatives are inadequate. Aristotle taught that we deliberate about means and not ends, and a rational approach to principles certainly looks like deliberation about ends. It is hard to know what a choice of principles could mean.

These categorical values and principles—Taylor's "limits to intelligibility"—define philosophic principles and modes of thought and define practical ends.[33] In practice, it was actions that are their own end that blocked the use of a common evaluative standard. In science, it was the paradoxical elevation of continuing inquiry into a value rather than a defect that defeated all single empirical tests. Similarly in philosophy.

Autonomous goods, including standards for rationality itself, prevent appeal to a neutral arbiter. It is not relativism and a denial of objective public values that defeats the reductionist end of ideology pragmatism. It is the existence of objective public values that cannot be specified in advance just because they are activities and thoughts that are their own end. For this reason, the reductive strategies for denigrating the categorical side of principles will not work—they are not survivals to be grown out of; they are not indirect devices for accomplishing ends that are not aimed at, but positively desirable and necessary properties of action and thought that is its own end. The categorical features of philosophy, like the ethical features of the self, defeat the pragmatic reduction in the name of autonomous values. From autonomous values as the engine of history and philosophy can emerge plural interpretations of rationality.

Pluralism and the Future of Pragmatism

Pragmatism, I have argued, has two sides that are always at tension and sometimes at war with each other. Pragmatism starts by bringing to bear on practice the successful problem-solving techniques of science. It also replaces instrumental values and preexisting ends by new autonomous values that are not simply reducible to problem-solving power. New intellectual virtues challenge traditional practical ideals.

Pragmatism in the narrow and reductive sense has a useful message for practice, one that Dewey and McKeon insisted on: practical agreement does not require agreement on philosophic principle. Practical agreement can take place even when we disagree about philosophic principles. That is the great attraction of the end of ideology side of pragmatism.

The reductive program for pragmatism, liberalism and philosophic rationality makes sense when ideas are instrumental and hypothetical, and that in turn makes sense when there is a common goal. Hobbesian liberalism is impossible unless people value peace not only over war but over autonomy, nobility and everything else, and so Hobbes engages in the rhetorical task of persuading people that fear of death is an overriding motive. He tries to convince people to abandon goals whose pursuit is incompatible with peace. Similarly, Humean skepticism undercuts people's beliefs in autonomous values and personal autonomy, and so rhetorically moderates and cools down our deepest commitments and enthusiasms. But people often want more from their ideas than a recipe for acting. The reductive side of pragmatism and liberalism has no room for autonomous value, autonomous activity and autonomous thought. The attraction of the end of ideology is precisely its denigration of autonomous values and acts that are their own end, because those are the things that cause all the trouble—we risk death for our ideals, fight religious wars over unverifiable enthusiasms, foolishly value honor over life itself. There is more to ideas than their "cash-value" or action-guiding nature. Ideas have symbolic, systematic, and allegiance-generating qualities, qualities erased when we look at ideas simply as hypotheses. The conflict between pragmatism as refinement of ordinary intelligence and pragmatism as reform here becomes acute. McKeon saw that ideas were more than hypotheses:

> Like the use of reason in the natural sciences, its use in practical affairs is an inference. . . . The inference is not from a proposition to a prediction, however, except in an analogical sense. Principles, theories, and statements are only one ingredient in the premises from which a practical inference proceeds. They are inferences and are made precise, in so far as they enter serious consideration, not by their truth but by their reliability as statements of intention, granted the circumstances, history, and character of their proponents. . . . Reason in application to practical questions therefore has, in addition to its direct inferential function of relating assumptions to conclusions [the function assumed in the so-called practical syllogism and in productive action], an inverse inferential or imputative function of relating proposals to the character and attitude from which they flow.[34]

McKeon's lines give a pragmatic reason, even an instrumental reason, for opposing the pragmatic reduction of ideas to hypotheses. There is a tactical reason to refuse reducing ideas to their consequences, which explains why reductive pragmatism is a rhetorical failure. To treat ideas as hypotheses is to search for those things that distinguish one idea from another. But in practice, we often want and need common ground. Treating ideas as hypotheses and searching for minimal morality and minimal rationality go together. Both try to make a permanent distinction between the things that ideas and people share—e.g., the institutions of justice—and the things that separate one idea and one people from another, e.g., conceptions of the good. When the one and the many, self and other, are intermingled, the separation of areas of agreement and of difference has only temporary, not principled, value. Pluralism, the deeper response to diversity, comes from autonomous practices that are their own end, not instrumental to and measurable by some common external end. With autonomy, there is no common goal or neutral measure of success.

It is easy to claim that we need a diversity of methods because each by itself is inadequate, and so several partial views are better than one. The end of ideology or reductive pragmatism and liberalism has two presuppositions, the neutral measure of success, and, we now see, a common task to which diverse parties can make contributions that can be added together. The rhetorical power of the reductive side of pragmatism, liberalism and procedural rationality comes from some background idea of inadequacy or partiality, which encourages people to distance themselves from their principles, thus not staking their characters on the validity of the principles.[35] That is exactly what it means to treat ideas as hypotheses. That rhetorical appeal is often successful. When I look outward at other controversialists, it is obvious to me that each is inadequate, and that these partial views need each other. I do not mind at all treating other people's moral convictions as preferences, and other religions as hobbies.

But I resist applying the same standards to myself, and I cannot help noticing that others return the favor. Hence the importance of Kant's second maxim, to think from the standpoint of everyone else. I can see other people's thoughts as inadequate, but I see no such partiality in my own thinking, and so the idea of treating ideas as hypotheses and values preferences fails because I cannot treat myself as I regard others. Pluralism advances over earlier forms of liberalism by showing how we need each other not because each by itself is so weak—as though proliferating falsehoods somehow produces truth—but through the strength and value of each. As Henry Richardson sums up this recent discovery,

> Liberalism [according to Barry, Raz, and MacIntyre] cannot be neutrally defended . . . because of . . . the depth and structure of competing conceptions of the good at large in society. If everyone took their good to hinge entirely on their own pleasure, then defending neutrality would be easier. In fact, however, people are attached to conceptions of the good that have a structure and depth—partly due to religious and political beliefs—that typically introduce other-regarding elements.[36]

These "other-regarding elements" break down the distinction between public and shared ideas of justice or minimal rationality against private conceptions of the true and the good. Taking autonomy seriously means, in philosophy, regarding diverse modes of rationality as each relatively adequate and self-sufficient. It is harder, but ultimately more philosophically honest, to account for and live with the diversity of method when each is by its own lights self-sufficient. The fruitful tension that I have called the engine of philosophy and history emerges when we take autonomy seriously. This is the difference between what Taylor calls clashes of truth, for which the pragmatism that treats ideas as hypotheses can be adequate, and the more radical clashes of intelligibility. Taking autonomy seriously will fully internalize pluralism, not just distance oneself from diversity by finding it in external relations only.

The Pluralist as Interpreter of Other Minds

Pluralism is what happens to pragmatism when there is no single test of success. Pluralism is what happens to liberalism when diversity is not simply a question of external relations, but when we encounter diversity within ourselves as well. Without a single test of success, the possibility of reducing ideas to hypotheses has to be abandoned. Without a single criterion, accusations of relativism are misplaced, since charges of relativism are made against an assumption of an independently ascertainable world to which the variety of claims are compared.[37] It's not that there is no single test of success because there is no real, objective, external world, as the relativists claim. There is no single test of success because autonomous values, acts that are their own end, and autonomous agents are their own measures of success, and so cannot defer to the neutral authority of a value-free array of facts specified in advance.

Without a single test, plural satisfactions of Kant's three maxims becomes a live option. When ideas are more than hypotheses, problems of relativism are replaced by problems of rhetoric and communication. As McKeon puts it,

> Recognition that the discovery of truth and the formation of thought are evidenced and tested only in communication need not lead to skepticism or relativism. On the contrary, the means to avoid sophism and dogmatism are provided by communication, and criteria of truth and value are translated into means of improving the content and efficacy of communication and of forestalling its use as an arbitrary and authoritarian instrument of control.[38]

Without a single test of success, philosophically satisfying pragmatism, as Dewey himself knew well, must broaden the ends of thought and the tests for successful thinking beyond actual to possible consequences. Otherwise pragmatism simply serves and preserves an existing order. A philosophically satisfying pluralism must expand even further, not only from actual to possible consequences, but beyond possible consequences to the constitution and vindication of agents and ideologies. A philosophically satisfying pluralism must broaden the means of evaluating diverse modes of thought by considering them not as hypotheses capable of verification and falsification, but as categorical systems.[39]

Pluralism is not a formula, and not even a method, but an intelligent and reflective confrontation between the two sides of my antinomy. The better I understand another, whether a great philosopher or a practically-minded individual of another culture or simply a neighbor and fellow-citizen with interests different from mine, the more persuaded I become of the reasonableness of his or her thinking, and the less I can see my own ideas as the unique embodiment of truth and goodness. In the lines I quoted before from Rorty, "It is hard to be both enchanted with one version of the world and tolerant of all the others." I have to understand others while still somehow retaining a distinction between self and other. The last section ended by my talking about how the encounter with diversity is deepened when we see the confrontations taking place among relatively adequate modes of thinking. When we see other thoughts as relatively adequate, then it becomes questionable how privileged my own thinking should be. Raising that issue—prefigured in my discussions of the rhetoric of assertion and supposal and of practical possibilities—is philosophical progress. We have discovered, at the heart of philosophic practice, a familiar problem faced by liberalism and liberals, a problem often framed in the words of Joseph Schumpeter quoted by Isaiah Berlin, and through him, by many others: "To realise the relative validity of one's convictions and yet stand for them unflinchingly, is what distinguishes a civilized man from a barbarian."[40] An ethics of choice for choosing principles among the real possibilities for my praxis, including what I called a rhetoric of assent and supposal, should allow us to develop more systematically the arts and virtues of pluralism that allow one to have principles, and character, without claiming unique status for them.

All along I have tried to show how philosophy rediscovers itself through new encounters with diversity, the one and the many. Plato invents philosophy by raising questions about the relation between ordinary practical virtues and the virtues of reflection and conversation. His method of hypothesis, elaborated in the *Meno* and the *Phaedo* and then with increased sophistication in other dialogues, presents a way of escaping given actualities and considering possibilities. Plato's method of hypothesis presents a way of moving from the actual to the possible that is opposed to the poet's withdrawal from a common world and public evaluation, foreshadowing the opposition of the philosophical and practical to the aesthetic and sophistic. My opposition between McKeon and Rorty as descendants of Dewey is thus a continuation of Socrates' ancient quarrel between philosophy and poetry.[41] When we saw philosophic systems and categorical limits to intelligibility appearing self-evident from the inside and arbitrary from the outside, we see re-enacted this struggle between philosophy and poetry for the title of liberators and legislators for mankind. Poetry, and rhetoric, see language and thought as opaque and self-referential while philosophy sees language and thought as transparent, and self-critical.

The history of philosophy is a series of encounters with diversity. I have claimed that the Greeks invented philosophy and politics through reflections on diversity. The strategy of removing divisive issues of principle by detaching people from principles and focusing instead on common practical goals is a way of reinstating unity, just as the market achieves unity by achieving agreement and forestalling questions of true value. That way of coping with diversity is too powerful to dismiss. But it is only a strategy. What I have called the engine of philosophy and history periodically shows that this pragmatic strategy will not always be successful, or appropriate, and that autonomous values, activities, ideas, and people that are their own end require deeper forms of pluralism. Hence the challenge of seeing the task of pluralism as plural fulfillment's of Kant's three maxims, and so of McKeon's insight that "to be of one mind is not to be of one opinion."

As my argument has developed, I have tried to show how philosophy in different ways requires the ultimate authority of the practical: in the need for an ethical relation between assertion and acceptance, in the irreducibility of what is possible for me to some other combination of the possible and the actual, and finally in the complex relation between philosophy and its history that makes new ethical demands on how we read the great thinkers of the past. The ultimate authority of the practical for philosophy is the truth of pragmatism. At the same time, where philosophy relies on the authority of the practical, I have also been exhibiting the authority of the philosophical over practice, by the inadequacy of the reductive side of pragmatism that would solve practical problems with a one-time inoculation against bad philosophy after which practice can continue happily with the end of ideology. The ultimate authority of philosophy for practice is the truth that pragmatism often misses. So, where philosophy reveals the ultimate authority of the practical, practice reveals the ultimate authority of philosophy. It is an achievement of McKeon's career to have exhibited this tension so clearly.

THE ECOLOGY OF CULTURE
PLURALISM AND CIRCUMSTANTIAL METAPHYSICS

Richard Buchanan

> "In the emerging community of the world the first problem
> of philosophy—the new metaphysics or at least the new pro-
> legomenon to all future metaphysics—will expound the sense
> in which truth is one, despite the multiplicity of the forms of
> its expression, and the sense in which what is on some
> grounds or in some circumstances true is at other times false
> and dangerous."
> RICHARD MCKEON, "A PHILOSOPHER MEDITATES ON
> DISCOVERY"

Exploration of metaphysics, or "first philosophy," was not a promising
direction for inquiry in the early decades of the twentieth century.
Theory about the nature of principles was typically rejected out of hand
for its supposed remoteness from the concrete facts and processes of our
lives, and attention focused on action and language for explanations
about the nature of the universe. But the study of principles and the investigation of metaphysical problems did not disappear. They quietly
reemerged in efforts to understand the structure of experience and the
organization and ends of expression, and they reemerged with practical
force in how we understand the evident diversity of principles held by
individuals and groups as the basis of their beliefs and actions. The

study of principles was transformed within the framework of a new philosophy of culture, turned in a direction that could not have been easily anticipated or predicted from an understanding of what metaphysics had been in the past. It was relocated within the context of communication, oriented toward the problems of how we order, disorder, and reorder our experience in an ongoing search for values and understanding within the ecology of culture.

John Dewey identified the metaphysical problem of our time in the relationship between knowledge and action, between our beliefs about the world and our beliefs about values. "The problem of restoring integration and cooperation between man's beliefs about the world in which he lives and his beliefs about the values and purposes that should direct his conduct is the deepest problem of modern life. It is the problem of any philosophy that is not isolated from that life."[1] Dewey's characterization of metaphysics represents a turn away from the study of fixed essences, or "natures," which dominated metaphysics in the past. For Dewey, the new orientation is toward philosophic consideration of the problems of experience and expression in a world that is open to change through the intentional operations of human beings. "There is then need of some theory on this matter. If we are forbidden to call this theory philosophy by the self-denying ordinance which restricts it to formal logic, need for the theory under some other name remains."[2]

What emerged from this new orientation in at least one form of philosophy is a systematic or scientific study of principles as they operate in discourse and, subsequently, as they influence action, thought, and the imputed structure of reality or Being. This is properly called a circumstantial metaphysics because it focuses on the circumstances of individual belief and the evident fact of pluralism in human expression and experience. In short, it focuses on what I have called the "ecology of culture," meaning by this term a subject which contrasts with other interpretations of both "ecology" and "culture" in authors such as Gregory Bateson, whose "ecology of mind" has its foundation in cybernetics and information theory.[3] The ecology of culture is the interrelation and interdependence of diverse perspectives in knowing, doing, and making in all areas of human activity. Circumstantial metaphysics is philosophic in vision and significance because it explores fundamental questions regarding the influence of principles on the discovery of new data for inquiry in all fields, the interpretation and establishment of facts, the operation of methods of thought and action, and the organization of learning. These are issues whose philosophic significance is only vaguely understood in the term "epistemology," which emerged in the social sciences of the twentieth century, where the popular imagination turned for better understanding of the diversity of beliefs in human experience.

One of the architects of circumstantial metaphysics and the scientific study of principles was Richard McKeon. McKeon's persistent exploration of causes in discourse and the development and influence of operative principles in all fields of thought and action is unmistakable. His exploration of metaphysics, shaped within the context of the philosophy of culture, is a central feature of his thought, evident in the importance of the concept of objectivity throughout his work.[4] However, McKeon was also one of America's foremost theorists of rhetoric, and throughout his work he displayed obvious concern for the rhetorical and circumstantial dimensions of thought and action that are characteristic of the twentieth century. Indeed, a careful reader will observe many signs that McKeon was an antimetaphysician—in current language, an antifoundationalist—deeply committed to pluralism and to the diversity of changing philosophic and practical perspectives whose interrelationship constitutes the ecology of culture. In keeping with this commitment, he developed a philosophy of process and change directed toward invention and inquiry, apparently displaying more concern for truths than for truth.

The combination of objectivity and process found expression in one of the most important ideas of McKeon's philosophy. "The objectivity of facts and values is not discovered or achieved in a structure of fixities but in an ongoing development of achievement and invention which is compounded of advancements of science, society, and art in the creation and expression of truths and values."[5] The idea that objectivity may be discovered in a world of diversity appears to have a subtle resonance with C. S. Peirce's understanding of truth and objectivity: "All propositions refer to one and the same determinately singular subject, well-understood between all interpreters and utterers; namely, to the Truth, which is the universe of universes, and is assumed on all hands to be real."[6] However, it also appears to contrast with Peirce's belief in absolute eternal truth. By stressing creation and invention in an ongoing process, McKeon is closer to Dewey in regarding objectivity as the goal and outcome of inquiry in the changing circumstances and complex processes of living. We will explore this issue more fully, but for now it serves as a beginning point in the discussion of circumstantial metaphysics. The relationship between objectivity and process is, as Bertrand Russell suggests, one of the fundamental problems of pragmatism and philosophy in general. How shall we relate thought and action in our lives?[7]

Reconciling the study of principles and criteria for objectivity with the pluralism of diverse truths and values in experience is the foremost challenge in understanding the transformation of metaphysics that McKeon sought. It is a paradox for traditional metaphysics and a challenge for philosophical investigation at the end of the twentieth century.

The issue of principles is deeply implicated in the intellectual and practical problems of modernism, postmodernism, and what comes afterward in the confused conflict among these and many other isms at the end of the twentieth century. The conflict of values that is evident in contemporary life is not fundamentally a problem of data, facts, or information. These we have in abundance. The problem is how we connect facts in thought and action, how we organize facts to reveal significance, and how we relate facts to the ends and values of our lives. Without better understanding of principles and the diverse expression of principles in individual behavior, shaped by varied cultural circumstances, there is little hope of achieving the peaceful and constructive reconciliation in human affairs that all sensible men and women seek for themselves and for their children.

Metaphysics and Antimetaphysics

The shortest sentence I have found in the writings of Richard McKeon is the terse, "My subject is, what is."[8] He must have chuckled when he wrote this opening to "Being, Existence, and That Which Is," the 1960 presidential address to the Metaphysical Society of America, because it is a surprising departure from the long, complex constructions that one normally finds throughout his work. However, he immediately returns to the distinctive style of thought and expression that characterizes his writings: an architecture of ideas and words that often puzzles the first-time reader and leaves no one indifferent to its effect.[9] To read McKeon requires uncommon discipline and concentration. The remainder of McKeon's essay is an examination of the metaphysical problems contained in that brief opening sentence, when "what is" is viewed in the twentieth-century context of existence, experience, and expression. Like all of his writings, the essay builds around a precise argument, where each sentence is an embryonic essay filled with the genetic code of its own possibilities for further elaboration through more examples and explanation.

I often wish that McKeon had elaborated his sentences into essays and his essays into books, because the amplification would have made his work more readily accessible to a wider audience. But he was less interested in building affordances for the reader than exploring the difficult philosophic problems that lie at the center of each essay. He always elaborated his thought with deliberate care and provided only as much detail and illustration as he believed necessary to reach the goal. In many cases this was a considerable amount. He was one of the most formidable scholars of his time, scrupulous in tracing the many lines of thought revealed in a philosophic examination of themes such as freedom, history, responsibility, human rights, dialectic, rhetoric, poetry, scientific method, and creativity. The effort produced an immense volume of work, notable for scholarly precision as well as philosophic insight. But in other cases, particularly the later essays, the architecture of sentences and paragraphs was like a bridge over wide waters. The purpose was not to elaborate facts, as they are usually understood in the twentieth century, but to rise above and demonstrate the integrity of the spans and arches of philosophic thought that make claims of fact meaningful in discourse and significant in action.[10] This was the culmination of McKeon's inquiries, with relevance for an age in which traditional metaphysics is usually regarded as irrelevant, abstract, or impossible.

McKeon took great care to distinguish his exploration of metaphysics from traditional as well as contemporary positions. He declined to follow the classical formulation of metaphysics as an ontology grounded in natural philosophy or mathematics in the manner of seventeenth- and eighteenth-century philosophers. He also declined to pursue an epistemological or methodological study of forms of thought such as that proposed by Kant and other nineteenth-century philosophers as a necessary preparation for proper metaphysical inquiry in the future. Even more significant, he declined to follow the broad substitutes for metaphysics that emerged in the twentieth century under the name of "unified science" or in various forms of linguistic and semiotic analysis. Instead, he preferred an empirical pluralism based on the study of concrete facts and values. He studied what people say and do about the world as expressions of their principles and beliefs.

> I am interested in metaphysics as a first philosophy or science of first principles. I do not think it is properly an ontology devoted to establishing certain first principles on the analogy of mathematical principles or the principles of natural philosophy; nor is it in need of a methodological propaedeutic devoted to the study of universal laws or particular values; nor does it depend on the establishment of a unified syntactic, semantic, and pragmatic, or on the construction of a universal grammar or of a general characteristical lexicon or of a moral technologized rhetoric. On the other hand, I am more interested in understanding the meanings, applications, and objectives of these programs for metaphysics than in refuting them as meaningless, impossible, or useless. They make use of ideas and methods that have always been part of the metaphysical enterprise broadly considered, and the long history of controversial opposition among them has apparently not lessened the attractiveness or reduced the effectiveness of any one of them. The metaphysics of the future should make use of

them as supplementary aspects rather than as incompatible opposites. I am convinced that the orientation of our times—in theory, practice, and art—is to the study of concrete facts of existence and experience, and I see no reason why the ontological study of principles and the epistemological study of methods should not find their propaedeutic in the study of concrete facts and values.[11]

McKeon argued that such a study would prepare the way for a new kind of inquiry that would encourage individual diversity but strengthen the philosophy of culture in troubled times of ideological division and uncertainty about the role of technology in social life.

McKeon's position on metaphysics grew out of problems that he regarded as central in twentieth-century culture. He identified these problems in various forms throughout a lifetime of work, but they all come back to a fundamental problem: the relation of the one and the many. He described his personal recognition of this problem in two autobiographical essays, offering an observation about twentieth-century culture with which others may easily identify.

> [P]hilosophic problems seemed to me to have taken on a new form from the new social, political, and moral problems of our times, and both problems, the philosophic and the practical, required a new philosophic approach. Our philosophic problems have centered, for the decades that have passed since I read Cicero and Plato together, in relativism and anti-intellectualism. . . . We are losing hold of truth because of the variety of ways in which it is expressed, and we are losing confidence in truth because of the degradations to which concepts, which were conceived to express ideals, and statements, which were thought to express truths, are put in their practical uses and manipulations.[12]

What McKeon describes is an indeterminate situation, a situation of doubt and perplexity surrounding the one and the many conceptions of truth operating in human culture. However, he turned this fundamentally indeterminate situation into a problematic situation for inquiry when he transformed the confused condition of the one and the many into the problem of order and the relation of human beings to order. McKeon's career subsequently developed around three specific forms of the problem. The first form was philosophical: our understanding of order in nature, in the relations of men, and in knowledge. The second form was educational: the preparation of men and women sensitive to the marks and uses of order. The third form was political and cultural:

the appreciation of differences in the modes in which people express order and seek fulfillment in accordance with it.[13]

Perhaps the first impression from this array of problems is that McKeon was concerned with order in the manner of classical metaphysics or ontology. Order in classical metaphysics is usually described as fixed, objective, and true, while the expression of order is described as changing, plural, and at best only partially true. Yet, this is not what McKeon means, because he explicitly states that the objectivity of facts and values is not discovered or achieved in a structure of fixities. To resolve the paradox of an objective order that is not discovered in a structure of fixities, McKeon believed that a new approach to philosophy was required, employing the ideas and methods of rhetoric as an art of communication. As a sign of this possibility, he cited the periodic emergence of rhetoric as a fundamental organizing art in culture: "Rhetoric has replaced metaphysics as an architectonic art, in the past, when the organization and application of the arts and sciences was based, not on supposed natures of things or perceived forms of thought, but on recognition of the consequences of what men say and do."[14] In this approach, order and expression are not treated as rigidly fixed and separate categories of thought. They are convertible, functional terms, best understood as places or topics of invention and discovery. In simple form, order is expression and expression is order. This echoes the classic problem of the relation of philosophy and rhetoric or wisdom and eloquence. Of course, lacking a robust philosophy of rhetoric—or a rhetoric of philosophy—in contemporary culture, the conditions for this convertibility are not easily understood. Nonetheless, McKeon believed that the conditions are potentially accessible through inquiry, and he investigated these conditions through a new science of first principles, a science that departs significantly from the classical form of metaphysics as a science of Being concerned with fixed essences and natures. As a sign of the extent of his departure, he argued that such a science has seldom if ever been developed throughout the long history of metaphysical discussion.[15]

The development of this science in McKeon's work has both biographical and philosophical dimensions. The biographical dimension deserves attention because it reveals the extent of McKeon's departure from Aristotle, a departure that demonstrates the absurdity of the occasional characterization of him by opponents as an "Aristotelian." Following World War I, McKeon observed the increasing diversity and variety of claims to truth. He also recognized, through his philosophic and scholarly studies in the United States and Europe, that any proposed statement of truth in the past has been subjected to degradation, misinterpretation, and misapplication. These combined in his mind to become the driving philosophic problem behind the understanding of order: the perplexity of the one and the many.[16]

To address this problem, he distinguished the various dimensions of discourse by which philosophies are developed and by which they are separated from each other in expression. In his words, he investigated "the aspects by which the forms of expression and proof may be differentiated and by which the criteria of continuing validity and value may be applied."[17] For McKeon, philosophies are distinguished from each other in four ways. First, they are distinguished by the subject matter addressed; second, by the methods used to treat the subject matter; third, by the assumptions and principles on which the methodical treatment of subject matter is based; and fourth, by the ends toward which such speculation is directed. Upon reflection, this is a startling set of distinctions. Taken together as the basis for studying philosophic discourse, we find no ready, robust precedent in the work of McKeon's contemporaries or recent predecessors. Indeed, if one seeks a precedent, it is perhaps best found in the history of rhetoric and in the influence of rhetoric on the course of philosophic discourse. For example, when Cicero discusses the nature of the art of rhetoric, he distinguishes the subject matter of the art, the function of the art, and the end or purpose of the art.[18] It appears that McKeon has drawn on this classic set of rhetorical distinctions and refined the middle area, broadening the function of rhetoric from civic discourse to an art of philosophic inquiry directed towards all communication. In short, he proposed to address the contemporary diversity of claims to truth in philosophy as a rhetorical problem, rather than as a logical, grammatical, or dialectical problem.[19]

This is the beginning of the perplexity and misunderstanding of McKeon by some of his contemporaries in the 1930s, 1940s, and 1950s. How many were prepared to understand the relentless and consistent development of rhetoric as a philosophic art? However, it is also the source of the continuing relevance of his work at the end of the twentieth century, when rhetoric has risen in importance as a philosophic and cultural art and when the implications of rhetoric for culture have become a subject of increasingly serious reflection. McKeon's body of work—rivaled most evidently by the work of another great American rhetorical theorist, Kenneth Burke—remains one of the few fully developed philosophies of our time based on a thoroughgoing rhetorical framework.[20]

McKeon's relationship to the philosophy of Aristotle and his departure from that philosophy emerge from the way discourse is understood and treated. The distinctions among subject matter, methods and principles, and ends are a broad framework for McKeon's study of discourse. But he refined these distinctions further, focusing on the middle area to generate some of his most important intellectual tools. For example, he added selection and interpretation to method and principle. For McKeon, these four terms—"selection," "interpretation," "method," and "principle"—are the key technical terms of semantic analysis. They are the fundamental issues of all discourse and communication, and they encompass the rhetorical act that takes place between our encounter with existence and the ends that we seek to achieve in the world. The rhetorical act involves four moments or modes of thought: we select the data, or simples, that will enter into discourse; we interpret the meaning of data to yield facts and claims of fact; we develop our interpretation by one or another method through a connected sequence of thought or action; and we base our discourse upon some principle that gives organization and fundamental significance to our communication.[21]

One may argue that McKeon did not develop a pure rhetoric, in the sense of the sophistic art that one often finds in contemporary twentieth-century rhetoricians, but a "rhetorical logic" or a "logical rhetoric."[22] The four moments of thought in the rhetorical act are a unique and innovative development of the four scientific questions of Aristotle, as those questions were transformed in the four master topics—the *constitutiones* or *quaestiones*—of Roman rhetoric and subsequently re-entered philosophic discourse.[23] *Is it?* broadens into the selection of data or simples from immediate existence. *What is it?* broadens into the interpretation of data that yields facts or claims of fact. *How is it qualified?* broadens into the question of method in creating sequences and consequences of thought and action. And, *Why?* broadens into the question of principles which organize discourse, thought, action, and things. In the biographical account of how he developed an understanding of the four differential aspects of expression, McKeon also explained how the four differentia are related to the four causes of Aristotle, adding an observation that clearly expresses the difference between his own study of causes and that of Aristotle.

> Once these differences have been elaborated, it is easy to recognize Aristotle's four causes in them; and since Aristotle has been able to find no more than four causes, there was some ground for the presumption that I should encounter no more in the writings of another two thousand years of philosophers. But whereas inquiry into the operation of causes led Aristotle to examine the first principles of being and to develop what was later to be called a metaphysics, inquiry into the operation of causes had apparently started me on an examination of first principles of philosophic discourse and to develop a form of what is now called semantics. If I had unconsciously borrowed the principles of my inquiry from Aristotle, I was committed to using them on a different subject matter.[24]

McKeon often observed that the terms and distinctions of Aristotle's philosophy have persisted throughout Western culture because of their utility in framing problems and suggesting lines of inquiry, but they have seldom been used with the meanings Aristotle intended or to the purposes that constitute Aristotelian philosophy. With this in mind, it appears that McKeon, too, has used Aristotle, but with different meanings and to different purposes.[25]

If the biographical account clarifies McKeon's relation to Aristotle, the philosophic development of McKeon's science of first principles—described in one aspect as "semantics" to distinguish it from traditional metaphysics—provides a sharp contrast with other contemporary versions of metaphysics that are often covert in their metaphysical claims. In "The Future of Metaphysics," he describes three types of metaphysical inquiry operating quietly in the twentieth century and contrasts these with a fourth, a circumstantial metaphysics of culture and communication. The three comprise skeptical, empirical, and transcendental or idealist philosophies, each asserting a metaphysical formulation of beliefs about the fundamental nature of reality, respectively based on language, materialism, and transcendental ideas.

> They are transformations of traditional beliefs that the ordering of science, action, art, and reflection is found by examining the structure of language, of things, or of ideas. Those beliefs are stated in the course of discovering and presenting the results of scientific inquiry, policy formation, moral judgment, and artistic creation and criticism. They do not require a separate inquiry, nor do they constitute the subject matter of a separate science.[26]

McKeon's final remark, that none of these forms of contemporary metaphysics requires a separate science to deal with metaphysical inquiry, deserves close attention. We will return to it later, since it has special significance for the tasks of circumstantial metaphysics. But the immediate bearing of this passage is its implication about the nature of pluralism in contemporary culture. If we interpret McKeon correctly, he implies that typical pluralism amounts to nothing more than temporary tolerance of the different beliefs that other people hold. It is tolerance based on a further belief that *they* are misguided in *their* beliefs, and that *our* beliefs, whether grounded in experience as scientists or as artists or as men and women of practical affairs, would finally be accepted as true if only others could experience what we have experienced.

In this context, philosophy is an attempt to clearly state beliefs that grow out of human activities in science, art, or practice. As McKeon observes, philosophers typically communicate with each other and with a general audience for three reasons: (1) to spread a personal vision of the truth; (2) to engage in a kind of technical or forensic critique, detecting errors of reasoning, proof, process, and procedure, and in this manner to validate or invalidate claims of fact; or (3) to speculate on the extension and consolidation of beliefs in a system. For McKeon, these are valid explorations of philosophy, but they do not address the problem of principles and order separately from the experiences out of which principles arise. In other words, they reduce human culture to language, things, or ideas, without recognition that the activity of ordering, disordering, and reordering is, itself, a central feature of culture that deserves attention in its own right. A particular order changes as human experience provides new circumstances, new perceptions of ends and purposes, and new means for living through the development of technology. But the activity of ordering, disordering, and reordering is continuous in culture, and this is a proper subject for investigation in a science of first principles. In such a study, the goal is not to establish a single order based on a reduction of culture to one or another kind of fixity. Rather, the goal is to reflect on the variety of orders that have been expressed in words and in actions and to find in those expressions the traces of ongoing inquiry into principles and operative causes—the "first" principles pursued continuously in the human community.

Circumstantial metaphysics is the science of studying all proposed principles and beliefs as the source of order in human experience. It is a study of the ecology of culture: the relations among human beings and the environment of communication and experience in which people express principles and beliefs about the world at large, seeking to order the world in words, things, ideas, and actions. This investigation is based on the diversity of human experience in all areas of endeavor. Yet, it is an independent science, because only an independent science can investigate the variety of principles that have been discovered and explored without reducing inquiry to the mere assertion of one or another of those principles. For example, how can a cognitive psychologist, who investigates the principles of thought processes occurring in the brain, assess the principles of poetic form without reducing them to principles of underlying cognitive behavior? Such a reduction would beg the question of the nature of order and principles and threaten to turn philosophers—or cognitive scientists or other investigators—into propagandists for their special field of inquiry or for their philosophic position.[27] How else can we objectively study principles in themselves than by a discipline which is independent of the many alternative principles that have been discovered or asserted in different fields of inquiry?

Similar to any other art or science, the characteristics of the science of circumstantial metaphysics may be identified by its subject matter, nature and method of investigation, and purpose or end. Its subject matter, as we have indicated, is the expression of principles and beliefs that are operative in human activity. Its nature and method is an independent and autonomous inquiry, not reducible to any of the methods or inquiries that it studies in the theoretical sciences, the domain of ethical and political action, or the fine and technological arts. Its end is wisdom and objectivity for the individual, without the need for consensus in a common ideology that reduces understanding to experience gained in the natural sciences, politics, or art.

The wisdom sought in a science of first principles is both theoretical and practical. It is theoretical in the sense that inquiry into the science of first principles is dynamic and ongoing, based on the continuous effort of individuals and groups to discover and explore principles of communication in their search for order. Circumstantial metaphysics is an ongoing investigation of the principles that human beings hold as the basis of their beliefs. It is practical in the sense that ongoing theoretical or scientific investigation also informs deliberation in all areas of human activity, where the circumstances and ends of action—as well as the new means of action provided by technology—are open to exploration in alternative directions. The understanding gained through circumstantial metaphysics in turn contributes to practical action, suggesting new alternatives or clarifying conflicts in beliefs.

However, the theoretical and practical dimensions of circumstantial metaphysics also resolve the paradox of being an individual while grasping universality or Being. The wisdom that is sought in circumstantial metaphysics is found in the unique position or standing of the individual in culture. To be a human being is to be an individual existing in coherent relationship with one's cultural context and the diversity of other human beings. To be is to be one and many.

> The unity of an ongoing philosophy of experience and humanity is a product of a plurality of perspectives focused on common experience rather than a consensus of opinions stated in a common belief. The universality it achieves is not a specification of generic inclusions but an expression of individuality or particularity placed in its context and traced through its coherences.[28]

The unique standing of an individual in culture is the only access one has to Being. We exist in communities, and communities afford us the opportunity to become our individual selves through thinking, saying, and doing.

A world community, like a cosmology, provides the conditions of our being, thinking, acting, and speaking. Objectivity is the inclusive principle of indifference by which it is recognized that being is grasped only in what we think, and say, and do about it.[29]

McKeon's use of the principle of indifference to capture the nature of objectivity in a world of communication and action is a critical recognition of the ultimate grounding of all human activities. The principle of indifference means that our thinking, saying, and doing is both a signifying of things and the things signified, with an interchangeability between the two. In an ultimate sense, to signify is to grasp the thing signified. This takes us to the roots of philosophy itself and its efforts to understand and address ambiguity in communication and logic. For example, referring to the *Categories* of Aristotle, John of Salisbury writes,

This book, more than the others, commends adherence to a principle of "indifference" [relative to variations in the meaning of words], which we always favor, and whose application is everywhere manifest to a careful student. While at one time the book is treating of things that signify, and at another of things signified, it uses their names interchangeably.[30]

One of the central problems of communication lies in how we interpret equivocal, univocal, and derivative terms across a spectrum of alternative philosophies—and how we use ambiguities to productive ends rather than seeking to crush ambiguity in favor of a single understanding of the world. For McKeon, univocal meanings are highly valued— hence, his extreme care in seeking to understand the work of other philosophers through his discipline of "philosophic and historical semantics"—but there is a deeper, consequent value in seeking to understand the irreducible ambiguities that distinguish different approaches to philosophy and that are revealed through circumstantial metaphysics. Circumstantial metaphysics leads us to the common experience of individuals.

Communication is central to the philosophy of culture because it is only through the interplay of individual perspectives that culture is continuously renewed. The activity of sharing ideas and deliberating about courses of action is the primary way in which an individual determines his or her unique standing in culture and, at the same time, contributes to the advancement of a common culture.

Culture is the framework within which many cultures are developed, interact, and communicate; the facts and values of culture and of cultures are seen and felt from the point of view of the individual man formed by his immediate culture. Common experiences and encountered existences are shared and stated in particular selections of facts and values. In this reorientation from fixed modes of being or fixed modes of thought to modes of action and statement, many of the old dichotomies of being and becoming, of reality and appearance, of objective and subjective, become dynamic functional relations rather than antinomical obstructions.[31]

McKeon's emphasis on the unique standing of the individual in culture appears to be in accord with the tendency of so-called postmodernist thought, which holds that the unifying ideals of modernism have failed to achieve an improvement in the human condition and that common or shared ideals are an illusion. However, McKeon's pluralism and philosophy of culture stand in stark contrast to such thought. Instead of arguing for a deconstructed or disintegrated view of contemporary culture in which the individual is isolated, he argues for increased participation in a common debate. The goal of this debate is not the creation of a new ideology. Nor is the goal one of consensus in a new set of beliefs about the nature of reality, which seems to be the only alternative to individuality or to the tribal and sectarian identity conceived in postmodernist thinking. The goal is continued exploration of the activity of ordering, with the introduction of new perspectives that may give unexpected insight into common problems and common values.

> The philosophic problem is not one for the speculation of the isolated scholar engaged in the construction of a personal doctrine. It depends for its statement and examination on the participation by a broadly educated public and on testing of basic doctrines and values against the fundamental presuppositions of other philosophies, religions, systems of values, and modes of life. Philosophic universality is easy to achieve by reducing all other views to the requirements and limits of one preferred creed and system, but it distorts the doctrines it refutes; and a similar easy and violent victory in imposing uniformity in political practices, with its consequences in suppression and hostility, is the only alternative to a political universality based on common understanding and on common values.[32]

McKeon's science of first principles is important in this context precisely because it turns attention away from disputes about beliefs and ideologies and toward the activity of ordering in the concrete circumstances of problems and experiences. The activity of ordering, disordering, and reordering in a wide community does not privilege one principle or belief over another. Rather, the activity is an ongoing exploration of possible principles, with continuous deliberation about their suitability in addressing common problems in particular circumstances. Danger arises when the community is too small or when individuals holding opposing views are inadvertently or deliberately prevented from participation. For McKeon, there is a corrective inherent in pluralism. The corrective does not come from temporary tolerance, the weak form of typical pluralism discussed earlier. It comes from the inevitable discovery of new possibilities for order when a subject is discussed from many perspectives.

> The philosophy of culture is a pluralistic interplay of ideas and methods, of facts and values, of commitments and inquiries. It is a quest, not for ideological consensus but for common problems to be examined in a variety of perspectives which focus on different aspects of a common problem and contribute to its reformulation and resolution and to the discovery of new problems in ongoing continuous sequence. It is a structure to which international discussions and congresses are admirably adapted, for it provides a rationale for the selection of the common problems to which they may be addressed in the constitution and enrichment of a renewing philosophy of culture.[33]

McKeon argues that the search for principles is always evident in human activity. Therefore, we may conclude that it is underway in contemporary culture as well. However, the search for principles today is the opposite of what many people expected it to be, based on their understanding of what the search has been in the past.[34] A proper scientific investigation of first principles does not lead to an ideology or to the systematization of a particular set of beliefs—theological, scientific, political, or aesthetic. Rather, it leads to further inquiry and to the renewed uses of philosophy in extending deliberation in matters of science, art, and policy. If our dilemma is how to achieve an order that does not stifle and oppress the individual, then we must understand and cultivate the activities of ordering, disordering, and reordering. This is what McKeon pursued in addressing the three interconnected problems of philosophy, education, and politics and culture.

Perplexity and Problems, Semantics and Inquiry

McKeon's work was so complete a departure from the practice of philosophy in his time that few contemporaries understood the direction of his work. Indeed, the frustration which many felt with the rhetorical and circumstantial dimension of his philosophy—in contrast with the fixities ordinarily ascribed to the old metaphysics and quietly smuggled into supposedly antimetaphysical philosophies of the twentieth century—is evident in one of the common complaints about him made by former students and colleagues, admirers and opponents, alike: he never takes a position on the issues that he discusses. This much is true as the basis for the complaint: he goes out of his way to ensure that a full array of alternative positions are represented in any discussion. If a position is not represented among actual interlocutors, he frequently voices the strongest alternative arguments that could be made. Thus, his writings typically present several perspectives on an issue. As a result, the impression is that McKeon takes no position of his own, and readers—caught up in the intricacies of alternative views—exercise little ingenuity in discovering the broader pattern of his position.

McKeon's implacable commitment to pluralism was often regarded as an annoying habit, and it distressed even some of the greatest admirers of his work. Instead of tolerance and intellectual honesty, it seems that they wanted a short-term rhetorical victory for his position and were not willing to stay the course of scientific inquiry, even McKeon's form of scientific inquiry. It was a doubly annoying habit for opponents who wanted a victory against his position or a vindication of their own but could not find a simple stance in his work to attack. Therefore, a further complaint is that McKeon's form of pluralism created needless perplexity without resolution. As if to compound the frustration of friends and opponents, alike, McKeon cheerfully accepted the accusation of creating philosophic perplexity. However, he gave a surprising turn to the idea and, characteristically, elevated the discussion to the nature of philosophy itself. "The Greeks thought that philosophy begins in wonder, and perplexity is an avenue to wonder. I have no objection to being detected in the enterprise of arousing perplexity."[35]

McKeon's explanation of the place of perplexity in his thought deserves attention, since it presents in unambiguous detail his view of the nature of philosophic discussion and, particularly, his way of shaping philosophic discussion in many of his essays and articles.

> A perplexity in a well-defined field is easily understood, but a perplexity which leaves no fixed meanings or references needs to be explained, if its purpose is more than merely to show that things are not as simple as they seem. . . . [I]ts purpose is to distinguish the task of stating and solving philosophic problems from the task of verifying and falsifying

> philosophic statements, that is, to separate philosophic inquiry from philosophic semantics.[36]

The distinction between inquiry and semantics is central to McKeon's thought. It is his equivalent of the classic distinction between invention and judgment, expressing a general philosophic issue which takes a variety of forms in traditional intellectual arts such as logic, grammar, rhetoric, and dialectic.

Semantics is an activity of judgment concerned with the examination of statements. It takes two forms, corresponding to whether the judgment is about what others have said or what we ourselves say. The first form is historical semantics: the analysis and interpretation of what others have said. It involves the examination of statements and their meanings determined by the relation of statements to what they are intended to signify. Historical semantics includes an appropriate recognition that the statements of others are properly judged in the immediate cultural context of related and opposed meanings applied to related situations and objects. The second form is philosophic semantics: the expression of one's own view of truth in a particular set of preferred terms, often with a philosophic characterization of alternative positions that may be related to historical semantics. It involves the expression of meaning determined by the relation of statements to truth or to what one believes to be true. In both forms of semantics, historical and philosophic, the activity of judgment is one of verifying or falsifying statements within a system of beliefs and the preferred terminology employed to express those beliefs. In essence, semantics is comparable to the rhetorical experience of reading a speech by another speaker, whether that speaker is ourself or someone else.

In contrast, inquiry is comparable to planning a new speech on a matter where no decision has yet been reached and where the audience is open to a new view. Inquiry is an activity of invention concerned with stating and solving substantive philosophic problems about what is and what is to be done. Unlike semantics, inquiry does not begin in belief or in the certainties embedded in a preferred terminology. It begins in perplexity, uncertainty, and doubt. It begins where prior semantic certainties and beliefs break down in confrontation with new circumstances. This is an indeterminate situation, and it cannot be resolved merely through an extension of old terminology. Rather, it requires a fundamental reconsideration of assumptions, principles, and beliefs. This leads to the formulation of new problems that transform the indeterminate into something problematic. And, eventually, this leads to a new semantic formulation to express the understanding gained through investigation.

Semantics and inquiry are closely related for McKeon, but they differ in a key respect: semantics express what inquiry discovers. This relation is elaborated by McKeon when he explains the relationship between invention and judgment.

> Invention is the art of discovering new arguments and uncovering new things by argument, while judgment is the art of testing arguments, proving conclusions, and verifying statements. In the context of inquiry and invention, judgment adds to the demonstrative arts of deducing from assumptions, the deliberative arts of examining consequences, and the judicial arts of falsifying alternatives, while invention extends from the construction of formal arguments to all modes of enlarging experience by reason as manifested in awareness, emotion, interest, and appreciation.[37]

Inquiry and invention are more useful than, and certainly prior in nature to, semantics and judgment. Inquiry is the origin and source of new ideas; it establishes the fundamental connection between human beings and their environment. Indeed, inquiry is the corrective for dogmatic entrapment in rigid beliefs that become disconnected or dissociated from the objective circumstances of experience and culture. Yet, most reading, discussion, and writing, McKeon suggests, takes place in the metarealm of semantics and judgment, where substantive problems of what is and what is to be done are transmuted into semantic problems of what we say and what we intend. In other words, most discussion is merely semantic analysis of what others say—or what we, ourselves, mean to say—cut off from the problems of inquiry that give significance to semantics. This is one reason why a circumstantial, rhetorical metaphysics is needed: to improve the level of semantic analysis and to distinguish semantics from philosophic inquiry so that philosophic discussion may resume a productive course. By itself, rhetoric helps us to understand communication from person to person, and in this context semantic analysis tends to focus on the creation and projection of meaning in signs, symbols, and gestures that we share with each other. In contrast, inquiry tends to focus on the environment within which the human being lives, treating the environment—both physical and cultural—as a medium within which we do, think, and feel. Rhetorical metaphysics seeks to reestablish the productive relationship between communication and experience that is sometimes lost in terminological disputes. More than this, however, rhetorical metaphysics points toward the sense in which our cultural environment is the medium of our lives—not a world of natural forces or eternal truths but an evolutionary clay with which we engage in a continuous reconstruction of experience, as Dewey suggests.[38]

Rejoining semantics and inquiry in proper relationship means redis-covering the relationship between rhetoric and philosophy.

McKeon, Dewey, and Pragmatism

As a former student of Dewey at Columbia, McKeon believed that his own work was best understood in the tradition of American pragmatic philosophy. There is considerable merit in this view and it goes a long way toward contextualizing his innovative exploration of rhetoric and the ecology of culture. The key lies in the concept of culture and in a problem that Dewey may not have entirely foreseen: through a reduc-tion to ideology, culture would too often in human affairs replace nature as the source of fixed and unchanging order in philosophy and politics.

McKeon's view of the intimate connection between inquiry and phi-losophy parallels the view expressed by Dewey, who argued that philos-ophy must take on a new role in formulating problems for inquiry in a period when the old metaphysical fixities have been put aside in favor of a new experimental approach to knowledge based on experience.

> Inquiry, in settling the disturbed relation of organism-envi-ronment (which defines doubt) does not merely remove doubt by recurrence to a prior adaptive integration. It insti-tutes new environing conditions that occasion new problems. What the organism learns during this process produces new powers that make new demands upon the environment. In short, as special problems are resolved, new ones tend to emerge. There is no such thing as a final settlement, because every settlement introduces the conditions of some degree of a new unsettling. In the stage of development marked by the emergence of science, deliberate institution of problems be-comes an objective of inquiry. Philosophy, in case it has not lost touch with science, may play an important role in deter-mining formulations of these problems and in suggesting hy-pothetical solutions. But the moment philosophy supposes it can find a final and comprehensive solution, it ceases to be inquiry and becomes either apologetics or propaganda.[39]

The new role of philosophy identified in this passage is a consequence of the so-called second Copernican revolution, described by Dewey as a re-orientation of the object of knowledge from fixed orders of Being or in-herent essences and natures to orders of change. Knowledge, he argued, now depends on the ability of science to produce facts experimentally, through "operations deliberately undertaken in conformity with a plan or project that has the properties of a working hypothesis."⁴⁰ However, the difficulty is that in the new orientation of knowledge there has been a tendency to substitute an equally fixed and rigid metaphysical distinction, the distinction between subject and object. Having discarded the distinction between the eternal and the changing, which is characteristic of the old metaphysics, modern thought has persistently substituted the distinction between "supposedly subjective and objective orders of Being."⁴¹ The human being, Dewey observed, becomes the extranatural knowing subject, set over the natural world as object. In philosophy, this leads to the dogmatic belief that there is a final and comprehensive solution to the problems of knowing, doing, and making, rather than the ongoing search and re-search of inquiry. Alternatively, it leads to the equally dogmatic belief in antiintellectual relativism: a distrust of analytical statements and rational proof and a belief that sensitivity and good intentions are enough for the individual and society.

To overcome the rigid distinction between subject and object, Dewey explains the sense in which human beings are not outside of the orders of change that they seek to understand but are part of it, through the intentional operations of inquiry. This is the shift that is characteristic of the second Copernican revolution.

> The old center was mind knowing by means of an equipment of powers complete within itself, and merely exercised upon an antecedent external material equally complete in itself. The new center is indefinite interactions taking place within a course of nature which is not fixed and complete, but which is capable of direction to new and different results through the mediation of intentional operations . . . There is a moving whole of interacting parts; a center emerges wherever there is an effort to change them in a particular direction. . . .
>
> . . . Mind is no longer a spectator beholding the world from without and finding its highest satisfaction in the joy of self-sufficing contemplation. The mind is within the world as part of the latter's on-going process. It is marked off as mind by the fact that wherever it is found, changes take place in a *directed* way, so that a movement in a definite one-way sense—from the doubtful and confused to the clear, resolved and settled—takes place. From knowing as an outside beholding to knowing as an active participant in the drama of an on-moving world is the historical transition whose record we have been following.⁴²

In Dewey's new philosophy, subject and object are not fixed categories but convertible and functional terms. The knowing subject easily becomes an object of knowledge, and the objects of knowledge, created through the intentional operations of inquiry, become the means and the subject matter for further inquiry.[43] The pattern of conversion is precisely the changing functional relation of order and expression in McKeon's philosophical rhetoric: principles become the subject of inquiry through their expression, and the study of expression gives rise to the pluralistic investigation of principles. Or, as McKeon says, the objectivity of facts and values is not discovered in a structure of fixities but in an ongoing development of achievement and invention.

As we suggested earlier, however, Dewey may not have foreseen that culture would eventually replace nature as the fixed and unchanging object in twentieth-century thought, creating a new kind of philosophic dilemma. How could culture, which Dewey regarded as another term for "experience" in his philosophy, become rigid and unchanging? The answer lies in the circumstances and use of language. For Dewey, culture is an essential part of the existential matrix of inquiry. "Problems which induce inquiry grow out of the relations of fellow human beings to one another, and the organs for dealing with these relations are not only the eye and ear, but the meanings which have developed in the course of living, together with the ways of forming and transmitting culture with all its constituents of tools, arts, institutions, traditions and customary beliefs."[44] Language, which is the means of capturing meaning, has an intrinsic connection with the community of action, and it is instrumental in the interaction of organism and environment. Indeed, culture is both a condition and a product of language. However, Dewey observed that written language tends to be the model of communication, leading to the separation of thought from communal operations and action.[45] The influence of written language as the model of communication amounts to an ongoing tendency towards the "hypostatization of Reason," which is evident in the formation of cultural, philosophic, and political ideologies.

Dewey believed his theory of logic adequately addressed this problem, allowing the continued development of the new kind of philosophy that he proposed. In retrospect, however, it may not have accomplished as much as he hoped in this direction. He may have underestimated the power of language to become detached from the ongoing flow of experience—that is, to become the vehicle for ideology, fixing culture in a seemingly changeless order and structure of thought that blocks inquiry. As a consequence, his tools of logic and inquiry were ground up among the blades of competing theories of grammar, linguistics, and symbolic logic, each based on a covert metaphysics of the type identified by McKeon. Indeed, one may argue that McKeon's conception of the problem of the one and the many—of order and expression in cultural process—emerges as a fundamental issue that must be resolved for continuation of the project of pragmatic philosophy. Where Dewey had confidence in the power of action to overcome ideological rigidity by infusing life with new experience, McKeon saw the value of a refined understanding of invention to inform new action. This is more than a methodological difference between Dewey and McKeon. It is ultimately a difference of principles, with Dewey emphasizing a pragmatic actional principle that tends to reduce theory to practice and with McKeon preferring to treat theoretical and practical problems separately in order to explore their productive, reflexive relationships. Therefore, while McKeon's work is perhaps best understood in the tradition of American pragmatic philosophy, it also represents a significant departure and development of that philosophy, with a subtle reminder of C. S. Peirce's distinction between theory and practice in his concept of pragmaticism and in his development of speculative rhetoric.[46]

The relation of theory and practice is where McKeon's philosophy begins, and this is where a new level of perplexity becomes important, shaped more explicitly by the art of rhetoric rather than formal logic.[47] Perplexity is the beginning point on the path toward the reformulation of problems and questions for inquiry. It is both a sign that further inquiry is needed and a tool to promote inquiry, in the sense that perplexity, methodically cultivated, may turn discussion from unproductive disputes that are fundamentally disputes over semantics and ideology into new problems of inquiry and philosophy that involve the invention of arguments suited to new situations of thought and action.

McKeon's form of perplexity involves the method of invention, adapted from rhetoric and directed toward the identification of questions, issues, and problems of philosophy prior to semantics and judgment.

> Method is needed in invention to define the question and to order the data pertinent to it. The distinction between the questions of philosophy and those of rhetoric may then be stated as an antithesis or as an assimilation of the two kinds of questions when rhetoric is transmuted into philosophy. Kinds of questions must be distinguished without predetermining the properties which will be found in the subject matter as a result of later discovery, and places must be formulated appropriate to the kinds of issues without anticipating the answers which will be discovered and explored by the use of them.[48]

The value of this activity lies precisely in avoiding dogmatic entrapment in ideology and unexamined assumptions and beliefs. It is not the end of philosophic discussion but the beginning, and it is relevant not only for professional philosophers but for that much larger group of nonprofessional philosophers who are engaged in concrete work in the arts, sciences, and practical affairs—thoughtful individuals who seek to "relate what they think, say, and do to contexts larger than the immediate consequences they anticipate or encounter."[49] In personal terms, McKeon explains his use of perplexity in this way:

> The question of the uses of perplexity is very close to the question of the nature of philosophic discussion. Why do I engage in philosophic discussion? What is my purpose? Is it to achieve understanding and to spread the truth as I see it? If that were my purpose, philosophic discussion, even in selected and enlightened company, is not a very efficient way of attaining it. . . . Discussion is neither a chain of understandings nor a chaos of misunderstandings; it is a complex of crossed monologues which occasionally spark, for a period of time or a period of discourse, into dialogue. This is the reason why I engage in discussion and use perplexity as a spark to melt the crossed monologues of semantic disquisition into a dialogue of philosophic inquiry. Even when I do not succeed in altering the course of the discussion at the meeting, I can take the fused bits of junctions home in memory, and discover what I did not understand, at some stages of the disputation, and get new insight into problems that had been discussed or that should have been discussed.[50]

Is McKeon's intellectual habit of tolerance and creating perplexity a personal vice or a virtue of philosophy? If the task of philosophy is merely to express beliefs, then his habit is clearly a vice, based on a questionable belief in the value of mere eclecticism and a desire to show that things are not as simple as they seem. He would do better to participate in the factionalism of the various schools of philosophy and assert his own beliefs in the war of many against many. In contrast, if the task of philosophy is to know and to investigate what is alleged to be known as orders of change, then McKeon's habit is a virtuous and disciplined practice of philosophic art, suited to confront a world of ideological fixities. It is not only appropriate but essential if one is to perpetuate the activity of knowing, seeking to spark discussion into a dialogue of philosophic inquiry that continually probes the nature of a Being that is knowable only in what we think, say, and do about it.

McKeon argues that a science of first principles is meaningless only if philosophy is unified in one science. In such a case, there would be no need for an independent, ongoing scientific investigation of principles, because principles would merely express beliefs about the nature of reality gained from the experience of some other science that one believes is more fundamental and more closely connected to being.[51] But if philosophy is not unified in a single science, then a science of first principles is not only meaningful but essential. It is the key to understanding the diversity of orders that are discovered and created in human activities in all of the arts and sciences. To this point, empirical evidence suggests that principles are exceptionally diverse in the ecology of culture, and, furthermore, that patterns and types of ordering recur across a wide range of human experiences in all times and places. Indeed, it is the plurality of principles proposed and defended in the course of inquiry in all areas of culture, as well as the persistent recurrence of patterns of ordering, that leads McKeon to their independent investigation.

McKeon's goal is the perpetual restoration of the *ecology* of culture, after reductions of culture to particular ideologies and rigid forms.[52] In the new turn of the revolution that began in the early decades of the twentieth century, culture is not a fixed ideology existing outside the individual. Culture is the center of indefinite interactions taking place within a world that is capable of direction to new and different results through inquiry. Culture is the activity of ordering, disordering, and reordering; it is what we do individually and collectively through communication when we take individual perspectives on common problems.

The Ecology of Culture and the Organization of Learning

For McKeon, the investigation of circumstantial metaphysics gives rise not only to a science of first principles but to a new organization of learning that is more adapted to the ecology of culture than the various organizations of knowledge that are inherited from the past. In the twentieth century, the organization of knowledge is usually based on facts, as stated in what are believed to be true substantive propositions. This perspective leads to an organization of knowledge that is typically divided into branches of science, periods of history, and forms of poetry and other arts of making. Other organizations are equally possible. Indeed, depending on the nature of the "facts" that are stated in true substantive propositions, different organizations of knowledge reflect principled divisions that are carried forward into institutions, professional societies, and culture at large. Philosophers and educators debate these organizations from time to time, and some reformations are particularly influential. Bacon's organization of the arts and sciences for the advancement of learning is one of many examples that have been carried into the contemporary world. But in the twentieth century, facts and claims of fact have expanded exponentially, until the possibility of integrative understanding and wisdom in action are threatened or rendered impossible. The traditional organizations of knowledge offer less and less help in providing integrations that are productive and relevant for the human community.

For McKeon, traditional and contemporary organizations of knowledge deserve study in their own right. They are part of the scientific study of principles in human culture, because they are expressions of beliefs and values gained through individual experience and often perpetuated in institutions and cultures without examination. Regarding their influence, he observes: "the education of a time and a people is a philosophy stated in genetic form and it serves to organize available knowledge and cogent beliefs in a kind of metaphysics of habitually accepted principles of action."[53] This indicates the perspective from which McKeon chose to study the ecology of culture, and it also indicates the perspective from which he proposed a new organization of learning rather than an organization of knowledge. Instead of studying the facts stated in true substantive propositions, he chose to study "the facts which marked the constitution and construction of a philosophically true substantive proposition."[54] In essence, he explored the organization of learning by the moments of the rhetorical act of constituting and constructing communication, creating a new kind of rhetorical *paedia* for the philosophy of culture.

The organization of learning and the problems of education are intertwined in the philosophy of culture and communication. "Most of the studies we prepare for a student in school and college, even when they are intended to stimulate his creativity and inventiveness, train him in a mastery of what is known, with little concern with the transition from the known to the unknown. We teach him how to solve problems, but not to discover problems, to explore the places of memory to the neglect of the places of invention, whereas problems are encountered and considered only if problem-solving is joined to problem-discovery."[55] The challenge is to discover new disciplines that give access to what is already known but orient thinking and action towards the problems of the unknown. Arguably, this is what is now underway in education with the merging of traditional disciplines and the transformation of their subject matters and methods. But the heat of current debate, involving so-called "culture wars" and the political battles between conservative factions and underprivileged or underrepresented peoples and classes, tends to obscure the broader pattern that McKeon observed. In the new circumstances of the philosophy of culture, he asked:

> What are the new disciplines, in the sense of subjects of inquiry, that are brought to our attention by considering the culture and problems of mankind? What are the new

disciplines, in the sense of arts and abilities, that will contribute to knowledge, art, community, and communication by transforming them and making them relevant to a developing world culture and to an altering organization of arts and science, technologies and politics?[56]

Consistent with the moments of the rhetorical act, McKeon argued that there are four subjects of inquiry in the new organization of learning. They are the stages in forming a complete communication in any area of human experience. *Topic* is the study of how people select and name data from what is encountered immediately in experience. One usually takes this selection for granted in studying what others have done, but it is the source of innovation and creativity, since what we select for examination may reorient perception and exploration, opening one's eyes to new problems and possibilities. *Hypothesis* is the study of how people have interpreted meaning in what they experience. It is the study of facts and how facts are constituted in communication by hypothesis and judgment. *Theme* is the study of connections among facts and the arts, sciences, and methods by which humans have stated facts and traced coherence in facts. It is the study of the sequences and consequences that are explored in discourse, action, and process. *Thesis* is the study of the principles that organize communication and experience into wholes and parts, giving fundamental significance to some facts rather than others. These four subjects of inquiry—topics, hypotheses, themes, and theses—do not exclude the study of what is already known. Indeed, they are significant only when explored in the context of what has already been said, written, and done in human culture. But the orientation is ultimately toward the unknown, toward how the individual student may find his or her own way in using what has been said and done to new purposes in addressing new problems.[57]

Doubtless some of the exhilaration that people felt when they heard McKeon speak, or feel when they read his essays, comes from the way he combines ideas and methods from a wide array of authors and disciplinary traditions when discussing a philosophic problem. He breaks conventional associations and suggests unexpected relationships that are intelligent and intriguing, often stimulating to new thinking. McKeon argued that the ability for innovation lies in most people and requires only cultivation through new ventures in education. The new organization of learning that he proposed and explored in his writing, teaching, and curricular reforms is the basis for such education.

This is why McKeon also included within the new organization of learning a set of intellectual arts that may be cultivated in the student. There are four arts, based on the need to distinguish different objectives and the use of different tools appropriate to each art. McKeon gives many different names to these arts throughout his writings, implying that the importance of these arts does not depend on what they are called but on what they allow individuals to do. What is perhaps most significant for the philosophy of culture is that all of the arts have an important connection with an expanded philosophical rhetoric. McKeon argued that the intellectual arts in our time are in the process of becoming arts of communication and action, variously understood and cultivated—and variously named, sometimes with traditional titles, sometimes with radically new titles, and frequently mixed and merged with borrowings of devices and tools that are put to new uses. In his later work, there is seldom a major essay in education and the philosophy of culture in which these arts are not named and described as new liberal arts.[58] From a broad perspective, the ecology of culture is unintelligible without understanding the continuous transformation of the arts of knowing, doing, and making.

While traditional organizations of knowledge seek to capture the facts about metaphysically stable subject matters, McKeon's organization of learning cuts across traditional organizations. He points toward the circumstantial nature of these organizations and the need for a more flexible organization that accords with new problems and a new philosophy of culture. "Since differences of subject-matter are produced by discovering and justifying answers to questions, the arts and sciences will not be organized according to differences in the subject-matter which they treat, but according to differences of questions, action, statement, valuation, and judgment. . . . A productive architectonic art produces subject-matters and organizes them in relation to each other and to the problems to be solved."[59] In the framework of his organization of learning, McKeon did not propose a synthesis of different philosophic approaches, whether among the schools of professional philosophers or the practices of thoughtful men and women in different fields of activity. Indeed, he argued that such a synthesis is impossible.[60] What he sought was a way to discover relations among different approaches so that an individual could avoid dogmatic entrapment in covert metaphysical beliefs and productively use pluralism to support new ways of thinking and acting.

Closure and Action

There is no conclusion to the study of circumstantial metaphysics. Circumstances change, and the search for order goes on through the work of disordering and reordering. But there is closure, based on more than the mere cessation of activities. Closure comes with each experience through the formation of an individual human being who is better prepared for action in new circumstances. For this reason, every essay and book by McKeon ends with a call to renewed action or a statement of the problems which must be overcome if one is to initiate action in the new circumstances that are created as a result of inquiry. The goal of philosophy and education is to "make men free in action, responsible in society, and wise in the pursuit of knowledge."[61]

McKeon's contribution to the development of American pragmatic philosophy requires further exploration in order to be well understood, but his contribution to the ongoing development of rhetoric in addressing the problems of contemporary culture is more easily understood. He showed, through argument and example, how rhetoric may be reformed and re-formed as a central art in the philosophy of culture.[62] The key lies in overcoming the separation between thought and expression that is a sign of our present cultural dilemmas. As a verbal art, rhetoric is a minor discipline among the other arts and sciences, typically confined in our universities to courses in English composition, technical writing, and service programs such as writing-across-the-curriculum. As an art of thought, joined to diverse forms of verbal as well as nonverbal expression, rhetoric becomes a source of innovation in addressing substantive problems in any field of thought or action. McKeon's contribution is through his philosophic investigations of circumstantial metaphysics and the ecology of culture. He restored thought to legitimacy in the rhetorical arts and showed how the rhetorical arts may be expanded beyond the bounds of a narrow technical discipline of verbal expression. He showed how philosophic thought is constructed through rhetorical acts in all areas of culture and how those acts lead to consequences for understanding and action.

MCKEON'S CONTRIBUTIONS TO THE PHILOSOPHY OF SCIENCE

Walter Watson

Richard McKeon wrote many articles on science and its relationship to philosophy. Since his articles on science are scattered and may be difficult to obtain, and since they have in any case received relatively little attention, I shall here give a brief account of them and indicate what I take to be their importance. Since philosophers generally have doctrines, and among them a doctrine about science, or a philosophy of science, it might seem that we could not do better than bring together the results of McKeon's articles in a unified and clearly formulated philosophy of science. Even a slight acquaintance with McKeon's philosophy, however, would suggest some doubts about this project. In the first place, it may be questioned whether McKeon's philosophy is properly a doctrine at all and does not rather belong with the nondoctrinal philosophies of the skeptical and rhetorical traditions—deconstruction, for example. And if its parts are semantics, topics, arts, and inquiry, it would seem that the philosophy of science is not a separable part of McKeon's philosophy, in which case to construct his philosophy of science would already be to depart from his philosophy. And if the philosophy of science is supposed to be concerned with the interpretation of science, this again departs from McKeon's views, for he conceived philosophy as already operative in scientific inquiries rather than as adding interpretation to their results. Describing the changes in the circumstances of philosophy that had taken place while he was pursuing his semantic inquiries into patterns of philosophical ideas and methods, McKeon says,

> Philosophy had progressed in its cultivation of technical disciplines. The discipline of philosophy had become distinct from the disciplines of the subjects that were treated in the philosophy of history, or the philosophy of language, or the philosophy of science. The historian of philosophy sought objectivity by avoiding commitment to a philosophy or by using his philosophy to identify the errors of the past; and scientists like Planck, Einstein, Bohr, Born, Schroedinger, and Heisenberg recognized the importance of philosophy by constructing philosophies for themselves as part of their scientific inquiries, while the interpretation of science was distinct from science in the philosophy of science. My studies were not history, or philosophy, or science, as they were understood in the newly changed circumstances of philosophy.[1]

McKeon's treatment of science differs from the prevailing philosophies of science not only in the way it is conceived. Nearly all of his articles on science advance views that are paradoxical in the sense of being opposed to received opinion. In this field his heterodoxy, not to say heresy, is particularly apparent, and his work illustrates what seems on the way to becoming his most famous remark, "I have always been a neoteric."[2] It should not be supposed, however, that to be opposed to received opinion means to be opposed to tradition, for the received opinion may be as wrong about tradition as about anything else. For McKeon, as for the Socrates of Plato's *Apology*, innovation and tradition are inseparable.

It is not so much the heterodoxy of McKeon's views concerning the nature and content of the philosophy of science that must give one pause in attempting to present them, however, as the way he himself has presented them. Each of his articles stands on its own as exemplifying a distinct possibility for inquiry, and nowhere are they brought together as parts of a systematic whole. Doubtless all the articles reflect the same fundamental convictions, but these are nowhere stated as such.

In these circumstances, if we are to stay as close as possible to McKeon's own mode of presentation, we can best proceed by surveying his articles in this field individually and in the order of their publication. This will permit attention both to the continuity of his work as an ongoing inquiry sustained over a period of many years and to the distinctive approach developed in each article. Reflections on the series as a whole may be reserved until after the articles have been examined individually.

At the outset of his career, in "Spinoza and Experimental Science" (1928),[3] McKeon undertook, in opposition to the prevailing empiricism, the unpromising task of resuscitating Benedict de Spinoza's ignored or forgotten arguments against Robert Boyle and the experimental method in general. McKeon examines the exchanges between Spinoza and Boyle, through Henry Oldenburg, in detail, and shows why each side found the other inadequate, although both were defensible in their own terms. It is clear from this account that Spinoza's criticism of the experimental method is integral to McKeon's philosophy and does not belong in a distinct philosophy of science and also that the philosophy of science as McKeon conceives it must be broad enough to have a place for the mathematical method of Spinoza, as well as for the experimental method of Boyle. Of Spinoza's position, McKeon says,

> In an age which glorified itself for having discovered the importance of observation and which had worked itself rapidly to the belief that all the secrets of nature might be forced out by manipulation of things, Spinoza held strictly to the requirements of rational speculation. His confidence in the mathematical method is only a symptom of his attitude: that all truths are so related to each other that they may be derived from a few postulates; that the method to discover the nature of things is to proceed carefully and on adequate warrant of inference from clear and simple ideas to others implied in them; and that the ways in which things affect the senses can reveal nothing of their nature.[4]

In "The Empiricist and Experimentalist Temper in the Middle Ages: A Prolegomenon to the Study of Mediaeval Science" (1929),[5] published in a volume of essays honoring John Dewey, McKeon again challenges prevailing preconceptions by exhibiting the empiricist and experimentalist temper of the Middle Ages. The facts and observations of the Middle Ages, McKeon argues, fit into an elaborate system of theory and explanation which gives them an interpretative significance comparable with that of the facts of later science. But since facts do not exist separate from the system of thought to which they are proper, these facts are not the facts of the modern world. Observation depends on thought no less than thought depends on observation.

There are, McKeon says, two traditions of science in the Middle Ages, based respectively on different types of causes—efficient causes and formal and final causes. The one is the tradition of technologies, the other of analogical explanation.

In the tradition of the technologies and the crafts was perpetuated the expert knowledge of how things are made, and
in that tradition the explanations of things are, therefore, in
terms of their efficient causes. The tradition of analogical explanation from which poetry, theology, magic, and astrology
grew, differed from the tradition of the technologies in that it
sought to explain the qualities of a thing by the essence of the
thing and sought therefore to know forms, not to produce
objects. The analogies of the one tradition and the efficien-
cies of the other were, of course, brought together eventually, and the explanation and the magic of modern science
resulted. But the efforts of the great thinkers of the middle
ages were exerted in varying ways to prevent the confusion
of the two traditions, for it was everywhere the conviction
that things and even events could not be explained by external and efficient causes.[6]

The philosophical study of science in this account is inseparable from
the study of philosophy, and philosophy and science are joined by their
common concern with causes.

The contrast between considering things in terms of their origin and
in terms of what they are that is presented in "The Empiricist and
Experimentalist Temper in the Middle Ages" reappears in "De Anima:
Psychology and Science" (1930).[7] Two conceptions of science, and the
psychologies that correspond to them, are distinguished. Speaking of the
prevailing psychology, McKeon says,

If science is formulated in the terms of psychology, it is the effect of sensation and experience ordered in the mind, or the active resolution of problems to which experience gives rise. But
if the sciences are considered in terms of what they are, rather
than in terms of their origin, that is, as bodies of knowledge
stable in propositions ordered in certain relations, they are
not caused by the data that enters into them . . . , but by the
ordering principle by which they are arranged. The sciences
are the effects of the soul which is potentially all things.[8]

The second conception of science, as bodies of knowledge ordered by
principles, requires the soul as a principle. The soul as defined by
Aristotle is a sound scientific concept, but this was not generally appreciated in 1930, even (or perhaps especially) by psychologists, and
McKeon's defense of the soul as a scientific concept is, in the audacity
with which it challenges accepted views, of a piece with his defense of
Spinoza's criticism of experiment and his account of the empiricism of

medieval thought. The use of the term "soul" in psychology is of course supported by Sigmund Freud as well as Aristotle, although James Strachey in *The Standard Edition of the Complete Psychological Works of Sigmund Freud* (1953–74) everywhere translates "*Seele*" as "mind" and "*seelisch*" as "mental." It was not until 1982 that Bruno Bettelheim pointed out that this is one of a set of mistranslations that systematically distort Freud in the interests of a particular conception of science. "Of all the mistranslations," Bettelheim says, "not one has hampered our understanding of Freud's humanistic views more than the elimination of his references to the soul (*die Seele*)."[9] McKeon, however, defends the concept of soul not for its humanistic but for its scientific value. He argues that the reflexivity by which the mind knows itself, and which leads to the logical paradoxes, makes a science of the rational soul impossible. Nevertheless, the recognition of the existence of the soul makes possible a theory of science that treats science not in terms of its genesis from data but in terms of its ordering by principles, and such a theory of science has its chief advantage over its rival in the recognition it permits of the characteristic activity of the soul reflecting on itself.

> The problem of the nature of science, in any case, is seen most sharply revealed in the science of psychology itself, for that science purports to study in part at least the faculty by which science is possible. To psychology without a soul, a science of the soul is meaningless; science itself, save in the sense of an ordering of data, is impossible; and true and false become terms of unending dispute and relativity. If the place of the soul is recognized, it is still impossible to have a science of the soul, since there are no self-evident propositions suitable to generate a demonstrative science of the soul, and the problematic propositions which experience might suggest are parts of the soul, not its principles. But the recognition of the nature of the soul will permit the statement of a theory of science that will transcend the mere statement of data collected and ordered; it will permit considerations of truth and falsity and the statement of first principles to be introduced without disguise or hesitation; and it will suggest a subject-matter in which what is possible of rational psychology may be worked out in terms of demonstration and the dialectical examination of arguments, rather than in terms of facility of learning, scope, and retention.[10]

It is appropriate in this context to note that in addition to his philosophic papers, McKeon also published a scientific paper in number theory in collaboration with H. H. Goldstine: "A Generalized Pell

Equation, I" (1940).[11] In this paper, the authors obtain all integral solutions of the equation $x^3 + 2y^3 + 4z^3 - 6xyz = 1$

A solution is a set of three integers which, when substituted for the variables x, y, and z in the equation, satisfy the equation. McKeon and Goldstine show that the solutions form a series that is infinite in both directions:

. . . (1,3,-3), (1,-2,1), (-1,1,0), (1,0,0), (1,1,1), (5,4,3), (19,15,12), . . .

The relation between successive solutions in the series, numbered n and $n + 1$, is given by the following equations:

$$x_{n+1} = x_n + 2y_n + 2z_n'$$
$$y_{n+1} = x_n + y_n + 2z_n'$$
$$z_{n+1} = x_n + y_n + z_n$$

These equations, together with one known solution, such as (1,0,0), determine all other solutions. The authors show that the solutions can also be obtained from the following equation, which gives the n-th solution in the series, beginning from (1,0,0), which is the solution obtained when $n=0$.

$$x + ya + za^2 = (1 + a + a^2)^n$$

where $a = 2^{1/3}$ and n may be any integer. Positive values of n give the solutions to the right of (1,0,0) and negative values give the solutions to the left.

One can recognize in the paper a disposition to solve problems in their general form and to give alternative formulations of their solution, but a more specific account of the relationship between the mathematics of the paper and McKeon's philosophic views I leave to others more able than I am to place in the context of alternative approaches to number theory. I do not find in the writing itself McKeon's characteristic thought and style.

"Democracy, Scientific Method, and Action" (1945)[12] challenges the fashionable tendency to analogize or identify scientific method and democratic processes. The analogy of scientific method to democratic processes is criticized in its bearing on three distinct problems: (1) the influence of democracy on science, (2) the influence of science on democracy, and (3) the characteristics of the respective processes and methods of science and democracy.

(1) With respect to the influence of democracy on science, McKeon concludes that all the evidence bearing on the question is ambiguous, and,

that when the proper qualifications are introduced, the question evaporates. The assertion of the dependence of science on democracy would require, as a theoretical proposition, a great deal more analysis and factual inquiry than is now available for its substantiation. Fortunately, the solution of the practical questions bearing on the dependence of science on democracy does not depend on the resolution of the theoretical problems.

> We do ourselves little credit and we endanger the advantages that democratic institutions do possess by arrogating to democracy a blanket natural predisposition to science. The practical problem is rather to be certain that the conditions of our democracy are truly favorable to science, that fundamental research is in fact being encouraged and executed, and that the immense material resources and intellectual ingenuity that are available for the advancement of science are employed efficiently to that end.[13]

(2) With respect to the influence of science on democracy, McKeon concludes that science has affected democracy by modifying political theory, social objectives, available devices for group action, and potentialities and materials for social amelioration. But in each form of its influence, science has raised problems as well as solved them, and the identification of the knowledge acquired by means of science with the knowledge essential to democracy consequently results in paralogisms. (3) With respect to the characteristics of scientific method and democratic processes, McKeon differentiates each of these in a series of respects. Problems are resolved scientifically when the solutions are based on grounds that in some sense involve the nature of things; problems are resolved democratically when the solutions are based on grounds that depend on the free decisions of individuals. He concludes:

> The supporting relations between science and democracy are strong, but their methods are distinct and, in the long as well as the short run, prejudgments and prejudices can be avoided and issues can be handled in accordance with democratic principles only by distinguishing carefully between science and politics.[14]

"Aristotle's Conception of the Development and the Nature of Scientific Method" (1947)[15] is a systematic exposition of Aristotle's conception of scientific method as it relates to the theories of philosophers, the nature of things, and the validation of propositions, or, briefly, as it relates to thoughts, things, and words. In distinguishing these three problems of method, as well as in the treatment of each, McKeon presents Aristotle as placing his method between the dialectical method of Plato, that assimilates things to thoughts, and the physical method of Democritus, that reduces thoughts to things. Thus, the article, in presenting the views of Aristotle, distinguishes three broad views of scientific method. The philosophy of science is again not distinct from philosophy, and philosophy and science are joined by their concern with method. McKeon's approach also challenges prevailing opinion by distinguishing multiple views of scientific method and by finding formulations of the different views in ancient philosophy. Here is McKeon's initial presentation of the contrast of the three methods:

> Aristotle makes frequent use of the contrast between the methods of Democritus and Plato to isolate problems of method and to indicate characteristics which he thinks the true scientific method should possess. Both with respect to the devices of analysis and inquiry which they employ and with respect to the metaphysical assumptions on which they are based, the two methods are contrary to each other, and their advantages and deficiencies are opposed and balanced. The true scientific method is distinct from both and should combine their advantages and avoid their errors. Democritus, because of the fidelity of his arguments to his subject matter, made a close approach to a scientific method appropriate to particular problems; but he was unable, within the scope of his method, to find any essence or definition of things beyond material configuration and color or any cause of motion other than the fact that things had been in motion or that what happened had happened in the same way before. He had a rudimentary conception of form, but he wholly neglected efficient and final causes. Plato, on the other hand, treated of essence and definition in his dialectic, but unfortunately his Forms were removed from sensible, changing things and without direct effect on them, and he was therefore unable, in the absence of an efficient case, to account for motion and change.[16]

"Aristotle and the Origins of Science in the West" (1949)[17] uses the threefold distinction of methods presented in "Aristotle's Conception of the Development and the Nature of Scientific Method" to show how the accounts of Aristotle's contribution to science are influenced by the different conceptions of the history and nature of science that Aristotle himself distinguished. Thus, since Aristotle in his scientific work is engaged in a connected series of continual experiments in the relation of facts and theories, he "occupies a prominent and important place in the history of science when the history of science is an account of the inter-relations established between the theories constructed to resolve problems and the facts they are adduced to explain. His contribution to science is slight when the history of science is a record of either the successive stages in the development of the atomic theory and the application of sensational empiricism or of the progressive elaboration of devices for the universal application of mathematics and the imaginative construction of mathematical models."[18]

McKeon uses Aristotle to distinguish the sense in which the history of science is short from the sense in which it is long, and finds a like distinction in modern versions of the history of science:

> The history of science is still short in modern versions for much the same reasons that persuaded Aristotle that it was no older than the generation before his own work. The scientist who is at work on a particular problem or on a specific subject can seldom find relevant data, appropriate methods, or plausible theories further back than the previous generation. Yet as hypotheses are adjusted and the general scheme of concepts shifts its form and coherence, vistas open in all directions, down the history of earlier inquiries as well as across subject matters to speculation in other fields.[19]

At the level of the short histories, of facts and theories, Aristotle's facts are now familiar or forgotten or false, and his theories have either been superseded or continue as generalizations in which only the sympathetic critic will see a likeness to the subtler formulation required in application to data later made available. At the level of the long histories, the level at which terms and ideas, distinctions and theories, recur and are influential, the peculiar contribution of Aristotle is the integrated system of distinctions on which his science is constructed, which laid down basic principles and differentiations frequently employed in later inquiry. Because Aristotle's conception of science distinguishes and relates theories and facts, his contribution to science must also be stated at a third level, for his philosophic generalizations force on the inquirer the realization that progress in science is achieved not merely by the meticulous observation and measurement of facts or by the elaboration of theories and the application of principles, but also by the substitution of theories which interpret the facts differently and the comparison of schemes of explanation established in ordering our various types of experience:

> It is the virtue of the Aristotelian analysis, whether applied to the data of the sciences or to the nature of the sciences

themselves, to identify and relate theory, which may seem to account for everything but which accounts for nothing precisely unless brought to specific application, and facts, which may seem to force their proper character on the attention of the inquirer without need of theory but which are unintelligible without insight into the reasons that govern proposed explanations. The effect of the distinctions which Aristotle introduced in elaborate system into the discussions of science and philosophy is to bring periodically to the forefront of attention the character of the abstractions to which we have grown accustomed in our explanations, the peculiarities of their interrelations, and the possible systematic changes in them. In this fashion precise formulations have contributed impulse and many of the elements to that ferment of thought in which new systems of explanation have been suggested, often by revealing the application of dialectic to experience or by developing the theory of empirical investigations.[20]

It is perhaps unnecessary to call attention to the novelty of these views of Aristotle's method, of his contribution to science, and of the history of science itself.

Various conceptions of science and scientific method are distinguished in the articles already considered. "Spinoza and Experimental Science" distinguishes the experimental method of Boyle from the mathematical method of Spinoza. "The Empiricist and Experimentalist Temper in the Middle Ages" and "De Anima: Psychology and Science" distinguish a science of efficient causes from a science of formal and final causes. "Democracy, Scientific Method, and Action" depends on a distinction between methods that makes literal distinctions and methods that use analogies to reduce literal distinctions. "Aristotle's Conception of the Development and the Nature of Scientific Method" and "Aristotle and the Origins of Science in the West" use a threefold distinction that places Aristotle's scientific method between the dialectic of Plato and the atomism of Democritus. These articles supply particular exemplifications of the general point that McKeon's formulations of his semantic schema of possible philosophies are also formulations of possible forms of science and scientific method. Long before Thomas Kuhn's account of the multiplicity of scientific paradigms, McKeon was distinguishing the multiple forms of science that result from different philosophic principles. The relation of the sciences to the semantic schema is made explicit in "Philosophy and Method" (1951)[21] and "Philosophy and Action" (1952).[22] At the beginning of "Philosophy and Method," McKeon is concerned with the reason why consensus and cumulative increase of knowledge are possible in the sciences but not in philosophy.

> In the sciences consensus is possible because the statement of laws and principles is tested by repeated use of the same method in application to the same things. The increase of knowledge is therefore cumulative in the history of science, since principles can be held by experts, at least for a time, and can be modified and improved to explain, order, or control the subject matters to which they are applied. The problems of science assume something of a philosophic character whenever the development of novel methods makes new or different facts relevant to a subject-matter or to a problem and whenever scientists differ on the interpretation of facts or the validity of principles. At such points the progressive accumulation of knowledge in the history of the sciences is punctuated by the abrupt formulation of new principles (or the reassertion of abandoned principles rendered more plausible by fuller knowledge) and by the recognition of new facts (or the rediscovery of discredited facts rendered more relevant by fuller exploration of their contexts).[23]

The appeal to science for the resolution of philosophic differences is inconclusive since it is involved in the same differences of method and principles exhibited in all philosophic discussions, and philosophy becomes scientific in accordance with the criteria of different philosophies of science. Dialectic, logistic, and inquiry, which correspond to the methods of Plato, Democritus, and Aristotle, are all presented as the method of science.[24] The operational method of the Sophists is added to the other three as a method of science in "Philosophy and Action,"[25] and thus the four methods of the semantic schema of "Philosophic Semantics and Philosophic Inquiry" (1966),[26] dialectical, operational, logistic, and problematic, are all methods of science.

After the 1952 formulation of the semantic matrix, with its columns of subject matter, method, principle, and purpose, McKeon turned his attention to the ways in which semantic differences, instead of generating fruitless controversies, could be used to further inquiry. "Process and Function" (1953)[27] is sharply critical of philosophers of science on this point. They have not learned from the sciences what they might have learned, which is how opposed principles can be used as alternative hypotheses in inquiry, and they have not made the contribution to the sciences that they might have made, which is to show the consequences of philosophic principles and to compare them in the sequence of problems they treat and in the structure of possibilities they open up by their respective definitions of basic concepts. As a result of these shortcomings, "scientists who have turned to the philosophic analysis of basic concepts involved in their inquiries and theories have . . . found in the language and technical devices of philosophers reasons for expressing intransigence in their assumptions rather than means of communication or clarification of differences."[28] That scientists have done better than philosophers at solving the philosophic problems of their disciplines is a recurrent theme in McKeon's writings. McKeon contrasts the way differences of principle are treated in the physical sciences with they way they are treated in philosophy:

> Progress in the physical sciences during the last fifty years has resulted from a clash of principles, but what has been discovered and expressed in terms of one set of principles has been assimilated to consequences that follow from the opposed principles and has been expressed in their terms, and inquiry has continued in the variety of directions that conflict. . . . Yet in spite of the happy result of the clash of principles in the scientific inquiries and ingenuity which they have stimulated, the philosophic discussion of opposed principles has proceeded on a double assumption, a metaphysical assumption that there must be one uniquely adequate and true set of principles to be expounded in "the philosophy of physics" and a semantic assumption that the same word refers to the same object when it is used as a basic concept and therefore when it occurs, differently defined in the context of different systems, one at least of the opposed theories must be incorrect and false.[29]

Basic concepts are for McKeon the meeting point of scientific and philosophic problems, and the philosophic discussion of basic concepts is the complement of their scientific use. "Process and Function" in its discussion of "process" and "function" presents two components of the philosophic discussion of science: it illustrates on the one hand the effect of scientific precisions on the differentiation of philosophic principles, and on the other the bearing of philosophic principles and distinctions on scientific problems. The first part of "Process and Function" shows how philosophic concepts might be rendered more precise if they are conceived as hypotheses and stated in terms of the inquiries that would follow from adopting them. The article begins with a comparison of the philosophic principles of Alfred North Whitehead and John Dewey and notes that in the sciences such principles operate in the selection of aspects of problems or of data and in the determination of programs of inquiry. The treatment of processes and functions in the sciences may, consequently, suggest means by which the related philosophic conceptions of process and function can be fruitfully compared. The first part of the article proceeds to analyze four scientific interpretations of process that are elaborated in terms of concepts that express opposed philosophical assumptions: Whitehead's "process," Albert Einstein's "invariance," Bohr's "complementarity," and Percy Bridgman's "operations."

The second part of "Process and Function" shows how philosophic examination of scientific principles can be given more content if the alternative hypotheses attached to alternative meanings of basic concepts are set in relation to each other—not as ultimates among which the philosopher must choose his truth, but as complementary emphases which contribute to the advance and scope of knowledge. It begins with a comparison between alternative hypotheses in science that are attached to alternative meanings of "process" and "function." Paul Weiss distinguishes between processes which are functional and those which are not, while Edwin Schroedinger uses physical processes to account for organic functions. The differences between process and function can be seen most fully, however, when they are used not only as principles for opposed hypotheses in scientific inquiry but also as grounds for opposed philosophies. McKeon returns to the philosophies of Whitehead and Dewey to develop the distinction between process and function, which is seen as the vanishing point in modern discussion of the ancient distinction between Being and substance.

McKeon's cycle of "general selections," in accordance with which successive historical periods seek principles in things, in thoughts, and in words and actions, provides a device for relating the scientific inquiries of different periods in two ways. One way is to seek the analogues of terms that are prominent in one phase of the cycle in another phase of the cycle, as process and function in the present pragmatic and semantic period are analogous to Being and substance in a metaphysical period. The other is to seek similarities among different periods that belong to the same phase of the cycle. This is illustrated in "Medicine and Philosophy in the Eleventh and Twelfth Centuries: The Problem of Elements" (1961).[30] The treatment of elements in the eleventh and twelfth centuries is examined in detail, but other periods in the same phase of the cycle exhibit similar patterns of opposed theories and end in a similar transition to new problems. In semantic and pragmatic periods such as our own, elements are principles, whereas in the succeeding metaphysical periods, causes are principles.

> Aristotle taught us that the Ionian and Italian philosophers used the "elements" as principles in their philosophies in "lisping anticipations" of his own use of "causes" as principles. . . . The theories of elements propounded in the medical

works of the eleventh century and the cosmologies of the twelfth century likewise provide the principles of the relevant sciences and prepare for the more diversified treatment, in the thirteenth century, of principles and sciences devised from the interpretation of Aristotle's works.[31]

The transition from the Renaissance to the seventeenth century is similar in what happened to the treatment of elements to the transition from the twelfth to the thirteenth century: more was known and the data were richer, but the opposed theories followed a similar pattern, and the discussion of elements again yielded to the discussion of laws and principles of motion—the issue in the seventeenth century was not primarily between Descartes' vortices, Leibniz' monads, and Newton's atoms but between their conceptions of mass and motion and their elaborations and applications of laws of motion. The Newtonian principles were used to organize a system of the world and a system of physical science in the eighteenth and early nineteenth centuries, but in the twentieth century our attention has turned again to elements and particles.[32]

We may note here the recent publication in book form of the transcript of McKeon's 1963 Ideas and Methods course, "Concepts and Methods: The Natural Sciences."[33] The course aims to apply McKeon's semantic schema to the concepts of motion, space, time, and cause as these appear in the works of Plato, Aristotle, Galileo Galilei, Sir Isaac Newton, James Clark Maxwell, and Einstein. The book includes transcriptions of both lectures and class discussions and thus serves to acquaint the reader with McKeon's teaching methods as well as with his analysis of scientific concepts. The contrast between the freer style of McKeon's introductory lectures to students and the carefully composed articles written for publication is striking. The lectures focus explicitly on his own schemata of interpretation and in their scope and suggestiveness recall Whitehead's recommendations for the stage of romance,[34] whereas the articles subordinate the schemata to the restricted problems they are attempting to solve.

"Hegel's Conception of Matter" (1963)[35] illustrates the use of the semantic schema not only to differentiate possible meanings of a term such as "matter" but also to help evaluate the different possibilities by structuring questions about their consequences. McKeon, in familiar fashion, distinguishes four conceptions of matter: Aristotelian matter as potentiality, Democritean matter as actuality and being, Protagorean matter as flux, and the matter of the Platonic tradition as negation and non being. He then goes on to ask what difference it makes that matter is conceived in one way or another by asking what the consequences are with respect to philosophical systems, with respect to methods of investigation and proof in philosophy and science, and with respect to the interpretation of physical laws.

"Spinoza on the Rainbow and on Probability" (1965)[36] centers on two scientific papers attributed to Spinoza, "Algebraic Calculation of the Rainbow, a Contribution to the Closer Connection of Physics and Mathematics" and "Calculation of Chances." The two works, McKeon argues, have a significant bearing on three interrelated problems: they present incidents from important stages in the history of modern mathematics; they permit a concrete reconstruction of the work and communication of a group of Dutch mathematicians with whom Spinoza was acquainted, including in particular Christian Huygens, John Hudde, and John de Witt; and they provide explicit reminders concerning conceptions of the methods of mathematics and the relation of mathematics to other disciplines that were widespread in the seventeenth century but are often ignored in interpretations of Spinoza's application of the geometric method to ethics. McKeon proceeds to treat all three problems in full historical detail, so that the article becomes an example of the history of science at its most concrete. With respect to the third problem, McKeon notes that the two works in question conceive the geometric method as a method of both discovery and proof and that the meaning of the method of discovery is further elucidated by the combination of the term "operation" (*Wirkung*) with "proof." McKeon's examination of the contents of the two works has the incidental result of supporting their attribution to Spinoza: "attention to the contents of the works increases rather than diminishes the probability that Spinoza was their author."[37]

"Philosophy as a Humanism" (1965)[38] distinguishes humanistic discussion of problems from nonhumanistic controversy about facts and thus continues the exposition of constructive ways of using philosophic oppositions. As one illustration of the humanistic discussion of problems, McKeon uses the discussion between Einstein, Wolfgang Pauli, Max Born, Bohr, and others, on the foundations of quantum mechanics as presented in *Albert Einstein, Philosopher-Scientist*.[39] "Scientists have on the whole," McKeon says, "used philosophy more wisely and effectively in testing and applying hypotheses than the postulates and rules which philosophers have built into their philosophies of science would have permitted."[40] The discussion between Einstein and others is one of three examples of humanistic discussions that McKeon uses to suggest methods which might be used to develop a new humanistic form of philosophy adapted to the problems and achievements of our times.

McKeon has no philosophy of science as distinct from philosophy, but, in "Philosophy and the Development of Scientific Methods"

(1966)[41] he proposes a philosophy of method. This proposal unites McKeon's continuing concern with scientific methods with his continuing concern to supplement controversy by inquiry. A philosophy of method, according to McKeon, is to be distinguished from controversies about method. Controversies about method

> employ a semantics of method to discover that words like "analysis" and "synthesis," "discovery" and "proof," "induction" and "deduction" have many meanings, and which move from that discovery to prove either that no problem of method is involved because the meanings do not refer to the same situation or issue, or that, if there is an opposition, one of the opposed sets of meanings does not apply to discovery and proof in science or is intrinsically meaningless or absurd.[42]

A philosophy of method, on the other hand, is needed

> to examine the many varieties of analyses and syntheses that have been used; to explore the kinds of discovery that are analytic and the kinds of discovery that are synthetic; to restate the kinds of induction that are methods of discovery and the kinds that are not, that is, the kinds of discovery that cannot be reduced to method and the kinds that can be.[43]

The article itself initiates the philosophy of method by surveying the accounts of method from the first uses of the word up to the present time. A glance at theories of method may serve, McKeon says, to differentiate methods of analysis and synthesis, discovery and proof, induction and deduction.

Of the articles we have discussed, those prior to "Process and Function" (1953) primarily are concerned to develop a semantics of science and philosophy, that is, a schema differentiating the various approaches to science and philosophy. The later articles, on the other hand, are more concerned to use this plurality of approaches to further scientific and philosophic inquiry. "Process and Function" argues that the different meanings attached to "process" and "function" express fundamental assumptions which may be stated as opposed hypotheses leading to lines of inquiry rather than as opposed doctrines evolved in endless and fruitless dispute. "Hegel's Conception of Matter" seeks not merely to distinguish Hegel's theory of matter from other theories of matter, but to examine its consequences for systems of philosophy, methods of philosophy and science, and interpretations of scientific law. "Spinoza on the Rainbow and on Probability" shows different methods functioning in the history of science. "Philosophy as a Humanism" distinguishes controversy about facts from discussion of problems. "Philosophy and the Development of Scientific Methods" distinguishes controversies about method from a philosophy of method.

"Scientific and Philosophic Revolutions" (1967)[44] continues this series by using the fact-problem distinction of "Philosophy as a Humanism" to contrast two modes of tracing the relation between science and philosophy: "The first is an account of the accomplishments of scientists and of the statements of philosophers as 'facts,' and the second is an account of the 'problems' treated by scientists and philosophers."[45] The difference between the two accounts reflects different conceptions of the relation between philosophy and science which extend back beyond the beginnings of modern science to problems of the relation of philosophy to scientia and to *episteme:* from the beginnings of philosophy some philosophers have conceived their task as the application of the methods of "science" to philosophic problems, and other philosophers have conceived their task as the refinement of the methods of knowing and philosophy as a culmination of the "sciences." The history of philosophy tends to be presented as a history of doctrines taken as facts, whereas the history of science tends to be presented as a history of problems investigated in inquiry. The result is a specious contrast between the history of philosophy and the history of science: "The difference between the history of science and the history of philosophy, as they tend to be presented, is due less to a difference between science and philosophy in fact than to a tendency to subordinate oppositions of doctrine to discussion of problems in the one history and to subordinate statement of problems to doctrines and their oppositions in the other."[46]

In "Scientific and Philosophic Revolutions," McKeon shows how, if the histories of both science and philosophy are treated as histories of problems investigated rather than as histories of accomplishments as facts, the two histories can be stated in terms of the same issues and problems. The period he chooses to investigate is the hundred years prior to the writing of the article, 1865–1965. This period includes the scientific and philosophic revolutions of the early twentieth century, and McKeon exhibits both as aspects of a single revolution. The history of science prior to the revolution is a history in which the universal mechanics stemming from Newton and the universal mathematics stemming from René Descartes provided methods to explain particular phenomena and to establish universal laws. The corresponding history of philosophy is a history in which the experiential tradition of J. H. Mill and William Whewell and the ontic tradition of William Hamilton and Auguste Comte both seek to determine the methods and structure of science. Corresponding paradoxes were encountered in both science and philosophy which led to the revolution of the early twentieth century. This revolution was from centering philosophic discussion of science on scientific method and order to centering it on scientific interpretation and explanation.

> The paradoxes of the late nineteenth-century controversy and discussion, inquiry and proof, had led to a change in the terms which formed the matrix of semantics and of inquiry. The nineteenth-century matrix had related the differentiation of method and science to the differentiation of phenomena and thought. The inductive method became dominant in the experiential tradition, and the synthetic method in the ontic tradition; the function of method in both traditions was to relate phenomena to principles. The paradoxes encountered in that enterprise suggested the reorientation of methodological inquiry to the facts of existence and experience rather than to the principles of systems. The matrix of semantics and of inquiry shifted from method and scientific system to interpretation and scientific statement, and from phenomena and thought to action and language.[47]

Of the various elements in McKeon's semantic schema, it is the general selection of categories that provides the basis for intellectual revolutions, for the general selection is the only semantic element that is characteristic of the whole philosophic communication of a period. "Medicine and Philosophy in the Eleventh and Twelfth Centuries: The Problem of Elements" traces the revolution from a semantic and pragmatic period to a metaphysical period, and "Scientific and Philosophic Revolutions" traces the revolution from an epistemological period to a semantic and pragmatic period.

"Philosophic Problems in World Order" (1968),[48] reprinted as "World Order in Evolution and Revolution in Arts, Associations, and Sciences" (1971),[49] examines the present as a time in which all assumptions are questioned and all things are investigated at once. In such a time, no framework remains within which to pose the resulting issues except world order. The article presents the encounters of sciences, communities, and arts with world order. In the sciences, the issues of the seventeenth century were stated in terms of fixed contrarieties:

> The issues of the seventeenth century were stated absolutely as oppositions between theories—between Cartesian and Newtonian laws of motion, between momentum and force, between vortices and absolute space, between particles and waves of light. One or the other theory must be eliminated.[50]

The encounter of the sciences with world order has led not only to the alteration of concepts of world order but also to reconsideration of what constitutes a fact or a theory and their relationship to each other, for when the opposed theories are extended to the whole of the world order and attention is focussed now on one aspect of processes, now on another, it is equally the case that neither theory is true and that both are true. The dissolution of assumption has altered the fixity of facts and the necessity of theories and has adjusted the relation of fact and theory in paradoxical truths which have displaced self-evident truths and self-contradictory antinomies. Physics and technology have provided a model for dealing with the new situation:

> Physics and technology have provided a model in the twentieth century for the discovery and treatment of issues of world order. It is a model, in the first place, for response to the need to abandon the fixed contrarieties of earlier theory. Physical theory has embraced paradoxes and made them principles. This has meant the abandonment of the absolutes of past theory—the Newtonian absolutes, of space, time, motion, and force—but it has also meant the preservation of the basic relations established by the Newtonian physics in a more diversified context of fact and formula. It is a model, in the second place, for use of the horns of a paradox to form alternative hypotheses which lead in their interplay to further progress. For decades the quantum physicists who base their theory on the conviction that the principle of indeterminacy is an irreducible fact of nature and those who base their theory on the conviction that the establishment of a general field equation will remove indeterminacy have each made contributions to quantum mechanics, have assimilated the knowledge acquired under opposed theories, and have moved on together to new problems.[51]

"Time and Temporality" (1974)[52] is an illustration of how the rhetorical device of the topic or commonplace can facilitate the productive interaction of opposed views. Commonplaces, McKeon tells us, are devices which the ancients used to discover arguments and relations among ideas and arguments. The vast literature on a concept such as time can be condensed into a pattern of topics or commonplaces. The commonplace of commonplaces is here "time and temporality," and this, McKeon says, is a formula to designate time in its circumstances, substantive and cognitive. It may be used as a device by which to develop and examine the variety of circumstances in which time acquires its variety of meanings in the context of a variety of problems, philosophical in nature but with consequences detectable and traceable in history, science, art, and social and cultural structures. McKeon contrasts the presentation of what has been said about time as a pattern of commonplaces with its presentation as an account of statements alleged to be true:

> If these variations in the meanings and instances of time were presented as an account of doctrines or of statements alleged to be true, they would each be in contradictory and incompatible oppositions to the others. Since they have been presented as a pattern of commonplace possibilities for analysis, inquiry, and application, they stand instead in the relation of alternatives which focus on different aspects of time brought to the attention by different temporalities from which time takes its meanings.[53]

Commonplaces are, McKeon says, "devices by which comparative philosophy may uncover, in its inquiries and analyses, not rigid structures of dead, past philosophies or of opaque alien philosophies, but living relations that animate past and unfamiliar inquiries and controversies and that are still relevant and operative in contemporary problems oriented to the emergence of new conceptions of time in the formulation and testing of new solutions to new problems."

McKeon's work on science runs through all the basic arts of his philosophy of culture: semantics, inquiry, topics, and arts. We have seen an increasingly articulated semantics of science, diverse inquiries in and about science and its history, and a pattern of topics or commonplaces relating to time and temporality. "The Organizations of the Sciences and the Relations of Cultures in the Twelfth and Thirteenth Centuries" (1975)[54] relates the development of science to structures of the arts. It presents McKeon's answer to the question currently addressed as the question of why modern science arose in the Western Christian tradition but not in the Chinese or Arabic traditions. McKeon's answer is that modern science arose precisely out of the impact of the Arabic tradition on the Western Christian tradition. He finds the beginnings of modern science in the meeting of two different cultural structures, the Arabic encyclopaedia of sciences and principles and the Latin Christian encyclopaedia of the liberal arts of words and things. The Latin arts of formulating disciplines were turned to structuring the sciences and methods introduced through contact with the Arabic tradition, and the result was a multiplicity of ways of seeking principles in new disciplines and new sciences.

> The consideration of cultures in terms of the structure or encyclopaedia of organizations of sciences suggests answers to

two puzzling questions about the contacts of cultures in the twelfth and thirteenth centuries: Why did the other Western traditions based on Greek culture learn about Greek science only from the Arabic tradition? and Why did the introduction of that knowledge into the Latin Christian tradition prepare the foundations for modern science? The Latin Christian encyclopaedia was an organization of arts and disciplines, which had tended to lay emphasis on the formulation of those disciplines, the arts of words and in particular the arts of logic and rhetoric, the arts of statement and proof, and of invention and judgment. The structure of the arts of things was implicit, however, in the arts of words, and the introduction of sciences of things and methods of inquiry into the nature and operations of things made explicit the interrelations of that methodological structure. The multiplicity of logics made it possible to seek the principles of motion and the laws of motion not only by induction from observed motions, but by the commonplaces of dialectic concerning motion, from the paradoxes of motion considered as a sophism, from the specificities and perspectives of motion suggested by rhetorical invention, from the numbers and proportions of calculation. Moreover, as the quadrivium became the subject of attention as second philosophy the double character of the quadrivium, as a homonym, as arts of mathematics and arts of things, laid the foundations for the two roads to the universal mathematics of Descartes and the universal mechanics of Newton. In a culture of disciplines contact with facts and sciences yields, when the tradition of disciplines is strong, new disciplines and new facts uncovered by the disciplines of new sciences.[55]

A final paper, "Philosophy and Theology, History and Science in the Thought of Bonaventura and Thomas Aquinas" (1975),[56] provides an appropriate conclusion to the series we have been examining. It presents and illustrates the paradox that Bonaventura and Aquinas, working before the development of modern history and science, provide a model for the pluralistic historical and scientific inquiries of the future. The paper applies to the different theologies of Bonaventura and Aquinas the distinction used in "Time and Temporality" between presenting different views on a subject as alternative possibilities for inquiry and presenting them as doctrines or statements alleged to be true and thus as incompatible with one another. Here, however, both sides of the distinction are treated in terms of commonplaces. Commonplaces of inquiry or discovery can be used to relate different approaches to common problems, while commonplaces of exposition or restatement can be used to place different conclusions in controversial opposition to one another. McKeon in this article uses commonplaces of inquiry as instruments of discovery and exploration to put in question commonplaces used as repositories of what everybody knows. Instead of distinguishing times of theology without science from times of science freed from theology, McKeon distinguishes two formulations of the science of theology: the affective science of Bonaventura in which cognition, action, and passion are inseparably joined, and the demonstrative science of Aquinas in which a subject matter is ordered by its proper principles and methods. McKeon proceeds to show how the differences between the affective and the demonstrative formulations of science extended beyond the science of theology and had fruitful as well as stultifying influences, as commonplaces of inquiry and commonplaces of exposition, in the interpretation of philosophers as well as saints, in the formulation of problems in other sciences as well as in theology, and in the systematic organization of the sciences. With respect to the second of these points, the influence of the differences between the two formulations on problems in sciences other than theology, McKeon says,

> The differences between the affective and the demonstrative formulations of science functioned in fruitful interaction and controversial opposition at the beginning of modern science. The use of the commonplace of inquiry concerning scientific problems and scientific methods in recent research has lessened the credibility of the broadly accepted commonplace that modern science had its beginnings in the sixteenth and seventeenth centuries. The Commentaries on the *Sentences* of the thirteenth and fourteenth centuries contain earlier discussions of motion, time, and space which prepared commonplaces for the inquiries of Galileo and Newton.[57]

McKeon concludes that we can learn from Bonaventura and Aquinas how to use, in both history and science, commonplaces of inquiry that put in question our commonplaces of exposition:

> We are fenced in by commonplaces of history which state the truths about the past. We destroy alternative interpretations as false and repair accepted interpretations in the light of evidence. Inquiry into problems of the past has little or no relevance to present problems. Bonaventura and Aquinas interpreted past occurrences and past thoughts in terms of their own problems. We dismiss their historical statements with the commonplace that they had no sense of history. We

might learn from them to use the past as a commonplace of inquiry and to ask not whether what they said about the sentences of Greek philosophers or Biblical interpreters is true or false but whether it suggests new ideas about the philosophy of Aristotle or Plato and about the problems of philosophy.

We state our problems of philosophy and theology and our problems of philosophy and science more nearly in the manner of the twelfth century than that of the thirteenth century. We have our book of sentences, and education consists in inculcating the truths established by the authorities in their fields. The authorities tend to be scientists rather than theologians, and theologians enter their sentences in our book by certifying them as scientific. We have not created a commonplace in which to treat those problems and to identify them as problems. Discussion of a problem tends therefore to be a joining of statements about different things. Theology is not architectonic but rather an imitation of a variety of sciences. Scientists develop their own philosophies to structure their scientific inquiries, and philosophers imitate scientific methods and construct philosophies of science. We might learn from Bonaventura and Aquinas how to use commonplaces to focus on the same problem and move from the battles of schools to common inquiry from different points of view. We would then celebrate their seven hundredth anniversary not by searching for something that they said which is true but by learning to recognize the insights which led them along fruitful lines of inquiry in which we might begin again to engage.[58]

In these terms it is evident that McKeon's effort, not only in this article but in the philosophy of science in general, is to use commonplaces of inquiry to call in question commonplaces of exposition.

Let us now return to the problems raised at the outset and ask what general results emerge from this survey of McKeon's contributions to the philosophy of science. One of the most striking features of his work in this field, as elsewhere, is his continual opposition to the views of most of his contemporaries, to the accepted commonplaces of his time. This opposition is not attributable merely to McKeon's personal contentiousness, but involves his acute awareness of a whole domain that was perceived only dimly, if at all, by most of his contemporaries. Like the prisoners in Plato's cave, we take the commonplaces of our time for truths and suppose that what we are not aware of does not exist.

What McKeon was aware of, and most of his contemporaries were not, is first of all the role of philosophic principles in all that we say and do, including science. Few if any philosophers have exhibited such a continual awareness of the relativity of statements and actions to philosophic principles. We fail to notice this relativity because we take our principles as given and dismiss alternative principles as evidently unsatisfactory. One consequence of the relativity of science to philosophic principles is that the philosophical discussion of science cannot limit itself to the interpretation of science, for philosophical principles are always operative within science. Another is that the philosophy of science is not separate from philosophy, for the philosophic principles operative in science are not of some special kind but are universal in their import. The generalizations that emerge from McKeon's writings on science, for example, which we are here seeking to formulate, apply not to science only, but to all subjects.

Closely related to this awareness of the role of philosophic principles in all that we say and do is an awareness that there are many different sets of philosophic principles that determine many possible philosophies. In science, as elsewhere, McKeon finds multiple possibilities arising from the multiplicity of possible philosophic principles. He is concerned in semantics to sort out these possibilities and inquiry to use them productively. Many of McKeon's earlier articles articulated the semantic differences of philosophies and scientific approaches, while many of the articles written after the formulation of the 1952 semantic schema avoided setting philosophical or scientific approaches in controversial opposition to one another and suggested ways in which the plurality of approaches can play a constructive role in inquiry. What is distinctive about the sciences, according to McKeon, is not that they do or do not exhibit a plurality of approaches, but that they make better use of this plurality than other disciplines, particularly philosophy. In the contemporary situation, the sciences rather than philosophy provide the best models of pluralistic inquiry.

McKeon's awareness of the role of philosophic principles in science, and of the plurality of such principles, leads to an awareness of the enduring significance and value of works that belong to the long rather than to the short history of science. Aristotle and the Medieval philosophers and Spinoza become directly relevant to contemporary problems in the philosophy of science. This was an awareness not generally shared by his contemporaries and one that tends to set his work apart from theirs. The four articles on the Medievals are particularly noteworthy in this respect, for the commonplaces of exposition would lead us to dismiss the thought of this period as unscientific and irrelevant to modern science. McKeon, however, as we have seen, finds an empiricist and experimentalist temper in the Middle Ages, a recurrent pattern in the opposed theories of elements in the eleventh and twelfth centuries, the origin of modern science in the encounter of Arabic and Latin encyclopaedias in the twelfth and thirteenth centuries, and a paradigm of pluralistic scientific inquiry in the work of Bonaventura and Aquinas.

McKeon's awareness of the role of philosophic principles in science, of the plurality of such principles, and of the longer histories in which they are manifest, leads to an awareness of new possibilities for inquiry. Most of McKeon's articles relating to science are exemplary in the sense that they not only resolve the particular problem with which they are concerned, but do so in a way that provides a paradigm for other inquiries of a similar kind. Thus "Spinoza and Experimental Science" shows the integral relationship between philosophy and science in the work of Spinoza; a similar relation might be found in the work of any thinker who treats both subjects. "Aristotle's Conception of the Development and the Nature of Scientific Method" uses Aristotle to develop a semantics of method; a similar inquiry could use philosophers other than Aristotle or investigate concepts other than method. "Aristotle and the Origins of Science in the West" shows how the history of a thinker's influence depends on the principles of the historian; the same might be shown for the history of the influence of any thinker. "Medicine and Philosophy in the Eleventh and Twelfth Centuries: The Problem of Elements" discovers a characteristic pattern in the theories of elements in one phase of the cycle of general selections; other phase-dependent patterns might be found. "Process and Function" shows how philosophy and science can complement each other in their treatment of two basic concepts, process and function; the same might be done for other basic concepts. "Hegel's Conception of Matter" distinguishes four meanings of "matter" and asks what their consequences are for the systems of philosophy, the methods of philosophy and science, and the interpretation of physical laws; the same might be done for other concepts. "Spinoza on the Rainbow and on Probability" is a contribution to the history of science centering on two scientific documents attributed to Spinoza; the same kind of contribution to history might be made by centering on the scientific documents of other authors. "Scientific and Philosophic Revolutions" treats the relationship between philosophy and science during a hundred-year period in terms of problems rather than positions; the same sort of history might be written for other periods or other subjects. "Time and Temporality" works out a pattern of commonplaces related to time and temporality; the same sort of pattern of commonplaces might be worked out for other concepts. "The Organizations of the Science and the Relations of Cultures in the Twelfth and Thirteenth Centuries" examines the relations of Arabic and Latin cultures through their respective organizations of the sciences; the same might be done for other relations of cultures. "Philosophy and Theology, History, and Science in the Thought of Bonaventura and Aquinas" treats the differences between these two thinkers by means of commonplaces of inquiry rather than commonplaces of exposition; the same might be done for the differences between other thinkers.

McKeon's presentation of his philosophy of science in diverse, independent articles rather than as a completed system thus serves to open up an enormous range of new possibilities for inquiry. A completed system, on the other hand, precisely in the respect in which it is complete, closes off rather than opens up possibilities of inquiry. McKeon is a great innovator rather than a systematizer, and his influence will be seen not in a common doctrine adhered to by his followers, but in the many and diverse ways in which his successors make use of his pioneering work.

FROM SEMANTICS TO PRAXIS

SOME OLD TRICKS FOR THE NEW PLURALISM

Thomas Farrell

> *"When accomplishment is marked by accumulation and value by place, humanistic studies offer less obvious attractions to young students than the precisions and effects of scientific studies or the utilities and problems of social studies . . . "*
> RICHARD MCKEON, "SPIRITUAL AUTOBIOGRAPHY"

I begin with a McKeonesque paradox, a personal note on method. My essay develops only in part through anecdote. But there are anecdotes aplenty. It will not move in that astonishingly distanced McKeon analytic, like those modern 3–D sight landscapes, where full form only emerges after agonizing reexaminations. All who knew McKeon know what I mean. My humble homage must necessarily steer a middle course.

However, I permit myself a small anecdote of mood, perhaps generalizable. Perhaps not. Using only myself as evidence, I would say the serious McKeon student was occupationally afflicted with a strange synthesis of manic-depression and an almost other-worldly serenity. The manic-depression is easy enough to explain, in largely intellectual terms. As we sat around the table, our large, and soon-to-be-shrinking group of genius scholar wannabes would await the next outwardly genial, probing question from the "teacher" in our midst (we went in order). And dread, full Kierkegaardian dread (the one thing McKeon was congenitally incapable of understanding), crept upon us as the buffer zone grew thin, and our moment was about to be. As we struggled to untie the imminent textual aporia, a little nod and smile from the master meant euphoria. A little head shake and pipecleaner reworking of the familiar McKeon prop meant something akin to, "We who are about to die salute you." I experienced the latter feeling enough times to believe in reincarnation. The former feeling was only experienced a few times, but it made life as a scholar my chosen path.

The reconciliation of such sharply divergent feelings would make any scholar (as many scholars purportedly are) a little weird. But I have not yet discussed the serenity. The serenity came from knowing early on that there was someone whose bootstraps one could never fasten, whose brilliance could never be approached, but only sensed, as over a distant horizon. For myself at least, the effect of this discovery was oddly reassuring. The pressure was off. I could just go ahead now, and as the athletes sometimes say, have some fun out there.

Richard McKeon did not just write about intellectual revolutions; he also instigated them. In my own would-be discipline of rhetorical studies, he charmed, cajoled and intellectually intimidated traditional scholars to reconsider their narrowing of the trivium. In recasting the traditional canon of *inventio* into an overarching lens of disciplinary vision and reconstruction, McKeon led scholars of the generation preceding my own on a sort of grand pilgrimage whose destination is still ambiguous. As I write, and as the humanities shrink before our eyes (I hope this is a coincidence), there has been considerable reexamination of the so-called architectonic turn in rhetoric. It proved to be a difficult movement to sustain for a variety of reasons.

One reason goes back to my opening anecdote. There was only one McKeon. And while he taught his students well and wisely, the very breadth of his philosophical stance defied two interrelated traits any successful intellectual movement must possess: ease of condensation and ease of transmission. Terms like "multiplicity," "difference," the "other" may and do mask many a garbled concept; but they summon forth ready facile enthusiasm. "Productive ambiguity" and even "architectonics" do not. The second reason has been introduced by former students, as well as fallen-away devotees. And it is the contention I will be wrestling with in this essay.

It is very difficult to extract a committed *practice* of rhetoric or politics from McKeon's work. Eugene Garver has argued recently an even broader position: namely that philosophical pluralism itself thwarts an activist political agenda.[1] Here I differ. But with McKeon's grand architectonics, one must concede the difficulty. Working from Aristotle's position that politics was the archetectonic art (since it instituted the conditions which made other arts and activities possible), McKeon borrowed the title and function of archetectonics for a rhetoricized philosophy. This would be an art of finding and forging conceptual relations among the pivotal lines of influence in the histories of Western (and even Eastern) philosophy. The result was a kind of politics of method, with a Westernized pluralism of freedom hovering over the whole proceedings like a silent observer at a General Assembly meeting.

McKeon's own tireless contributions to postwar institutional politics are well-documented. And even today, one might well imagine the uses of productive ambiguity and tolerance for the multiplicities of "other" in our midst. But in an age of identity-outrage, and scourging polemics of every stripe, the McKeon politics of method must appear as it retrospectively is: rather standoffish and remote.

I want to probe for the reasons behind this standoffishness, and then try and push McKeon's pluralistic semantics in a more explicit doctrinal direction. To do this I will need to read some of what McKeon has said allegorically and also introduce some asymmetries into a system that valorizes coherence over all else. This is my way of admitting that McKeon would no doubt not approve of this. But since the best I ever received from him was an A minus, I will remain serene and hopeful of some modest gains for a pluralist praxis.

Let us begin with an intimation of the problem. McKeon's system of philosophical analysis has proved to be so encompassing and therefore imposing that it literally defies any attempt by mere mortals to get enough breadth of perspective to venture an analysis of it. Again, an anecdote may help. McKeon would begin opening seminars on Aristotle's *Organon* with the observation that these works introduce philosophic method "without presuppositions or foundations." Seasoned philosophy students would just shake their heads at this apparent aporia. To this day, I do not know whether this was McKeon's sincere profession of faith or (as was known by many) a bit of opening-round bravado. What I do know is that some of this same symbolic "spreading" pervades the quiet tyranny of philosophic semantics.[2] Any suspicious interlocutor pointing to an apparent omission in the program is likely to be either wrong or guilty of the "fails to" argument; i.e. pointing to an object of neglect that what was never part of the system's intent in the first place.

I am brazenly following the latter course in trying to express what it was that we wanted that we never quite received, why it was that philosophy seemed with McKeon to begin with wonder only to end with bewilderment. In an exhaustingly brilliant series of studies, the work of McKeon showed us all the differing arrays of "moves" (a favorite word of his, as an amateur boxer) philosophies could and did, and may have but did not, make. Did he have, as Aristotle purportedly did not, any presuppositions, any doctrinal commitments, any foundations? In my opinion, there was only one, and not a terribly satisfying one at that. It was that language gives us the resources to analyze and learn about the infinitely rich possible relationships among things, thoughts, and terms.

Why is this not satisfying? If one were to ask McKeon, as a popular soft-drink commercial (and a popular recent philosophy book) did, "What does it all mean?," the answer would be such as to befuddle Buddha: "It depends." And so I come to my point. May a system inclusive of potentially everything be exclusive of something pragmatically needful? I believe that it may. In two neglected essays McKeon authored during the height of the Cold War, "Power and the Language of Power" and "The Ethics of International Influence,"[3] McKeon rather explicitly owns up to what he is leaving out of his system as well as points us in the direction we will need to follow, if we are to invent a much needed renewal of political praxis. We turn now to these essays.

In "Power and the Language of Power," McKeon traverses territory his great teacher, John Dewey, visited several decades earlier in the essay "Force, Violence, and Law."[4] It is always dangerous to summarize or essentialize a McKeon study. But I suspect McKeon was doing with the concept of "power" something analogous to what Dewey attempted with the notion of "force." And that is to show its inescapability, while simultaneously alluding to the needs and avenues for linguistically constituted civic constraints. However, in the intervening time there had been two world wars, a fierce doctrinaire struggle between superpowers, and something else: an almost Romantic, (I suspect) Kantian-derived, fixation on *power* as somehow imbued with certain value-loaded properties. For the Kantian, there needed to be some a priori point "beyond" power. For Hannah Arendt, echoing Martin Heidegger, power would not be power unless it also expressed some preternatural good. Oversimplifying to make my point, if Dewey was saddled with the task of overturning the presumption that force is evil, McKeon strikes me as struggling with newly emerging pseudocontraries: that power may be totalized as good, but that power that is not our power is evil.

Already I have committed one McKeonesque fallacy: motive attribution (I am sure there will be more). But it may help to explain, in a Burkean sense, what is going on in this essay. Taking great care not to define power (I am sure others have noticed that McKeon always took great care not to define much of anything), McKeon's analysis echoes Dewey's treatment of force in finding that power is ubiquitous. Any conceptual analysis that imagines either the disappearance of power or its substantive irrelevance must therefore be suspect. The question, rather, is how to approach, understand, appropriate highly divergent senses of power in an obviously dangerous world. This may be enough to begin our "situation" of this philosopher who defies situation.

Taking as his point of departure the crisis of superpower rivalry, McKeon is eager to rid power of its false and wrong-headed presumptions. Along with the notion that power is ubiquitous, must come the notion that power has no *inherent* value-laden essence. It is neither good nor evil. Here is his historically revealing statement of power's pliability:

> The good and the true are advanced by powers of adherence and resistance.
>
> Power defines a good to which it is directed and an evil which it avoids. Both are patterns for dictators as well as saints and prophets . . . The difficulties and dangers which both transformations encounter also illustrate an identical pattern of forces:
>
>> the improvement of morals inspired in the followers of a saint is degraded when the fraternities and orders they form become corrupt and worldly, and the rules by which they live after having renounced the world stand in need of periodic reform . . . renunciation of power is a method of accumulating power of a different sort and it is usually practiced with provisos that recognize limits beyond which nonviolence is ineffective.[5]

I have pulled together a series of consecutive excerpts, because it helps to show just how all-encompassing McKeon's overarching perspective can be when it encounters an equally pervasive concept (such as power).

McKeon never worked through a system as pedestrian as claims and position summaries. However, this essay, and its companion piece, "The Ethics of International Influence," seem to rotate around a number of key propositions. First, that power is ubiquitous; there is no archimedian point outside of its pervasive influence that one could stand, either for purposes of critique or celebration. Second, that power correspondingly must take on many forms; as McKeon noted earlier, even the renunciation of power is itself a mode of securing power in different guise. Whether a golden mean is implied or not, McKeon even sketches a sort of grid, bounded by extremes. At one end might be the Machiavellian's position implying that might makes right. At the other end is the warm, abstract idealism that knowledge of the good is the only real power. But to my own theme: Is there some sort of political doctrine or political praxis here? Is there a grounded direction for responsible political action?

Other than a sort of resistance to suspicion and an eagerness to include, McKeon's writings on most political subjects explicitly refuse doctrinal adhesions. This is, one is tempted to say, one of the few things he is adamant about: "What is needed in discussion is not a single philosophy, however tempting that prospect may be to those who view their own philosophies as peculiarly suited to fill that purpose, but a common language to bring the issues of power and theory, of sentiment and reason, to a common focus."[6] Here the metaphor is as clear as the wonderfully subtle wit. We need a language comprehensive enough to include the wildly various monistic candidates for world philosophy. We need a proper procedural venue for an Olympics of the mind.

It would not be fair to suspend the analysis at this point, however. McKeon's steadfast academic style always left room for sly and subtle subversions of the materialism of his time. He quite clearly deplored the mindless conformism of the fifties, as well as the Cold War. While no apologist for our postwar antagonists, McKeon took great pains (perhaps even risks) in decrying the irrational logics of imputation during the late fifties. This suggests several important qualifiers and hedges to any categorical critique of the McKeon position.

First, McKeon had no intention of inventing and deploying a practical political program, what he calls (somewhat disparagingly) a "doctrine." Failing to have what one never intended to propose is, by most scales and measures, a less than lethal flaw. Second, there are compelling historical reasons for McKeon's reluctance to take to the podium for overt political advocacy. The context for the essays I have cited was a Cold War climate so polarizing that any call for rationality or common sense could be viewed as weakness, a softness on communism. As McKeon sensed, it was the self-sealing insularity of doctrines themselves that was largely responsible for the historic difficulties. In arguing forcefully against philosophies of imputation, McKeon sought to preserve room for what he regarded as the true mission of philosophy: a language of discussion, where ambiguities and commonalties of value could be sorted, spread, and served.

Was this enough? Yes and no. It depends. McKeon believed strongly enough to repeat the assertion in both essays that, "The grave problems which concern statesmen and moralists take their origin, not in the relations between man and the state, but in the relations between states."[7] The statement is a revealing one for several reasons. At the time he authored these sentiments, they were well-founded. Given the wrenching turbulence of racial injustice and seemingly insurmountable civil strife, the sentiments are perhaps less plausible today. But a second, and virtually unexamined, reason why the statement is revealing comes to us from its implicit eventfulness. In a system so inclusive as to allow speculative thought to begin virtually anywhere, it is rather startling to encounter an overt proclamation of exigence.

While we might agree or disagree with McKeon's actual statement of priorities and origins, the very inclusion of the concept points to a nagging difficulty in the archetectonics project. It simply fails to land any-where where actual priorities are at stake. Here is an example: "There is no pre-established priority of being, cause, or rule among things, thoughts, actions, and statements; each in turn may be made fundamen-tal in deliberation or judgment or demonstration. Speculation concern-ing discourse must avoid the fixities of categories, doctrines, methods, and assumptions which discourse assumes in any one form of philoso-phy or inquiry, if it is to include all the forms which discourse takes in philosophy and in inquiry, action, and production."[8] This strangely hor-tatory statement preaches an almost Utopian loftiness of inclusion through an avoidance of doctrinal program. Should this be judged a fault? At the very least, I would judge it a rhetorical deficiency.

Not long ago, Edwin Black observed that the problem with McKeon's archetectonic pluralism was that it lacked a "referent."[9] I know what Black was trying to get at, but I would put the matter dif-ferently. McKeon's discursive philosophy invents and varies a dizzying array of referents while managing to juggle them all at arms length. There are no mistakes, corrections, improvements. Only endless reinter-pretations. The result is a rhetoric of method. Such a rhetoric features endlessly fascinating speculative inquiry, but at the expense of another sense of rhetoric: namely, as a civic practice. And so, we come to the core question of this essay. Can we, dare we, consider reformulating the McKeon lexicon so as to invite a more praxis-centered vision of rheto-ric? Much in the spirit of the grease monkey adjusting a bolt or two on Richard Petty's race car, I attempt a modest adjustment or two here.

It would do damage to alter McKeon's method of analysis, notori-ously analytical as it is. But what might be at least proffered as a mod-est amendment is the suggestion that methods are invented too. And occasionally concepts may emerge which alter the unit of analysis itself. If McKeon has been luminously reflective on methods of speculation other than his own (perhaps most notoriously in "Dialectic and Political Thought and Action,"),[10] he remained silent on the unground-ed priority accorded to his own method of analytic. Might there not be an inventional emergence that changes the nature of the system, per-haps even its units of analysis? Instead of things, thoughts, terms, ac-tions, could there be "thing-thoughts?" Edmund Husserl and Hans Gadamer thing-thought so. And how about "term-actions," what Mikhail Bakhtin would call "utterances"? This is, in my opinion, what is the great, gaping omission in McKeon's grand design: an absence of cultural-situatedness in discourse practices of actually speaking and an-swering subjects. His archetypical paradigm for the world society, dis-cussion, still seems remarkably correct and on target. But of what does discussion consist? Surely not things, thoughts, terms and even actions, any more than marriage vows consist in bunches of atoms and particles intersecting in peculiarly configured ways. If discussion is even to occur in meaningful manner, it must consist of utterances. I consider this modest wrinkle in the McKeon program at least loosely consistent with his overall aims; indeed, the aforementioned essays (on power and international influence) were both interested in developing a historically situated understanding of the concept "accountability." The question we must now ask is whether this revision might help us to relocate rhetoric in a less abstract sense, to find its operation in recognizable world situations.

I believe that it might. And in the treatment that follows, I will be examining one unduly neglected utterance type, that of "confession," in search of an inventional rhetoric in praxis. While this treatment cannot exactly be dubbed McKeonesque, if for no other reason than McKeon never published extensive readings of speech-texts, it is intended to be at least consistent with an appreciative alternative sense of invention; the ways we are able to individuate recognizable form. It also is in tribute to McKeon's prototypical communal aim: discussion.

Confessional Rhetoric

This is a genre which would seem almost antithetical to ordinary understandings of rhetoric. Granted, the harlot of the arts may have plenty to fess up to, particularly in this century. But it is typically the case that those most in need of confession rarely, if ever, do it. The younger Cicero does tell us about something called concessio,[11] but it seems closer to a form of plea bargaining than of genuine confession. Nor is apologia confession, other than in the form of a last-ditch, "throw yourself at the mercy of the public" tactic. It is perhaps understandable that confessional rhetoric has received so little attention. Fully developed cases of its enactment are difficult to locate. However, I think it is an important enough rhetorical activity that it deserves closer attention, even in its absence.

For one thing, we have heard much about a return to teaching virtue, building character, developing ethical norms, and even forgiving those who trespass against us. Confessional rhetoric is the flip side of forgiveness. In fact, I suspect (though I am not sure I can prove the matter) that real forgiveness is not possible without some modest attempt at confession. For one not convinced at all that she has strayed, to be forgiven could only be viewed as something of an insult. To make matters more complicated, confession is not always obviously moral, or even the "right" thing to do. Stephen Carter presents the case of a man's deathbed confession of a long-ago infidelity to his loyal wife as an act closer to cowardice than nobility.[12] He has tarnished a loving partner's memories just to get "something off his chest." What could be said, I think, is that rhetorical confession is always morally charged, and ethically significant.

Why is confession rhetorical? Not all confession is. But rhetorical confession (not yet defined) is so because it involves public utterance before an audience at a moment of uncertainty, involving personal diminishment over wrongdoing. Like traditional rhetoric, confessional rhetoric is also evocative of judgment; only in this case, the judgment is of the self by the self. It is for the other to forgive or not.

We may be able to appreciate the place of magnitude in rhetorical confession by spelling out some symbolic act conditionals for its successful performance. Both caricature and confession have perlocutionary and illocutionary features. Those of confession are easier to express in succinct form. One thing that might need to be said early on is that rhetorical confession does not need to be religious confession. While members of certain doctrines may well believe that they are confessing to God in the form of another person, I do not believe that this belief is necessary for rhetorical confession to occur. Here is what would seem to be necessary:

(1) An explicit admission of wrongdoing is made.
(2) The admission must be true.
(3) There is remorse for the act committed. (This is the sincerity condition.)
(4) The confession is made before the proper party; either the aggrieved party or—failing this, an audience/ agency empowered to acknowledge and forgive.
(5) The magnitude of the offense must be worth the effort and burden of confessing.

I think the above matters are reasonably straightforward. The admission of wrong is really what constitutes the locutionary feature of the act. The truth condition is necessary because there are, on many a police blotter, those who compulsively confess to things they have not done. Remorse is needed for rhetorical confession; nothing may be forgiven unless the act is thought to be wrong. Propriety of party and magnitude are relational conditions. If I confess to my drinking buddy that I've been cheating on my wife, it does no good for him to forgive me. And those who confess to minor offenses to avoid confronting major ones usually are found out long before they realize it. In the discussion which follows, I explore three attempted "confessions." The first two are rhetorical failures, for quite different reasons. Only the last confession, which is treated in more detail, meets our somewhat rarefied criteria for a genuine rhetorical confession.

For our first example of "failed confession," it seems only fair to cross the political aisle and observe President Bill Clinton in one of his own less than exemplary moments. President Clinton was no stranger to the discourse of disclosure and evasion. An undeniably able and charismatic public figure, it was the president's personal character that seemed to be subjected to nearly constant suspicion and scrutiny. Throughout two terms of office, his therapeutic style seemed to join uneasily with the outward form of apology. Clinton professed not only to "feel our pain," but to be a sort of unofficial envoy for cathartically redressing our respective pent-up grievances. So he apologized to African Americans for racism. He apologized to Japanese Americans for their own wartime internment, to native South Africans for the slave trade.[13] Interestingly, in each of these rhetorically charged episodes, the personal character of Clinton was conspicuously not at fault.

Where his own personal actions were concerned, the president could be considerably more ingratiating and circumspect. Before an astonished Democratic Party, the president apologized to an audience of well-heeled campaign contributors for raising taxes too much. And then, in what might otherwise have been the apogee of his triumphant public popularity, William Jefferson Clinton was eventually forced to address the single subject that made his vast constituency most uneasy: himself.

In January 1998, charges were widely circulated that the president had carried on a clandestine adulterous relationship with a much younger woman, a White House intern. These charges emerged within the already oppressive climate of a sexual harassment lawsuit filed by a former Arkansas state worker, as well as a seemingly interminable investigation of Clinton by special prosecutor Kenneth Starr. In addition to compounding the president's personal problems, the charges fueled a nearly year-long tabloid media spectacle, complete with tawdry rumors of intrigue, greed, betrayal, obstruction, and sexual transgression. "A dirty job," the media seemed to be saying, "but somebody has to do it."

By late summer 1998, the "alleged affair" had become the single most widely covered story of the year. Two other unexpected events in the developing drama abruptly reversed the president's fortunes. First, the alleged consensual partner in the alleged affair broke her own silence and was able to negotiate immunity from prosecution with the special prosecutor. And second, the president was forced to honor a subpoena and thus became the first sitting president to testify before a grand jury. These events, plus a mounting array of incriminating evidence, continued to erode the president's credibility.

Bill Clinton faced a most paradoxical situation. He remained an extremely popular president. But his presidency could be lethally damaged, even ended, by proof that he had lied about something a great many persons have lied about: their own undeniably private conduct. In the face, then, of the most damning circumstances, it was decided that the president should make a confession.

On the evening of August 17, the president delivered what was arguably the most unusual speech he, or any recent president, had ever delivered. It was brief, seemingly blunt, largely devoid of rhetorical flourish. It grappled with most of the traditional aspects of forensic rhetoric generally, acknowledging guilt, taking blame, explaining motive, vowing (personal) reform. If this were all it did, or attempted to do, I suspect it might have been hugely successful; and the comeback kid would have confounded the special pleading of his critics still another time. But for once, this one time, the speech did not prove to be the rhetorical sorcery the president had accustomed himself to performing. In the opinion of almost every self-appointed observer, the speech proved to be a colossal rhetorical failure. The question of the moment is why.

The answers are far from obvious; for on the surface, the Clinton speech appears to touch each condition for the confession utterance. In carefully measured words (perhaps too carefully measured), it admits wrongdoing: "Indeed, I did have a relationship with Miss Lewinsky that was not appropriate. In fact, it was wrong." One assumes that this admission is—at long last—factual. On the ambiguous matter of remorse, the president at least appears to be clear: "I know that my public comments and my silence about this matter gave a false impression. I misled people, including even my wife. I deeply regret that." While one might agree with the president's right to privacy, this confession, once made, is surely performed before the proper party: a mass public audience. In fact, if the president is to rebuild confidence and trust, this is the one audience that needs properly to forgive him. So where does the speech go wrong?

It is in the issue of magnitude, the weight of the matter, where the utterance begins to unravel. Since magnitude is a topos of proportion, it reflects relationally between subject and object. Not only must the transgression be of significant magnitude to warrant confession, but the utterance itself must be of sufficient depth and compass to measure properly the weight of offense. Yet in a variety of subtle, and not so subtle, ways, Clinton's speech sought to diminish the weight of his offense and even to underscore the myopia of his chief accusers. The overall effect of this tactic was to make the expressed conditions of Clinton's utterance appear to be tepid, reluctant, occasionally defiant, and ultimately unsatisfying.

Begin with the obvious matter of the speech's brevity. Parsimony never having been one of the president's rhetorical virtues, it was not a bad idea to make a short, candid statement. This was not the age for Nixonian histrionics. One suspects there was also the intent of trivializing by contrast the mountains of testimony, the sheer largesse of the Starr fishing expedition. But whatever the motive, the scripted Clinton performance simply tried to do too many tasks for one discourse of barely five hundred words.

The president telegraphed his initial reluctance to be forthcoming from the very beginning of his speech by terming the subjects of his morning's testimony: "questions no American citizen would ever want to answer." This misguided attempt at identification seems barely to conceal a more brazen version; i.e. "should ever have" to answer. It is only after this that Clinton qualifies, "Still, I must take complete responsibility for all my actions, public and private. And that is why I am speaking to you tonight." Before making his actual confession, Clinton pauses to qualify his earlier January testimony, "While my answers were legally accurate, I did not volunteer information." Translation? "I did not perjure myself." And immediately following his forceful disclosure and characterization ("It constituted a critical lapse in judgment and a personal failure on my part for which I am solely and completely responsible"), there is this remarkable qualifier: "But I told the grand jury today and I say to you now that at no time did I ask anyone to lie, to hide or destroy evidence or to take any other unlawful action." Translation? "I did nothing impeachable." What a guy! (I can imagine Clinton's addressee to be thinking). Rather more seriously, it has been Clinton himself doing the lying. And this is where the fancier footwork ensued.

Clinton could not quite bring himself to the same blunt words about this aspect of his transgression. He conceded his public comments and his silence "gave a false impression." He says "I misled people," a statement which—if taken literally—would be even more damning than "mere" prevarication. But Clinton did not appear to think so, although this is where he musters his only palpable sign of remorse: "I deeply regret that." Interestingly, his regret seems directed at his deceptions, rather than the affair itself. This may be one reason why so many Americans felt that the president had not really apologized.

Another reason may be the series of motivations the president immediately produced to explain his deception: "First, by a desire to protect myself from the embarrassment of my own conduct. I was also very concerned about protecting my family" (apparently not concerned enough to abstain from transgression in the first place). The last motivation is the kicker: "The fact that these questions were being asked in a politically inspired lawsuit, which has since been dismissed, was a consideration too." What is one to make of this? That on an equal ethical plane as lying to protect self and family is lying because one's accusers are politically motivated? One senses an ample contribution from Hillary Clinton's legal pad at this point. An interesting missing motivation, for instance, would be lying to protect the honor of the other party to this liaison. Apart from Clinton's early admission, the "other party" has completely disappeared from this speech.

It is at this point that the speech began to career wildly out of control. Alternately grim and defiant, the president issued less than memorable injunctions such as: "Even presidents have private lives," and "It's nobody's business but ours." Much more could (and will) be written about the downward spiral of bathos in this latter portion of the Clinton speech. But perhaps enough has been said to underscore my point. In its understandable effort to diminish the magnitude of his offense, the president failed to negotiate one of the critical conditions for successful confession: the condition of sincere contrition.

Our second example of confession comes from a literature that is all but obsessed with this rhetorical form. The work of Fyodor Dostoevsky stands as an implacable monument to a human condition "rotten with perfection." His bleak and brooding characters, with emotions, vices, and secrets larger than life, are always on the verge of some dark admission to each other, as therapist, judge, and executioner. In the greatest of this work, such as *The Possessed,* we have premonition within premonition, as Dostoevsky himself anticipates a new generation with only demons to guide it. Published in installments in the early 1870s,[14] this great work was greeted with waves of episodic outrage throughout its creation. While its history may be dubious, its anticipation of history's moods is absolutely uncanny. The corrupt emptiness of tradition and the tragedy of modernity have never been rendered in less compromising, or more hilarious, terms.

Within Dostoevsky's own premonition, there is the reckless mission of his nihilist central characters, Peter and Nikolai. A fanatic, like a fetishist, is a person for whom only one thing matters. And when we have two such single-minded individuals, nothing else need distract or undermine the task at hand. When the end in view is murky or lost, we simply redouble the effort. *The Possessed* is a harrowing view of this existential dedication. It is a vision of hell, without any glimpse of heaven. Whether or not anything may be found, everything must first be lost. The enemy is every trace of cultural convention: the bourgeois class taking literally Marx's counsel about "destroying itself."

Nikolai, the mysteriously charismatic interloper, is the central character. And by the time of the pivotal event of his confession, he has drawn an unlikely cast of co-conspirators together, largely through his exploitation of their own self-destructive instincts. Taken together, this band of miscreants seems a cross-section of every existential malady in the late nineteenth century. That these "possessed" are together even for a time is also due in no small amount to the power of personality exerted by the towering figure of Nikolai himself. Nikolai, like Dostoevsky's greatest creations, never is experienced as a creation. We never feel as if we can even withstand his utterly pitiless regard for others, let alone comprehend what so obviously eludes his own grasp. For all this, Dostoevsky seems to regard his masterpiece with a sort of ambivalence occasionally bordering on sympathy. Nikolai will ride out his furiously self-critical honesty wherever it takes him, saddled to dark forces that seem to elude even the "God's eye" of the writer. Like the indifferent God of old, this author seems to have made up this universe and then let things play themselves out however they will. We find this only rarely in Dostoevsky's work (*The Underground Man* comes to mind). But with this character in this work, someone else entirely seems to be driving here.

Can such a figure as this really make a confession? That is, in part, the question we need to face. Some idea of what and whom we are up against emerges in a relatively early exchange between Nikolai and another justly famous character, Kirolov. Kirolov has just expressed to Stavrogin the idea which will so endear him to modern existential philosophers (such as Albert Camus): the logical, one is tempted to say, *theo*logical suicide. Stavrogin, on the verge of ridicule, makes this crude attempt at a rejoinder:

> "I can understand a man's shooting himself, of course," Stavrogin said, frowning slightly, after a three-minute silence. I've thought of it myself sometimes. And I've often said to myself, "Suppose I committed a crime?—I mean something really disgraceful, unspeakable, ridiculous . . . something people would remember with disgust for a thousand years. And then I'd think, 'One shot in the temple and there'll be nothing left. So, what do I care about people and whether they'll loath me for a thousand years?' Don't you agree?"[15]

No stranger to ridicule, Kirolov responds: "'You call that a new idea?'" Stravrogin is forced to resort to a most revealing allegory: "'Let's say you've been living on the moon,'" Stavrogin interrupted him, anxious to work his thought through to the end,

> "and let's say you've done all those loathsome, ridiculous things there. Well, when you get here, you know that, back there, they'll keep laughing and spitting at the mention of your name for thousands of years to come, all over the moon. But now you're on earth and you look at the moon from here and why should you care what you did over there and whether your name had been disgraced on the moon for thousands of years?"[16]

Framed here with an almost sociopathic detachment, not only action but character itself may be compartmentalized. Our moral responsibility for what is done may be as close, or as far away, as those afflicted by our conduct are to us. Note also how space crosses and effaces time. What has been done is not only "over there;" it is also "back there." That was then. This is now. Out of sight. Out of Mind. Kirolov either does not "get it," or decides to remind Stavrogin of old familiar appearance. "I've never been to the moon," he says.[17]

This sort of public confrontational therapy goes on throughout *The Possessed*. And it has led some commentators to conclude that the typical Dostoevsky character must have had no fear of ridicule. This is, I think, a confusion of Dostoevsky's uniquely voyeuristic posture toward the displaying of his character's psychic secrets, with the obvious dread of cultural rejection displayed by the characters themselves. Nowhere is this dread made more manifest than in "Stavrogin's Confession."

> The problem of *confession* in cases being investigated for trial (what has made it necessary and what provokes it) has so far been interpreted only at the level of laws, ethics, and psychology. Dostoevsky provides a rich body of material for posing this problem at the level of a philosophy of language (of discourse): the problem of a thought, a desire, a motivation that is authentic.[18]

The immediate, albeit disputed, context for Stavrogin's confession is a section of *The Possessed* called the "Fairy-Tale Prince." In this section, Nikolia and his co-conspirator, Peter, nearly come to blows over differences in their views of the insurrection they have been planning. Peter, having grown exasperated with Nikolai (as well as being flush with drink), confronts Nikolai with a rather dubious action step:

> "What's the matter with you, anyway?" Stavrogin cried. But Peter kept trotting along beside him without answering, staring at him with the same beseeching yet relentless look. "Let's make it up!" he whispered again. "Listen, I have a knife hidden in my boot just like Fedka, but I'm still willing to make it up with you." "But what the hell do you want from me, anyway?" Stavrogin exploded in a mixture of anger and indignation. "What's the big mystery? . . . Listen, we'll create political unrest," Peter muttered, as though in delirium. "Don't you believe we can do it? We can cause such a mess that everything will go flying to hell. Karmazinov is right: there's nothing to hold on to. Karmazinov is very smart. Only ten cells like that in Russia and no one will be

able to touch me." "You mean cells made up of the same sort of idiots?" Stavrogin couldn't help remarking?[19]

What happens next is a series of wild mood swings by Peter as he tries to convert Nikolai's radical questioning into anarchist doctrine. First, he will hand his newly leveled world over to the pope. Stavrogin sneers that this is stupid. Peter, delirium personified, says: "Listen, I'll drop the Pope . . . " Next, Peter throws himself at Stavrogin, "I love beauty. I'm a nihilist, but why shouldn't I love beauty? As if nihilists couldn't love beautiful things! Nihilists can't love idols, though, but me—I love idols and you're my idol! . . . You are the leader, the sun, and I'm your worm."[20] If we know anything at all about Stavrogin by now, we can predict his nauseated reaction, as his would-be anarchist ally melts in sentimentality. It is at this point that Peter announces that Stavrogin was to be his "Fairy-tale Prince," in his secret plan to seize control. When Stavrogin asks the next coldly logical question, "What for?" Peter explodes: "So, you just don't feel like it! I might have known it" Verkhovensky shouted in a fit of mad fury. "You're lying, you miserable, lecherous, perverted son of the rich! I don't believe you!"[21] There are times in this great work when it appears that the elusive Stavrogin is something of a stand-in for Dostoevsky himself. This is one of those times. But as we are about to learn, it is impossible to identify with Stavrogin for very long. Faced with the bleak comedic fact of anarchy in disarray, Stavrogin decides to visit the retired Bishop Tikhon. His purpose? As always, this is elusive—even to our antihero himself. Upon discovering that his mother has also been to see the old bishop, Stavrogin becomes even more agitated and blurts out, "And she must have told you, of course, that I'm insane?" Responds the bishop, "No, not that you're insane, although I've heard that said by others."[22] Following several more awkward exchanges, here is Stavrogin: "'I really have no idea why I came here in the first place,' he said with distaste, looking Tikhon straight in the eye as though challenging him to answer." And in what must be one of the great understatements in modern literature, Tikhon responds: "You seem a little out of sorts too."[23]

Stavrogin's stated reason for coming to see the bishop is that he has been suffering from hallucinations and is plagued by devils. A lengthy discursus on the reality of devils and deities follows. Finally, while professing no need to share his dark secrets, Stavrogin imposes his prepared document upon the poor bishop. Further contexts abound, as if Dostoevsky himself is not sure what to make of Stavrogin's text. It was a prepared document from some time in the past. It displays "a grim, naked need for punishment, for a cross, for public execution."[24]

And of the document? It is a curious affair, recounting in tediously exacting manner a dissolute life. The principle details of this narrative are that Stavrogin has meticulously arranged a series of deceptions involving his lovers, his landlady, and even the landlady's victimized twelve-year old daughter. The daughter is made to suffer a vicious beating for taking Stavrogin's knife (an act she obviously has not committed). Later, upon finding his knife, Stavrogin tells no one, allowing the daughter to remain under suspicion. He describes, with apparent relish, the ecstatic pleasure he derives from this pointlessly vile act. To culminate his shocking tale, Stavrogin apparently seduces the poor girl, at least to the point of taking indecent liberties with her. Since this pivotal episode, Stavrogan has been plagued with guilt and terror. He decides that he must kill the girl. Instead, Metryosha (the girl) becomes ill, and a short time later hangs herself. Having told no one of his involvement in this sorry affair, Stavrogin then secretly marries a lame, half-witted cleaning woman (because he finds the freakish taboo aspects of the union, "thrilling"). However, neither this nor subsequent shocking lifestyle escapades are able to still the memory of his role in Metryosha's death. Following a strangely Utopian dream (of innocence reborn, one suspects), Stavrogin signs off, ready to "face the music." He will have three hundred copies of this incriminating document printed and circulated. "If summoned, I will go wherever I'm wanted."[25]

What are we to make of this extraordinary document? It has all the outer trappings of what we have called a confession. A serious wrong has been committed. While we lack a precise vocabulary for measuring magnitudes of evil, Dostoevsky's scale is clear enough. And the unwarranted suffering of the already victimized child is so horrific as to anticipate the Grand Inquisitor's charges against God himself. We also have a would-be perpetrator who acknowledges willful complicity. The perpetrator is tormented by the psychic costs of his offense and makes the acknowledgment—in part, at least—to alleviate these costs. Moreover, he makes the acknowledgment to a bishop. In other words, this looks a lot like a real confession. But watch, as Dostoevsky's own rhetorical genius unfolds and we witness the "evil one's" confession unravel.

The first clue that this might happen precedes the confession itself. Stavrogin makes the surprising disclosure that if he is to share his secret with the bishop, he might as well share it with everyone else. In other words, Stavrogin is not willing to grant his confessor any special status as agency of forgiveness. If the bishop is to stand in for anything, it is not "God," but man. But, it gets worse.

Following Tikhon's reading, there is an agonizing delay (during which Stavrogin repeatedly insists on publicizing his sin). Then Tikhon undermines one of our conditionals by voicing a suspicion of motive. He says: "'Repentance can go no further than the courageous choice of self-inflicted punishment that you are contemplating, if only—' 'If only what?' 'If it really *is* repentance and really a Christian thought.'

'Hairsplitting,' Stavrogin muttered absently."[26] Tikhon further challenges Stavrogin's regard for those who might judge his evil deeds: "'But even now, you hate and despise all those who will read your confession . . . ,'" And later, "'you want hatred from them so you can answer them with an even greater hatred." Stavrogin grows pale, as his would-be confessor continues to deconstruct his motives: " At one point you even try to convince the reader that the child's threatening you with her fist no longer impressed you as ridiculous, but terrifying. What I want to know is, how could the girl's shaking her fist have seemed funny to you, even for a second—"[27] Clearly, this is not going the way Stavrogin had in mind.

Stavrogin seems lost at this point. He pointlessly insults his host: "I understand now why they say you're not fit to be a spiritual guide." He takes back the "locutionary force" of his own utterance: "Perhaps I don't really suffer so much as that suggests—perhaps I even made up much of it against myself." (See condition two.) Later on, he is even more explicit) ". . . well, let me tell you that I despise them all as much as I despise myself or as a matter of fact, more—infinitely more. Not one of them is fit to sit in judgment over me, I wrote that nonsense just because I fancied—out of sheer cynicism." Clearly our antihero is confused. It takes Tikhon to cut to the chase by posing the essential question. If someone forgave Stavrogin, an anonymous party, "'silently, without saying a word to anyone—tell me, would the knowledge of it make you feel better or wouldn't it make any difference?" Stavrogin concedes, "I'd feel better . . ."[28] and we seem headed in a more promising direction.

But this encounter is doomed. Stavrogin refuses to reciprocate forgiveness and "couldn't bear universal pity with humility. . . ." Worst of all, he is afraid of what might happen when Stavrogin goes public with his terrible secret: "'You're afraid I won't be able to stand it? To stand their hatred? "'Not only their hatred.' 'What else then?' 'Well—their laughter,' Tikhon whispered as though squeezing the words out of himself with great effort."[29] Stavrogin loses it completely at this point. Camus and others have observed that Dostoevsky's characters have no fear of ridicule. Tell that to Stavrogin. In his fury, he demands to know what Tikhon finds so ridiculous in his confession. Tikhon responds, "Why? Why do you keep worrying about its ridiculousness?"[30]

But if we know anything about confession, we know the answer. The penitent's worst nightmare is that behind the sliding door our foul disclosure has stirred peals of laughter. Walter Benjamin has found, in Stavrogin's confession, the origins of Surrealism.[31] There surely is the sense that evil and good might spring from the same inventional source, that each might admit to a primal purity that eludes the judgment of conventional morality. And so far has conventional morality fallen in this dark tale, that unimaginable evil might be greeted with laughter and derision. There is further evidence here that caricature and confession are dialectical blood-brothers under very different skin. While one would ridicule the other outside, the failure of its partner ends in conspicuous ridicule to the self. Not even the bishop can forgive Stavrogin. The abject horror (and humor) of this would-be confession concludes not with forgiveness, but with a premonition of even greater villainy to come by Stavrogin. Stavrogin's final thoughts on the matter? "You damned psychologist!"[32]

Guilty as charged, perhaps. In his early work, *Stigma*, the social psychologist Erving Goffman wrote a little theorem of disclosure that might apply to our overwrought antihero:

> the more there is about the individual that deviates in an undesirable direction from what might have been expected to be true of him, the more he is obliged to volunteer information about himself, even though the cost to him of candor may have increased proportionally.[33]

Bernadin's Confession

On March 23, 1995, Joseph Cardinal Bernadin of the Archdiocese of Chicago was invited to the Hebrew University of Jerusalem to receive an honorary fellowship. On such an occasion, one can imagine a fairly large array of fitting rhetorical responses. But Bernadin knew, as surely did his hosts, that 1995 also offered a fifty-year marker for the conclusive documentation of the century's great crime: the Holocaust. And so the cardinal took on a more challenging assignment. He delivered a major speech on the topic, "Anti-Semitism: The Historical Legacy and the Continuing Challenge for Christians."[34] When I first encountered this speech-text some time after the event, its title struck me as odd. Why would Bernadin be posing his principal "challenge" for Christians, when the vast preponderance of his audience at the Hebrew audience would have to have been of a decidedly different doctrinal persuasion? The deceptively simple answer is that a great deal of this speech is a performative utterance made on behalf of Christians generally and Catholics specifically. The performative utterance, I hope to illustrate, is that of confession.

Bernadin opens his quite detailed and lengthy remarks in appropriately modest tone as well as praise for his hosts:

> Ladies and gentlemen, I am greatly honored by your conferral upon me of the Honorary Fellowship of the Hebrew University of Jerusalem. It is a humbling experience, indeed,

to receive such an honor from this distinguished scholarly community. I am also very grateful for this opportunity to address you on the subject of antisemitism from a Catholic point of view."[35]

In framing his subject from "a Catholic point of view" (which he presumably represents), Bernadin positions himself to meet his controversial subject head-on. For centuries, the Catholic point of view itself was regarded as anti-Semitic. Most notoriously, perhaps, fifty years earlier a cowardly pontiff (Pope Pius XII) had caved in completely to Italian fascism, while ignoring the pleas of a small but concerned international community for a more active interventionist role. It is interesting to note, however, that Bernadin steers clear of orthodoxy and takes pains to maintain a distinct autonomy in this delicate situation. His is a Catholic point of view; it is not necessarily the Catholic point of view. The body of the Bernadin address unfolds as his title promises. It is scholarly and formal in tone, albeit carefully inclusive of all prevailing sentiments. I am tempted to say it is very close to what I suspect McKeon had in mind by discourse "of discussion," addressed to other minds in the interest of common opinion. This is another way of saying that it eventuates in a form of power as McKeon understands it. But this is only because it manages to be, indeed it intends to be, accountable. It is accountable from the very beginning.

The first full passage of Bernadin's address, in the form of a report, presents a stunning admission: "In recent years the Catholic Church has undertaken important efforts to acknowledge guilt for the legacy of antisemitism and to repudiate as *sinful* any remaining vestiges of that legacy in its contemporary teaching and practice."[36] This is an extraordinarily inclusive pronouncement. *The* Catholic Church has, of course, sequestered its many variations in reification from time immemorial; so there is nothing new here. What is new are "the important efforts to acknowledge guilt . . ." (an interesting turn of phrase; apparently it has not been easy) and the repudiation of such conduct as "sinful."[37] At least from Bernadin's activist perspective, his version of the church is not only saying things; it is performing actions. It is a promising, even somewhat startling, beginning to an address of considerable consequence.

The body of Bernadin's address is divided into four parts: (1) the roots of anti-Semitism in Christian history; (2) contemporary developments in Catholic theology; (3) thoughts on the relationship between anti-Semitism and Nazism; and (4) actions that can be taken to ensure that anti-Semitism is not part of the future. This may seem to be strangely ordered, shifting as it does between the forensic and the deliberative. However, a closer reading suggests that Bernadin is actually moving, in a McKeonesque way, between causality in the history of ideas and accountability in the affairs of persons and nations. There is nothing deceptive or manipulative about this movement, at least to this reader. What Bernadin seems to be after is an interpretation of history that is fair to the climates of opinion, as well as the motives of chief participants. It is an interpretative frame that seems, dare I say it, humanistic.

The lengthy history of anti-Semitism holds too close an affiliation with Christianity to find its connections dismissed outright. Yet this is exactly what much revisionist church history has sought to do. Bernadin knows full well that he is reopening old wounds when he intones: "Inclusion of this history, as painful as it is for us to hear today, is a necessary requirement for authentic reconciliation between Christians and Jews in our time."[38] Bernadin's history is a complex one, including cultural prejudices rampant at the time, the ill-fated Jewish revolt against Rome, negative stereotyping of Jews throughout the New Testament, and the Patristic theology throughout early Christianity itself. Bernadin does not shrink from the responsibilities of early Church Fathers in his accounting:

> In the East, St. John Chrysostom (344–407 CE) clearly linked the now permanent exilic condition of the Jews with the "killing of Christ." And St. Augustine of Hippo (354–430 CE) in his classic work, *City of God*, speaks several times of the Jews as having "their back bend down always." While the Patristic writings were far more than an extended anti-Jewish treatise, Christians cannot ignore this shadow side of patristic theology, which in other respects remains a continuing source of profound spiritual enrichment. Jews are very well aware of the "shadow side" of this theology; unfortunately, Christians generally are not.[39]

These are, it hardly needs to be added, extraordinarily blunt and bold words from a Catholic cardinal. So much so that they place the Cardinal in something of a dilemma. Is this theology simply wrong? If so, there may be reason to question the emerging doctrines of the New Testament itself, literally the foundation of Christianity.

Bernadin negotiates the conundrum with utmost care. He concedes that there are "negative passages" throughout the New Testament, particularly in John's gospel, where John has Christ pronouncing that Jews are the children of the devil (this, one must concede, is a difficult hermeneutic challenge). But this is balanced by an extensive review of recent declarations of the Vatican Council that "Jews remain a covenanted people, revered by God."[40] The passages, he concedes, do require patient biblical retranslation along with prayerful reflection. This is presumably the burden of Bernadin's lengthy scholarly excursus on what he terms "Contemporary Developments."

But the critical section of this discourse must confront the event that will not yield to hermeneutics, translations, semantics: the Holocaust itself. Granting the legacy of anti-Semitism within at least some early church doctrines and granting, as Bernadin does, that "the theology of perpetual divine judgment upon Jewish people did not vanish overnight,"[41] what responsibility did and does the church bear for this crime? For fifty years, dark questions of accommodation and silence have been evaded and ignored by church hierarchy. The moment has arrived for Cardinal Bernadin's confession.

Bernadin begins where he must, by acknowledging what scholars of many doctrinal persuasions have concluded:

> there is little doubt that classical Christian presentations of Jews and Judaism were a central factor in generating popular support for the Nazi endeavor, along with economic greed, religious and political nationalism, and ordinary human fear. For many baptized Christians, traditional Christian beliefs about Jews and Judaism constituted the primary motivation for their support, active or tacit, of the Nazi movement. Some even went so far as to define the struggle against the Jews in explicitly religious and theological terms. In the Church today, we must not minimize the extent of Christian collaboration with Hitler and his associates.[42]

He calls this collaboration a "profound moral challenge." But this portion of the address could also be read as extenuating circumstances. After all, the doctrinal stereotypes were all in place; and people were greedy and afraid. Bernadin needs, for his confession to be performed properly, to find an accountable party for this historic accommodation. The accommodation of Christians generally, it must be said, simply blurs the true issue.

Bernadin chooses an ingenious course to make his candid plea. He proclaims that, despite the convivial surroundings for the Holocaust created by centuries of Christian anti-Semitism, "at its depths, it (the Holocaust) was profoundly as anti-Christian as it was anti-Jewish, evidenced by the fact that at least one of its theoreticians attempted to rewrite the new testament totally based on Nazi concepts."[43] Whether convincing or not, this ringing pronouncement accomplishes two goals simultaneously. First, it frees the "core Christian" doctrine from the stigmatic connection to the anti-Semitism of the Nazis. Second, it sets the scene for violations of integrity, failures to accord with one's own principles, to be confessed publicly: "We must be prepared to deal honestly

and candidly with the genuine failures of some in the Christian church-
es during that critical period."[44]

The apogee of this address comes with an acknowledgment of guilt
and the open call for repentance:

> Above all, in light of the history of anti-semitism and
> Holocaust, the Church needs to engage in public repentance.
> As I remembered the six million Jewish victims of the Shoah
> this morning at Yad VaShem, I was reminded of the Holy
> Father's call upon the Christian community, in preparation
> for the celebration of the third millennium of Christianity to
> foster a genuine spirit of repentance for the "acquiescence
> given, especially in certain centuries, to intolerance and even
> the use of violence in the service of truth."[45]

This is a beginning, but it is characteristically papal; in other words,
vague. Bernadin goes further, citing with approval a statement by
German bishops, "in which they took responsibility for the failure of the
Catholic community during the *Shoah*." Bernadin continues: "And then
they go on to add a point with which I wholeheartedly concur: 'The
practical sincerity of our will of renewal is also linked to the confession
of this guilt and the willingness to painfully learn from this history of
guilt.'"[46]

The utterance has been completed. But in this remarkable speech,
the most remarkable feature may be its peroration. For two millennia,
the church has sought to propagate its faith with the eventual aim of
converting the world. Bernadin believes:

> there is need to find ways to cooperate for the development
> of a genuine peace among Christians, Jews, and Muslims,
> Arabs and Israelis, that includes living faith communities
> with full opportunity for economic justice. Jerusalem, my
> brothers and sisters, cannot become a mere monument to
> peace. it must be a true city of living communities of peace,
> a true *Neve Shalom*. That is my prayer. That is my hope.
> That is my dream![47]

Conclusion

The speech of Joseph Cardinal Bernadin seems a particularly apt illustration for the McKeon ideal of discussion. In this discourse, centuries'
old doctrines are positioned within larger parameters of language-mean-
ings, all in the interest of enhancing a grounded sense of accountability.

The result, at least in part, is that highly visible representatives of traditional antagonists (neither of which could be deemed a bastion of pluralism) are repositioned in more harmonious understanding. I think, in other words, that the master pluralist we celebrate would have liked Bernadin's speech.

But I am not so sure that the McKeonesque lexicon could fully explain the speech. There is an event-centeredness about the speech that—for all of Bernadin's own history of ideas—cannot be reduced to pure discourse of principles, selections, methods, and terms. This speech is decidedly about something intractable. And actually, the speech would be incoherent without it.

Something else perhaps more important. This speech, like most speeches, is not only about something. It is also doing something. Alone of the three illustrations included here, this speech I regard as a successfully performed utterance of confession. Working in reverse order, the magnitude of the loss casts its shadow over the century, so much so that failure to resist becomes an accountable moral offense. We cannot confess to those murdered, at least not in this life. But we can and must confess to those who understand and are in a position to acknowledge and forgive. We also are the proper party to be doing the confessing. While not perhaps explicitly guilty ourselves, we are the highest visible representative from our nation of the doctrines dishonored by official misconduct. We have remorse, and our remorse is well-founded. Our admission is true. And here, finally, the admission is made. Bernadin's courageous remarks do not close the books. Nothing, I believe, could ever do that. But they do something that may be more important. They reopen the conversation.

In this essay, I have sought to offer an appreciative commentary upon McKeon's imposing philosophic hermeneutic. For all its brilliant metalinguistic archetectonics, the rhetorical program seems to invent everything but an enlightened civic practice. McKeon would surely and properly brand this alleged oversight a classic case of the "fails to" argument (since he no doubt never had any such intention in mind). Nonetheless, my own view is that the neglect of such an important domain of rhetoric has probably contributed to the less-than-widespread enthusiasm for his visionary agenda. Taking my cue from McKeon's own treatment of discussion in two important articles, I have sought to relocate the actional domain of discussion in rhetorically rich notion of the "utterance." My three examples of one utterance-type, the confession, sought to overview the importance of both good faith and referentiality in attempting to perform a successful rhetorical confession.

The subject of our own discussions, Richard Peter McKeon, appreciated the value of such invention as well as anyone this century has produced. This essay, which could never fully emulate his inquiring spirit, has sought at least to perform it.

RICHARD MCKEON'S PLURALISM
THE PATH BETWEEN DOGMATISM AND RELATIVISM

Wayne C. Booth

As I struggle one more time to probe a few of Richard McKeon's foundations, overt and covert, remembering how skillful he was in finding flaws in such efforts, I keep thinking of my first experience with him.[1] In a way it explains why many of his interpreters have thought of him as a dogmatist. It also pushes me inescapably into the two questions that will be my center here: why did so many of his critics and even some of his disciples think of him as a relativist, and why were they wrong in ignoring his universals?

In 1943, I escaped for a few hours each week from my chores as a Mormon missionary by enrolling in a course on Plato's *Republic*. The chairman of the University of Chicago English department, Napier Wilt, had in effect ordered me to take the course, taught by a professor I'd never heard of before, one Richard McKeon. Since Wilt had provided my scholarship funds, I felt obliged to obey him, though I wondered whether a course in the *Republic*, a work I had already read on my own, would perhaps be a waste of time.

As it turned out, there was only one other student in the course—one we then must have called a "co-ed." Since she said hardly a word throughout the ten weeks, the greenhorn Mormon missionary found himself in every three-hour class forced into a kind of deep philosophical probing he'd never before even dreamed of.

McKeon's first assignment was to read the whole of *The Republic* and come back prepared to discuss it. I re-read it, and found it again fascinating but full of outlandishly obvious logical fallacies—absurd "proofs" that I wrote about scornfully to a friend back in Utah.[2] At the beginning of our first real session, McKeon asked us what we thought of the work. The conversation between the two of us—what the young woman was thinking through it all I'll never know—went something like this:

"Oh, I found it on the whole delightful, especially the section on the cave."

"Delightful? Only the story parts? What about the arguments?"

"Oh, they're interesting, but logically really messy."

"Mr. Booth, has it never occurred to you that reading a philosophical work is not like reading a novel? Here we'll not be looking for the 'exciting' parts. We're looking for the argument." (Of course I have no literal record of his statements, but I swear that my report comes pretty close to reality: his words seared themselves into my timid soul. I remember these words as precisely what he spoke; the rest of the conversation really occurred, but I couldn't swear to any one wording.)

"Well," I replied, disguising my terror, "as I said, the arguments are often just plain silly. For example . . ."

And I pointed to one or two of Plato's "obviously absurd" analogies.

McKeon punched hard.[3] "Mr. Booth, you have not really read the book; you've only toyed with it." And from that moment on, he patiently and decisively wiped the floor with me, uncovering careless "literary" and "logistical" misreadings that I still remember. For every objection I raised, he had an answer that would stump me, always referring to the text as his authority: "Hasn't it occurred to you to compare how *this* analogy relates to what he says in Book X, or to the larger analogy between the soul and the state?"

In short, Plato, with McKeon's help, had an answer for every objection I could contrive. After a few weeks of this treatment, I happened on Professor Wilt in the quad. The conversation went something like this:

"How's the Plato going?"

"Oh, it's challenging. (I didn't want to say terrifying.) But I really don't think it's good to be such a dogmatic Platonist as Mr. McKeon is. He's got this absolute conviction that Plato's 'ideas' are real, and he even agrees with Plato that literature, and even music, should be judged by *real* moral standards. He even defends that crazy stuff about the moral effects of distinct musical modes. I'll stick it out, but I do find his dogmatic Platonism weird."

"Oh, is that so? Have you not heard that Richard McKeon is thought to be a dogmatic Aristotelian?"

I had not heard. Having never had a course in philosophy, I had not even the foggiest notion of what an "Aristotelian" might be, let alone a dogmatic one. McKeon had mentioned that Aristotle had spent a life-time *unsuccessfully* trying to refute Plato. What kind of mind was I then dealing with?

Well, it was the same kind that I met in a later course with him after the war, that of an absolutely dogmatic Humeian, not just eager to de-fend Hume from every conceivable attack but brilliant at exposing the stupidities of any of us who raised what seemed to us obvious objections to Hume. It was the kind of mind that had earlier produced a "dogmat-ically Spinozist" book on Spinoza, that obviously heroic geometrist of ethics who cannot easily be fitted under the umbrella of either a Platonist or an Aristotelian or a Humeian. As any reader of McKeon might predict, I later met in him an equally persuasive dogmatic de-fender of Democritus, of Cicero, of Kant, of Dewey, and—somewhat pe-ripherally from McKeon's point of view but highly important in my own thinking—of Anselm: reading McKeon's account of Anselm's ontologi-cal proof left me never again able to say flatly that "I don't believe in the existence of God." I had learned from McKeon's reconstruction of Anselm—and then from Anselm himself—that only a fool could say that.[4]

The question of where the real McKeon is to be found, beneath such a variety of radical defenses of seemingly contradictory systems, has plagued many of his serious students, and it is inevitably faced by several contributors to this volume. The real McKeon traveled in his works over the whole range of life and of thought about life—a range that he himself classifies autobiographically under three extremely broad headings: the history and methods of philosophical inquiry; the aims and possibilities of education in all of its intricacies; the hopes and practices of politics, especially on the international scene.[5] He does not himself deal with these three McKeons as in real conflict, but those of us who look at them closely have no easy task in drawing them to-gether.

George Plochmann, for example, in his biography, works hard to decide just where the real McKeon would be placed on his own schema of philo-sophical possibilities (the incredibly complex full chart McKeon long with-held from publication; it appeared only after his death). See pp. 57–59.

"Where does McKeon himself fit?" Plochmann asks, and finally places the master, cautiously but firmly, by interrelating four out of the sixteen key terms in one of McKeon's various schemata: he has "reflex-ive Principles, essentialist Interpretation, linguistic Selection, and opera-tional Method: two Aristotelian and two stemming alternatively from the Sophists and the Operationalists."[6] While I do not see such precise placements as utterly pointless, I know from experience that they always end in controversy with other McKeonites who would place him else-where on his own various charts.[7] Still, in spite of this slipperiness, I want to argue that Plochmann is right in not reducing McKeon to any kind of relativist: he was "not a chameleon."[8] Though he cannot be accused of utter relativism, his multifaceted forms of inquiry are genuinely always pluralist, and thus threatening to all monists who, as true believers, are sure that some one system will someday sew everything up.[9]

As my opening anecdote illustrates, McKeon really, genuinely, passionately, unfalteringly believed that *when properly pursued,* the diverse projects of Plato *and* Aristotle *and* Kant *and* Dewey *and* an indeterminate number of others were sound, true—though true, as it were, only in their own way; they revealed structures of genuine truths, and methods for pursuing truths, that were and are ultimately, finally, irrefutable. They are not irrefutable in the sense pursued by one of his students, Richard Rorty, turning it all into a hodge-podge of pointless controversy.[10] Rorty's campaign to undermine the importance of systematic philosophizing would have distressed McKeon.

For McKeon, the major philosophies are irrefutable in the sense that they each reveal one true path to one vision of one genuine aspect of truth. Platonic inquiry will forever yield real truth, when pursued by full-fledged Platonists: not just a corner or slice or aspect of truth but a total vision that is so profound, so persuasive, that it can *seem,* to any true believer, to embody a refutation of all the others; McKeon was not just playing an admirable game in that Plato course.[11] Yet the same can be said for Aristotle and a small list of others, only some of whom I have already named. The list of the fully *comprehensive* philosophies, in contrast to the fragmented ones, was never very long for him, but there was never a moment, after his twenties, when he offered the hope, either to himself or any future philosopher, of developing a single philosophy that would genuinely refute or encompass all those others.[12]

Such a plural commitment means, among other things, that there can be no single right angle from which to photograph the center of this multifaceted figure. The quest for common values, or universals that somehow unite or harmonize the many McKeons and his many heroes, will work in different ways for different questers, depending on where they in turn come from: just which first principles, methods, purposes, and notions of commonality of subject matter they adhere to.

Leaving for others to detect where my own multiple selves can be located, I shall here simply consider three McKeons—not identical but overlapping those he traces in the "Spiritual Autobiography": (1) *the historian of thought* who discovered how and why thought is always to some degree circumstance-bound, subject to shifts in political realities and intellectual fashions; (2) the *philosophic semanticist* who reconstructed the major philosophies with more genuine and penetrating "entry" than any other prober I've encountered;[13] and (3) the *philosopher*

who, moving beyond or beneath history and circumstance and mere semantic interpretation, was all the while committed to a wide range of
truths underlying philosophical diversities: (3a) the moralist, (3b) the
committed educator, (3c) the political activist, and finally (3d) the
metaphysician who postponed until quite late the unmasking of his ultimate fundamentals, as described in Buchanan's essay here. (Some have
chosen, as I've said, to harmonize these various selves under the general term "rhetorician"; I can understand that, but I fear that the term has
for most current readers seriously misleading connotations; besides, it
implies a neglect of the sense in which he was a metaphysician or even
theologian: that's why we perhaps need a new term like "rhetorolo-
gist.")

The Historian of Thought

The problem of discovering the true believer underlying all of his sympathetic reconstructions as an insider is complicated by many factors.
Perhaps most important is his passionate and incredibly learned historical pursuit of what earlier philosophers had actually said—what might
be called the historical "facts" in contrast to the caricatures constructed
by other historians of philosophy. His "historical semantics," the effort
not just to understand but to "think the thoughts" (as Garver puts it
here), that other thinkers really thought, as they wrote in a variety of
philosophical vocabularies, was practiced so diligently that his reconstructions always sound—as in my Plato class—almost like what a dogmatic disciple would have said, even when one can find evidence
elsewhere that McKeon saw the author as sadly misguided or at least as
so limited as to be finally of little use.

As Plochmann points out, he very rarely spends energy attacking
other philosophers; when he dismisses them at all it is usually for their
having only a corner on some truth—not a single, grand ultimate truth
but one of the truths that was treated more fully by one or another of
the fully comprehensive philosophies he most respected. His criticisms
were most often not claims that a given thinker was just plain wrong but
that he (invariably he) had in effect stopped too soon, having started on
one possible path.

In his article on G. E. Moore, for example, it is clear that McKeon
has not in any sense tried to refute Moore but rather somehow to place
him on the right platform—a platform that Moore rightly sensed as
much lower, for McKeon, than McKeon's own. Re-reading Moore's
three-sentence reply to McKeon's twenty-seven-page critique, it's not
hard to see why Moore might have had trouble deciding just what he
could reply to. McKeon has both understood and acceded to most of

Moore's major points: he has thought Moore's thoughts, and has then simply insisted that Moore's lines have all been cut off too short and thus compartmentalized and trivialized. As Moore said, "I can quite understand anyone [like McKeon] thinking that the things I have not dealt with are far more important than those I have dealt with."[14]

The Historian of Ideas

When we take seriously this historical semanticist, the historian of ideas—the one who more than any other performed tracings of fully developed, comprehensive ideas, not of the fragments that Arthur Lovejoy made fashionable with his *The Great Chain of Being*—we discover a kind of identical twin: the *philosophical* semanticist who is not doing just history of what others believed but who is—to repeat—*thinking with* those others. He is thinking with them not just in order to do justice to them historically but to take in fully the truths they offer and relate them to other philosophies, doing full justice to radical ambiguities in key terms. This is the man who recognizes the full truth of diverse truths, and thus falls into a variety that is overwhelming both to him and to those of us who would like to discover the real McKeon. He again and again makes it clear that the quest for a single overarching complete philosophy is absurd—the point that Rorty has picked up and inflated.

Is the quest for a coherent Richard McKeon, the man who embraced so many versions of the whole, equally absurd? It all depends on the meaning of the word "coherent." What cannot be doubted is that when you probe his writings in a search for the final, ultimately correct, version of the range of philosophical possibilities, hoping for a single philosophy of everything, you are doomed; studied carefully, his final schema will yield far more than just 16 X 16 squares but thousands of legitimate possibilities.

In his later years, whenever anyone made some hard-and-fast claim about the supreme validity of any one of these possibilities, he would almost snarl, "You're entitizing!" That is to say, you are pinning things down that are inherently, essentially, forever *un*pindownable. He carried this habitual deconstructing so far that most of us who were strongly influenced by this fluid, evasive McKeon have been much less troubled by the deconstructionist revolution than disciples of other earlier schools have been; McKeon had already deconstructed us with his attack on entitizing.

Thus, it can be said that a fair share of the claims made by Jacques Derrida and others against literal fixations of truth through precise language had long since been made by McKeon, and indeed by many of his most admired forebears. Perhaps the most shocking of these, to traditionalists, was his repeated argument that facts are not as much found as made. They are constructed by the particular philosophical perspective of the constructor. A careless reader of some parts of his work could easily—and quite falsely—lump him with the more extreme positions mocked by Alan D. Sokal in his recent spoof that trapped the editors of *Social Text* into publishing his satire without recognizing it for what it was.[15] But McKeon's claim that facts are always in some sense made by us was never extended to the claim that Sokal's mock-speaker makes: a denial that "there exists an external world, whose properties are independent of any individual human being."[16]

It was this deconstructionist side that confirmed some critics in their accusation that he was a relativist: he had sold out all first principles, betraying his original commitment to Spinozist, or Aristotelian, or even Ciceronian/rhetorical/operationalist groundings; he was simply saying "Anything goes, so long as you make it complicated." Even though he again and again declared that he was pursuing a path between dogmatism and relativism, his refusal to slide decisively and finally into any one philosopher's home plate inevitably led superficial readers to declare, in effect: "Since I can't find a fixed label for him, or even a short list of philosophical principles that he declares as primary, he can only be called a relativist." Such critics either did not know, or could not understand, his many statements like this one: "There is *doubtless* a *single inclusive truth,* but there are no grounds for supposing that it will ever receive full and exclusive expression in any human philosophy, science, religion, art, or social system" (my italics).[17] The word "doubtless" in that sentence is to me extremely important; McKeon never doubted the existence, at our center, of a central, though elusive, truth. He was an ontological monist, while laboring as a philosophical pluralist.

The Philosopher-as-Man, and His Universals

What did he see, or feel, or choose to live with, as that center? Dodging the larger philosophical issue of where he fits on any philosophical grid, especially his own, I shall now rephrase the search for *the* McKeon as the search for just what universal values can be discerned, if any, as underlying all of his quests. Did he find, as he sometimes suggested, that all of the philosophers for whom he shows greatest respect embraced certain shared universals, though in different vocabularies? Did they all in some sense end up with the same truth, though in different languages? A full treatment of this question, looking in detail at how his heroes could be reconciled, would require a book in itself, with a detailed look at two or more philosophies that seem to clash right down to the ground. And it would require a much fuller treatment than I can manage of a troublesome question that I come to later: how is his pluralism to deal with what look like flat contradictions in practical decisions that seem to stem from philosophical orientations?

My various questions can be brought down to earth quite simply: can a McKeonite pluralist embrace, and even fight for, any one universal, any one standard, any one value, seen as valid in all cultures and historical periods and thus defensible in all defensible philosophies? Since the word "universal" is radically ambiguous, some redefining will be required along the way.

The questions can be divided into three parts, depending on which kind of universal one is seeking. (1) Does McKeon the man exhibit a consistent practice of character-virtues that none of "his" philosophers would question? (2) Are there discernible "intellectual virtues," universals about how to think, exhibited by all of his heroes, universal habits of thought that underlie the striking differences of methods and principles and purposes? (3) Would all true philosophies finally come to agreement on practical judgments of the toughest questions about right and wrong behavior: questions like the legitimacy of slavery, of torture, of totally free speech, and so on?

(1) Did McKeon himself express and practice a strong adherence to any recognizable set of virtues, values that he himself never questioned—and that thus were universal in his own biography?

This one, unlike the others, can be answered simply and clearly: yes. His writings like the rest of his life reveal an intense commitment to a broad-ranging, relatively conventional code, most of it shared by most of us, and most of it, so far as I can discover, never questioned by him. The classical virtues, for example, most notably the four cardinal virtues, permeate every nook and cranny of his writings, as they do the writings of his philosophical heroes, and as they did most of his encounters with those of us who worked with him personally.[18] Such obvious virtues are of course widely shared, much more widely indeed, even among nonphilosophers, than many cynics in our time care to recognize. (On another occasion it would make an amusing project to probe the work of the great relativists and "nominalists" [Rorty's term for himself], uncovering the substantial list of universals that their actual codes abide by.) In a longer account, one might provide anecdote after anecdote and quotation after quotation to support the claim that McKeon lived at least the following virtues. Though listing them is inevitably banal—since they are so widely embraced—it underlines just how he differs from any true relativist.

Wisdom? All of his heroes honored it and pursued it vigorously, under one definition or another. It's a major end of all of their projects. It exists, somewhere; pursue it! McKeon pursued it day and night, in every classroom, in every article.

Courage? What serious thinker has ever claimed that cowardice is superior to courage? And what could take more courage than attempting, as all of them did, to encompass it all? And does it not require even more courage to undertake, as McKeon does, to understand the whole of philosophical history and produce a dialogue among the heroes? (I ignore for the moment the obvious fact that courage, like other virtues, is sometimes hard to distinguish from excesses like rashness, intemperance, blind indifference to fate, and so on.)

Temperance? None of his real heroes were intemperates of the Friedrich Nietzsche kind, say, or even René Descartes with his intemperate worship of certainty through the logistical method.[19] It may be unfair to claim that in McKeon's view Descartes was intemperate, but for the mature McKeon the logistical method when combined with the existential interpretation was never fully inviting and indeed represented the intemperance that results from overconfidence in any hard-proof method. Intellectual intemperance was one of McKeon's *bête noirs*: it's another term for dogmatism. The freedom he extolled was never a freedom from rational standards and pursuits.

Justice? Whether defined as political and social and economic justice or as responsibility to treat other philosophers fairly and honestly, justice is at least verbally honored by all major thinkers, and it would not simply be verbally honored but was recommended at length and *practiced* by McKeon. (For how the concept of responsibility relates for him to justice, see "The Development and the Significance of the Concept of Responsibility." Or have a look at the word "responsibility" in the index of Zahava McKeon's edition of *Freedom and History*.)

Already here we have a rather impressive list of universal virtues, however conventional. McKeon was always aware that the banality of a concept does not diminish its importance, if its surface meanings are "deconstructed"—a word he did not use—and its full range of possible meanings explored. Stimulated by his way of approaching key terms, I have often asked beginning students, before they've even heard of the cardinal virtues, to list the qualities they most admire in their friends. The resulting list always includes something like "guts," for courage; "being fair," for justice; "being smart," for wisdom; and "being cool," for temperance (or perhaps also for wisdom). When they then read Plato, say, they usually recognize that they join him, in all their postmodernity, in embracing at least four universals. To embrace them as ideals, however, is a much different thing than practicing them, as McKeon seemed to, at every moment of every day.

Thus, pluralism of McKeon's kind fully eschews relativism: real values really exist and should be practiced by all of us on all occasions. Any thinker who seriously violated any one of the four—and one can find such thinkers throughout history—simply would not enter McKeon's pantheon.

It is true that the four cardinal virtues often conflict with others—as justice can conflict with mercy, or courage with prudence. But even those who celebrate mercy or prudence do so with a full acknowledgment that justice and courage are real values, whether or not they conflict with others. I shall later look further at the question of "incommensurability" and the necessity of casuistry if and when we embrace McKeon's universals.[20]

(2) The second question—Are there more specifically intellectual universals?—overlaps with number one but leads to greater complexities. I find in McKeon's work an impressive list of never-questioned intellectual virtues and goals.

The most obvious of these, perhaps, is the one that reformulates justice as the McKeonesque passion for a kind of golden-rule-of-scholarship: treat other thinkers' ideas with as much care as you would hope they would treat yours. Put universally: it is *always* wrong, regardless of your philosophical position, to attack ideas you have not tried honestly to understand. He reports often on his belated discovery of his youthful violations of such justice, as in his account of his most important philosophical discovery, when finally putting together the seemingly conflicting views of Plato and Cicero:

> I had read the great philosophers with something less than intellectual ingenuity or sensitive insight, *as functions of my own limited point of view* rather than as presentations of problems, to be considered in their own right before being dismantled to solve my problems. . . .[21]

In short, to raid a philosopher without really attempting to think his thoughts was for McKeon a blatant intellectual vice.[21] Any of us who lived closely with him would testify to a grand difference between his actual practice of this form of justice and the practice of most people who claim to accept it.[23]

Followed honestly, this virtue leads to a second one: the "commandment" from the nature of things (or from human nature, or—as he never puts it—from God's creative intent) that we ought, in all intellectual encounters, to pursue mutual understanding, not controversy but dialogue. Essay after essay concludes—especially in the period when he was working with UNESCO on the problem of universal rights—with statements like the following (in these quotations, the italics are mine: McKeon rarely used italics; indeed he refused to employ most standard devices for heightening rhetorical effect):

> Analyses of arguments for communication, separated from analyses of arguments for demonstration, may provide not

merely the method by which to advance dialogue in philosophy but also materials by which to lessen tensions and oppositions between cultures. . . . Mutual understanding in the
sense of agreement concerning what the question is and what
is required in a satisfactory solution is *necessary* if philosophers are to resume their dialogue, or even continue their efforts to convince each other of the truth of their respective
positions, and it is *essential* also to the solution of social and
political problems—to make possible agreement on common
courses of action for different reasons, appreciation of alien
values, and confidence based on understanding.[24]

Followed honestly, this virtue, the habitual pursuit of understanding,
leads to a third sibling, concerning education: every thinker should not
just think but join other thinkers in working on how to educate thinkers
who know how to understand: "Thou shalt be a teacher, and a teacher
of teachers," working to educate people who themselves practice the intellectual virtues. In his own autobiographical account, something like a
full one-third of his life was devoted to teaching and educational reform.[25] Though he does not state outright that in doing so he was following a universally valid commandment from God, or from human
nature and its inherent, universal needs, he implies that commandment
throughout. In the following he makes it explicit:

I urged (as we tried to develop the University of Chicago
College curriculum) three objectives: the development in the
student of taste and broad acquaintance with the arts, literature, history, and philosophy, sufficient to direct his interests
and afford guidance into the rich satisfactions and improvements which exploration in these fields might afford; the formation of abilities which are necessary to the recognition and
appreciation of artistic, cultural, and intellectual values, as
opposed to the random associated reflections which frequently accompany the attentive attitude and proper remarks
that pass for appreciation; and, finally the analytical abilities
needed to integrate taste and interest, on the one hand, and
critical judgment and discrimination, on the other hand, into
the context of the principles—philosophic and social, theoretic and practical—which are particularized in the character
and attitudes of a man, and universalized in the philosophies
and cultural communities men share.[26]

Followed honestly, this virtue of the passionate educator leads to a
fourth: every thinking educator should educate not just local students

but citizens of the whole world: the world's hope for the future depends on educating everyone to share what he again and again calls "common values": to engage in the necessary politics, locally, nationally, internationally, that might ensure future generations of inquiring, dialogical world citizens. He became obsessed with multicultural issues that are now on everyone's mind: how can we produce dialogue across cultures, when both practical codes and seeming ultimate principles clash so obviously?[27] "World community consists in understanding *common values,* even when embodied or expressed in different ways, and in cooperative action for the furtherance or achievement of those values."[28]

This point deserves a full quotation from his long concluding paragraph about the "double commitment of philosophers," in "Philosophy and Freedom in the City of Man." That double commitment is:

> the explication of the theoretic elements which have become imbedded in practical oppositions and are the tags and identifying marks of parties in the opposition, *and* the defense, in the course of that explication, of the freedoms which afford the *best means* for the peaceful resolution of such oppositions. . . . [A] world community is achievable in which *all citizens* are, in a degree, philosophers as they understand the problems of their communities and participate in their responsibilities of joint actions. . . . [T]he philosopher can assume a responsible role in practical issues and in so doing contribute something to saving philosophy from the two accusations which philosophers have in recent years vied most in applying to each other: the inconclusiveness of [those] philosophers who have dealt with important problems [such as the dialecticians in the European tradition] and the triviality of problems in which [other] philosophers [the ordinary language crowd, for example] have achieved precision.[29]

When followed honestly, as he follows it, this passion for international education of a world citizenry of philosophically minded folk leads him inevitably to further universals, most notably freedom and responsibility (or one could say, these two lead him to the previous ones). Thus, in the paragraph from which I just quoted, he says:

> When oppositions of doctrines become doctrinal oppositions of parties, there is danger that the stronger will be found to be right, and the plea that force be placed in the hands of those who possess knowledge and love justice is easily converted into the assumption that those in power

are well informed and wise. Political freedom is *essential* to
the resolution of international and national political problems precisely because political wisdom *must be shared by
all* who are to benefit by it . . . Justice in the interaction of
competing and co-operating philosophies and cultures is
the concrete form of the pursuit of inquiries *essential* to political freedom.

(Note that three of the four character-virtues reappear here as intellectual virtues; maybe even courage is implied).

Followed honestly, these virtues lead to another universal, one that
is openly celebrated in almost all of his writing and implicitly present in
all: the drive for invention, creativity, discovery—for keeping the intellectual life fluid by what he sometimes calls "preserving perplexity,"
sometimes merely "openness." The art of rhetoric, in his elaborate wide-
ranging definition of that much-abused term, is largely the art of listen-
ing to conflicts in such a way as to keep honest perplexity alive, and thus
to lead to new inventions/discoveries (he tended to favor the second of
these terms, in my view because he really did believe that the truth, "the
One," is really *there,* waiting to be discovered). This clearly depends on
the universals of freedom and responsibility as necessities.

Again here I see him as a powerful postmodernist: if anyone has ever
gone beyond preaching and actually practiced the golden rule of fully attending to "the other," not just with bland tolerance or benign empathy,
but with understanding, a full entering into where the other resides,
McKeon is the man.

(3) We come now to the most difficult of the three questions about
universals: where do these universal character-virtues and intellectual-
virtues lead in the contentious world of practical controversy? What
would the pluralist have to say, for example, about the much contested
universalist claims of Amnesty International that torture is always in all
circumstances and cultures morally indefensible?[30] Or about the claim,
which I would share with Garver, that slavery is universally indefensible? Or about the claim that infanticide is always wrong, regardless of
any culture's specific needs for or uses of it? Or about the claim that love
is, in all cultures and climes, superior to hate and should be cultivated
by societies and pursued by all individuals? Or—to choose another value
that at least seems implicit in what we've met already—the claim that
the use of violence in resolving controversy is *always* not just inferior to
the use of dialogue but in fact morally wrong?

Add your own list of universals (if you admit to having any) and
thus make the question acute: Where does McKeon, the grand pluralist,
stand—if anywhere—on universalist claims that have produced radical

controversy not just in the political domain but among highly competent philosophers, including his own heroes?

To deal with this tough question we must consider again how the three different McKeons would work together in answering it. The *historian of thought* dealt with conflict in the world of thought historically, as a historian should: what is the truest possible history of what has been thought and said in the past? *Do not cover up the conflict.* He constructed systematic accounts of how the cycle of fashions in philosophical subject matter had in effect duplicated itself at least four times: from those seeking truth about the Truth, ultimate substance, or nature; to those giving up on the search for such inaccessible substance and moving instead to the nature of thought, or epistemology; on to those who, becoming convinced that studying thought leads into hopeless controversy, turn instead to action, or pragmatics; and finally to those who, like most in our time except for the pragmatists, see philosophy as boiling down to inquiry about language: linguistics, semantics, ordinary language, deconstruction.[31]

This historian of thought seldom worried openly about whether the practical consequences of the systems jibed or clashed. Let's just get the history straight, and avoid dogmatism by embracing the truth of multiple perspectives embedded in this overwhelmingly complex history.

Meanwhile the *philosophic semanticist* was busily at work, pursuing the goal of discovering common ground (the pursuit that I've lately been labeling "rhetorology," in order to avoid the widespread pejorative sense of "mere rhetoric)." His goal was to uncover the full meaning of particular philosophies and then to resolve the conflicts and ambiguities of language that are revealed in any one philosophical controversy. This decipherer usually did not worry much about the determining, accidental effects of culture, of historical circumstance. The goal here was not historical validity or placement but the recovery of multiple possibilities independent of historical fashion. Having, as philosophic historian, pursued Plato's claim that "what is on some grounds or in some circumstances true is at other times false and dangerous" (with the lurking threat of relativism), he was simultaneously pursuing Cicero's claim, equally true, that "despite the multiplicity of the forms of its (truth's) expression, 'truth is one.'"[32]

And meanwhile again, *the philosopher* eager to pursue and promulgate certain universal values in the practical world had to grapple with unlimited conflicts: his philosophical heroes often in practical affairs conflicted with his own views. It is one thing to reconstruct, as semanticist, what a major philosopher is really saying, and quite another to deal with major disagreements. What happens, to choose a prime example, when McKeon, philosophical celebrator of freedom and responsibility and universal dialogue, encounters a hero who, like Aristotle, defends slavery, cogently, meticulously, in what can be claimed to be full harmony with his own principles about what is natural?[33] McKeon the philosopher knows that slavery always violates the universal value, freedom, and that the slave owner violates the command to work with full responsibility for the education of anyone within his domain. McKeon the historical semanticist, however, knows that Aristotle makes a highly cogent case, one that was accepted—just like his arguments about women's natural inferiority—by myriads of readers over centuries.

Here I think one of McKeon's "selves" that I have not so far mentioned takes over: the philosophical progressivist who had a deep hope for and commitment to intellectual progress. Despite the many cycles of truth and error he had seen us go through in our quest for a better grasp of truth, he believed that since truth really exists, we can hope to obtain better handles on it. Indeed, his whole pluralistic project was designed in the hope that we could all be led to do philosophy better, and that hope included implicitly the acknowledgment that universals are not universally grasped, and that some universals, especially of the kind he was pursuing in UNESCO with its drive for universal human rights, were discovered by humankind later than others. Thus, though it has always in all cultures been wrong to violate with slavery the basic freedoms, it took Western cultures a long time to get relatively clear about it, and there are still cultures that have not yet made the discovery.

To take this move, siding in effect with Abraham Lincoln and Richard McKeon and Wayne Booth and Eugene Garver against McKeon's hero, Aristotle, leaves us still with the problem that even the firmest of universals may clash with some other universal: universals are not absolutes in the sense of precluding the necessity for thought about when and how they should be applied. If, for example, I happened to become president of a country practicing slavery, I might very well, like Lincoln, allow my respect for other virtues like prudence and tolerance to postpone my open declaration against it. Or if I happened to be prince of a kingdom so committed to and dependent on slavery that to ban it out of hand would lead to mass starvation and a destroyed kingdom, I might be justified in some sort of (temporary) compromise.

In other words, every universalist who believes in the full range of McKeon's universals, including hopes for the full education of all cultures into efforts at mutual understanding, must sooner or later become a casuist who refuses to treat any one universal as an absolute, beyond discussion. Cases usually land us in conflicts of universals that cannot be ultimately hierarchized into a fixed code. Casuistry, in the partly forgotten meaning of the term, is the art of looking closely at the particulars of a case, discovering how diverse values are embodied in the case, and then choosing—employing whatever wisdom one can muster—between those incommensurable values.[34]

McKeon does not talk much openly about the need for such casuistry, but I see built into his philosophic semantics a casuistry that is implicitly demanded by the historical semanticist. The twentieth-century philosopher has discovered these international universals—the drive for peace, the drive for unfettered inquiry (freedom), the drive for universal responsibility to all peoples—and he knows that many powerful earlier philosophers did not accommodate such views in their visions. In judging the importance of Aristotle, for example, one would not reject the potentialities of his principles, methods, and purposes just because they enabled him to prove both the justice of slavery and a lot of other matters, such as the inferiority of women to men. Aristotle's circumstances, his historical moment with its various forms of scientific ignorance, led his philosophy astray there, as it led his astronomy astray, and it took millennia before most of us could arrive at agreement on the proposition, all slavery is wrong, just as it took millennia before astronomers could correct his highly plausible beliefs about how stars travel.

But casuistry is not merely historical placement: it is placement of one genuine universal value against another, and facing the necessity to decide which of two values a given case requires us to violate. To torture someone for having spoken something objectionable is always a wrong, in all circumstances. But that does not settle the question of whether to torture someone to save the lives of others is, though a violation, a necessary violation at this moment: a wrong that is right. The most honorable and virtuous of agents might be forced to commit the wrong, to avoid committing a worse wrong.

If my family were threatened by a terrorist, and I had reason to think that in torturing that terrorist I could learn where the bomb is and when it would go off, I might have to commit the atrocity—but I should never tell myself that in doing so I did something that was just plain right; it was necessary, but still a violation of a universal value. It would be like the action of a priest I once heard telling of his "wrong" behavior when the Nazis came to his door and asked whether he was hiding Jews in his house. "I lied," I remember him saying. "I lied deliberately. I believe that *all* lying is wrong, but I *had* to lie. And that night in my prayers I asked forgiveness for lying—for having *had* to lie. And I'm pretty sure that the Lord forgave me."

Here we see the distinction I've already referred to: between universals and absolutes. I do not find McKeon fully articulating it, though he must have lived with it constantly: There are probably no absolutes, in the sense of values unalterable by cases, circumstances.[35] There are, however, universals, in the sense of values that no one should ever violate without in effect praying to the One for the violation of its nature.

His life thus implies for me some such summary as this: we all should recognize that actually embraced values are often in utter conflict, because this or that culture has not yet discovered the values that underlie all human aspirations. The history of cultural discovery should not be confused with the goals of philosophical inquiry: history must always be in part a history of irresolvable conflict. Philosophy is a search for truth, but it is inescapably embedded both in historical circumstance and the complexities produced by the reciprocal priorities among modes of thought. Only a pluralistic embrace of the Many can do justice to the One.

How should an account of a project as complex and elusive as Richard McKeon's be concluded? He himself offers a fine (characteristically dense) summary of much that I have tried to say, as he concludes his "Spiritual Autobiography" (because of the density, I have added a few comments in brackets, and again a few italics):

> Philosophical universality is easy to achieve by reducing all other views to the requirements and limits of one preferred creed and system, but it distorts the doctrines it refutes; and a similar easy and violent victory in imposing uniformity in political practices, with its consequences in suppression and hostility, is the *only alternative* to a *political universality based on common understanding and on common values.* *True universality* in intellectual, as well as in practical relations, depends on insight into the diversities of cultures, philosophies, and religions, and on acquaintance with the methods and consequences of science.

After then looking briefly at how "integration" and "universality" are to be achieved in the three areas of his lifetime commitment—intellectual inquiry, educational improvement, and international understanding— he turns finally once again to universal values:

> Values are based on the peculiarities of cultures [through a long history], but they are understood and appreciated, even by those who share the culture in which they originated, because of their *universality,* and international understanding is based on the recognition of *common values* in the vast diversity of their forms and idioms. Understanding has a practical bearing both on action (because education and knowledge can build a *foundation* for international cooperation and world institutions) and on theory (because understanding and the preservation of peace are *indispensable* conditions for the progress of science, the construction of values, and the cultivation of the good life). These three—the *understanding* of order in nature [the progress of science], in the

relations of men [the progress in our grasp of practical universals], and in knowledge [philosophy and theology, etc.], the *education* of men sensitive to the marks and uses of that order [the construction of communities that respect universal values], and the appreciation of differences in the modes in which peoples express that order and seek their fulfillment in accordance with it [the cultivation of cultures that practice his kind of pluralism!]—are the three related aspects [why, oh cautious McKeon, why that weasel word "aspects" when you clearly mean something like "universally valid commitments"?] of a problem which *we all* face in our individual lives, our communities, and in the world relations in which *all* communities have been placed."[36]

I am tempted to conclude then by labeling this great cautious inquirer into universals as a deeply religious man. His worship of the One, the inaccessible incomprehensible single truth, was in my experience always oblique, tacit, even a bit dodgy. Knowing how the very word "religion" sets off controversy that freezes dialogue and blocks understanding, he almost always kept silent about his own parallels with the great theologians. But anyone who pursues the works I have neglected here—his great edition of Abailard's *Sic et non,* or the unparalleled collection of medieval thinkers—will discover a man who respects the great believers far more than he respects the great doubters.[37] Though many of us have described him, finally, as an "operationalist" or "rhetorician," my current label has to be something like "rhetorical theologian" or even "rhetorological prophet." Few other thinkers in our time or any other have probed as deeply and constructively into the mysteries of a value-laden creation that permanently eludes our efforts to pin "It" down. He pursued that probing religiously, in both senses of the word: he was at it steadily and aggressively at every moment of every day, and he was all the while motivated spiritually: he felt driven by his connection to the *mysterium tremendum,* the One.

Notes

Preface

In addition to their publication in multiple journals, many of McKeon's essays were gathered in collected works. Often when citing one of McKeon's articles, both its original publication site and its appearance in a particular collection of essays are noted. The abbreviations that are used in these notes are a key to the collected essays and are described in the bibliography.

1. "Spiritual Autobiography" (1953g), p. 36, and *FHOE.*
2. "The Circumstances and Functions of Philosophy" (1975a), p. 111.
3. "Fact and Value in the Philosophy of Culture" (1969c) and *SW₁,* p. 432.

Philosophy and the History of Philosophy

1. This paper is a somewhat revised version of a chapter I wrote for the *Columbia History of Western Philosophy* (New York: Columbia University Press, 1998), pp. 772–778.
2. Benedict de Spinoza, *A Theological Political Treatise,* trans. R. H. M. Elwes, chap. 7, p. 113.
3. "History of Philosophy and Reconstructing Philosophy" in the *Columbia History of Western Philosophy,* p. 758–771.
4. In the *Columbia History of Western Philosophy,* p. 31–51.

McKeon: The Unity of His Thought

1. "A Philosopher Meditates on Discovery" (1952d), par. 8; also *REID,* p. 202 and *SW₁,* p. 48. Since the pagination of the original articles is changed each time they are printed in collections, I have given section and paragraph numbers as well as page numbers of the collections in which the articles appear.
2. Ibid., par. 10; also *REID,* p. 204 and *SW 1,* p. 48.
3. Ibid., par. 9; also *REID,* pp. 202–3 and *SW 1,* pp. 47–8). McKeon mentions in paragraph 7 (*REID,* pp. 200–201 and *SW 1,* p. 46) that he was studying with Dewey at this time, and at a dinner with the Stony

Brook Philosophy Department on January 4, 1966, following a talk that presented more informally what he had just said in the Carus Lectures, McKeon gave a variant account of the origin of his pluralism that gives Dewey a more significant role. He said that it was from Dewey's courses in Types of Philosophic Thought and Types of Logical Theory that he had gotten "my idea."

4. Ibid., par. 11; also *REID*, p. 204 and *SW 1*, p. 49.

5. "The Circumstances and Functions of Philosophy" (1975a), par. 4.

6. "Facts, Values, and Actions" (1972b), last paragraph, and *SW 1*, p. 446.

7. The generative paradox of McKeon's pluralism is dramatically stated by the playwright Richard Wynne in an unpublished sketch, "McKeon as Tragic Figure." He begins,

> First, he mastered all philosophies:
> — positively, he could adopt and maintain the view of any thinker, on any matter;
> — negatively, he could refute the views of any thinker, on any matter, from the standpoint of any other.

What follows? Such a person, "his power balked by his power," can no longer have a philosophy in the traditional sense, and Wynne sees this as a tragedy.

8. For the argument that pluralism is possible in any philosophic mode, see Walter Watson, "Types of Pluralism," *Monist* 73 (1990): 350–66.

9. Eugene Garver, "Why Pluralism Now?," *Monist* 73 (1990): 388.

10. For illustrations of the types of pluralism, see Watson, "Types of Pluralism," pp. 350–66.

11. "The Empiricist and Experimentalist Temper in the Middle Ages" (1929), par. 4.

12. "The Philosophic Bases of Art and Criticism" (1943), par. 1, and *CC*, p. 464.

13. "Facts, Categories, and Experience," The Paul Carus Lectures, delivered at the annual meeting of the Eastern Division of the American Philosophical Association in New York, December 27–29, 1965, beginning of Lecture Two, "Appearances and Occurrences." The lectures are unpublished and the quotation is from a typescript prepared by Douglas Mitchell, March 2, 1989, p. 14.

14. "The Uses of Rhetoric in a Technological Age: Architectonic Productive Arts" (1971c), par. 14, and *REID*, p. 12.

15. "The Interpretation of Political Theory and Practice in Ancient Athens" (1981), par. 1.

16. Ideas and Methods 372: Methods—Dialectic and Logic, taught by McKeon at the University of Chicago in the Winter Quarter, 1970. Transcript prepared by Marcia Moen and Joseph Englander, Lecture 9.

17. "Discourse, Demonstration, Verification, and Justification" (1968d), par. 16, and *REID*, p. 49). In "Fact and Value in the Philosophy of Culture: (1969c), par. 5 (*SW 1*, p. 431), McKeon adumbrates similar steps of selection and interpretation in the constitution of facts and values from immediate experience:

> Reality in the philosophy of culture is the experienced. Any immediate concrete experience has an infinite richness of distinguishable aspects which may be made the subject of attention or examination. Facts and values are selections among these phenomenal possibilities and interpretations of what is given in such a selection in the perspectives selected. A statement about the experientially given in such a selection is a hypothesis concerning what is the case and what properties characterize it. The step from assertion to discovering and establishing a warrant for assertion, to validification, evaluation, actualization, is the step from hypothesis to objectivity.
>
> . . . The selection and interpretation of aspects of an original immediate experience in science, or in action, or in art, are the constitution of concrete facts and values.

18. A bibliography listing ten books and 142 articles was published in 1975 in *Philosophes critiques d'eux-memes,* Vol. 1, ed. A. Mercier and M. Svilar (Bern und Frankfurt/M, 1975), pp. 131–42. Students and friends of Richard McKeon compiled a bibliography privately printed by the University of Chicago Press in 1980 that includes eleven books and 154 articles. After McKeon's death in 1985 the *Journal of the History of Ideas* for October–November, 1986, reprinted the 1980 bibliography with the addition of four articles published by McKeon after 1980.

19. Andrew J. Reck, *The New American Philosophers: An Exploration of Thought since World War II* (Baton Rouge, La.: Louisiana State University Press, 1968), p. vi.

20. I am indebted to Douglas Mitchell of the University of Chicago Press for propounding two of the principal questions addressed in this paper, why McKeon's philosophy is expressed in a plurality of articles and what role paradoxes play in his thought.

21. "Facts, Categories, and Experience" The Paul Carus Lectures, second lecture, p. 26. For a more formal statement, see the original introduction to *The Basic Works of Aristotle* (1940), also unpublished, but mimeographed by students from the galley proofs, p. 3:

Aristotle has been remembered, since the Middle Ages, chiefly in terms borrowed from the Romans to express the more violent reaction of men of the Renaissance against the impracticality, inelegance and technical specificity of the scholasticism with which they lumped the philosophy of Aristotle. From this disrepute and opprobrium he has been rescued during the last fifty years by scholars who have applied a learned and delicate sensitivity to the task of discerning stages of development in his doctrine, but this new-found respectability is dearly bought, for the philosophy is distributed into periods at the cost of sense and pertinence except as the expressions in which ideas are stated happen to bear, not on those ideas, but on the newly constituted historical and philological problems.

22. "Criticism and the Liberal Arts: The Chicago School of Criticism" (1982), sec. 4, par. 1.

23. Interview by James E. Ford, April 6, 1982, transcribed by D. C. Mitchell, February 17, 1987, p. 1.

24. Conversation of McKeon with Robert Sternfeld, Walter Watson, and Harold Zyskind at the American Philosophical Association meetings in New York, December, 1962.

25. *Apology,* trans. F. J. Church (New York: Liberal Arts Press, 1956), 33a.

26. "A Philosopher Meditates on Discovery" (1952d), par. 13. Also in *REID,* p. 206 and *SW1,* p. 50.

27. "The Organization of Sciences and the Relations of Cultures in the Twelfth and Thirteenth Centuries" (1975b). Discussion, McKeon's penultimate speech.

28. "Spiritual Autobiography" (1953g), par. 4, also *FHOE,* p. 6.

29. This set can be viewed as the master topic of McKeon's philosophy. For its use to determine three-stage cycles in the history of philosophy, see "The Philosophic Bases of Art and Criticism" (1943), sec. 1. par. 9, also in *CC,* p. 476; "Democracy, Scientific Method, and Action" (1945), par. 9, also in *SW1,* p. 340; "Freedom and History" (1952), sec. 1 (*FHOE* pp. 160–70); "Philosophy and Action" (1952b), par. 6, also in *SW1* p. 409); "A Philosopher Meditates on Discovery" (1952d), pars. 14–21, also in *REID,* pp. 207–12 and *SW1* pp. 50–54; "Imitation and Poetry" (1954), sec. 4, par. 1, also in *TAP,* pp. 155–56); "Communication, Truth, and Society" (1957e), par. 4, also in *FHOE,* p. 90 and *SW1* p. 396); "Principles and Consequences" (1959b), sec. 1, par 5; "Medicine and Philosophy in the Eleventh and Twelfth Centuries: The Problem of Elements" (1961d), par. 5 and last

par.; "The Flight from Certainty and the Quest for Precision" (1964e), par. 2, also in *SWi* pp. 229–30; "Facts, Categories, and Experience" (1965), p. 2; "The Methods of Rhetoric and Philosophy: Invention and Judgment" (1966b), par. 1, also in *REID*, p. 56; "Philosophical Semantics and Philosophical Inquiry" (1966), par. 15, also in *FHOE*, pp. 251–52 and *SWi*, p. 216; "Scientific and Philosophic Revolutions" (1967a), par. 34, also in *SWi*, p.80; "Ontology, Methodology, and Culture" (1969d), par. 3; "Fact and Value in the Philosophy of Culture" (1969c), par. 3, also in *SWi*, p. 430; "The Future of Metaphysics" (1970b), sec. 1, par. 9, and sec. 2, par. 3; "The Philosophy of Communications and the Arts" (1970d), par. 5, also in *REID*, p. 98; "The Uses of Rhetoric in a Technological Age: Architectonic Productive Arts" (1971c), par. 15, also in *REID*, p. 12; "Facts, Values, and Actions" (1972b), par. 3, also in *SWi*, p. 437; "The Circumstances and Functions of Philosophy" (1975a), par. 4; "Person and Community: Metaphysical and Political" (1978a), pars. 1–2.

30. For a sketch of the development of the semantic schema, see Walter Watson, "McKeon's Semantic Schema," *Philosophy and Rhetoric* 27 (1994): 85–87.

31. For various accounts of these arts, see "Renaissance and Method in Philosophy" (1935); "Suggestions Concerning Organization and Contents of Course Observation, Interpretation, and Integration" (1943), see note 72; "The Liberating Arts and the Humanizing Arts in Education" (1964); "The Future of the Liberal Arts" (1964c); "Discourse, Demonstration, Verification, and Justification" (1968d), also *REID*, p. 37; "Character and the Arts and Disciplines" (1969a); "Philosophy of Communications and the Arts" (1970d), also *REID*, p. 95, "The Future of Metaphysics" (1970b); "The Uses of Rhetoric in a Technological Age: Architectonic Productive Arts" (1971c), also *REID*, p.1; and "Facts, Values, and Actions" (1972b), also *SWi*, p.436.

32. For the use of this topic to distinguish components of McKeon's philosophy, see *The Philosophy of Spinoza* (1928), p. vii; "A Philosopher Meditates on Discovery" (1952d), par. 28, also in *FHOE*, p. 218 and *SWi*, p. 59; *Freedom and History* (1952), sec. 2, par. 12, see also *FHOE*, p. 179; "Philosophic Semantics and Philosophic Inquiry" (1966), par. 2, also *FHOE*, p. 243 and *SWi*, p. 209; "Scientific and Philosophic Revolutions" (1967a), last par, also *SWi*, p. 81; "Discourse, Demonstration, Verification, and Justification" (1967), par. 4 of the oral statement, referring to par. 3 of the written statement, and *REID*, p. 38; "Philosophy of Communications and the Arts" (1970d), sec. 2, par. 1, also *REID*, p. 107; "Philosophy and Theology, History and Science in the Thought of Bonaventura and Thomas Aquinas" (1975c), sec. 1, par. 6, also *SWi* p. 115; "The

Circumstances and Functions of Philosophy" (1975a), last par. Douglas Mitchell has worked out its application to the articles on rhetoric in "Richard McKeon's Conception of Rhetoric and the Philosophy of Culture," *Rhetorica* 6 (1968): 395–414.

33. "Ontology, Methodology, and Culture" (1969d); "Fact and Value in the Philosophy of Culture" (1969c), also *SW1*, p. 429; "Facts, Values and Actions" (1972b), also *SW1* p. 439; and "The Circumstances and Functions of Philosophy" (1975a).

34. "Philosophy as a Humanism" (1965d), also *SW1*, p. 23.

35. "Philosophy of Communications and the Arts" (1970d), also *REID*, p. 95.

36. "The Uses of Rhetoric in a Technological Age: Architectonic Productive Arts" (1971c), also *REID*, p. 1.

37. "The Problems of Education in a Democracy" (1943c).

38. "Philosophy and the Development of Scientific Methods" (1966a), also *SW1*, p. 165.

39. "The Interpretation of Political Theory and Practice in Ancient Athens" (1981), par. 4.

40. For the architectonic significance of the *politeia-politikos-nomoi* distinction, see Walter Watson, "Dogma, Skepticism, and Dialogue," in *The Third Way: New Directions in Platonic Studies*, ed. Francisco J. Gonzalez (Lanham, MD: Rowman & Littlefield, 1995), pp. 205–10.

41. Conversation of McKeon with Harold Zyskind, Walter Watson, and others, American Philosophical Association Meeting, New York, December, 1962.

42. "The Circumstances and Functions of Philosophy" (1975a), par. 6.

43. "Mankind: The Relation of Reason to Action" (1964d), Sec. D, par. 5. For the distinction between persistent and emergent problems, see "Ethics and Politics," *Teachers College Record*, Vol. 62, No. 7 (April 1961): 564–75, reprinted in *Ethics and Bigness*, ed. Harlan Cleveland and H. D. Lasswell (New York: Harper & Brothers, 1962), pp. 471–87.

44. Interview with Richard McKeon by James E. Ford, April 6, 1982, transcribed by D. C. Mitchell February 17, 1987, p. 8.

45. "A Philosopher Meditates on Discovery" (1952d), par. 28, also *REID*, p. 218 and *SW1*, p. 59.

46. "The Philosophic Bases of Art and Criticism" (1943), last paragraph, also *CC*, p. 544.

47. *Freedom and History* (1952), sec. 2, par. 13, also *FHOE*, p. 180.

48. "A Philosopher Meditates on Discovery" (1952d), par. 28, also *REID*, p. 219 and *SW1*, p. 59.

49. "Dialogue and Controversy in Philosophy" (1956), next-to-last par., also *FHOE*, p. 124.

50. "The Uses of Rhetoric in a Technological Age: Architectonic Productive Arts" (1971c), par. 14, also *REID*, p. 11.

51. "*Pride and Prejudice:* Thought, Character, Argument, and Plot" (1979a), concluding sec., par. 2.

52. Interview with Richard McKeon by James E. Ford, March 16, 1982, transcribed by D. C. Mitchell February 16, 1987, p. 11.

53. Interview by James E. Ford, pp. 8–9.

54. Interview by James E. Ford, pp. 8, 6.

55. "The Battle of the Books" (1967b), par. 22.

56. Interview by James E. Ford, pp. 6, 10.

57. For the paradoxes of the *Apology,* see "Dogma, Skepticism, and Dialogue," p. 191.

58. See, for example, Warner Wick, "Philosophy in Community and Communication," *Ethics* 67 (1952): 282–92, and McKeon's reply, "Communication and Community as Philosophy" (1953c), pp. 190–206, or McKeon's reply to Eliseo Vivas in "Imitation and Poetry" (1954), n. 247, also *TAP,* pp. 277–85.

59. "The Flight from Certainty and the Quest for Precision" (1964e), par. 1, also *SW1,* p. 229. "A Philosophy for UNESCO" (1948d) begins from a similar paradox: "Although, in one sense, no consideration could be more important in estimating the significance of statement or the probability of action than the philosophy which animates the agent, whether one person of an association of persons, it is nonetheless true that the 'philosophies' presented in explanation of ideas or actions are often irrelevant adornments and, at best, symptoms rather than reasons." The section of "Philosophy and History in the Development of Human Rights" (1970c) begins, "The ambiguities of philosophic problems are frequently stated as paradoxes. One of the most persistent paradoxes which men have faced has been the paradox of right and law." See also *FHOE,* p. 53.

60. *Spiritual Autobiography* (1953g), par. 3, also *FHOE,* p. 4.

61. "Philosophy and Theology, History and Science in the Thought of Bonaventura and Thomas Aquinas" (1975c), sec. 1, par. 5, also *SW1,* p. 115.

62. "Pluralism of Interpretation and Pluralism of Objects, Actions, and Statements Interpreted" (1986), par. 3.

63. "Philosophic Problems in World Order" (1968a), par 3.

64. "The Organization of the Sciences and the Relations of Cultures in the Twelfth and Thirteenth Centuries" (1975b), discussion, par. 8:

> Then the *sophismata* come in. *De Motu* is, in the fourteenth-century sense, a sophism, a series of sophisms. The sophism provides as a principle the paradox. Therefore, one of the innovations is that in a good respectable science from the fourteenth century on, instead of seeking a principle which is clear and certain and intuitively verifiable, a good science can

be respectable only if it gets a principle which is a paradox. And this is still going on in science. Physics can afford paradoxes. The less exact sciences cannot.

65. "Philosophical Problems in World Order" (1968a), par. 4:

Physics and technology have provided a model in the twentieth century for the discovery and treatment of issues of world order. It is a model, in the first place, for response to the need to abandon the fixed contrarieties of earlier theory. Physical theory has embraced paradoxes and made them principles. This has meant the abandonment of the absolutes of past theory—the Newtonian absolutes, of space, time, motion, and force—but it has also meant the preservation of the basic relations established by the Newtonian physics in a more diversified context of fact and formula. It is a model, in the second place, for use of the horns of a paradox to form alternative hypotheses which lead in their interplay to further progress. For decades the quantum physicists who base their theory on the conviction that the principle of indeterminacy is an irreducible fact of nature and those who base their theory on the conviction that the establishment of a general field equation will remove indeterminacy have each made contributions to quantum mechanics, have assimilated the knowledge acquired under opposed theories, and have moved on together to new problems.

66. *Apology*, 34e-35a, trans. F. J. Church (New York: Liberal Arts Press, 1946), p. 41.

67. For an account of McKeon as a teacher, see Wayne C. Booth, *The Vocation of a Teacher* (Chicago: University of Chicago Press, 1988), pp. 289–92.

68. *Symposium,* trans. Benjamin Jowett (New York: Appleton, 1899), 215b.

69. "Facts, Values, and Actions" (1972b), last par., also *SW1*, p. 446.

70. "Fact and Value in the Philosophy of Culture" (1969c), pars. 6–7, also *SW1*, p. 432; see also "The Future of Metaphysics" (1970b), sec. 3, par. 6.

71. An exception was Philosophy 393, Esthetics and Criticism, taught in the Spring Quarter 1950, which made use of "The Philosophic Bases of Art and Criticism" (1943), also *CC*, p. 463. The course was not, in my judgment, one of his more successful.

72. The original design for the course is presented in "Suggestions Concerning Organization and Contents of Course Observation,

Integration, and Interpretation: Or the Organization, Factual Bases, and Theoretical Formulations of the Arts and Sciences," University of Chicago College, 1943, mimeographed. The course is also described in "Spiritual Autobiography" (1953g), sec. 2, pars. 11–13, also *FHOE*, pp. 21–24. McKeon also designed a component for the history integration course in the college that examined the treatment of space and time in philosophy, art, and science. See "Illustrations of the Second Variety of Historical Evolution and Integration Described in the Report of the History Review Committee," Appendix A to "Report of the Review Committee for History to the Faculty of the College," March, 1948, mimeographed.

73. The Humanities sequence is sketched in "Spiritual Autobiography" (1953g), sec. 2, par. 9–10, also *FHOE*, pp. 20–21.

74. "Latin Literature and Roman Culture in Modern Education" (1977).

75. For the new liberal arts, see "The Liberating Arts and the Humanizing Arts in Education" (1964a) and the subsequent articles listed in Note 31. The new arts were used to design the curriculum at the New School College during the 1960s under the leadership of Dean Allen Austill.

Between Pragmatism and Realism

1. William James, *North American Review* 121 (1875): 201. Quoted in Robert Richards, *Darwin and the Emergence of Evolutionary Theories of Mind and Behavior* (Chicago: University of Chicago Press, 1988), p. 433. The line from Lovejoy comes from Arthur O. Lovejoy, "The Thirteen Pragmatisms," *Journal of Philosophy* 5 (1908): 36–39.

2. Quoted in Richards, *Darwin and the Emergence*, p. 427.

3. John Dewey, "From Absolutism to Experimentalism," in G. P. Adams and W. Montague, eds., *Contemporary American Philosophy* (New York: MacMillan, 1930), 2: 24.

4. John Dewey, "The Influence of Darwinism on Philosophy," in John Dewey, *The Influence of Darwinism on Philosophy and Other Essays* (New York: Henry Holt, 1910).

5. Sidney Hook, *The Metaphysics of Pragmatism* (Chicago: Open Court, 1927).

6. Rudolf Carnap, "Empiricism, Semantics, and Ontology," *Revue Internationale de Philosophie* 9 (1950): 20–40, reprinted in *Pragmatism*, ed. Amelie Rorty (New York: Doubleday, 1966): 396–411. See also Willard van Orman Quine, "Ontological Relativity," in *Ontological Relativity and Other Essays* (New York: Columbia University Press, 1966).

7. John Dewey, "Nature, Communication, and Meaning," in *Experience and Nature* (New York: Dover, 1958 [1925]).

8. Nor was Dewey much of a cultural pluralist, as his debates in the thirties with Horace Kallen and Alain Locke about this issue reveal. The issue is treated well in Robert Westbrook, *John Dewey and American Democracy* (Ithaca: Cornell University Press, 1991).

9. Richard Rorty, "Dewey's Metaphysics," in Richard Rorty, *Consequences of Pragmatism* (Minneapolis: University of Minnesota Press, 1982): 72–89.

10. The rise of professionalism in American philosophy, and the hostility of most professionalizers to pragmatism, is told well in Daniel J. Wilson, *Science, Community, and the Transformation of American Philosophy* (Chicago: University of Chicago Press, 1990).

11. Adams and Montague, *Contemporary American Philosophy*, 2: 433. Frederick Woodbridge is known today among Plato scholars as a pioneer of the so-called "dramatistic" interpretation of Plato's Dialogues, which asserts that no philosophical doctrines can be extracted from Plato's play-like dialogues. The view goes back to Friedrich Schliermacher, and was probably picked up by Woodbridge by way of his education in Germany during the silver age of German idealism. In my view, Woodbridge was insufficiently dogmatic about Plato precisely because he was overly dogmatic about Aristotle.

12. "A Philosopher Meditates on Discovery" (1952d), in *REID*, p. 200. First published in *Moments of Personal Discovery*, Robert M. MacIver, ed. (New York: Jewish Theological Seminary, 1952).

13. See David Depew, "Introduction to Part II," in *Pragmatism: From Progressivism to Postmodernism*, ed. Robert Hollinger and David Depew (Westport, Conn.: Praeger, 1994), pp. 109–21. Also see Daniel J. Wilson, *Science, Community*.

14. "Philosophy of Communications and the Arts" (1970d), in *REID*, p. 104. First published in *Perspectives in Education*, ed. H. Keifer and M. Munitz (New York: SUNY Press, 1970).

15. "A Philosopher Meditates on Discovery" (1952d), in *REID*, p. 207.

16. Ibid., p. 204.

17. Ibid., p. 205.

18. Ibid., p. 198.

19. "Spiritual Autobiography" (1953g).

20. Elder Olson, "Richard McKeon," in *Remembering the University of Chicago*, ed. Edward Shils (Chicago: University of Chicago Press, 1991), p. 306.

21. Walter Watson, *The Architectonics of Meaning: Foundations of the New Pluralism* (Albany: SUNY Press, 1985).

22. This matrix is adapted from McKeon's fullest and clearest presentation of philosophical semantics, "Philosophical Inquiry and

Philosophical Semantics" (1990). *Freedom and History and Other Essays* (Chicago: University of Chicago Press, 1990), pp. 242–56.

23. "A Philosopher Meditates on Discovery" (1952d), pp. 206–7.

24. Plato, *Protagoras,* 339a.

25. The "stuff" out of which arguments are made in the classical Greek world are thing-like, Plato's Forms and Parmenides's Being no less than Democritus's atoms. Thus, we need not mention selection further in our thought experiment about Greek archic profiles. It took an epistemological turn after Aristotle to make thoughts or ideas into the elements of arguments. That sort of turn happens again in modern philosophy, as in Locke's "new way of ideas." Epistemological turns are often succeeded by linguistic turns, in which terms not only constitute the elements on which mental computation is performed but elicit acts or performances by acting as cues rather than referring to concepts. The rhetorical turn of our own time, which McKeon was among the first to recognize and develop, depends on this major fact about twentieth-century thought, the consequences of which are still unfolding.

26. See David Depew, "Introduction to Part II," in *Pragmatism: from Progressivism to Postmodernism,* ed. Robert Hollinger and David Depew.

27. See Rudolf Carnap, "Empiricism, Semantics, and Ontology," and, for an even more strenuous turn toward pragmatism considered as conceptual relativism, W. V. O. Quine, "Two Dogmas of Empiricism," both reprinted (in part) in *Pragmatic Philosophy,* ed. Amelie Rorty (New York: Doubleday, 1966).

28. Watson, *Architectonics,* p. ix.

29. "A Philosopher Meditates on Discovery" (1952d) in *REID,* p. 207.

30. Watson, *Architectonics:* ix. My italics.

31. In his creative appropriation of McKeon's work, Watson proposes an entirely new approach, in which selection is replaced by a fold-fold scheme of perspectives: diaphantic or revelatory, disciplinary, objectivist, and personal. These categories make a better fit with the *personae* who speak in the Greek dialectic I have sketched. Plato is diaphantic, Aristotle disciplinary, Democritus objectivistic, and Protagoras personal. But they take McKeon's work in a direction much more oriented toward the preoccupations of a perennial philosophical than McKeon's and away from the use of McKeon's rubrics as commonplaces for invention and judgment of concrete issues.

32. This means, I suspect, that McKeon's own archic profile is: reflexive principles, agonistic methods, essentialist ontology. By contrast, Dewey (by McKeon's own account) has: actional principles, problematic method, and essentialist ontology. The greater sensitivity to discursive plurality that is picked up by McKeon's use of the agonistic method of

debate is blunted by his claim that each speaker can get to the one essence of things in his own way and that the entire system is as reflexively self-stabilizing as Aristotle's *causa sui* (in the "way of things") or Descartes' *cogito* (in the "new way of ideas"). Dewey's essentialist interpretation is the point of intersection with McKeon. But his use of creative or actional beginning points rather than of reflexive first principles embodies the turn to *praxis* over *theoria,* in terms of which I have interpreted the pragmatist-realist debate.

33. "A Philosopher Meditates on Discovery" (1952d), in *REID,* p. 203.

34. The quotations in this paragraph are taken from *REID,* pp. vii–xi.

35. See "Creativity and the Commonplace" (1973) in *REID,* pp. 25–36.

36. "The Use of Rhetoric in a Technological Age" (1971c) in *REID,* p. 15. First published in Lloyd F Bitzer and Edwin Black, *The Prospect of Rhetoric* (Englewood Cliffs: Prentice-hall, 1971), pp. 44–63.

37. If McKeon had taken the turn that Backman claims he did, his project would probably have come closer to that of lifelong friend and fellow graduate student in philosophy at Columbia, Kenneth Burke, whose conceptual relativism is indeed self-consciously rhetorical and whose politics are, as my argument predicts, more left-wing than McKeon's. Burke made different, but no less interesting things out of the same intellectual and cultural materials that McKeon was working with. It should be noted that Burke has always been regarded by the members of McKeon's Committee for the Analysis of Ideas and Study of Methods at Chicago as an insightful, worthy discourse partner. So indeed he is.

38. "A Philosopher Meditates on Discovery" (1952d), in *REID,* p. 201. My italics.

39. Ibid., p. 203. My own view is that a close reading of Cicero's philosophical dialogues, such as *On Duties* and *On the Nature of the Gods,* will fail to turn up much to support McKeon's interpretation.

40. McKeon, "A Philosopher Meditates on Discovery" (1952d), in *REID,* p. 198.

41. See Rorty, *Consequences of Pragmatism.*

42. "Spiritual Autobiography" (1953g).

43. For example: "Yet the reasons for writing about the circumstances which influenced one's thoughts and about the processes and events in which they are involved can be only that the significance of thoughts, which is broader than the occurrences of one man's life, can be grasped concretely only in the particularities of expression and implication which are parts of biography rather than of metaphysics and logic." "Spiritual Autobiography" (1953g).

44. My thanks to Eugene Garver for soliciting this paper and to Merrill Rodin and Michael Calvin McGee, among others, for critically reading it. No implication follows that they agree with what I have said.

I want especially to acknowledge Walter Watson for the most productive discussions of McKeon I have ever had and for his insightful dissent from the direction this essay takes. It pains me greatly to have disagreed with him on various points. I know, however, that Walter honors his friends for their attempts to honor the truth, and that he can be counted on to ascribe as many disagreements as possible to merely conventional elements. In this spirit, I dedicate this essay to Walter Watson.

Theory and Practice Revisited

1. An earlier version of this essay was presented at the Conference on Pluralism and Objectivity in Contemporary Culture: Departures from the Philosophy of Richard McKeon, The University of Chicago, March 13–14, 1992. For assistance in its revision I am indebted to Craig Calhoun and Doug Mitchell.

2. George Plochmann, *Richard McKeon: A Study* (Chicago: University of Chicago Press, 1990).

3. Those unfamiliar with the work of either will probably find these figures opaque, and some may find them uncongenial. To begin to represent the power and significance of these schemata would take a small book for each. I can only hope that they may whet the appetites of some readers and not alienate others.

4. *Talcott Parsons: Theorist of Modernity*, ed. Roland Robertson and Bryan S. Turner (London: Sage Publications, 1991), p. 17.

5. Walter Watson, "McKeon: The Unity of His Thought," Paper presented at the Conference on Pluralism and Objectivity in Contemporary Culture: Departures from the Philosophy of Richard McKeon, University of Chicago.

6. Ibid., p. 1. See also "Fact and Value in the Philosophy of Culture" (1969c), p. 507.

7. Jeffrey Alexander, *The Modern Reconstruction of Classical Thought: Talcott Parsons* (Berkeley, Ca.: University of California Press, 1983).

8. "Fact and Value in Philosophy of Culture" (1969c), pp. 505–6.

9. 1952b.

10. "Philosophical Semantics and Philosophic Inquiry" (1990), p. 250.

11. Talcott Parsons, "The Place of Ultimate Values in Sociological Theory," *International Journal of Ethics* 45 (1935): 282.

12. Talcott Parsons, *The Social System* (Glencoe, Ill.: Free Press, 1951), pp. 195–98.

13. Talcott Parsons, "A Tentative Outline of American Values." Theory, Culture, and Society 6, no. 4: 557–612. Reprinted in Robertson and Turner 1991, pp. 37–67.

14. Stephen R. Warner, "Toward a Redefinition of Action Theory: Paying the Cognitive Element Its Due," *American Journal of Sociology* 83 (1978): 1317–49. However, Alexander, pp. 460–62, offers trenchant argument to show that Warner overstated this criticism.

15. Talcott Parsons, "Social Science: A Basic National Resource," in *The Nationalization of the Social Sciences,* ed. Samuel Z. Klausner and Victor M. Lidz, pp. 41–112 (Philadelphia: University of Pennsylvania Press, 1986).

16. Morris Janowitz, "Sociological Models and Social Policy," Archives for Philosophy of Law and Social Philosophy LV (1969): 307–19. Reprinted as "Theory and Policy: Engineering versus Enlightenment Models," in *Morris Janowitz on Social Organization and Social Control,* ed. James Burk, pp. 86–95 (Chicago: University of Chicago Press, 1991).

17. Although the taxonomy that follows is my own, not McKeon's, the type of thinking it embodies has clearly been inspired by McKeon.

18. Aristotle, *Nicomachean Ethics,* 2, 6, 1106b20–24; 2, 9, 1109a25–29.

19. Ibid., 6, 1141b14–22, 1142a23–28.

20. Karl Marx.

21. Plochmann, *Richard McKeon,* p. 92.

22. Pp. 11–12. See also "A Philosopher Meditates on Discovery" (1952d), pp. 120–23.

23. Donald N. Levine, *Visions of the Sociological Tradition,* Part I (Chicago: University of Chicago Press, 1995) applies this cyclical mode in another context—to interpret a sequence of shifts in the types of narrative used by sociologists over the past century—including Parsons, *The Structure of Social Action*—to represent the history of their disciplinary tradition.

24. Plochmann, *Richard McKeon,* p. 91.

25. On this point, my gloss on the Freudian schema cuts across that of Parsons as represented in Figure 2.

One Mind in the Truth

1. Richard Rorty, *Philosophy and the Mirror of Nature* (Princeton: Princeton University Press, 1980), p. 366, quoted in *REID,* p. ix.

2. Susan Bordo, "The View from Nowhere and the Dream of Everywhere: Heterogeneity, Adequation and Feminist Theory," *APA Newsletter,* March 1989, 88:2.

3. Ibid., p. 21. The quotation is from Carroll Smith-Rosenberg, *Disorderly Conduct* (Oxford: Oxford UP, 1985) p. 291.

4. Addressing the pressing issue of the legal challenge to Bertrand Russell's appointment at CCNY, McKeon reviews the plight of every philosopher from Socrates to Spinoza. "The Problems of Education in a Democracy" (1943c.) pp. 91–130. Even in "personal" circumstance McKeon could not resist the historical array. His presidential address for the APA delivered at an after-dinner occasion was a stunning scholarly review of all after dinner speeches from Plato's *Symposium* to Luther's *Tischreden.* "Love and Philosophical Analysis" (1954), also in *TAP.*

5. An amusing example of McKeon's non-Western interest was a tale he told about meeting a group of Syrian philosophy professors while traveling in the Middle East. He queried them about what they were teaching. Russell, Whitehead, positivism. McKeon was aghast and asked why they weren't teaching Avicenna, Alfarabi, and the like. Well, they didn't know much about those philosophers. The next thing, McKeon offered to give (and then gave) a set of lectures in Damascus on Arabic philosophy.

6. McKeon, "A Philosopher Meditates on Discovery" (1952d) in *Moments of Personal Discovery,* ed. Robert MacIver (New York: Harper & Row, 1952), p. 201.

7. "Communication, Truth, and Society" (1957e), p. 91.

8. Ibid.

9. "Viable communication moves in four dimensions: it relates man to man, and that relation determines and is determined by what man can become, by the ideals which inspire him, and by his conception of the objective circumstances which environ him." "Communication" (1957e), pp. 93–94. (Since he was a classical scholar, one will generously suppose that in all such passages McKeon is unconsciously translating the neutral *anthropos* as "man" in an "ungendered" sense.)

10. "Communication" (1957e), pp. 94–95.

11. Ibid., pp. 94–95.

12. Ibid., p. 95.

13. Ibid.

14. Ibid., p. 94.

15. Ibid., p. 95.

16. Plato, *Republic,* 414.

17. "Communication" (1957e), p. 98.

18. Ibid., p. 99.

19. Ibid., p. 94.

20. When I went to Princeton in 1957, one of the most precious possessions of the department was a photocopy of the mimeographed notes which constituted the Blue Book and the Brown Book. These sketches for the sketches that were to be published as *Philosophical Investigations*

were hot underground property for those not privileged to have attended the master's arduous seminars at Cambridge during the 1930s.

21. Ludwig Wittgenstein, *The Blue Book* (Oxford: Blackwell, 1958), pp. 58–59.

Memoirs of a Pluralist

1. There is a story—probably only a story—that Bertrand Russell, as sponsor/inventor of the account of implication in which this statement makes its "counter-intuitive" sense, was once asked how it was that "two and two is five" implies "Russell is the pope." "You say two and two is five, but I can prove that two and two is four. Thus four is equal to five and two is one. The pope and I are two; therefore the pope and I are one." The story bears witness to Russell's reputation for quick wit and a certain sense of humor, if nothing else.

2. About this same time, for example, his friend Kenneth Burke was developing another analysis of the plurality of "the philosophical schools" based not on logical commonplaces but those of the ethical and rhetorical treatment of action and motivation. *A Grammar of Motives*—a work destined to become increasingly influential over succeeding decades—was published in 1945.

3. This phenomenon is most obvious in an academic community—perhaps particularly among "researchers"—because their activity and "work product" tend to be more explicitly intellectual: some sort of argument or inquiry. Also, most of them are happy, even anxious, to explain what they're doing, and occasionally such explanation becomes genuinely reflective—philosophically sophisticated.

4. *Appearance and Reality,* 2nd. ed. (Oxford: Oxford University Press, 1906), pp.1–2.

5. "Dismiss" as *logic*—he thought (or at least said) that it was good psychology, but of course it was not logic. (I do not know whether he ever said this in print; I certainly heard him say it.)

6. F. C. S. Schiller.

7. I remember sitting in a hotel room at the end of a day of sessions of the Western Division of the American Philosophical Association while McKeon explained, at the special request of two Catholic theologians, how the books of the *Metaphysics* constituted an intelligible sequence of investigation. Since he did it from memory and with a drink in hand I suppose it counts as something of a "stunt." The significant point is that this is the sort of feat for which he was at that time renowned. (This would have been in the fifties. Was it in Minneapolis?)

Pluralism and the Virtues of Philosophy

1. One of the lessons all his students learned from McKeon is to avoid as uninformative and misleading all talk of "isms." By liberalism, I mean only the practical arrangements that separate church and state, ethics and politics, and the theoretical and rhetoric resources used to justify and make sense of such separations, just as by pluralism I mean whatever the reflective and intelligent response to the predicament of diversity turns out to be. I leave for another time questions about the precise connections between liberalism and pluralism.

2. John Dewey, *The Quest for Certainty* (New York: Capricorn Books, 1929), pp. 160, 228.

3. Alasdair MacIntyre, *Whose Justice? Which Rationality?* (South Bend, Ind.: University of Notre Dame Press, 1988), p. 384. "Just because and insofar as the internationalized languages-in-use of late twentieth-century modernity have minimal presuppositions in respect of possibly rival belief systems, their shared criteria for the correct application of such concepts as 'is true' and 'is reasonable' must also be minimal."

4. "A Philosopher Meditates on Discovery" (1952d), p. 205. "Changes in the world situation [make] the relations of peoples, nations, classes, and in general all associations profoundly philosophic problems. Men of all cultures, of all nations, and of all philosophies have been brought into contacts that affect every aspect of their lives."

5. Charles Larmore, *Patterns of Moral Complexity* (Cambridge: Cambridge University Press, 1987), p. 49. "Classical utilitarianism fails to be neutral . . . because it subscribes to a subjectivistic conception of the good and thus of the good life that many will reasonably not share. For much that is good is not a matter of our experiences, but rather of what we do; and such nonexperiential goods can often be constitutive of some ideal of the good life. The utilitarian principle would force many to understand the value of what they pursue in a manner alien to what makes it of value to them.

"There is, I think, an important lesson to be learned from the classical utilitarians' failure. They adopted what may well be a wrong strategy for arriving at a position neutral with respect to different conceptions of the human good. They thought that neutrality would be secured if they could find what each such conception *has in common*. For them this common denominator was a certain sort of experience. . . . But we should be skeptical whether there is any sort of common denominator to all that can reasonably be considered good. The human good may be irreducibly various, incommensurable with respect to any single standard."

6. John Dewey, "From Absolutism to Experimentalism," in *Later Works: 1925–1953* (Carbondale: SIU Press, 1984), V: 154–55. "Nothing could be more helpful to present philosophizing than a 'Back to Plato' movement; but it would have to be back to the dramatic, restless, cooperatively inquiring Plato of the Dialogues, trying one mode of attack after another to see what it might yield; back to the Plato whose highest flight of metaphysics always terminated with a social and political turn, and not to be artificial Plato constructed by unimaginative commentators who treated him as the original university professor."

7. John Dewey, *Freedom and Culture,* pp. 145–146.

8. Bernard Williams, *Descartes: The Project of Pure Enquiry* (Atlantic Highlands, N.J.: Humanities Press, 1978).

9. Onora O'Neill, "Ethical Reasoning and Ideological Pluralism," *Ethics* 98 (1988): 718.

10. See Cynthia Farrar, *The Origins of Democratic Thinking: The Invention of Politics in Classical Athens* (Cambridge: Cambridge University Press, 1988).

11. John Dewey, *The Public and Its Problems* (Chicago: Gateway Books, 1946), p. 126. First published by Henry Holt, 1927.

12. *Critique of Judgment* (Section 40. 160–1/294). See also *Anthropology* 228; 96–97, *Logic,* 63. The plurality of methods explicated systematically by McKeon also has affinities to Ian Hacking's recent description of "Styles of Scientific Reasoning," in *Post-Analytic Philosophy,* ed. J. Rajchman and C. West (New York: Columbia University Press, 1985), pp. 145–65. See, e.g., p. 155. "Logic is the preservation of truth, while a style of reasoning is what brings in the possibility of truth or falsehood. . . . Styles of reasoning create the possibility for truth and falsehood. Deduction and induction merely preserve it." An important earlier exploration of plurality of rationality by a student of McKeon's is William Sacksteder, "Inference and Philosophic Typologies," *Monist* 48 (1964): 567–601. I find this appeal to the *Critique of Judgment* a more useful approach to pluralism than that indicated by McKeon's long-time comrade in the explorations of pluralism and rhetoric, Chaim Perelman. See Chaim Perelman and L. Olbrecht-Tyteca, *The New Rhetoric: A Treatise on Argumentation,* trans. John Wilkinson and Purcell Weaver (South Bend, Ind.: University of Notre Dame Press, 1969), pp. 48–50. "To reconcile philosophical claims to rationality with the plurality of philosophical systems, we must recognize that the appeal to reason must be identified not as an appeal to a single truth but instead as an appeal for the adherence of an audience, which can be thought of, after the manner of Kant's categorical imperative, as encompassing all reasonable and competent men."

13. "Communication, Truth, and Society" (1957e), p. 99. The idea of plural modes of thought is more radical, and a more productive way of

thinking about ultimate diversity of thought, than the more common way of conceiving diversity as a conflict of fundamental beliefs, which we find, for example, in Nicholas Rescher, *Pluralism: Against the Demand for Consensus* (Oxford: Clarendon Press, 1993).

14. Collingwood, *Speculum Mentis,* pp. 190–1. There are similarities between the projects and careers of Collingwood and McKeon worth noticing. Both were interdisciplinary thinkers vitally concerned with the relations between philosophy and its history and between philosophy and practice. Both were admired by other philosophers but not taken as part of the dominant community of discourse among philosophers.

15. *Ethics and the Limits of Philosophy,* pp. 148, 167–69.

16. Jonathan Sacks, *One People? Tradition, Modernity and Jewish Unity* (London: Littman Library of Jewish Civilization, 1993), p. 147. See also David Sidorsky, "Moral Pluralism and Philanthropy," *Social Philosophy and Policy* 4 (1987): 100. "The justification for religious tolerance was the similarity of value commitment in the other religion that deserved to be tolerated. In that sense, pluralism required the relegation to insignificance of such 'outward' or secondary aspects of religion as ritual, language, and form and style of worship, and appropriate appreciation of the 'inward' or major substance of moral value. In the parable of Lessing's play *Nathan the Wise,* which is paradigmatic for religious tolerance in the Enlightenment, the authentic magical ring transmitted over generations can only be distinguished from the counterfeit ring by its *moral* powers. All religions share, in this view, the *core* of ethical culture."

17. Richard Bernstein, "The Varieties of Pluralism," *American Journal of Education* 95 (1987): 511. "A primary reason why philosophers have recently become so obsessed with radical relativism and incommensurability is that this reflects what is happening in our everyday lives where we experience the phenomenon of becoming entrenched in limiting languages, horizons and paradigms."

18. *Relativism and the Social Sciences* (Cambridge: Cambridge University Press, 1985), p. 158. I have applied this sense of the possibilities of history, and the current dilemma, to Machiavelli in "After *Virtù:* Rhetoric, Prudence, and Moral Pluralism in Machiavelli's *Discourses on Livy*," *History of Political Thought,* forthcoming, and to contemporary discussion of critical thinking and rhetoric in "Point of View, Bias, and Insight," *Metaphilosophy* 24 (1993): 47–60.

19. "The Priority of Democracy to Philosophy," in *The Virginia Statute of Religious Freedom,* ed. Merrill Peterson and Robert Vaughn (Cambridge: Cambridge University Press, 1988), and reprinted in Alan R. Malachowski, *Reading Rorty* (Oxford: Blackwell, 1989), p. 293. "There is a moral purpose behind this light-mindedness. It helps make the world's inhabitants more pragmatic, more tolerant, more liberal,

more receptive to the appeal of instrumental rationality. Moral commitment, after all, does not require taking seriously all the matters which are, for moral reasons, taken seriously by one's fellow citizens. It may require just the opposite. It may require to josh them out of the habit of taking topics so seriously. There may be serious reasons for so joshing them. More generally, we should not assume the aesthetic is always the enemy of the moral. I should argue that in the recent history of liberal societies, the willingness to view matters aesthetically . . . to be content to indulge in what Schiller called 'play' and to discard what Nietzsche called 'the spirit of seriousness' has been an important vehicle of moral progress." I have looked at Rorty's development of Dewey's thought in "Pragmatism and the Unity of Practical Reason," in *In Search of the Public,* ed. George Graham, forthcoming. Insofar as Rorty and McKeon represent divergent ways of developing pragmatism further through the encounter with plurality, that piece could be regarded as a companion to this one. Compare Allan Bloom (*Closing,* p. 35), who thought that religious wars were proof that partisans took "their beliefs seriously," and conversely that the lack of people dying, and killing, for ideas means that ideas are no longer central to their lives.

20. For personality as either arbitrary or necessary, see, among many others, Michael W. McConnell, "Religious Freedom at the Crossroads," in *The Bill of Rights in the Modern State,* ed. Geoffrey R. Stone, Richard A. Epstein, and Cass. R. Sunstein (Chicago: University of Chicago Press, 1992), pp. 115–94. I have developed the sense of *êthos* under discussion here, and shown its central place in Aristotle's *Rhetoric,* in *Aristotle's Rhetoric: An Art of Character* (Chicago: University of Chicago Press, 1995).

"Love, Self, and Contemporary Culture" (1968e), p. 15. "Each of the paradoxes [of self-knowledge, self-determination, and self-realization] yields, on one side, an apparent relativity of the person to his conditioning external circumstances and, on the other side, an irresistible objectivity of the person internally reflexive to himself. This reflexivity makes it possible to cultivate diversity without disorder, pursue pluralism without relativism, and set up criteria without dogmatism or constraint. The opportunity of the self in contemporary culture is to use the new possibilities of reflexivity to achieve freedom and to assume responsibility as opposed to the automatic conformism and the aggressive irrational self-assertion which are the heteronomous effects of new circumstances frequently presented as the dominant characteristics of the age."

21. Thus Aquinas proposes tolerating Jews, since they could remind Christians of the meaning of what they had rejected, while there was no practical threat that Christians would be attracted to these rejected ideas. But at the same time, Aquinas will not tolerate Christian heretics,

because they presented live possibilities that were too tempting to regard with equanimity, or confidence. *Summa Theologica* 2a 2ae 9–11.

22. Bernard Williams, *Ethics and the Limits of Philosophy* (Cambridge, Mass.: Harvard University Press, 1985), p. 160.

23. "Dialectical and Politcal Thought and Actions," 23.

24. *Philosophical Investigations* (Oxford: Blackwell, 1963), p. 125. Cf. Bernard Williams, "Conflicts of Values," p. 222. "Where conflict needs to be overcome, this 'need' is not of a purely logical character, nor a requirement of pure rationality, but rather a kind of social or personal need, the pressure of which will be felt in some historical circumstances rather than others." Charles Taylor, "Rorty in the Epistemological Tradition," in Alan R. Malachowski, *Reading Rorty* (Oxford: Blackwell, 1989), pp. 260–61. "What makes consistency? Now there is a story which was injected into our philosophical bloodstream by the Vienna School that consistency is a matter of logic. Propositions are consistent, and they are so when they fail to contradict each other. But this doesn't get to the interesting questions. We use logical inconsistency to point up and articulate what's wrong with a position, but that's not how we identify it as wrong. For instance, we might say to a holder of a self-indulgent view: 'How nice and convenient! If your artistic and love life, you're always quoting Sartre, and rejecting any human essence. Then when you want to denounce the Junta, suddenly you're talking about their violating this essence. You can't have it both ways.'"

25. David Hume, *Essays,* pp. 252–53. Laurence Thomas, "Statistical Badness," *Journal of Social Philosßophy* 23 (1992): 34–35. "An irrational and negative attitude about a car model that one does not correct in light of the facts available to one is just that—an incorrect, irrational, and negative attitude towards a particular model of car. Not so with human beings. A mistaken, negative, and irrational attitude about a group of human beings that one does not correct in light of the facts readily available to one constitutes a prejudice." Hume's place in the history of pluralism is a main theme of my "Why Pluralism Now?" *Monist* 73 (1990): 388–410. See also Arendt's comment on Eichmann, *Eichmann in Jerusalem* (New York: Viking, 1963), p. 255: "For politics is not like the nursery; in politics, obedience and support are the same."

26. Lee H. Yearly, "Education and the Intellectual Virtues," in *Beyond the Classics: Essays in Religious Studies and Liberal Education,* ed. Frank E. Reynolds and Sheryl L. Burkhalter (Atlanta, Ga.: Scholars Press, 1990), p. 100. Something similar occurs at the end of Richard Popkin's autobiography, where he reports that he is "psychologically hostile to orthodox Jewish practice in a way in which I am not hostile to Catholic or Shi'ite practices. . . . The dogmatic restrictions orthodoxy imposes on daily life in Israel makes me want to start a Church of the Blessed Benedictus (Spinoza) to advocate now and forever the sacred

separateness of Church and State, and the basic moral law. I do not have the same reaction to Catholicism or Shi'ite Islam, though I understand historically how their views and practices developed. These are not live options in my world, so I can explain them as an outsider." Richard Popkin, "Intellectual Autobiography: Warts and All," in *The Sceptical Mode in Modern Philosophy: Essays in Honor of Richard H. Popkin,* ed. Richard A. Watson and James E. Force (Dordrecht: Nijoff, 1988), pp. 148–49.

27. Richard Rorty, "Postmodernist Bourgeois Liberalism," *Journal of Philosophy* 80 (1983): 587. See also Jonathan Sacks, *The Persistence of Faith: Religion, Morality and Society in a Secular Age* (London: Weidenfeld and Nicolson, 1991), p. 64. "Precisely because liberalism gained power in the nineteenth century it was able to take for granted a high degree of shared morality and belief, without having to reflect too carefully on the institutions that sustained it. Pluralism takes much further the idea that there is no such shared basis of society. Public policy should be neutral in matters of religion and should merely adjudicate impartially between conflicting claims. The problem is that pluralism gives rise to deep and intractable conflicts while at the same time undermining the principles by which they might be resolved. It disintegrates our concept of the common good."

28. "Relativism, Power, and Philosophy," in *Relativism: Interpretation and Confrontation,* ed. Michael Krausz (Notre Dame, Ind.: University of Notre Dame Press, 1989), p. 201. Hans Küng, "Dialogability and Steadfastness: on Two Complementary Virtues," in *Radical Pluralism and Truth: David Tracy and the Hermeneutics and Religion,* ed. Werner G. Jeanrond and Jennifer L. Rike (New York: Crossroad, 1991), p. 243. "The [inclusivist position] holds that one religion is the true one but that all religions share in their own way in the truth of the one religion! Does this not in actual fact debase the other religions to a lower or partial cognition of truth? Does this not elevate one's own religion from the start to a super system which is slipped over all other religions, thus raking them into the net? Actually, what looks like tolerance proves in practice to be a sort of conquest by hugging, an integration by relativization and loss of identity."

29. Ernest Gellner, *Relativism and the Social Sciences* (Cambridge: Cambridge University Press, 1985), p. 160. "George Santayana observed somewhere that our nationality is like our relations with women—far too implicated in our moral nature to be changed honourably, and far too accidental to be worth changing. This corresponds exactly to the Wittgensteinian double basis for the legitimation of the hold which conceptual custom has over us: the rules of language are far too implicated in our whole way of life to be changeable without deep disruption, and at the same time they are far too contingent to deserve

reform. They bind us because they are oh so ultimate *and* because they are ever so trite and ordinary. They are too ultimate to be changed and too optional to be worth changing. This is the double vindication: they stand both beyond and beneath the compliment of rational opposition." Lenn Goodman, "Six Dogmas of Relativism," in *Cultural Relativism and Philosophy: North and Latin American Perspectives,* ed. Marcelo Dascal (Leiden and New York: Brill, 1991), p. 79. "Since paradigms are ultimately matters of intention, no behavioral evidence or overt sign can ever convey to an outsider the categorical intentions of a language user; these are inevitably opaque to all who do not share them. They are equally miraculously transparent (thus invisible) to those who do share them."

30. "Communication, Truth, and Society" (1957e), p. 98: "We have tended in our analysis of communication to reduce the minds of men to opinions and to neglect active attitude and ability."

31. Richard Rorty, "The Priority of Democracy to Philosophy," in *Reading Rorty,* ed. Alan R. Malachowski (Oxford: Blackwell, 1989), pp. 294–95. Rorty's derogatory use of "enchantment" resembles Hume's similar use of "enthusiasm." For an argument that there are good Kantian grounds for treating oneself differently from others, see Claude Levi-Strauss, *Tristes Tropiques* (New York: Atheneum, 1981), p. 392. "Other societies are perhaps no better than our own; even if we are inclined to believe they are, we have no method at our disposed for proving it. However, by getting to know them better, we are enabled to detach ourselves from our own society. Not that our own society is peculiarly or absolutely bad. But it is the only one from which we have a duty to free ourselves: we are, by definition, free in relation to the others. We thus put ourselves in a position to embark on the second stage, which consists in using all societies—without adopting features from any one of them—to elucidate principles of social life that we can apply in reforming our own customs and not those of foreign societies: through the operation of prerogative which is the reverse of the one just mentioned, the society we belong to is the only society we are in a position to transform without any risk of destroying it, since the changes, being introduced by us, are coming from within the society itself."

32. "Philosophy and Its History," in *Philosophy in History,* ed. Richard Rorty, J. B. Schneewind, and Quentin Skinner (Cambridge: Cambridge University Press, 1984), p. 29. Frederick L. Will, "Reason, Social Practice, and Scientific Realism," *Philosophy of Science* 48 (1981): 15. "One begins to appreciate some of the logical momentum at work in [the Copernican revolution] when one begins to look upon the rival theories in question, not as sentences to be parsed, or logical propositions to be analyzed, but more importantly, as rival programs for the governance of practices and of the intellectual institution of which these

practices are features; when one thinks of what sort of institution astronomy had been in the centuries preceding Copernicus, and of what sort of institution, according to certain tendencies in it, it might become. If astronomy, hitherto primarily an institution for celestial calculation, was in the process of giving increased emphasis to another mission, that of developing an acceptable cosmology, and was therefore in the process achieving a new identity among the cognitive and other institutions of the time, then there was strong logical impetus to the change, rooted in the inner dynamics of the governance of practices in these institutions." David Tracy, *Plurality and Ambiguity,* p. 73, suggests some ways in which the instrumental pragmatic response can be inadequate to clashes of intelligibility. "We can trust ourselves to conversation and argument when our only problem is error. But if we face something more elusive and profound than error, if we face systemic distortion, then another intellectual strategy is also called for. That other strategy we name a hermeneutics of suspicion." The difference between conflicts of truth-claims and clashes of intelligibility is a reason why, as I said before when discussing Kant's maxims, plural modes of thought is a more radical conception of pluralism than plural ultimate beliefs.

33. In *Aristotle's Rhetoric: An Art of Character* (Chicago: University of Chicago Press, 1995), I rely on the distinction between "given ends," which get all practical reasoning going in the first place, and "guiding ends," which are the purposes which practices develop, and which answer to their own standards of excellence. When there is a neutral test, the following lines from Gellner depict the development of dual loyalty, to one's own preferred theory or faith, and to public standards of justification, that is, to the good and to the right. Ernest Gellner, "An Ethic of Cognition," in *Essays in Memory of Imre Lakatos,* ed. R. S. Cohen, P. K. Feyerabend, Marx W. Wartofsky (Dordrecht: Reidel, 1976), p. 168. "Ideologies are so constructed that they are not refutable from inside. They generate, each of them, a world so neatly rounded off that, though it is well fed by confirmations, no refutation can occur within it. But, though this is an important characteristic of ideologies, it is not the only one. Another one of the first importance is: they are all bilingual. Though they speak a language which is closed and generates a full-circle world, they must invariably—if only for purposes of proselytizing, defense, and so forth—also entertain diplomatic-conceptual relations with other worlds, and meet on more or neutral ground, or at any rate ground not wholly controlled by either side."

34. "Dialectic and Political Thought and Action" (1954a), p. 26.

35. Michael J. Sandel, "Moral Argument and Liberal Toleration: Abortion and Homosexuality," *California Law Review* 77 (1989): 522. "Those who argue that law should be neutral among competing conceptions of the good life offer various grounds for their claim, including

most prominently the following: (1) the *relativist* view says law should not affirm a particular moral conception because all morality is relative, and so there are no moral truths to affirm; (2) the *utilitarian* view argues that government neutrality will, for various reasons, promote the general welfare in the long run; (3) the *voluntarist* view holds that government should be neutral among conceptions of the good life in order to respect the capacity of persons as free citizens or autonomous agents to choose their conceptions for themselves; and (4) the *minimalist,* or pragmatic view says that, because people inevitably disagree about morality and religion, government should bracket these controversies for the sake of political agreement and social cooperation."

36. Henry Richardson, "The Problem of Liberalism and the Good," in *Liberalism and the Good,* ed. R. Bruce Douglass, Gerald M. Mara, and Henry S. Richardson (New York and London: Routledge, 1990), p. 16. Brian Barry, "How Not to Defend Liberal Institutions," in *Liberalism and the Good,* ed. R. Bruce Douglass, Gerald M. Mara, and Henry S. Richardson (New York and London: Routledge, 1990), p. 55. "The problem with neutrality is that it asks people with moral convictions to treat them as external preferences or matters of personal opinion." The difference between a philosophic pluralism based on relative inadequacy of each mode of philosophy taken singly and a philosophic pluralism based on relative adequacy is illustrated in Walter Watson's development of McKeon in Walter Watson, *The Architectonics of Meaning: Foundations of the New Pluralism* (Albany, N.Y.: SUNY, 1985), second edition (Chicago: University of Chicago Press, 1993).

37. Donald Davidson, "On the Very Idea of a Conceptual Scheme," *Proceedings and Addresses of the American Philosophical Association* (1974): 5–20.

38. "Communication: Making Men of One Mind in Truth" (1965d), p. 5.

39. For pragmatism as restricted to actual consequences, and as therefore protective of the status quo, see Max Horkheimer, "On the Problem of Truth," in *The Essential Frankfurt School Reader,* ed. Andrew Arato and Eike Gebhardt (New York, 1982), p. 423. "The pragmatic concept of truth in its exclusive form . . . corresponds to limitless trust in the existing world. If the goodness of every idea is given time and opportunity to come to light, if the success of the truth—even after struggle and resistance—is in the long run certain, if the idea of a dangerous, explosive truth cannot come into the field of vision, then the present social structure is consecrated. . . . In pragmatism there lies embedded the belief in the existence and advantages of free competition." For pragmatism extending beyond possible consequences to the constitution of agents, see Dewey, *Human Nature and Conduct,* p. 150: "The thing actually at stake in any serious deliberation is not a difference of quantity,

but what kind of person one is to become, what sort of self is in the making, what kind of a world is making."

40. Isaiah Berlin, "Two Concepts of Liberty," in *Four Essays on Liberty* (Oxford: Oxford University Press, 1969), p. 172. To which Berlin replies: "To demand more than this is perhaps a deep and incurable metaphysical need; but to allow it to determine one's practice is a symptom of an equally deep, and more dangerous, moral and political immaturity." I have discussed Berlin's version of pluralism in "After *Virtù*: Rhetoric, Prudence, and Moral Pluralism in Machiavelli's *Discourses on Livy*," *History of Political Thought* 17 (1996): 1–29.

41. They differ just because McKeon thinks that philosophy can be pluralistic while for Rorty philosophy is necessarily monistic and "Platonic," and only poetry can be pluralistic. Richard Rorty, *Achieving Our Country: Leftist Thought in Twentieth-Century America* (Cambridge, Mass. and London: Harvard University Press, 1998), p. 118. "Literature . . . is as inevitably polytheist and agonistic as Plato's invention, philosophy, is inevitably monistic and convergent."

The Ecology of Culture

1. John Dewey, *The Quest for Certainty: A Study of the Relation of Knowledge and Action* (New York: G. P. Putnam's Sons, 1929), p. 255.

2. Dewey, *The Quest for Certainty*, p. 67.

3. Gregory Bateson, *Steps To An Ecology of Mind* (New York: Ballantine, 1972), pp. 399–410. See also Norbert Wiener, *The Human Use of Human Beings: Cybernetics and Society* (New York: Houghton Mifflin, 1950).

4. While developing his own concept of objectivity, which we will discuss later in this paper, McKeon did not hesitate to discuss the alternative criteria of objectivity that mark the pluralism of thought. See "Has History a Direction? Philosophical Principles and Objective Interpretations in *Essay, Oral Presentation, Reply to Queries, and Commentary"* (1968c), also in *FHOE*, pp. 144–45.

5. "Fact and Value in the Philosophy of Culture" (1969c), also in *SWI*, p. 432.

6. *Collected Papers of Charles Sanders Peirce*, ed. Charles Hartshorne and Paul Weiss, Vol. 5 (Cambridge: Harvard University Press, 1931–35), p. 506.

7. Bertrand Russell, "Foreword," in James Feibleman, *An Introduction to Peirce's Philosophy: Interpreted as a System* (New York: Harper & Brothers, 1946), p. xvi.

8. "Being, Existence, and That Which Is" (1960b), also in *SWI*, p. 244.

9. "Unhappily for America, our two greatest rhetoricians, Kenneth Burke and Richard McKeon, are for most people very hard to understand." Richard Lanham, *The Electronic Word: Democracy, Technology, and the Arts* (Chicago: University of Chicago Press, 1993), p. 165. See Eugene Garver, "Richard McKeon and the History of Rhetoric, or Why Does McKeon Write So Funny," *Rhetoric Society of America Quarterly* 14 (1984), pp. 3–14.

10. "The Circumstances and Functions of Philosophy" (1975a), pp. 107–8.

11. "The Future of Metaphysics" (1970b), p. 293.

12. "A Philosopher Meditates on Discovery" (1952d), also in *SWI*, p. 49.

13. "Spiritual Autobiography" (1953g), p. 36.

14. "The Uses of Rhetoric in a Technological Age: Architectonic Productive Arts" (1971c), also in *REID*, p. 18.

15. "The Future of Metaphysics" (1970b), pp. 290–91. "Paradoxically, the history of metaphysics since this beginning has been a history of controversial oppositions among fundamental beliefs about the nature of reality—oppositions of idealism, materialism, and skepticism—in which an independent science of first principles has seldom if ever been propounded."

16. "A Philosopher Meditates on Discovery" (1952d), also in *SWI*, p. 49. In addition to providing the broader historical context and personal experiences that led up to his insight, McKeon describes the actual moment of discovery as the conjunction and opposition of two passages that he read in ancient philosophy, one from Plato and one from Cicero.

17. Ibid., also in *SWI*, p. 50.

18. Cicero, *De Inventione,* trans. H. M. Hubbell (Cambridge: Harvard University Press, 1960), p. 15.

19. Developing from McKeon's early explorations, Walter Watson continues the investigation of the foundations of pluralism along a related but different pathway. Walter Watson, *The Architectonics of Meaning: Foundations of the New Pluralism* (Albany: SUNY Press, 1985).

20. See Thomas M. Conley, "Philosophers Turn to Rhetoric," *Rhetoric in the European Tradition* (New York: Longman, 1990), pp. 285–307. Conley focuses on the work of McKeon, Stephen Toulmin, Chaim Perelman, and Jürgen Habermas to demonstrate a "new Ciceronianism" in twentieth-century thought.

21. For a discussion of McKeon's modes of thought as functional distinctions, based on the circumstances of discourse and inquiry, see Kenneth A. Telford, "McKeon's Modes of Thought," *Hypotheses: Neo-Aristotelian Analysis* 17 (spring 1996): 10–13. On similar issues, see Watson, *The Architectonics of Meaning.*

22. Such syntheses are common enough in the history of the intellectual arts in Western culture, where rhetoric, grammar, logic, and dialectic undergo periodic mergings in one form or another with inventive results. McKeon often described such innovations in the course of his writing. "Greek Dialectics: Dialectic and Dialogue, Dialectic and Rhetoric" (1975d).

23. "The Methods of Rhetoric and Philosophy: Invention and Judgment" (1966b), also in *REID*, pp. 56–65. Aristotle, *Posterior Analytics* ii.1.89b23–35, and Cicero, *De inventione* i.8.10 and 11.16.

24. "A Philosopher Meditates on Discovery" (1952d), also in *SWI*, p. 50.

25. Questions also arise concerning McKeon's relation to Hegel and a variety of other philosophic traditions. For example, McKeon studied not only with Dewey but the dialectician F. J. E. Woodbridge at Columbia, and in his autobiographical essays he acknowledges the combined influence of these two men on his later work. However, just as Dewey expressed his respect for Hegel but denied that his own work was Hegelian or "continental" (in response to Bertrand Russell's attacks), McKeon also displayed nothing more than respect for Hegel and a host of other philosophers whose work he studied. McKeon's response is perhaps best summarized in this passage. "The professors under whom I studied philosophy had all, in their times, been introduced to philosophy by idealists. In the place of the idealisms they had discarded, they presented me with a choice among realisms . . . and when I continued my studies in Europe, I was able to add to this array, neocriticism, neothomism, and phenomenology. . . . It did not seem necessary to me to assume that one of these modes of philosophizing was the unique true philosophy, or that what other philosophers said and did had to be thought odd, absurd, or meaningless, as it was said to be in the light of the true philosophy. The later revolts of neopositivism, analytical, linguistic, and existentialistic philosophies provided further diversification of materials and orientations with even less temptation to be converted to the new testaments." McKeon, "The Circumstances and Functions of Philosophy" (1975a), p. 104.

26. "The Future of Metaphysics" (1970b), p. 306.

27. One is reminded of Peirce's argument against Comte regarding whether truth is identical with what is verifiable. "Truth is to be distinguished from what is verifiable, and Peirce argued against Comte and the positivists of his day that to make truth identical with what is verifiable is to resort to another form of the theory according to which truth is subjective." Feibleman, *An Introduction to Peirce's Philosophy*, pp. 212–13.

28. "Fact and Value in the Philosophy of Culture" (1969c), also in *SWI*, p. 432.

29. "The Circumstances and Functions of Philosophy" (1975a), p. 111.

30. John of Salisbury, *The Metalogicon: A Twelfth-Century Defense of the Verbal and Logical Arts of the Trivium,* trans. Daniel D. McGarry (Berkeley: University of California Press, 1962), p. 156.

31. "Fact and Value in the Philosophy of Culture" (1969c), also in *SWI,* p. 432.

32. "Spiritual Autobiography" (1953g), pp. 35–6.

33. "The Circumstances and Functions of Philosophy" (1975a), p. 112.

34. "The Future of Metaphysics" (1970b), p. 307.

35. "Discourse, Demonstration, Verification, and Justification," *Oral presentation and response* (1968d), p. 86.

36. Ibid.

37. "The Methods of Rhetoric and Philosophy: Invention and Judgment" (1966b), also in *REID,* p. 59.

38. For Dewey, social life and communication are identical; both are educative; and they are the continuous reconstruction of experience in the environmental medium we call culture. John Dewey, *Education and Democracy* (New York: Free Press, 1966), p. 76.

39. Dewey, *Logic: The Theory of Inquiry* (New York: Holt, Rinehart and Winston, 1938), p. 35. Dewey's view is also expressed in this passage from an earlier work: "Philosophy has often entertained the ideal of a complete integration of knowledge. But knowledge by its nature is analytic and discriminating. It attains large syntheses, sweeping generalizations. But these open up new problems for consideration, new fields for inquiry; they are transitions to more detailed and varied knowledge. Diversification of discoveries and the opening up of new points of view and new methods are inherent in the progress of knowledge. This fact defeats the idea of any complete synthesis of knowledge upon an intellectual basis. The sheer increase of specialized knowledge will never work the miracle of producing an intellectual whole. Nevertheless, the need for integration of specialized results of science remains, and philosophy should contribute to the satisfaction of the need. . . . The situation defines the vital office of present philosophy. It has to search out and disclose the obstructions; to criticize the habits of mind which stand in the way; to focus reflection upon needs congruous to present life; to interpret the conclusions of science with respect to their consequences for our beliefs about purposes and values in all phases of life. The development of a system of thought capable of giving this service is a difficult undertaking; it can proceed only slowly and through cooperative effort." Dewey, *The Quest for Certainty,* pp. 312–13.

40. John Dewey, "By Nature and By Art," *Philosophy of Education* (Totowa, N.J.: Littlefield, Adams, 1971); reprint ed., *Problems of Men* (New York: Philosophical Library, 1946), p. 288.

41. Ibid., p. 289.

42. Dewey, *The Quest for Certainty,* pp. 290–91.

43. Dewey expresses the functional relation in this way. "The name *objects* will be reserved for subject-matter so far as it has been produced and ordered in settled form by means of inquiry; proleptically, objects are the *objectives* of inquiry. The apparent ambiguity of using 'objects' for this purpose (since the word is regularly applied to things that are observed or thought of) is only apparent. For things exist *as* objects for us only as they have been previously determined as outcomes of inquiries. When used in carrying on new inquiries in new problematic situations, they are known as objects in virtue of prior inquiries which warrant their assertibility. In the new situation, they are *means* of attaining knowledge of something else. In the strict sense, they are part of the *contents* of inquiry as the word content was defined above. But retrospectively (that is, as products of prior determination in inquiry) they are objects." Dewey, *Logic,* p. 119.

44. Ibid., p. 42. "The acquisition and understanding of language with proficiency in the arts (that are foreign to other animals than men) represent an incorporation within the physical structure of human beings of the effects of cultural conditions, an interpenetration so profound that resulting activities are as direct and seemingly 'natural' as are the first reactions of an infant. To speak, to read, to exercise any art, industrial, fine or political, are instances of modifications wrought *within* the biological organism by the cultural environment."

45. Ibid., p. 48.

46. "The delicate balance of the just proportion of the truth by which pragmaticism is maintained is a delicate balance from which it is possible to fall off on the one side by concentration upon practice, action, contemplation, and on the other by an overemphasis on rationality, relations, prediction. Having demonstrated the relations which hypotheses have to practice, and hence the reality of actuality, it became necessary to show once more, to those who had gone too far in the direction of practice, that pragmaticism is involved also in the reality of generals, and hence the reality of possibility." Feibleman, *An Introduction to Peirce's Philosophy,* p. 308.

47. The revival of interest in Dewey's logic at the end of the twentieth century owes much to the development of rhetoric as an important intellectual and philosophic art, as in the work of Stephen Toulmin, Chaim Perelman, and McKeon. However, the connection between logic and rhetoric is not explored by a recent commentator, who merely observes: "Dewey's logical theory will therefore appear to be relatively unusual by current standards. One might want to say that he was doing something else besides 'logic,' perhaps developing instead a generalized theory of scientific method." Tom Burke, *Dewey's New Logic: A Reply to Russell* (Chicago: University of Chicago Press, 1994), p. 3.

48. "The Methods of Rhetoric and Philosophy: Invention and Judgment" (1966b), also in *REID,* pp. 59–60.

49. "A Philosopher Meditates on Discovery" (1952d), also in *SWI*, p. 59.

50. "Discourse, Demonstration, Verification, and Justification," *Oral presentation and responses* (1968d), pp. 88–89.

51. "The Future of Metaphysics" (1970b), p. 290.

52. In this sense, McKeon's goal is very close to that of Dewey in education. "The idea of education . . . is formally summed up in the idea of continuous reconstruction of experience, an idea which is marked off from education as preparation for a remote future, as unfolding, as external formation, and as recapitulation of the past." Dewey, *Democracy and Education,* p. 79.

53. "Spiritual Autobiography" (1953g), p. 34.

54. "The Circumstances and Functions of Philosophy" (1975a), p. 108.

55. "Honors Courses and Honors Programs of Study" (1976b), p. 16. Also see, "A Philosopher Meditates on Discovery" (1952d), also in *SWI*, p. 48. "Discovery does not result from reading about facts or discourses which follow from or accord with one's basic beliefs; at most such reading leads to the accretion and substantiation of doctrines and the increase and solidification of schools and sects."

56. "Honors Courses and Honors Programs of Study" (1976b), p. 16.

57. The subject matters of inquiry are usually described by McKeon as new fields for investigation. They are identified as *topics, hypotheses, themes,* and *theses* in works such as in "The Circumstances and Functions of Philosophy" (1975a). They are also identified as the fields of *invention, recovery, presentation,* and *action.* For example, see "The Liberating Arts and the Humanizing Arts in Education" (1964a), pp. 159–81.

58. For example, "Character and the Arts and Disciplines" (1969a), pp. 51–71, and "Philosophy of Communications and the Arts" (1970d), also in *REID*, pp. 95–120.

59. "The Uses of Rhetoric in a Technological Age" (1971c), also in *REID*, p. 6.

60. "Has History a Direction? Philosophical Principles and Objective Interpretations," *Essay, Oral Presentation, Reply to Questions, and Commentary* (1968c), also in *FHOE*, p. 148.

61. "Love and Wisdom: The Teaching of Philosophy" (1964b), p. 49.

62. For a discussion of the significance of McKeon's work in rhetoric, see Richard Lanham, "The 'Q' Question," *The Electronic Word,* pp. 155–94.

McKeon's Contributions to the Philosophy of Science

1. "The Circumstances and Functions of Philosophy" (1975a), par. 7, vol. 1, p. 107. Cf. "Philosophy and Theology, History and Science in

the Thought of Bonaventura and Thomas Aquinas" (1975c), last par., also in *SW1*, p. 136: "Scientists develop their own philosophies to structure their scientific inquiries, and philosophers imitate scientific methods and construct philosophies of science."

2. "The Battle of the Books" (1967b), par. 22, p. 191.

3. "Spinoza and Experimental Science," in Richard McKeon, *The Philosophy of Spinoza: The Unity of His Thought* (1928), pp. 130–57.

4. Ibid., par. 8, pp. 138–39.

5. "The Empiricist and Experimentalist Temper in the Middle Ages: A Prolegomenon to the Study of Mediaeval Science" (1929), pp. 216–34.

6. Ibid., par. 7, p. 223.

7. "De Anima: Psychology and Science" (1930a), pp. 673–90.

8. Ibid., sec. III, par. 3, p. 688.

9. Bruno Bettelheim, "Reflections: Freud and the Soul," *New Yorker* (March 1, 1982): 84.

10. "De Anima: Psychology and Science" (1930a), last par., p. 690.

11. "A Generalized Pell Equation, I" (1940a), VII: 165–71.

12. "Democracy, Scientific Method, and Action" (1945), also in *SW1*, pp. 335–93.

13. Ibid., sec. II, last par., p. 357.

14. Ibid., sec. IV, last par., p. 393.

15. "Aristotle's Conception of the Development and the Nature of Scientific Method" (1947a), also in *SW1*, pp. 256–89.

16. Ibid., sec. I, par. 16, p. 13.

17. "Aristotle and the Origins of Science in the West" (1949a), also in *SW1*, pp. 290–303.

18. Ibid., par. 8, p. 295.

19. Ibid., par 2, pp. 290–91.

20. Ibid., next-to-last par., p. 302.

21. "Philosophy and Method" (1951a), also in *SW 1*, pp. 183–208.

22. "Philosophy and Action" (1952b), also in *SW1*, pp. 406–28.

23. "Philosophy and Method" (1952b), par. 3, p. 184. See also par. 6, pp. 185–86, where the interrelations of commitments to subject matter, method, and principle are discussed.

24. Ibid., par. 37, pp. 205–6.

25. "Philosophy and Action" (1951a), par. 9, p. 411.

26. "Philosophic Semantics and Philosophic Inquiry" (1966), also in *FHOE*, pp. 242–56.

27. "Process and Function" (1953b), also in *SW1*, pp. 82–111.

28. Ibid., sec. I, par 20, p. 99.

29. Ibid., par. 19, pp. 98–99.

30. "Medicine and Philosophy in the Eleventh and Twelfth Centuries: The Problem of Elements" (1961d), pp. 211–56.

31. Ibid., par. 5, p. 213.

32. Ibid., last par., pp. 255–6.

33. *On Knowing—The Natural Sciences,* compiled by David B. Owen and edited by David B. Owen and Zahava K. McKeon (Chicago: University of Chicago Press, 1994).

34. Alfred North Whitehead, "The Rhythm of Education," chap. 2 of *The Aims of Education* (New York: Macmillan, 1929).

35. "Hegel's Conception of Matter" (1963b), pp. 421–25.

36. "Spinoza on the Rainbow and on Probability" (1965c), pp. 533–59.

37. Ibid., par. 2, p. 534.

38. "Philosophy as a Humanism" (1965d), also in *SW1*, pp. 23–40.

39. *Albert Einstein, Philosopher Scientist,* ed. Paul Arthur Schilpp (Evanston: Northwestern University Press, 1949).

40. "Philosophy as a Humanism" (1965d), par. 29, p. 36.

41. "Philosophy and the Development of Scientific Methods" (1966a), also in *SW1*, pp. 165–82.

42. Ibid., par. 2, p. 166.

43. Ibid., par. 3, p. 166.

44. "Scientific and Philosophic Revolutions" (1967a), also in *SW 1*, pp. 61–81.

45. Ibid., par. 3, p. 62.

46. Ibid., par. 8, p. 65.

47. Ibid., par. 34, pp. 80–81.

48. "Philosophic Problems in World Order" (1968a), pp. 160–83.

49. "World Order in Evolution and Revolution in Arts, Associations, and Sciences" (1971d), pp. 209–30.

50. "Philosophic Problems in World Order" (1968a), "Issues of World Order as Cosmos or Encountered Structures," par. 3, p. 169.

51. Ibid., par. 4, pp. 169–70.

52. "Time and Temporality" (1974b), pp. 123–28.

53. Ibid., par. 10, p. 127.

54. "The Organization of Sciences and the Relations of Cultures in the Twelfth and Thirteenth Centuries" (1975b), pp. 151–92.

55. Ibid., last par., pp. 183–84.

56. "Philosophy and Theology, History and Science in the Thought of Bonaventura and Thomas Aquinas" (1975c), also in *SW1*, pp. 12–136.

57. Ibid., sec. 3, par. 6, p. 124.

58. Ibid., last two paragraphs, pp. 135–36.

From Semantics to Praxis

1. Eugene Garver, *Aristotle's Rhetoric: An Art of Character* (Chicago: University of Chicago Press, 1994), pp. 237–40.

2. McKeon's most famous unpublished essay has finally appeared as, "Philosophic Semantics and Philosophic Inquiry" (1990), pp. 242–56.

3. "Power and the Language of Power" (1957a), pp. 143–63 and "The Ethics of International Influence" (1960a), pp. 187–203.

4. John Dewey, "Force, Violence, and Law," *Journal of Philosophy* 11 (1916).

5. "Power and the Language of Power" (1957a), p. 103.

6. Ibid., p. 106.

7. Ibid.

8. McKeon, "Discourse: Demonstration, Verification, and Justification" (1968d), p. 45.

9. Edwin Black, "*The Prospect of Rhetoric:* Twenty-Five Years Later," Plenary Session of *Rhetoric Society of America,* Seventh Biennial Conference "The Prospect of Rhetoric," May 30, 1996, Tucson, Arizona.

10. McKeon, "Dialectic and Political Thought and Action" (1954a), pp. 1–33.

11. Marcus Tullius Cicero, *De Inventione,* II, xxxi, 95.

12. Stephen L. Carter, "The Insufficiency of Honesty," *Atlantic Monthly* 277, no. 2 (1996): 74–75.

13. William J. Clinton, "Presidential remarks," reported in *New York Times,* Nov. 3, 1995.

14. Marc Slonim, "Afterword," Fyodor Dostoyevsky, *The Possessed* (New American Library, 1962), pp. 695–696.

15. Dostoyevsky, *The Possessed,* p. 223.

16. Ibid.

17. Ibid.

18. Mikhail Bakhtin, *The Dialogic Imagination: Four Essays,* ed. Michael Holquist, trans. Caryl Emerson and Michael Holquist (Austin: University of Texas Press, 1983), p. 350.

19. Dostoyevsky, *The Possessed,* p. 398.

20. Ibid., p. 400.

21. Ibid., p. 404.

22. Ibid., p. 409.

23. Ibid., p. 410.

24. Ibid., p. 412.

25. Ibid., p. 432.

26. Ibid., p. 432.

27. Ibid., p. 434.

28. Ibid., p. 436.

29. Ibid., p. 437.

30. Ibid., p. 439.

31. Walter Benjamin, "Surrealism," in *Reflections: Essays, Aphorisms, and Autobiographical Writings,* ed. Peter Demetz (New York: Harcourt Brace Jovanovich, 1978), p. 187.

32. Dostoyevsky, *The Possessed,* p. 443.

33. Erving Goffman, *Stigma* (New York: Free Press, 1964), p. 133.

34. Joseph Cardinal Bernadin, "Anti-Semitism: The Historical Legacy and the Continuing Challenge for Christians," Address to Hebrew University," March 23, 1995. Text courtesy of Chicago Archdiocese.

35. Ibid., p. 1.

36. Ibid.

37. Ibid.

38. Ibid., p. 3.

39. Ibid., p. 6.

40. Ibid., p. 15.

41. Ibid., p. 7.

42. Ibid., p. 16.

43. Ibid., p. 17.

44. Ibid., p. 19.

45. Ibid., p. 22.

46. Ibid., p. 23.

47. Ibid., p. 24.

Richard McKeon's Pluralism

1. I am indebted to Eugene Garver and Richard Buchanan for critical suggestions incorporated here.

2. I later learned that many an ordinary language and analytical philosopher had been attacking these proofs more solemnly, even insisting that Plato was really not worth bothering about. The current scene tends to overlook, or even to forgive, the absurd reductionisms of many mid-century philosophers.

3. For some of his students the punches were destructive, and for some, like the angry Robert Pirsig who attacked McKeon as "The Professor" in *Zen and the Art of Motorcycle Maintenance,* the destruction was felt as deliberate. My own view is that McKeon never intended to destroy the arguer, only the fallacious argument or reading. His profound probing did, however, produce some personal tragedies.

4. See *Selections from Medieval Philosophers* (1929–1930), I: 142–84.

5. He "covers" these three dimensions of his career—the scholarly philosopher, the educator, and the pursuer of international justice and understanding—in his "Spiritual Autobiography."

It is hard sometimes to avoid a sense of gloom as one thinks about the fate of McKeon's three grand projects. His philosophical work is still largely ignored, in spite of many who share my sense that he was their strongest intellectual influence. His educational project, both for graduate and undergraduate education, is in most institutions and minds fragmented beyond recognition, both home and abroad. His visions for UNESCO and for the world political dialogue seem even more hopeless than they could have seemed in his own time. So what do we gain by attempting to keep "him" alive? We keep those hopes alive, in a world that has always made such hopes questionable.

6. George Plochmann, p. 93.

7. There does seem to be some agreement among many that "operationalist" or "rhetorician" is the best single label. See the essays here by Garver and Buchanan. My original intention for this essay was to explore how McKeon-the-rhetorical-theorist jibed or clashed with McKeon-the-rhetorician and McKeon-the-universalist. But as Kenneth Burke has God say, in the wonderful dialogue with Satan at the end of *The Rhetoric of Religion: Studies in Logology,* "It's more complicated than that." (Boston: Beacon Press, 1961).

8. Plochmann, , p. 91.

9. For McKeon a favorite "monist" target was Rudolf Carnap, with his pursuit of a unified language of all the sciences. I think today he would have fun exhibiting the flaws in E. O. Wilson's recent totalizing effort in *Consilience: The Unity of Knowledge* (New York: Knopf/Random House, 1998).

10. Richard Rorty, *Contingency, Irony, and Solidarity* (New York: Cambridge University Press, 1989).

11. For a full development of the "reciprocal" relation of philosophies, in the McKeon view—both their inevitable capacity to refute one another, each of them "prioritizing" in a different way, and their inescapable dependence on one another, see Walter Watson's excellent account in *The Architectonics of Meaning* (Albany, N.Y.: SUNY, 1985); second edition (Chicago: University of Chicago Press, 1993).

12. His accounts of his youthful arrogance about ultimate mastery are amusing. "The three chief ingredients of which it [my youthful "system"] was composed were a scientific basis in behaviorism . . . , a normative criterion in pragmatism . . . , and a symbolic system . . . . It was a highly satisfactory philosophy, because it could be applied to a succession of subject matters and problems with little need for adjustment and with only a minimum of knowledge of the particular subject matter to which it was to be accommodated. I have never since been able to achieve comparable scope of system or convenience of method." "Spiritual Autobiography" (1953g), also in *SW1*, p. 7.

For an excellent account of how "true" philosophies can, because they place different subjects and methods in priority, seem to refute all other philosophies—how they can engage in unjustified/justified "reciprocal refutation," see Watson, esp. Chapter One, "Archic Variables."

13. Only Leibniz, in my experience, seems to work as hard at genuine "entry" as McKeon, though Aristotle often can impress any reader who is as ignorant of his targets as I am. Two major contrasts to McKeon in this matter are John Dewey, with his absurdly reductive treatment of earlier philosophers in the otherwise fine book, *Reconstruction in Philosophy* (Boston: Beacon Press, 1950), and Bertrand Russell, with his even worse reductions in his *History of Western Philosophy* (London and New York: Simon and Schuster, 1945). Perhaps in part because of its aggressive bias, Russell's book "proved the main source of my income for many years," and had "a success which none of my other books have had" (*The Autobiography Of Bertrand Russell* [Boston: Little Brown, 1968; original 1951], II: 340. To make their own projects work, both major philosophers felt driven to commit what McKeon steadily resisted: refuting the others to "make mine look like the best one." Russell answered the justified charges of bias with the anti-McKeonite claim that "a man without bias cannot write interesting history. . . I regard it as mere humbug to pretend to lack of bias" (pp. 340–41). Is it any wonder that McKeon's lifetime "history of philosophy" never "sold," while Russell's brief and often shoddy effort made him rich.

Of course it remains true, as revealed later here, that McKeon's pluralism is itself a kind of "system," that claims to refute at least the exclusivist claims of each philosopher he admires and thus could be accused of being a very special version of "bias."

14. *The Philosophy of G. E. Moore,* ed. Paul Arthur Schilpp (New York: Tudor Publishing Company, 1952), p. 676.

A major exception to McKeon's "incorporative" style, as reported by Plochmann, is his aggressive refutation of Dilthey, in "Imitation and Poetry" (1954). I would say that the most misleading (even unfair?) of his rejections, was performed through the near absolute silence throughout his work of any reference to the work of his lifetime friend and debating rival, Kenneth Burke. Burke is in my view the only twentieth-century thinker who can be said to rival him in the breadth and depth of his rhetorical studies—in the deepest philosophical sense of the word "rhetoric." It is also lamentably true that Burke remains aggressively silent about McKeon. Did these "friends" really dislike other? Could they not endure the thought of thinking about how their two projects overlapped? At one stage in this essay I had planned a set of parallel columns about their similarities and differences—but again Burke's God intervened to say, "It's more complicated than that." Both of them knew that almost everything is more complicated than "anyone else" had ever admitted.

15. Alan D. Sokal, "Transgressing the Boundaries: Toward a Transformative Hermeneutics of Quantum Gravity." *Social Text,* Spring/Summer, 1996 (Durham, N.C.: Duke University Press).

16. Ibid., introduction. The great historian Arnold Momigliano once met with a group of us professors who had been influenced by McKeon—long before "post-modernism"—and there was a terrific and unresolved battle with him over our assertion that even historical and scientific facts are "constructed": "real" enough—some of them at least—but always depending, in our formulations of them, on the McKeonite four-fold scheme: our first principles (whether comprehensive, reflexive, simple, or actional), our methods (whether dialectical, operational, logistic, or problematic), our interpretations (whether ontological, entitative, existentialist, or essentialist), and our selections (whether of hierarchies, of matters, of types or of kinds). We could hardly provide in two hours a "McKeon-education," for that highly learned traditionalist, Momigliano, and he left seeming to feel—as many who read Derrida leave feeling—that the rational store has been sold to the barbarians. (I wonder as I think of it now whether we really listened honestly to his arguments, as he failed to grasp ours.)

17. "World Community and the Relations of Cultures" (1950c), p. 801, my italics.

18. Were there serious violations of the four? That's hard to determine. We can assume so—he was a human being. There were certainly violations of value placements that others would insist on—such as mercy-over-justice, or toleration-over-truth. But were they violations of his own code? It's a complicated and unanswerable question—at least until some probing biographer studies his entire life. Here we pursue mostly the "publishing" McKeon.

19. You'll search in vain in his works for favorable references to Nietzsche as a real philosopher. Descartes fares somewhat better. He was embraced by the young McKeon seeking full certainty and mastery ("Spiritual Autobiography," [1953g] p. 8); later, as the product of his placement in history and culture, Descartes nicely exemplifies "the logistic method with reflexive principles and existentialist interpretation" ("Philosophic Semantics and Philosophic Inquiry," in *SW1*, p. 254).

20. Eugene Garver has suggested to me that McKeon did a somewhat inadequate job on the subject of the casuistry required in dealing with incommensurable real values. I agree with him that many contemporary thinkers like Isaiah Berlin have done a somewhat more *direct* job on the tricky topic.

21. "A Philosopher Meditates on Discovery" (1952d), also in *SW1*, p. 200; my italics.

22. See Garver, this volume.

23. Some philosophers might argue that practicing any one of the cardinal virtues, while a good thing in itself, may not make one a better philosopher. The answer to this objection would depend on one's definition of good philosophy. To spend time dealing justly with every contender might well hamper a philosopher's work on some special theory that is unrelated to most of what other philosophers have had as their center. Bertrand Russell was obviously one of the great modern philosophers, yet I can think of no philosopher who does as much injustice to previous thinkers as he does in his *A History of Western Philosophy* (New York: Simon and Schuster, 1945). Yet if Russell had spent as much time as McKeon spent attempting a just account of previous philosophers, he no doubt could never have produced the *Principia Mathematica*—at least not in anything like the present quality. So, practicing justice will make you a good philosopher in McKeon's sense, but it may make you a poor philosopher in Russell's sense. The same qualifications would apply to every other virtue. For McKeon, the "good philosopher" practices intellectual justice in the search for a radically different vision than Russell, brilliant as he was, could ever aspire to.

24. "Dialogue and Controversy in Philosophy" (1955b), also in *FHOE,* p. 163.

25. "Spiritual Autobiography," pp. 14–25.

26. Ibid., p. 20.

27. See especially the conclusion of "Philosophy and the Diversity of Cultures" (1950e). For a much celebrated current effort to grapple with similar problems raised by the "hybridity" of cultures, and what would-be thinkers can do about it, see Homi Bhabha, *The Location of Culture* (London: Routledge, 1994). I wish that I could wave a magic wand and produce a dialogue between McKeonites and Homi Bhabha and other "postcolonial discourse" scholars. They would be surprised by the great overlap, and they could learn from one another.

28. "World Community and the Relations of Cultures," p. 810.

29. "Philosophy and Freedom in the City of Man," p. 161.

30. See my "Individualism and the Mystery of the Social Self; or, Does Amnesty Have a Leg to Stand On?" in *Freedom and Interpretation: The Oxford Amnesty Lectures 1992,* ed. Barbara Johnson. (New York: Basic Books, HarperCollins, Inc., 1993), pp. 69–102.

31. Perhaps the clearest accounts of this history is that given in "A Philosopher Meditates on Discovery," reprinted in *REID,* pp. 207–212. See also "Philosophy and Method." (1951a). If he were writing in the late nineties, I'm pretty sure he would note—along with all other postmodernists—that we are at a new turn, with struggles about where the turn from language-as-center should go: back toward "pragmatics" and "action" or even "further back" to "substance" or even nature itself.

32. "A Philosopher Meditates on Discovery," in *REID*, p. 220.

33. *Politics*, Book I, chapter 4–5. A cogent argument that Aristotle's explanation of slavery cannot easily be excised from his full philosophical position can be found in Eugene Garver "Aristotle's Natural Slaves: Incomplete *Praxeis* and Incomplete Human Beings," *Journal of the History of Philosophy* 32 (1994): 1–22.

34. Of several recent works reviving interest in casuistry, the only ones I've read with real profit are Albert Jonsen's and Stephen Toulmin's *The Abuse of Casuistry: A History of Moral Reasoning* (Berkeley: Univ. of California Press, 1988), and James Chandler's *England in 1819: The Politics of Literary Culture and the Case of Romantic Historicism* (Chicago: University of Chicago Press, 1998), especially pp. 39–41 and chapters 3, 4, and 9.

35. Except perhaps for one: "Thou shalt always try to adjust your universally valid values to the case at hand."

36. "Spiritual Autobiography," in *FHOE*, pp. 35–36.

37. See *Selections*, especially (from my perspective) the accounts of Augustine, Anselm, Abailard, and Aquinas.

❖ Richard McKeon ❖
A Bibliography of His Published Works

Articles are listed according to their first publication. For those reprinted in the collections of McKeon's essays and in collections which contain one or more of McKeon's essays the following annotations are also
used.

CC   *Critics and Criticism*. Ed. R. S. Crane. Chicago:
University of Chicago Press, 1952.

FHOE   *Freedom and History and Other Essays: An
Introduction to the Thought of Richard McKeon*. Ed.
Zahava K. McKeon. Chicago: University of Chicago Press,
1990.

REID   *Rhetoric: Essays in Invention and Discovery*. Ed.
Mark Backman. Woodbridge, Conn.: Oxbow Press, 1987.

SW1 *Selected Writings of Richard McKeon, Volume 1:
Philosophy, Science, and Culture*. Ed. Zahava K. McKeon
and William G. Swenson. Chicago: University of Chicago
Press, 1998.

TAP *Thought, Action, and Passion*. Chicago: University of
Chicago Press, 1954.

Books

1928. *The Philosophy of Spinoza: The Unity of His Thought*. New
York: Longmans, Green and Co.

1929–30. *Roger Bacon to William of Ockham*. Vol. 1 of *Selections from
Medieval Philosophers*. New York: Charles Scribner's Sons.

1941. *The Basic Works of Aristotle*. New York: Random House.

1947. *Introduction to Aristotle.* New York: Random House (Modern Library). Second edition, revised and enlarged. Chicago: University of Chicago Press, 1973.

1951. *Democracy in a World of Tensions: A Symposium Prepared by UNESCO.* Chicago: University of Chicago Press. Author of "Forward," pp. v–xi, 194–213.

1952. *Freedom and History: The Semantics of Philosophical Controversies and Ideological Conflicts.* New York: Noonday Press.

1954. *Thought, Action, and Passion.* Chicago: University of Chicago Press.

1957. With Robert K. Merton and Walter Gellhorn. *The Freedom to Read: Perspective and Program.* New York: R. R. Bowker Co. Author of "Introduction," pp. xi–xvii, and "Censorship and the Freedom to Read," pp. 1–66.

1959. With N. A. Nikam. *The Edicts of Asoka.* Chicago: University of Chicago Press. Phoenix paperback edition, 1966. Indian edition, Bombay: Asia Publishing House. 1962.

1971. *Gli studi umanistici nel mondo attuale.* Rome: Armando Armando Editore.

1976–77. With Blanche B. Boyer. *Peter Abailard,* Sic et Non: *A Critical Edition.* Chicago: University of Chicago Press.

Articles

1927a. "A Note on William of Ockham." *Speculum* 2:455–56.

1927b. "Spinoza and Experimental Science." *Psyche* 8:55–77.

1928a. "Spinoza and Medieval Philosophy." *Open Court* 42:129–45.

1928b. "Thomas Aquinas' Doctrine of Knowledge and Its Historical Setting." *Speculum* 3:425–44.

1929. "The Empiricist and Experimentalist Temper in the Middle Ages: A Prolegomenon to the Study of Mediaeval Science." In *Essays in Honor of John Dewey,* pp. 216–34. New York: Henry Holt and Co.

1930a. "*De Anima:* Psychology and Science." *Journal of Philosophy* 27: 673–90.

1930b. "Causation and the Geometric Method in the Philosophy of Spinoza." *Philosophical Review* 39:178–89, 275–96.

1931. "Bericht über die 1928–1931 erschienenen amerikanischen Arbeiten zu Patristik, Scholastik und Renaissancephilosophie." *Archiv für Geschichte der Philosophie* 41:534–44.

1933. "Utility and Philosophy in the Middle Ages." *Speculum* 8:431–36.

1934. "The Science of Criminology." Part 3 of "*Crime, Law and Social Science:* A Symposium," with Beardsley Ruml and K. N. Llewellyn. *Columbia Law Review* 34:291–309.

1935. "Renaissance and Method in Philosophy." In *Studies in the History of Ideas,* 3:37–114. New York: Columbia University Press.

1936. "Literary Criticism and the Concept of Imitation in Antiquity." *Modern Philology* 34:1–35.

1937. "Education and the Disciplines." *Ethics* 47:370–81.

1938. "The Development of the Concept of Property in Political Philosophy: A Study of the Background of the Constitution." *Ethics* 48:297–366.

1939. "Aristotelianism in Western Christianity." In *Environmental Factors in Christian History,* pp. 206–31. Chicago: University of Chicago Press.

1940a. With H. H. Goldstine. "A Generalized Pell Equation." *Travaux de l'Institut mathématique de Tbilissi* 8:165–71.

1940b. "Plato and Aristotle as Historians: A Study of Method in the History of Ideas." *Ethics* 51:66–101.

1940c. "The Way We Talk." *The University of Chicago Magazine* 1:12–14.

1941a. "Aristotle's Conception of Moral and Political Philosophy." *Ethics* 51:253–90.

1941b. "Moses Maimonides, the Philosopher." In *Essays on Maimonides: An Octocentennial Volume,* pp. 2–8. New York: Columbia University Press.

1941c. "The Problems of Education in a Democracy." In *The Bertrand Russell Case,* pp. 91–130. New York: Viking Press.

1942a. "Propositions and Perceptions in the World of G. E. Moore." In *The Philosophy of G. E. Moore,* ed. Paul E. Schilpp, pp. 453–80. Evanston: Northwestern University.

1942b. "Rhetoric in the Middle Ages." *Speculum* 17:1–32. (=*REID,* pp. 121–166).

1943. "The Philosophic Bases of Art and Criticism." *Modern Philology* 41:65–87, 129–71.

1944a. "Discussion and Resolution in Political Conflicts." *Ethics* 54:235–62.

1944b. "The Philosophic Problem." In *New Perspectives on Peace*, pp. 196–226. Chicago: University of Chicago Press.

1944c. "Saadia Gaon." In *Rab Saadia Gaon: Studies in His Honor*, pp. 97–106. New York: Jewish Theological Seminary of America.

1944d. "The Liberal Arts and Democracy." *Ripon Alumnus* 18:26–36.

1945. "Democracy, Scientific Method, and Action." *Ethics* 55:235–86. (=*SW1*, pp. 335–93).

1946a. "Aristotle's Conception of Language and the Arts of Language." *Classical Philology* 41:193–206, 42:21–50.

1946b. "Poetry and Philosophy in the Twelfth Century: The Renaissance of Rhetoric." *Modern Philology* 43:217–34. (=*REID*, pp. 167–93).

1947a. "Aristotle's Conception of the Development and the Nature of Scientific Method." *Journal of the History of Ideas* 8:3–44. (=*SW1*, pp. 256–289).

1947b. "Economic, Political, and Moral Communities in the World Society." *Ethics* 57:79–91.

1947c. "The Meeting of the Executive Board of UNESCO." *World Affairs* 110:170–76.

1947d. "Les fondements d'une déclaration internationale des droits de l'homme." *Synthèses* 2:274–87.

1948a. "Philosophie et liberté dans la cité humaine." *Les études philosophiques*, n.s. 3:164–74. English translation, *Ethics* 49:155–61.

1948b. "UNESCO in Action: The UNESCO Program for 1947 and 1948." *Report of Meetings, 1947*. U.S. Department of State publication no. 3173, pp. 37–44. Also published in *Learning and World Peace* (New York: Harper & Brothers), pp. 577–91.

1948c. "The Philosophic Bases and Material Circumstances of the Rights of Man." *Ethics* 58: 180–87. Also published *in Human Rights: A Symposium Edited by UNESCO* (London and New York: Allan Wingate), pp. 35–46.

1948d. "A Philosophy for UNESCO." *Philosophy and Phenomenological Research* 8:573–86.

1948e. "UNESCO in Its Second Year." *Educational Record,* April 1948, pp. 137–44.

1948f. "The United States Student Abroad." In *Conference on International Student Exchanges,* pp. 36–45. New York: Institute of International Education.

1949a. "Aristotle and the Origins of Science in the West." In *Science and Civilization,* pp. 3–29. Madison: University of Wisconsin Press. (=*SW₁*, pp. 290–303).

1949b. "The Nature and Teaching of the Humanities." *Journal of General Education* 3:290–303.

1949c. "The Pursuit of Peace through Understanding." *Yale Review,* n.s. 38:253–69.

1949d. "Should Communists Be Allowed to Teach in Our Schools?" *Talks* (A quarterly digest of addresses presented in the public interest by the Columbia network), July 1949, pp. 10–18.

1950a. "Introduction to the Philosophy of Cicero." In *Brutus, On the Nature of the Gods, On Divination, On Duty* (Chicago Edition of Cicero), pp. 1–65. Chicago: University of Chicago Press.

1950b. "An American Reaction to the Present Situation in French Philosophy." In *Philosophic Thought in France and the United States: Essays Representing Major Trends in Contemporary French and American Philosophy,* pp. 337–62. Buffalo, N.Y.: University of Buffalo Publications in Philosophy. Second edition, Albany: State University of New York Press, 1968. Also French translation in *L'activité philosophique contemporaine en France et aux Etats-Unis* (Paris: Presses Universitaires de France, 1950), 2:359–91.

1950c. "World Community and the Relations of Cultures." In *Perspectives on a Troubled Decade,* pp. 801–15. New York: Harper & Brothers.

1950d. "The Funeral Oration of Pericles." In *Great Expressions of Human Rights,* pp. 29–41. New York: Harper & Brothers.

1950e. "Philosophy and the Diversity of Cultures." *Ethics* 60:233–60.

1950f. "Problems of Democracy." *Common Cause* 3:404–15.

1951a. "Philosophy and Method." *Journal of Philosophy* 48:653–82. (=*SW₁*, pp. 183–208).

1951b. "Evidence in History." In *Freedom and Reason: Studies in Philosophy and Jewish Culture,* pp. 201–22. Glencoe, Ill.: Free Press.

1951c. "Philosophic Differences and the Issues of Freedom." *Ethics* 61: 105–35.

1951d. "La philosophie et l'action." *Bulletin de la Société française de philosophie* 45:93–129.

1952a. "International Relations and Morality." In *Moral Principles of Action: Man's Ethical Imperative*. New York: Harper, pp. 343–77.

1952b. "Philosophy and Action." *Ethics* 62:79–100. (=*SW1*, pp. 406–28).

1952c. "Knowledge and World Organization." In *Foundations of World Organization: A Political and Cultural Appraisal*, pp. 289–329. New York: Harper & Brothers.

1952d. "A Philosopher Meditates on Discovery." In *Moments of Personal Discovery*, pp. 105–32. New York: Harper & Brothers. (=*SW1*, pp. 41–60). (=*REID*, pp. 194–220).

1952e. "Semantics, Science, and Poetry." *Modern Philology* 49:145–59.

1952f. "Symposia." In *Proceedings and Addresses of the American Philosophical Association (1951–1952)*, 25:18–41.

1952g. "Philosophie et culture." *Les études philosophiques*, n.s. 7:75–95.

1952h. Reprinted in *Critics and Criticism, Ancient and Modern*. Ed. Ronald Crane Chicago: University of Chicago Press.:

> "Literary Criticism and the Concept of Imitation in Antiquity," pp. 147–75.
> "Aristotle's Conception of Language and the Arts of Language," pp. 176–231.
> "Rhetoric in the Middle Ages," pp. 260–96.
> "Poetry and Philosophy in the Twelfth Century: The Renaissance of Rhetoric," pp. 297–318.
> "The Philosophic Bases of Art and Criticism," pp. 463–545.

1953a. "Philosophy and the Diversity of Cultures." In *Interrelations of Cultures: Their Contribution to International Understanding*, pp. 11–42. Paris: UNESCO.

1953b. "Process and Function." *Dialectica* 7:191–231. (=*SW1*, pp. 82–111).

1953c. "Communication and Community as Philosophy." *Ethics* 63:190–206.

1953d. "Experience and Metaphysics." In *Proceedings of the XIth International Congress of Philosophy*, 4:83–89. Amsterdam: North Holland. (=*SW1*, pp. 222–228).

1953e. "The Teaching of Philosophy in a Big American University." In *The Teaching of Philosophy*, pp. 158–83. Paris: UNESCO. (French translation)

1953f. "Thinking, Doing, and Teaching." *Ethics* 64:52–55.

1953g. Contribution to *Thirteen Americans: Their Spiritual Autobiographies*. Ed. Louis Finkelstein, pp. 77–114. New York: Harper & Bros. (=*FHOE*, pp. 3–36).

1954a. "Dialectic and Political Thought and Action." *Ethics* 65:1–33.

1954b. "Symbols, Myths, and Arguments." In *Symbols and Values: An Initial Study*, pp. 13–38. New York: Harper & Brothers. (=*REID*, pp. 66–94).

1954c. "Contemporary French Philosophy." *Proceedings of the American Catholic Philosophical Association* 28:17–36.

1954d. "Human Values and Technology." In *The Conference on Student Life and Education in the United States*, pp. 36–46. Chicago: University of Chicago Press.

1954e. "World Understanding." *Chicago Review* 7:81–98.

1955a. "Philosophical Presuppositions and the Relations of Legal Systems." In *University of Chicago Law School Conference on Jurisprudence and Politics*, pp. 3–19. Chicago: University of Chicago Press.

1955b. "Dialogue and Controversy in Philosophy." In *Entretiens philosophiques d'Athènes*, pp. 161-78. Athens: Institut international de philosophie. Reprinted in *Philosophy and Phenomenological Research* 17:143–63. (=*FHOE*, pp. 103–25).

1956a. "A Report on Roundtable Discussions in India and the United States of America—Human Relations and International Obligations," pp. 257–96. Bangalore: W. J. Jidge.

1956b. "Action and the Uses of the Humanities." *Comprendre* 15:69–83.

1956c. "The Choice of Socrates." In *Great Moral Dilemmas in Literature, Past and Present*, ed. R. M. MacIver, pp. 113–33. New York: Harper & Brothers.

1956d. "Communication—Making Men of One Mind in Truth." In *Conference on Communication: Problems of Communication in a Pluralistic Society*, pp. 1–22. Milwaukee: Marquette University Press.

1957a. "Le pouvoir et le langage de pouvoir." *Annales de philosophie politique* 1:1–32. Also as "Power and the Language of Power" in *Ethics* 68:143–63.

1957b. "Encyclopaedia." In *Encyclopaedia Britannica* 8:424–30. In 1968 edition, 8:363–70.

1957c. "The Development and the Significance of the Concept of Responsibility." *Revue internationale de philosophie* 34:3–32. (=*FHOE*, pp. 62–87).

1957d. "The Practical Uses of a Philosophy of Equality." In *Aspects of Human Equality: Fifteenth Symposium of the Conference on Science, Philosophy and Religion*, pp. 1–24. New York: Harper & Brothers.

1957e. "Communication, Truth and Society." *Ethics* 67:89–99. (=*FHOE*, pp. 88–102), (=*SW*, pp. 394–405).

1957f. "Aristotle's Conception of Scientific Method." In *Roots of Scientific Thought: A Cultural Perspective*, ed. Philip P. Wiener and A. Noland, pp. 73–89. New York: Basic Books. Reprint of 1947 article.

1957g. "Introduction: The Meanings of Justice and the Relations among Traditions of Thought." *Revue International de Philosophie* 41: 253–67.

1958a. "The Humanities and Action." In *Les rapports de la pensée et de l'action: Entretiens philosophiques de Varsovie*, pp. 16–17, 104–17, 164–67, 185–200. Warsaw.

1958b. "Freedom and Value." *Relazioni introduttive del XII. congresso internazionale di filosofia*, pp. 105–20. Florence: Sansoni.

1958c. "Culture and Humanity." In *Encyclopaedia Britannica*. Vol. 5, p. 743.

1959a. "Universities in the Modern World." In *Issues in University Education*, ed. Charles Frankel, pp. 1–23. New York: Harper & Brothers.

1959b. "Principles and Consequences." *Journal of Philosophy* 56:385–401.

1960a. "The Ethics of International Influence." *Ethics* 70:187–203.

1960b. "Being, Existence, and That Which Is." *Review of Metaphysics* 13:539–54. (=*SW1*, pp. 244–55).

1961a. "The Judgment of 'Judgment.'" In *Atti del simposio di estetica Venezia, 1958*, pp. 222–35. Padua: Edizioni della Rivista di estetica.

1961b. "Freedom and Value." In *Atti del XII. congresso internazionale di filosofia*, 3:500–505. Florence: Sansoni.

1961c. Official Speeches of the Closing Session. Ibid., 12: 424–29.

1961d. "Medicine and Philosophy in the Eleventh and Twelfth Centuries." *The Thomist* 24:211–56.

1961e. "Introduction: The Meanings of Society and the Relations among Traditions of Thought." *Revue internationale de philosophie* 55:3–16.

1962. First Lyman Bryson Lecture, "Ethics and Politics." In *Ethics and Bigness*, ed. Harlan Cleveland and H. D. Lasswell, pp. 471–87. New York: Harper & Brothers.

1963a. "Justice and Equality." In *Justice: Nomos VI*, ed. Carl J. Friedrich and John W. Chapman, pp. 44–61. New York: Atherton Press. (Yearbook of the American Society for Political and Legal Philosophy.)

1963b. "Hegel's Conception of Matter." In *The Concept of Matter*, ed. Ernan McMullin, pp. 421–25, 428–29. Notre Dame: University of Notre Dame Press. Discussion of other conceptions of matter, 75–78, 140–42, 242, 570–72.

1964a. "The Liberating Arts and the Humanizing Arts in Education." *Humanistic Education and Western Civilization: Essays for Robert M. Hutchins*, ed. Arthur A. Cohen, pp. 159–81. New York: Holt, Rinehart and Winston.

1964b. "Love and Wisdom: The Teaching of Philosophy." *Journal of General Education* 15:239–49.

1964c. "The Future of the Liberal Arts." In *Current Issues in Higher Education, 1964*, ed. G. Kerry Smith, pp. 36–44. Washington, D.C.: Association for Higher Education, National Education Association of the U.S.

1964d. "Mankind: The Relation of Reason and Action." *Ethics* 74: 174–85.

1964e. "The Flight from Certainty and the Quest for Precision." *Review of Metaphysics* 18:234–53. (=*SW1*, pp. 229–243).

1965a. "Rhetoric and Poetic in the Philosophy of Aristotle." In *Aristotle's "Poetics" and English Literature*, ed. Elder Olson, pp. 201–36. Chicago: University of Chicago Press. (=*SW1*, pp. 137–164).

1965b. "The Relation of Logic to Metaphysics in the Philosophy of Duns Scotus." *The Monist* 49:519–50.

1965c. "Spinoza on the Rainbow and on Probability." In *Harry Austryn Wolfson Jubilee Volume*, pp. 533–59. Jerusalem: American Academy for Jewish Research.

1965d. "Philosophy as a Humanism." *Philosophy Today* 9:151–67. (=*SW1*, pp. 23–40).

1966a. "Philosophy and the Development of Scientific Methods." *Journal of the History of Ideas* 27:3–22. (=*SW1*, pp.165–182).

1966b. "The Methods of Rhetoric and Philosophy: Invention and Judgment." In *The Classical Tradition: Literary and Historical Studies in Honor of Harry Caplan*, ed. Luitpold Wallach, pp. 365–73. Ithaca: Cornell University Press. (=*REID*, pp. 56–65).

1966c. "Philosophy and Human Rights." In *Le fondement des droits de l'homme: Actes des entretiens de l'Aquila (14–19 septembre 1964), Institut international de philosophie*, pp. 90–101. Florence: La Nuova Italia. Discussion, pp. 183–85; 346–48; 383–90; on dialogue, Séance de clôture, pp. 399–402.

1966d. "The Concept of Mankind and Mental Health." *Ethics* 77:29–37.

1967a. "Scientific and Philosophic Revolutions." In *Science and Contemporary Society*, ed. Frederick J. Crosson, pp. 23–56. Notre Dame: University of Notre Dame Press. (=*SW1*, pp. 61–81).

1967b. "The Battle of the Books." In *The Knowledge Most Worth Having*, ed. Wayne C. Booth, pp. 173–202. Chicago: University of Chicago Press.

1967c. "Analysis and Synthesis," "Methodology (Philosophy)," "Synthesis." In *New Catholic Encyclopedia*.

1968a. "Philosophic Problems in World Order." In *Science, Philosophy and Culture: Essays Presented in Honour of Humayan Kabir's Sixty-second Birthday*, pp. 160–83. Bombay: Asia Publishing House.

1968b. "Man and Mankind in the Development of Culture and the Humanities." In *Changing Perspectives on Man*, ed. B. Rothblatt, pp. 271–94. Chicago: University of Chicago Press.

1968c. "Has History a Direction? Philosophical Principles and Objective Interpretations." In *La compréhension de l'histoire*, ed. Nathan Rotenstreich, pp. 29–32, 38–39, 63–101, 159–62. Jerusalem: Israel Academy of Sciences and Humanities.

1968d. "Discourse: Demonstration, Verification, and Justification." In *Demonstration, Verification, Justification: Entretiens de l'Institut international de philosophie, Liège, septembre 1967*, pp. 37–55. Louvain: Nauwelaerts. Oral presentation, pp. 55–63; responses, pp. 67–69, 78–92; interventions, pp. 125–27, 217–18, 259, 397–99. (=*REID*, pp. 37–55).

1968e. "Love, Self, and Contemporary Culture." In *East-West Studies in the Problem of the Self*, ed. P. T. Raju and A. Castell, pp. 13–33. The Hague: Martinus Nijhoff.

1968f. "The Individual in Law and in Legal Philosophy in the West." In *The Status of the Individual in East and West*, ed. Charles A. Moore. Honolulu: University of Hawaii Press.

1968g. Foreword to *The Political Theory of John Dewey* by A. H. Somjee, pp. vii–ix. New York: Teachers College Press.

1969a. "Character and the Arts and Disciplines." In *Approaches to Education for Character: Strategies for Change in Higher Education*, ed. Clarence H. Faust and Jessica Feingold, pp. 51–71. New York: Columbia University Press. Also in *Ethics* 78:109–23.

1969b. "Principles of Modal Logic, Aristotelian and Modern" (Summary). *Acta Logica* 12:231.

1969c. "Fact and Value in the Philosophy of Culture." In *Akten des XIV.internationalen Kongresses für Philosophie, Wien, 2–9 September 1968*, 4:503–11. Vienna: Herder. (=*SW1*, pp. 429–435).

1969d. "Ontology, Methodology, and Culture." In *Contemporary Philosophy: A Survey*, ed. Raymond Klibansky, 3 (*Metaphysics, Phenomenology, Language and Structure*): 96–116. Florence: La Nuova Italia. Includes three pages of bibliography.

1970a. "Concluding Remarks on 'Metaphysics, Politics and Contemporary Unrest.'" *Metaphilosophy* 1:85–90.

1970b. "The Future of Metaphysics." In *The Future of Metaphysics*, ed. Robert E. Wood, pp. 288–308. Chicago: Quadrangle Books.

1970c. "Philosophy and History in the Development of Human Rights." In *Ethics and Social Justice*, ed. Howard E. Kiefer and Milton K. Munitz, pp. 300–322. Albany: State University of New York Press. (=*FHOE*, pp. 37–61), (=*SW1*, pp. 447–67).

1970d. "Philosophy of Communications and the Arts." In *Perspectives in Education, Religion and the Arts,* ed. Howard E. Kiefer and Milton K. Munitz, pp. 329–50. Albany: State University of New York Press. (=*REID*, pp. 95–120).

1971a. "Humanism, Civility, and Culture." In *God, Man and Philosophy: A Symposium,* ed. Carl W. Grindel, C.M., pp. 65–72. New York. St. John's University Press.

1971b. "Knowledge, Community and Communication." In *A Center for National Goals and Alternatives: Collected Papers,* pp. 245–72. New York: National Industrial Conference Board.

1971c. "The Uses of Rhetoric in a Technological Age: Architectonic Productive Arts." In *The Prospect of Rhetoric,* ed. Lloyd F. Bitzer and Edwin Black. Report of the National Development Project Sponsored by the Speech Communication Association, pp. 44–63. Englewood Cliffs, N.J.: Prentice-Hall. Report of discussion group, pp. 182–85. (=*REID*, pp. 1–24).

1971d. "World Order in Evolution and Revolution in Arts, Associations, and Sciences." In *Evolution-Revolution: Patterns of Development in Nature, Society, Man and Knowledge,* ed. Rubin Gotesky and Ervin Laszlo, pp. 209–30. New York: Gordon and Breach. Reprinted in *Philosophy Forum* 11:221–42.

1972a. "History and Philosophy, Art and Science, Validity and Truth," In *Vérité et historicité: Institut international de philosophie, Entretiens de Heidelberg, 12–16 septembre 1969,* ed. Hans-Georg Gadamer. The Hague: Martinus Nijhoff.

1972b. "Facts, Values, and Actions." In *Les sciences humaines et le problème des valeurs: Institut international de philosophie, Entretiens d'Amsterdam, 8–11 septembre 1971,* ed. K. Kuypers, pp. 73–85. The Hague: Martinus Nijhoff. (=*SW1*, pp. 436–46).

1972c. "The Transformations of the Liberal Arts in the Renaissance." *In Developments in the Early Renaissance,* ed. Bernard Levi, pp. 158–223. Albany: State University of New York Press. Includes sixteen pages of bibliography.

1972d. "Where We Are and Where We Are Going." The 339th Convocation Address. *University of Chicago Record,* June 5, 1972, pp. 69–71.

1973. "Creativity and the Commonplace." *Philosophy and Rhetoric* 6:199–210. (=*REID*, pp. 25–36).

1974a. "Censorship." In *Encyclopaedia Britannica,* 15th ed.

1974b. "Time and Temporality." *Philosophy East and West* 24:123–28.

1974c. "Logos: Technology, Philology, and History." Proceedings of the XVth World Congress of Philosophy: Varna, Bulgaria, September 17–22, 1973 (Sofia: Sophia Press Production Center: 974), 3:481–85.

1975a. "The Circumstances and Functions of Philosophy." In *Philosophers on Their Own Work,* ed. André Mercier and Maja Svilar, 1:95–142. Bern and Frankfurt am Main: Verlag Herbert Lang.

1975b. "The Organization of Sciences and the Relations of Cultures in the Twelfth and Thirteenth Centuries." In *The Cultural Context of Medieval Learning,* ed. J. E. Murdoch and E. D. Sylla, pp. 151–92. Dordrecht: D. REIDel.

1975c. "Philosophy and Theology, History and Science in the Thought of Bonaventura and Thomas Aquinas." *Journal of the History of Ideas* 36:387–412. Reprinted *in Journal of Religion Supplement* 58:S24–S51. (=*SW1*, pp. 112–136).

1975d. "Greek Dialectics: Dialectic and Dialogue, Dialectic and Rhetoric." In *Dialectics/Dialectiques,* ed. Ch. Perelman, pp. 1–25. The Hague: Martinus Nijhoff.

1975e. "Arts of Invention and Arts of Memory: Creation and Criticism." *Critical Inquiry* 1:723–39.

1976a. "Canonic Books and Prohibited Books: Orthodoxy and Heresy in Religion and Culture." *Critical Inquiry* 2:781–806.

1976b. "Honors Students and Honors Programs of Studies." Paper delivered at National Collegiate Honors Council meeting.

1977. "Latin Literature and Roman Culture in Modern Education." *Journal of General Education* 28:296–302.

1978a. "Person and Community: Metaphysical and Political." *Ethics* 88:207–17.

1978b. "Philosophy as an Agent of Civilization." In *Philosophy and Civilization: Proceedings of the First Afro-Asian Philosophy Conference, March 13–16, 1978,* ed. Mourad Wahba, pp. 127–37. Cairo. (=*SW1*, pp. 468–482).

1979a. "*Pride and Prejudice:* Thought, Character, Argument, and Plot." *Critical Inquiry* 5:511–27.

1979b. "The Hellenistic and Roman Foundations of the Tradition of Aristotle in the West." *Review of Metaphysics* 32:677–715. (=*SW1*, pp. 304–334).

1981. "The Interpretation of Political Theory and Practice in Ancient Athens." *Journal of the History of Ideas* 42: 3, 12.

1982. "Criticism and the Liberal Arts: The Chicago School of Criticism." *Profession 82*:1–26.

1983. "The Background of Spinoza." In *Entretiens in Jerusalem on Spinoza—His Thought and Work: Proceedings of a Conference of the International Institute of Philosophy, September 6–9, 1977*, pp.1–40.

1986. "Pluralism of Interpretation and Pluralism of Objects, Actions and Statements Interpreted." *Critical Inquiry* 12:576–596.

1990. "Philosophic Semantics and Philosophic Inquiry." in *Freedom and History and Other Essays: An Introduction to the Thought of Richard McKeon*, ed. Zahava K. McKeon, pp. 242–256 (Chicago, University of Chicago Press). (=*SW1*, pp. 209–221.

◆ Contributors ◆

Wayne C. Booth is George M. Pullman Distinguished Service Professor Emeritus at the University of Chicago and former dean of the college at the University of Chicago. He is the author of many books, including *The Rhetoric of Fiction* (winner of the Phi Beta Kappa Christian Gauss Award), *Critical Understanding: The Powers and Limits of Pluralism, Modern Dogma and the Rhetoric of Assent, The Rhetoric of Irony, Now Don't Try to Reason with Me: Essays and Ironies for a Credulous Age,* and *The Vocation of a Teacher: Rhetorical Occasions, 1967-1988.*

Richard Buchanan is professor of design and head of the School of Design at Carnegie Mellon University. He received his Ph.D. from the Committee on the Analysis of Ideas and the Study of Methods at the University of Chicago. He was the inaugural holder of the Nierenberg Chair of Design at Carnegie Mellon University. He writes on the theory and practice of design, with special interest in the philosophical and rhetorical thinking that lies behind technology and the humanmade world, including the relation of words and images in industrial, communication, and interaction design. He is coeditor of *The Idea of Design* and *Discovering Design: Explorations in Design Studies.* He is also coeditor of the international journal *Design Issues: History, Theory, Criticism.*

David J. Depew is professor of rhetoric of inquiry and communication studies at the University of Iowa. With Bruce H. Weber, he is the author of *Darwinism Evolving: Systems Dynamics and the Genealogy of Natural Selection* , and and he is coeditor, with Robert Hollinger, of *Pragmatism: From Progressivism to Postmodernism.* He has written on the influence of Aristotle's biological works on his political theory and of Aristotle's reception by Marx and Dewey. He is currently coauthoring a book on the history of the philosophy of biology with Marjorie Grene.

Thomas B. Farrell (Ph.D., University of Wisconsin) is a professor of rhetoric and political communication at Northwestern

University. He has published more than seventy articles and monographs dealing with rhetoric and public culture. In 1990 Farrell received the Charles H. Woolbert Award for "scholarship of exceptional originality and influence." His study of modernity and rhetorical tradition, *Norms of Rhetorical Culture,* won the 1994 Winans-Wichelns Award for "distinguished scholarship in rhetoric and public address." In 1998 Farrell's collection *Landmarks in Contemporary Rhetorical Theory* appeared, and Farrell was also named "Outstanding Scholar in Rhetoric and Communication Theory" by the division of the same name in the National Communication Association. Farrell is interested in the ways public symbols, images, and figures channel our participation toward partisan ends and collective projects.

Eugene Garver is Regents Professor of Philosophy, Saint John's University. He is the author of *Machiavelli and the History of Prudence* and *Aristotle's Rhetoric: An Art of Character,* as well as many articles on Aristotle's ethical and political philosophy, Aristotle's rhetoric, and contemporary rhetorical theory. His work is a series of considerations of the ways in which practical wisdom and character are articulated by different philosophers and how those ideas change with changing ethical and political circumstances.

Donald N. Levine is the Peter B. Ritzma Professor of Sociology and former dean of the college at the University of Chicago. For the past decade he has edited The Heritage of Sociology series for the University of Chicago Press, and in 1996-1997 he served as chair of the Theory Section of the American Sociological Association. His books include *Georg Simmel on Individuality and Social Forms* (1971), *The Flight from Ambiguity: Essays in Social and Culture Theory* (1985), and *Visions of the Sociological Tradition* (1995).

Dennis O'Brien is a graduate of Yale University and the University of Chicago, Ph.D. He has held academic positions at Princeton, Middlebury, and Bucknell Universities and at the University of Rochester. He was dean of the college at Middlebury and president of Bucknell (1976-1984) and Rochester (1984-1994). He is the author of *Hegel on Reason and History* (1975) and most recently *All the Essential Half-Truths about Higher Education* (1997), as well as numerous articles in scholarly and popular journals. He currently lives in Middlebury, Vermont.

Richard H. Popkin is professor emeritus at Washington University, St. Louis, as well as adjunct professor of history and philosophy at the University of California, Los Angeles. He is the author of *The History of Scepticism from Erasmus to Spinoza* as well as many other books and more than three hundred articles. *The Columbia History of Western Philosophy,* which he edited, appeared in 1999. He was a founding editor of the *Journal of the History of Philosophy* and the *International Archives of the History of Ideas.*

Walter Watson is professor emeritus at the State University of New York at Stony Brook, where he taught in the Department of Philosophy. He is the author of *The Architectonics of Meaning: Foundations of the New Pluralism* (1985). He writes on a wide range of subjects in philosophy, and he currently lives on Long Island.

Charles W. Wegener is professor emeritus at the University of Chicago, where he served as chair of the Committee on the Analysis of Ideas and the Study of Methods and dean of the New Collegiate Division. He is the author of *Liberal Education and the Modern University* (1978) and *The Discipline of Taste and Feeling* (1994). He currently lives in Chicago.

Index

288